BATS, BALLS & BAILS

www.**rbooks**.co.uk

Also by Les Scott

End-to-End Stuff: The Essential Football Book
(endtoendstuff.co.uk)

LES SCOTT

BATS, BALL'S & BAILS

THE ESSENTIAL CRICKET BOOK

BANTAM PRESS

LONDON • TORONTO • SYDNEY • AUCKLAND • JOHANNESBURG

TRANSWORLD PUBLISHERS
61–63 Uxbridge Road, London W5 5SA
A Random House Group Company
www.rbooks.co.uk

First published in Great Britain
in 2009 by Bantam Press
an imprint of Transworld Publishers

A CIP catalogue record for this book
is available from the British Library.

ISBN 9780593061466 (cased)
9780593061473 (tpb)

Addresses for Random House Group Ltd companies outside the UK
can be found at: www.randomhouse.co.uk
The Random House Group Ltd Reg. No. 954009

The Random House Group Limited supports The Forest Stewardship
Council (FSC), the leading international forest-certification organization. All our
titles that are printed on Greenpeace-approved FSC-certified paper carry the FSC logo.
Our paper procurement policy can be found at
www.rbooks.co.uk/environment

Typeset in 9.75/13pt Scala Sans by
Falcon Oast Graphic Art Ltd.
Printed and bound in Great Britain by
CPI Mackays, Chatham, ME5 8TD

2 4 6 8 10 9 7 5 3 1

Mixed Sources
Product group from well-managed
forests and other controlled sources
www.fsc.org   Cert no. TT-COC-2139
© 1996 Forest Stewardship Council
FSC

For Jane, Lauren, Ruby and Charley – my favourite cricket team, and everything else too.

Additional illustrations by Lauren Scott and Ruby Scott

Contents

Cricket is a team game: likewise the production of a book. I would like to express my sincere thanks to the following for playing a blinder in this particular team and for making this book far better than it might have been: Julian Alexander and all at literary agents Lucas Alexander Whitley; Ken and Jean Bolam; Andy Boot; all in the PE Department at Chasetown Specialist Sports College; Scott Cordon; Phillip Dann and Dean Statham; Giles Elliott, Doug Young, Vivien Garrett, Dan Balado and all at Transworld Publishers; Matt Hardman; Arthur Montford; Dave and Christine Scott; John Turnock; Mark Williams; Wisden, and every County Championship club.

All records in *Bats, Balls & Bails* apply, unless otherwise stated, up to and including June 2009.

Back in the sixties the seasons were clearly defined. As soon as the fixtures of the last Saturday of the football season were completed, someone would say, 'Time to get the cricket bat out!' It would never occur to my pals or me to play football in June or July. That would have been akin to setting off fireworks in April, or singing carols in May. We played cricket until the football season started again, but watched the county season to its denouement.

The Durham I grew up in was a Minor County; attendance at a 'proper' cricket match meant going to watch Sunderland in the then Durham Senior League. We envied those boys who had Lord's, Trent Bridge or even Grace Road on their doorstep. To us it appeared that cricket, like life, was happening elsewhere. In fact everywhere and anywhere but where we lived.

We played cricket at school, but the real cricket was played in the back lanes of Sunderland, which for the best part of my childhood were of the cobbled variety. These games were played with a proper cricket ball – proper in the sense it was a ball of cork, the leather having long since given up the ghost. The meat of the blade of the one bat we possessed was swathed in so much sticky yellow tape it appeared to be wearing a lifebelt, which was appropriate in that we belted the life out of both bat and ball. The bat was hardly from the school of Gunn and Moore: the rubber grip and binding string of the handle had long since perished so one was left holding what amounted to little more than a stick. As for the wicket, that was sponsored: an old orange box donated by the local greengrocer.

No one, of course, possessed pads or gloves. Should today's schoolteachers see boys bearing as many bruises as we did they'd be on the phone to Social Services right away. Back then no one thought anything untoward about a boy splattered with bruises the size of saucers, least of all the boy himself.

Bowling on cobblestones had its moments. Many was the time the bowler delivered the ball only for it to hit a jutting cobble and rebound straight back to him – unfailingly a source of much amusement and usually accompanied by cries of 'Too much back-spin!' At junior school we played on a rubber-mat wicket laid on a concrete strip. When I was 11 years old I attended grammar school where I played on my first grass wicket, flummoxed as to why there was no actual grass on it and totally alienated by the talk of my new team-mates about the wicket 'having pace in it' or being 'conducive to spin'.

'What sort of wickets have you been used to bowling on?' the PE master once asked.

'Cobbled ones,' I replied.

'Oh, yes,' replied the master, 'I've known groundsmen such as that.'

That's how my great love-affair with cricket began. Like all great romances there was love at first sight, only for a deeper, more meaningful and rewarding love to develop over time. It was a love fostered by my dad and, in particular, my older brother, who spent countless hours bowling to me in our backyard.

Now I spend countless hours bowling to my two young daughters, not in a back lane or backyard, but a back garden. Of course things are different now, rightly and happily so. My daughters benefit from coaching at school, play for their respective school cricket teams and enjoy the use of equipment that would have been beyond the wildest dreams of me and my boyhood pals.

Cricket, particularly at professional level, has changed irrevocably in recent years. The plethora of international matches and competitions; two, often three different touring teams visiting each summer – all serve to over-egg the pudding. The money generated will guarantee the future of cricket, but what sort of future will it be?

But when the football season ends and my daughters turn to me and say, 'Time to get the cricket bat out!', my worries fade. Hearing those words has a profound effect on me, for when there is cricket, no matter what the standard or where it is taking place, the world appears to be a far, far better place.

We can't have cricket in the winter, but we can read about it, and hopefully this book will bring some warmth and sunshine into the coldest and darkest of days, keep you going until some sprightly youngster lifts your heart by uttering those magical words: 'Time to get the cricket bat out!'

Les Scott, 2009

Alfred Lyttelton (Cambridge University) represented England at both cricket and football. He played in four Tests for England (1880–84), for Old Etonians in the 1876 FA Cup Final, and was capped by England against Scotland in 1877. An outstanding wicket-keeper, Lyttelton was called upon to bowl in the 1884 Test against Australia at the Oval and took 4 for 19 while still wearing his pads. Five of his brothers also played first-class cricket and one, Edward, also played football and was capped once for England, against Scotland in 1878.

Hornby double? Oh! Albert Hornby (Lancashire) was the first double international in cricket and rugby union and the first man to captain England at both sports (1882). Having made his Test debut in 1879, he went on to captain England in his third Test in 1884, against Australia at the Oval. He gained nine caps for England at rugby union (1877–92) and played his club rugby for Preston Grasshoppers and Manchester. A true all-round sportsman, he also played football for Blackburn Rovers. Along with fellow Lancashire opener Dick Barlow he provided the inspiration for the Francis Thompson poem 'At Lord's', written in 1907, which included the line 'Oh my Hornby and my Barlow long ago'.

Sam Woods was born in Sydney in 1867, played Test cricket for Australia against England and went on to play both cricket and rugby for England. Woods came to England in 1884 to attend Brighton College and represented the college at both cricket and football, on one occasion playing for the college football team against Burgess Hill FC, whose team included C. Aubrey Smith.

Cultured Barbarian. Andrew Stoddart (Middlesex) captained England at both cricket and rugby union. He led England on the 1894–95 and 1897–98 tours to Australia having previously toured there with England, then won 10 caps for England at rugby union and was captain of the Barbarians in their first ever match, in 1890–91.

Reg Spooner opened the innings for Lancashire for nigh on 20 years, apart from a three-year spell when he served in the Boer War. He was offered the England captaincy for the tour of Australia in 1920–21 but had to withdraw due to an injury sustained when playing rugby for Liverpool. He won one cap for England at rugby union, against Wales in 1903.

One evening I read in the stop press 'R. H. Spooner b. Wilson 0'. R. H. Spooner was my favourite cricketer, and whenever he failed much of the savour went out of my life. The next evening, or the evening after, a worse blow befell me. Again I turned to the 'close of play' score and there, in cold print, was this announcement: 'R. H. Spooner b. Wilson 0'. A pair of spectacles for him! I hadn't the heart that summer evening to play cricket with my schoolmates. I wandered the streets blighted.
NEVILLE CARDUS

Reginald 'Tip' Foster is the only man to have captained England at both cricket and football. Foster made his Test debut against Australia at Sydney in December 1903 and has the distinction of having the highest individual score on a Test debut – 287 not out. He later went on to captain England in the Test series against South Africa. Between 1900 and 1902 he won five caps for England at football, captaining his country against Wales. He had also represented Oxford University at cricket, football, golf and racquets. Sadly his career was cut short by diabetes: he died at the age of 36 while, according to one report, 'attempting to eat a boiled egg' (was this really of relevance?). Tip had six brothers all of whom, like him, played cricket for Worcestershire.

C. B. Fry (Sussex and Hampshire) represented England at both cricket and football and also Great Britain at athletics. Fry played in 26 Tests for England in a first-class career that spanned the years 1892 to 1921. He was capped at football by England and played for Southampton in the 1902 FA Cup Final against Sheffield United (1–2 after 1–1. Sheffield United's winning goal in the replay was scored by Ernest 'Nudger' Needham who also played county cricket, for Derbyshire.) Days after appearing for Southampton in the 1902 FA Cup Final replay, Fry played for England in a Test against Australia. In March 1893 he set a world long jump record of 7.17m.

Johnny Douglas played cricket for Essex and captained England in 18 of his 23 Tests, from his first, when deputizing for Pelham 'Plum' Warner in 1911. He was capped for the England amateur football team and as a middleweight boxer won a gold medal at the 1908 Olympics.

Prolific batsman Elias 'Patsy' Hendren (Middlesex) was a dual international who played in 51 Tests (1920–35) and also played football for Brentford, Queens Park Rangers, Manchester City and Coventry City. He was also capped by England, against Wales in 1919.

Joe Payne, who on 13 April 1936 set a Football League record by scoring 10 goals for Luton Town against Bristol Rovers, played Minor Counties cricket for Bedfordshire for whom, in 1952, he scored a century in 90 minutes.

Denis Compton's elder brother, Leslie, kept wicket for Middlesex (1938–56) and also played football for Arsenal and England (two caps). The Compton brothers have the rare distinction of having played together in a County Championship-winning team, in 1947, and also a Football League Championship-winning team (Arsenal, in 1947–48). Both represented England at football, though only Denis played Test cricket for England.

Denis Compton was the all-round sportsman. The hero worship I felt for him then cannot be described in fewer than three volumes, with footnotes and full index. He once addressed two words to me, and if you have a long evening to spare I'll give you the full story.
MELVYN BRAGG

Arthur Jepson, who played 390 matches for Nottinghamshire between 1938 and 1959, also played professional football as a goalkeeper, appearing in over 300 Football League and FA Cup matches in a career that encompassed Mansfield Town, Port Vale, Stoke City and Lincoln City. While still playing for Nottinghamshire, in the winter he also had a spell as player-manager of Hinckley United, and later managed Hinckley Athletic. Following his retirement as an active sportsman, Jepson became a renowned first-class umpire, officiating at many Test matches.

Maurice Turnbull (Glamorgan) played cricket for England, and rugby and hockey for Wales. Turnbull is regarded as one of Glamorgan's greatest captains and many believed he would have captained England after the Second World War. Tragically this was never to be: he was killed in action during the D-Day landings while serving with the Welsh Guards. When news of his death reached Cardiff, Glamorgan were playing the Fire Service at Arms Park. After the announcement a crowd of over 5,000 spontaneously took to their feet and stood in silence for five minutes.

He spanned two sports. Everton Weekes (West Indies) is the only Test cricketer who was also an international bridge player, for his native Barbados.

Bruce can do for the Kangaroos. Bruce Dooland represented Australia at both cricket and baseball.

Having played for Cambridge University in the Varsity matches of 1936 and 1937, Norman Yardley (Yorkshire) was one of those cricketers who missed his peak years due to service in the Second World War. He succeeded Wally Hammond as England captain in 1947 and was captain of Yorkshire from 1948 to 1955. He played hockey and amateur football in the Sheffield area and was North of England squash champion for six years in succession.

Thirteen county cricketers also played football for Arsenal: Brian Close, Denis and Leslie Compton, George Cox, Ted Drake, Andy Ducat, Joe Hulme, Arthur Milton, Don Roper, Jim Standen, Harry Storer, Ray Swallow and Steve Gatting.

Arsenal chairmen Samuel and Denis Hill-Wood both played for Derbyshire.

In 1947 Eric Houghton was in his twentieth season as a footballer with Aston Villa when he made his first-class debut for Warwickshire, against India at Edgbaston.

Willie Watson (Yorkshire and Leicestershire) played in 23 Tests for England (1951–59), won four caps for England at football (1949–50) and was a member of England's 1950 World Cup squad. Watson played his club football with Huddersfield Town (for whom his father had played professionally), Sunderland and Halifax Town.

In the early 1950s Fred Trueman played for Lincoln City reserves while doing his National Service in the RAF. When demobbed he was offered full-time professional terms but decided to concentrate on a career in cricket.

Alan Oakman (Sussex) played in goal for Hastings United (Southern League) and once wrote to Arsenal requesting a trial but never received a reply. Undaunted, he then wrote to Brentford and Queens Park Rangers. After failing to receive a response from either of these clubs he decided, very wisely as it turned out, to pursue a career in cricket with Sussex.

Glamorgan's Don Shepherd had trials with both Cardiff City and Leeds United and also played badminton for Swansea.

Maurice Tremlett (Somerset and England) was an accomplished golfer, playing off a handicap of five for 20 years. He holed in one seven times, including three times in a month.

Trevor Bailey (Essex) played in 61 Tests for England (1949–59) and in 1952 won an FA Amateur Cup winners medal with Walthamstow Avenue, for whom his Essex team-mate Doug Insole also played.

Brian Taylor (Essex) signed as a professional footballer for Brentford in 1950 and played for three years for the club when Tommy Lawton was player-manager. He continued to play non-league football as a part-time professional while playing cricket for Kent, his last club being Dover, then (1967) of the Southern League.

John Pretlove (Kent) was a Cambridge Blue at both cricket and football. When he retired as a cricketer he went to work for Blue Circle (Cement).

Len Shackleton gained three caps for England at football – a meagre reward for a player of consummate skills, the fact that he made no secret of his contempt for the sport's officialdom not helping his case. He joined the Arsenal groundstaff in 1936 but was released and began his senior career in football with Bradford Park Avenue. He then played for Newcastle United and Sunderland, and while in the north-east he played cricket regularly in the Durham Senior League, and also qualified as a boxing referee.

Ray Illingworth (Yorkshire, Leicestershire and England) was a talented footballer who at the age of 18 was offered trials by Huddersfield Town, Bradford City and Aston Villa. The Villa scout's report on the young Illingworth described him as 'the best two-footed player I have seen'. On the advice of his father, Illingworth declined the offers from all three Football League clubs to concentrate on a career in cricket.

In 1956–57 three Kent players, Stuart O'Leary, Sid O'Linn and Derek Ufton, and Surrey's Micky Stewart, were all regular players with Charlton Athletic.

In the late 1950s the Glamorgan team included Alan Durban, who went on to enjoy a successful career in football both as a player (Cardiff City, Derby County and Wales) and manager (Stoke City and Sunderland).

Alan Durban was not the only high-profile footballer to have appeared for Glamorgan. In 1968 former Welsh international Trevor Ford, whose clubs included Swansea Town, Aston Villa, Sunderland and Cardiff City, was in the field against Nottinghamshire at Swansea, the match in which Gary Sobers famously hit six sixes in a single over off the bowling of Malcolm Nash. As Ford quipped, 'I was one of the players who went to retrieve the ball from a nearby street, and had to pay to get back in the ground.'

In the late 1950s and early 1960s Derbyshire's Ian Buxton, Ian Hall and Ray Swallow spent the winters playing League football for Derby County.

Australian captain Brian Booth also played hockey for his country and was a member of the Australia hockey team at the 1956 Olympic Games.

The Nawab of Pataudi (Sussex) played cricket for England and also cricket and hockey for India.

Gilbert Parkhouse (Glamorgan and England) retired from first-class cricket in 1964 and became an international hockey umpire, officiating at international hockey matches in Spain and Belgium as well as in the UK.

Ted Hemsley and Jim Standen played in the Worcestershire team that won the County Championship in 1964 and 1965 and also enjoyed successful careers as footballers. Hemsley played for Shrewsbury Town, Sheffield United, Doncaster Rovers and Halifax Town. He made his Football League debut for Shrewsbury in 1961, and a few months later played his first game for Worcestershire Seconds. Standen played for Arsenal and West Ham United. In 1964 he won an FA Cup winners medal with West Ham and later that summer achieved a remarkable 'double' as a member of the Worcestershire team that won the County Championship.

In the 1960s the hat-trick hero of England's 1966 World Cup-winning team, Geoff Hurst, played for Essex. Not as successfully as he did for West Ham and England, however: Hurst scored more goals in the 1966 World Cup Final than he did first-class runs for Essex.

Jim Coombes, a mainstay of the Worcestershire team of the 1960s and early 1970s, also enjoyed a career as a goalkeeper with Aston Villa.

In the 1960s and 1970s Graham Cross was a regular member of the Leicestershire team, and played 599 matches for Leicester City. He appeared for Leicester City in two FA Cup Finals and two League Cup Finals and won 11 Under-23 caps for England. He made his debut for Leicestershire in 1961 and is the only man to have played in cup finals at both Wembley (1963 and 1969) and Lord's, where he was a Benson & Hedges Cup winner with Leicestershire in 1975.

Balder-Dash. Chris Balderstone also played in that Benson & Hedges Cup Final, and he too was a noted footballer, with Huddersfield Town, Carlisle United and Doncaster Rovers. On 14 September 1975 Balderstone was playing for Leicestershire against Derbyshire at Chesterfield and at close of play had made 51 not out in a match in which Leicestershire gained a first-innings lead and four bowling points which confirmed them as county champions. Rather than celebrating with his team-mates, at close of play Balderstone set off for Doncaster and played for Rovers in a Fourth Division match against Brentford (1–1). After that game, Balderstone then played for the Doncaster Rovers players' darts team against a team of Rovers fans in the Supporters Social Club before setting off to join his Leicestershire team-mates at their Derby hotel. The following morning he resumed his innings, taking his overnight score to 116 before being run out. Not only is Balderstone the only man to have played county cricket and a Football

League match on the same day, he must be the only man to have played a Football League match midway through a first-class hundred.

Arthur Milton played cricket for Gloucestershire (1948–74) and was also a professional footballer with Arsenal and Bristol City in the 1940s and 1950s. He represented England at both cricket and football and was capped in the latter sport after only 12 games for Arsenal. His Test debut came in 1958 against New Zealand at Headingley and he made an unbeaten 104 in his first innings. Arthur died in 2007, in all probability the last of the 'dual' internationals.

Viv Richards (Somerset, Glamorgan and West Indies) is the only man to have played in both the cricket and football World Cup, having turned out for Antigua in the qualifying stages of the 1978 World Cup.

Steve Gatting (Middlesex), brother of Mike, played League football for Arsenal, Brighton and Charlton Athletic. Steve's son, Joe, played cricket for Sussex and football for Brighton and Hove Albion.

When I was in my mid-teens I played both football and cricket and was invited for trials by Heart of Midlothian football club and Derbyshire. After the trials I was told I showed great promise as a right-hand batsman and had all the makings of a good centre-forward. Unfortunately, Hearts went on to say they had no need for a right-hand batsman and Derbyshire didn't want a centre-forward.
MICK CULLERTON (Hibernian, Port Vale and Derby County)

Sir Ian Botham played football for Scunthorpe United (1980–85), albeit intermittently due to winter tours with England. His son, Liam, played cricket for Hampshire. Liam also played both rugby union and rugby league – among the clubs he represented were Newcastle Falcons (union) and Leeds Rhinos (league).

Gary Lineker played football for Leicester City, Everton, Barcelona and Tottenham Hotspur and won 80 caps for England. A promising cricketer, in his teens he joined Leicestershire and once scored a century for the Second XI. While still enjoying considerable success as a footballer he played for the MCC against Germany at Lord's in July 1992. After being dismissed for 1 in this match he quipped, 'At least I've maintained my record of always having scored one against Germany.'

Tim Buzaglo, who sensationally scored a hat-trick for non-league Woking against West Bromwich Albion in the third round of the FA Cup in 1991, also played international cricket for Gibraltar.

 He was an all-rounder, which means he was average at more things than the average player.
FRED TRUEMAN

In 1876 James Lillywhite's touring professional team played a match against Goulburn in Australia during which play was interrupted when six hares and two kangaroos chased about the pitch.

On 30 August 1892 a runaway horse and cart stopped play during Yorkshire's match against the MCC at Scarborough.

No, you go and get it. On 12 July 1934 during a match in Sohar, India, a ball from Sohar's Birkat Ullah was hit into the sea and immediately swallowed by a shark.

On 3 July 1936, during the match between the MCC and Cambridge University at Lord's, Cambridge's Jehangir Khan killed a sparrow in mid-flight when bowling to T. N. Pearce. Days later the sparrow was well and truly stuffed again, this time by a taxidermist. It continues to see out its days in the MCC museum.

Jiminy Cricket! A plague of grasshoppers stopped play during the match between South Australia and Queensland at Adelaide in 1947.

Ewe gotta be joking. On 4 August 1948 play was stopped in the match between Glamorgan and Gloucestershire at Ebbw Vale when a flock of sheep wandered on to the pitch. Even when the last of them had been shepherded away play did not resume for another 10 minutes – until the 'presents' they had left had been removed.

Play was stopped during the match between Maharashtra and the MCC at Poona in December 1951 when a monkey ran on to the field and for some minutes avoided attempts by players and officials to capture it.

In 1953, during a County Championship match between Worcestershire and Leicestershire at New Road, a drive from Leicestershire's G. A. Smithson hit and killed a pied wagtail that was walking along the boundary.

Eh, two Brutus. A dog named Brutus stopped play during Test matches at Headingley in both 1961 and 1962. The dog, which lived in a house overlooking the ground, somehow gained entry and after running about the field for some minutes, causing consternation among players, officials and police, on both occasions evaded capture before exiting via a gate at the Kirkstall Lane End. The dog was considered a lucky omen by the England players: on both occasions England went on to win the Headingley Test.

In June 1962 a swarm of bees stopped play during the match between Oxford University and Worcestershire at The Parks.

A 'very large' swarm of bees stopped play during Lampeter CC's match against Bronwydd at Lampeter in June 1988.

On 5 August 1963 the match between Southern Schools (Public, of course) and The Rest was halted when a black cat walked on to the field and, unconcerned that play was in progress, lay down on the pitch in front of the non-striker's wicket.

The only animal to have appeared in the 'Obituaries' in *Wisden Cricketers' Almanack* (1965) is a cat named Peter which resided at Lord's for 12 years until it expired in November 1964.

Had a mare. In 1976 play was abandoned at Tintwistle CC (Cheshire) when two runaway horses tore across the field and their hooves dug up the pitch.

In August 1984 the match between Launceston CC and Old Suttonians at Launceston was stopped when, much to the surprise of the Cornish players, camels walked on to the field. The animals were appearing in a circus nearby and had broken free from their tethers. What a pity it didn't happen at Camelford.

England wicket-keeper Bruce French (Nottinghamshire) was attacked and bitten by a dog while on a training run during England's 1985–86 tour of the West Indies. (It was not a Jack Russell.)

'Mackerel Stopped Play' during the Cricketer Cup first-round tie between Old Cliftonians CC and Stowe Templars at Bristol in 1986. Simon Hazlitt was batting for Old Cliftonians when a mackerel fell from the sky and splattered across the pitch. The fish had been dropped by a seagull which, it transpired, had taken it from the sea lion pen at Bristol Zoo.

An iguana stopped play when it settled on the pitch during Young Sri Lanka's match against Young England at Colombo in February 1987.

The first match of the 1987 season at Swardeston CC in Norfolk was halted when two bulls rampaged across the pitch.

Play was stopped during the match between Mumbles CC and Skewen in August 1989 when stoats ran across the pitch.

In 1989 at Kentisbeare, a new ball was summoned when the original in the match between Kentisbeare CC and Exmouth was swallowed by a cow.

Ant and decked. On 11 August 1990 play was halted during the match between Chard CC and Sampford Arundel when a swarm of flying ants invaded the area around the pitch.

During 2003–04, cane toads encroaching on to the pitch stopped play in four separate matches in Queensland, Australia.

Raging Bull. A bull stopped play during the Second XI fixture between Derbyshire and Leicestershire at Dunstall in June 2005. The bull found its way into the ground from a nearby field via a low fence, chased the players from the field and resisted all attempts at capture for 20 minutes.

So gullible. In September 2005 Glamorgan lost to Nottinghamshire by eight wickets at Sophia Gardens. The Glamorgan players blamed their defeat on a wet patch at one end of the pitch. Bemused as to why this should be so, Glamorgan officials decided to investigate. They discovered the wet patch was the result of seagulls having pecked holes in the tarpaulin cover, which the Nottinghamshire seam bowlers had subsequently exploited to their advantage.

Birds or animals (real or mythological) feature on the badges of seven County Championship clubs: Durham (dragons), Kent (horse), Leicestershire (fox), Nottinghamshire (stags), Somerset (dragon), Sussex (martlets) and Warwickshire (bear). And, of course, the England badge features lions.

A team of players who played Test cricket who share their names with those of animals, birds or fish:

Morice Bird (England)
Geoff Chubb (South Africa)
Alfred Dipper (England)
Arthur Dolphin (England)
Ryan Hinds (West Indies)
Wavell Hinds (West Indies)
Bradley Hogg (Australia)
Allan Lamb (England)
Joe Partridge (South Africa)
Cliff Roach (West Indies)
Ashley Woodcock (Australia)
Manager: Arthur Chipperfield (Australia)

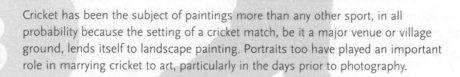

3

Cricket has been the subject of paintings more than any other sport, in all probability because the setting of a cricket match, be it a major venue or village ground, lends itself to landscape painting. Portraits too have played an important role in marrying cricket to art, particularly in the days prior to photography.

Artists began to portray cricket from the game's earliest days. Several prominent artists of the eighteenth century found inspiration in the rural settings of matches. Among the earliest representations are *The Cricket Match* by L. P. Boitard, dated 1740, and *Gentlemen v. Players at Brading, Isle of Wight* by Francis Hayman, arguably the best-known painter of cricket scenes during this period, dated 1749.

The most famous artwork of the late eighteenth and early nineteenth centuries, and arguably the work of most historical significance, is not an individual painting but 12 watercolour drawings by George Shepherd (1770–1842), who played for Surrey. The watercolours appear on a single sheet taken from one of Shepherd's art books. As for why this single sheet was removed and alone survived no one can be sure. Shepherd's sketches depict nine named cricketers at Lord's circa 1790, among them Lord Frederick Beauclerk, Henry Tufton, Charles Lennox, Edward Bligh and two of Thomas Lord. The work also contains three unique action portraits of Hambledon players Tom Walker, David Harris and William Beldham. This single sheet from Shepherd's art book is owned by the MCC.

Many cricket paintings of the nineteenth century have, over the years, been reproduced as prints. The most famous and most consistently reproduced is *The Scorer* by Thomas Henwood (1842). The subject is William Davis, the scorer at Lewes Prior Cricket Club, who appears as an old rustic, bearded, bewhiskered and bespectacled, hunched over a detailed scorebook while smoking a churchwarden pipe. It is estimated some 10,000 prints of *The Scorer* were sold between 1860 and 1914.

Famous cricketers often consented to having their portraits painted, though art critics have never considered such portraits to be of outstanding artistic merit. Among the best known are those of W. G. Grace, by A. Stuart-Wortley; Herbert Studwick, by Frank Eastman; and *Impression of Jack Hobbs* by George Belcher. A fine portrait of Sir Leonard Hutton by Henry Carr is now owned by the Hutton family.

By far the most popular subjects are matches in progress at famous grounds, many of which now also serve as a historic record of the ground in question and a depiction not only of cricket but of society at the given time. Such paintings include *The Oval, 1849* by C. J. Basbe; *Hastings* and *Lord's*, both by Charles Cundall; and *Edgbaston* by C. T. Burt.

Nineteenth-century artists were also keen to portray minor cricket in rustic settings, often featuring village greens ringed by what we might now term 'chocolate box' cottages and the traditional thatched country pub – again, the appeal is the landscape setting. Particularly fine examples of this 'landscape' genre are *Landscape with a Cricket Match in Progress* by Paul Sandby (1850); *Cricket Match with a view of Christchurch Priory and countryside*, artist unknown, thought to date from c. 1840; *Village Cricket* by John Ritchie (1855); and *A Cricket Match at Parkers Piece, Cambridge* by L. Ullman (1860 and/or 1861).

In the 1860s and 1870s cricket-themed paintings of a very sentimental, 'sugary' and idealized nature became very popular with the public. Such paintings were invariably reproduced as prints and sold cheaply, and they adorned thousands of walls in Victorian homes. Among the most popular 'cricket sentimentals' were *An Old Cricketer* and *Her First Lesson*. The titles are self-explanatory, both the work of James Hayllar.

For some artists the actual cricket match was incidental to the main body of the work, the match or players just 'creeping' on to a canvas that recorded a setting often depicting a particular element of Victorian society, or contrasting social spheres. A famous example is *Eton v. Harrow, 1886* by Albert Chevalier Taylor, which features a single fielder by the boundary to the upper left of the painting. The main body of the work is devoted to what appear to be the families of the players, dressed in their finery and seated primly in rows under the roof of a buff-coloured low-level grandstand. Social etiquette dictates they sit impassively, in contrast to the unbridled enthusiasm being displayed by some 'working-class' spectators purposefully portrayed much further down the line.

Match de Cricket à Bedford Park, Londres, painted by Camille Pissarro in 1897, shows a match in progress as viewed by the artist over a hedge from a vantage point in a neighbouring field, suggesting that the French impressionist felt he was forever to be distanced from the sport and, where the complexities and nuances of cricket were concerned, that he would always be an 'outsider'.

The impressionist Claude Monet visited London towards the end of 1899, primarily to paint scenes of mist and fog on the Thames. Monet had previously come to London in 1871, it is said with plans to paint a cricket scene at Lord's, only to abandon the idea on being told there was no cricket at Lord's in November.

The landscape theme continued in cricket art well into the twentieth century, though there was a desire among artists to capture the whole scene rather than an element of play, and often to make a personal statement. *England v. Australia at Lord's, 1938* by Charles Candall offers a panoramic view of proceedings from behind a body of spectators looking out across the pitch with the pavilion in the far background. The pavilion is featured just off centre which indicates, in opposition to the view held by the MCC, that the artist may not have viewed Lord's as the epicentre of the English cricket scene.

After the First World War, caricatures of cricketers became a very popular mode of art. The most famous exponent of this genre was Tom Webster. Webster began drawing caricatures of cricketers (and other sportsmen) for the *Daily Mail* but later worked as a freelance producing inventive pen-and-ink and charcoal drawings for many newspapers and magazines as well as his own publication, *Tom Webster's Annual*, which was published until 1960. Among his lasting impressions of cricketers are those of Don Bradman, George Duckworth, Percy Fender, Patsy Hendren, Jack Hobbs and Maurice Tate. Webster was the inspiration for several later sporting caricaturists, most notably Roy Ullyett, whose drawings and cartoons of cricketers for the *Daily Express* perfectly captured the events of the time and proved immensely popular with readers.

Most pavilions at County Championship clubs boast portraits of players and scenes from past matches. There are any number of paintings of relatively recent times, commissioned in grateful recognition of outstanding achievement and years of service to the club in question – for example the portrait in oils of Basil D'Oliveira which hangs in the members bar at New Road, Worcester.

 There hangs in the pavilion of Kent Cricket Club at the St Lawrence ground, Canterbury, an old print, in the Hogarthian manner, of a ladies cricket match. Married v. Single I believe. It is not a delicate or aesthetic scene. Mid-wicket is an object of fun, having, like the mariner's wife of Mr Jacobs, lost her good looks and found others.
R. C. ROBERTSON-GLASGOW

Upon his retirement as a cricketer in 1967, Godfrey Evans (Essex) became an accomplished artist.

Cricket art is not confined to painting, it encompasses all aspects of art from sculpture (that of W. G. Grace at Lord's) to pottery. After the Second World War, Royal Worcester produced a series of fine bone china gilt-edged plates on an annual basis which featured facsimile signatures of the tourists. The most collectable is the 'Ashes', produced in 1953 to commemorate the series between England and Australia, and which featured facsimiles of both teams and signatures.

Today there are numerous companies selling paintings and prints of cricket and cricketers of varying quality, all of whom have websites. There are also several contemporary artists who specialize in cricket scenes, among them:

Terry Harrison, who depicts contemporary scenes at famous grounds in watercolour and acrylic.

Jocelyn Galsworthy, the Isle of Wight-based artist who has travelled the world and is renowned for her paintings of cricket scenes in oils and other mediums, the settings of which range from famous grounds to club and village cricket.

Colin Richards, the Kent-based artist whose work has been exhibited at the Royal Academy. Richards' work tends to concentrate on parks and club cricket rather than major matches, the simplicity and basic techniques used in his paintings reflecting the nature of cricket at grass-roots level. He also paints scenes from amateur football matches, a notable work being *Kick and Run.*

The best-known contemporary artist specializing in cricket scenes is the former Gloucestershire and England wicket-keeper Jack Russell. His career as a painter began in 1987 when rain stopped play during a Gloucestershire match and he started to sketch to pass the time. Although his subjects are varied, he is best known for his cricket paintings. He opened his own gallery in Chipping Sodbury in 1994 and has since enjoyed numerous sell-out exhibitions of his work. Among his most famous paintings are *Fond Memories*, a scene of Stroud CC, the club he joined as an 11-year-old; *Moment of Victory*, which depicts a scene during England's defeat of the West Indies in Jamaica in 1990; *The Old Tavern*, commissioned by the Lord's Taverners, which he painted from old photographs as the Old Tavern had been demolished in 1968; and *Sydney Cricket Ground, 1995*, which was a private commission. Russell is also a keen military historian, and this features in his work, as do scenes from Slad Valley in Gloucestershire, commonly known as 'Laurie Lee country'.

AUTHOR: In what way would you say you differed from Jack Russell?
ALAN KNOTT: Well, for a start, I can't paint.

The greatest collection of cricket paintings can be found in the Long Room at Lord's. They are accessible to all, simply book for the MCC Museum Tour. Among the most famous is *The Conversation Piece*, which features cricket legends Godfrey Evans, Trevor Bailey, Peter May, Brian Statham, Denis Compton, Alec Bedser, Colin Cowdrey, Fred Trueman, Ted Dexter and Tom Graveney enjoying a chin-wag in the Long Room itself.

In 2004 L. S. Lowry's *The Cricket Match* sold for £600,000 at auction, a record price for a cricket painting.

One born every minute? Within two days of having started to attend an art class in Brighton in 2005, former Middlesex and England bowler Phil Tufnell sold his first painting – for £1,100. Described as being 'a red whirling window into Tufnell's soul', the piece was purchased by dance DJ Fatboy Slim (Norman Cook).

Surrey County Cricket Club 6d.

SURREY v. YORKSHIRE
at Kennington Oval, Sat., Mon., Tues., Aug. 14th, 16th, 17th, 1965

SURREY — First Innings

				Second Innings	
*1 M. J. Stewart	lbw b Taylor	29		N/O	9
2 J. H. Edrich	st Binks, b Close	12		N/O	
3 W. A. Smith	c Boycott, b Wilson	39			
4 K. F. Barrington	c Hampshire, b Hutton	54			
5 R. A. E. Tindall	b Hutton	15			
6 S. J. Storey	c Boycott, b Wilson	11			
7 D. Gibson	not out	60			
‡8 A. Long	c Illingworth, b Wilson	0			
10 R. Harman	c Sharpe, b Wilson	5			
9 D. A. Marriott	c Padgett, b Hutton	2			
11 D. A. D. Sydenham	b Waring	12			

Total 248

Fall of the wickets 1—28 2—81 3—97 4—152 5—159 6—175 7—179 8—199 9—216 10—248

Bowling Analysis 1st Ins. O. M. R. W. Wd. N.b. 2nd Ins. O. M. R. W. Wd. N.b.

	O.	M.	R.	W.
Hutton	28		85	4
Waring	19	3	91	1
Close	15	4	47	1
Taylor	6	1	20	1
Wilson	26	10	70	4

TEST MATCH AT THE OVAL, ENGLAND v. SOUTH AFRICA, AUG. 26th–31st, AND GILLETTE CUP FINAL AT LORD'S, 4th SEPT., 1965

Please call at the Office or write to the Secretary, S.C.C.C., S.E.11., for information concerning advance bookings.

YORKSHIRE — First Innings

	Second Innings
1 G. Boycott	
‡ K. Taylor	92
2 P. J. Sharpe	
3 D. E. V. Padgett	
4 J. H. Hampshire	
*6 D. B. Close	
7 R. Illingworth	
8 R. A. Hutton	
‡9 J. G. Binks	
10 J. Waring	
11 D. Wilson	

Fall of the wickets 1—96 2—97 3—105 4—169 5—190 Total 251 Dec

Bowling Analysis 1st Ins. O. M. R. W. Wd. N.b. 2nd Ins. O. M. R. W. Wd. N.b.

*Captain ‡Wkt.-keeper

Umpires—A. E. Fagg & R. S. Lay

Toss won by—YORKS.

Hours of play—1st day 11.30—6.30. 2nd day 11.30—6.30. 3rd day 11.0 to 5.30 or 6.0. Lunch 1.30 all days

NEW BALL may be taken by the fielding captain after 85 overs.

SUPPORTERS' ASSOC. URGENTLY NEED AGENTS. Apply at the Office by Press Entrance

On 29 August 1882 England lost to Australia for the first time on home soil, and a number of publications subsequently carried mock obituaries mourning the 'death' of English cricket. The first of them appeared on 31 August in *Cricket – A Weekly Record of the Game,* a magazine edited by Charles Alcock: 'Sacred to the memory of England's supremacy in the cricket field which expired on the 29th day of August at the Oval. Its end was Peate (the last England batsman to lose his wicket that day).' But it was the one that appeared in the *Sporting Times* that has enjoyed lasting fame and has been credited with the creation of the term 'the Ashes':

In Affectionate Remembrance
of
ENGLISH CRICKET
Which Died At The Oval
On
29th August, 1882
Deeply lamented by a large circle of sorrowing friends and acquaintances
RIP
NB – The lady will be cremated and the ashes taken to Australia

On 9 September 1882 *Punch* magazine ran with a poem lamenting the death of English cricket which began:

Well done, Cornstalks!
Whipt us fair and square,
Was it luck that tript us, was it score,
Kangaroo lands, demons,
Or our own want of devil, cool, nerve and backbone?

Some weeks after the cricket season ended, an English team captained by the Honourable Ivo Bligh (later Lord Darnley) set off to tour Australia. Bligh vowed to the press he would 'return with the ashes'. This must have been a direct reference to the mock obituary in the *Sporting Times,* but no one attached any great credence to the term as it was not yet in common usage.

Prior to a match being played, on Christmas Eve 1882 Ivo Bligh and the English team were guests of Sir William Clarke on his Rupertswood estate in Sunbury, Victoria. It was at this gathering that a group of Melbourne women presented a small terracotta urn to Bligh as a memento of his visit. The 'urn', some six inches (15cm) in height, was in all probability a perfume jar and, rather than a trophy to be contested by England and Australia, a personal gift to Bligh. It is often written that the 'Ashes' urn contains the ashes of one of the bails (or both) used in the Oval match of 1882, but as the urn was presented as a gift to Ivo Bligh on Christmas Eve in 1882, this is not the case.

In February 1883 Mrs Ann Fletcher, the daughter of Joseph and Marion Clarke (née Wright), made a velvet bag in which to keep the 'Ashes' urn and presented it to Ivo Bligh.

Following the return of Bligh and the English team from Australia, little was heard of the urn and its bag as they were kept at the Bligh family home. The next known reference to the term 'the Ashes' was in 1899 when, in Australia, George Giffen published his memoirs, *With Bat and Ball,* and mentioned the term.

In 1903 Pelham 'Plum' Warner took an England team to Australia and in an interview given to the English press promised to 'regain the Ashes'. It was following Warner's reference that the press first latched on to the term.

Following England's success in Australia, in 1904 Plum Warner wrote a book, *How We Recovered The Ashes.* There is, however, no reference to the term 'the Ashes' within its pages. This being the case, in all probability the title was the brainchild of the publisher who deemed it a marketable title for the book. It is not known for sure when 'the Ashes' came into popular usage as a term to describe the series between England and Australia, but certainly after the publication of Warner's book people were referring to 'the Ashes'.

In 1904 an 'Ashes' urn was presented to Plum Warner, and one to Australian captain M. A. Noble in 1909. One wonders where these urns are now.

The first mention of 'the Ashes' in *Wisden* occurred in 1905. The first *Wisden* account of the legend featured in the 1922 edition.

In 1925 *The Cricketers Annual* printed a poem which included the following lines:

> So here's to Chapman, Hendrie and Hobbs,
> Gilligan, Woolley and Hearne;
> May they bring back to the Motherland
> the 'Ashes' which have no urn.

In 1927 Ivo Bligh (now Lord Darnley) died and his widow presented the original 'Ashes' urn to the MCC. This was to prove the key event in the establishment of the urn as the physical embodiment of the legendary Ashes series.

Later in 1927 the MCC placed the urn on display in the Long Room at Lord's. It is often mistaken as the official trophy of the Ashes series, when in fact it is a private memento. For this reason the idea of presenting the actual 'Ashes' urn was never entertained by the MCC. For many years no trophy was presented to the winners of what was now termed 'the Ashes'. In 1934, however, an urn containing 'ashes' was presented to Australian captain W. M. Woodfull. Subsequent winning captains of the Ashes series have also been presented with a replica of the original urn.

In 1953 the 'Ashes' urn was transferred from the Long Room to the cricket museum at Lord's. It remains on display in the MCC museum along with the velvet bag and a scorecard of the 1882 match at the Oval.

Due to the very fragile condition of the original urn only twice has it made the journey to Australia. The first occasion was in 1988 as part of Australia's bicentennial celebrations, and it was also the centrepiece of the MCC Travelex Ashes Exhibition in 2006–07, which visited seven museums in six Australian states and attracted in excess of 105,000 visitors.

In the late 1990s, in recognition of the desire of England and Australia teams to compete for an actual trophy, following discussions with the ECB and Cricket Australia the MCC commissioned an urn-shaped Waterford Crystal trophy. It was first presented to Mark Taylor following Australia's victory over England in the 1998–99 Test series. Since then the trophy has been presented to the winning captain at the end of each Test series between England and Australia except in 2005, when a replica of the Ashes urn was presented to winning captain, Michael Vaughan.

In 1998 Lord Darnley's daughter went on record as saying that far from containing the ashes of a piece of cricket equipment, some years ago her mother had revealed to her that the original urn in fact contained the ashes of a veil she had once owned. The MCC official responsible for the safety of the urn during the 2006–07 visit to Australia said the veil story had been discounted but did not offer any evidence as to why. Well, he wouldn't, would he?

Despite this, the Ashes is now synonymous with the Test series between England and Australia, and while not an actual trophy, it is revered throughout the sporting world.

ENGLAND v AUSTRALIA at MANCHESTER

2nd INNINGS OF AUSTRALIA

BATSMEN		HOW OUT	BOWLER	TOTAL	MINS
1	C.C. McDonald	c Oakman	Laker	89	341
2	J.W. Burke	c Lock	Laker	33	106
3	R.N. Harvey	c Cowdrey	Laker	0	2
4	I.D. Craig	lbw	Laker	38	263
5	K. Mackay	c Oakman	Laker	0	8
6	K.R. Miller	b	Laker	0	17
7	R.G. Archer	c Oakman	Laker	0	3
8	R. Benaud	b	Laker	18	107
9	R.R. Lindwall	c Lock	Laker	8	44
10	I.W. Johnson	not out		1	27
11	L. Maddocks	lbw	Laker	2	8
	EXTRAS			16	
	TOTAL			205	

FALL OF WICKETS: 1 28, 2 55, 3 114, 4 124, 5 130, 6 130, 7 181, 8 198, 9 203, 10 205

BATSMAN: Harvey, Burke, Craig, Mackay, Miller, Archer, McDonald, Benaud, Lindwall, Maddocks

Unlike football clubs, historically cricket clubs have never kept meticulous attendance records, primarily because club members never had their attendance registered or recorded by passing through a turnstile. Where records were kept, many figures were rounded up to the nearest thousand, again because accurate figures were difficult to establish due to members coming and going, often on the same day of play. There have also been numerous instances of spectators being allowed free admission to matches nearing completion on the final day of play.

Aggregate attendances for County Championship matches were not regularly available prior to 1947 because clubs were not officially bound to keep a record of match attendances for individual games.

The attendance on the final day of the very first Test match between Australia and England in 1877 at the Melbourne Cricket Ground was 3,000.

The record aggregate attendance for a County Championship match at Headingley is 78,792, for Yorkshire against Lancashire (three days) in 1904.

The record aggregate attendance for a County Championship match is 80,000 at the Oval for the match (three days) between Surrey and Yorkshire in 1906.

The record aggregate attendance for a County Championship match at Old Trafford is 76,617, for Lancashire against Yorkshire (three days) in 1926.

The 1936–37 Test series between Australia and England was attended by a record total of 943,000 spectators. The aggregate attendance for the Melbourne Test was 350,534. Match receipts for the series totalled £87,963.

In 1945, the fourth Victory Match between England and Australia at Lord's (three days) was seen by an aggregate of 93,000 spectators.

The record aggregate attendance for a Test match in England is 158,000, for England against Australia at Headingley in 1948. The Lord's Test in this series had an aggregate attendance of 137,915.

In 1948 the touring Australians attracted large numbers wherever they played. The tourists' match against Essex at Southend produced a capacity crowd of 16,000 (a record for the ground) on each day of play.

The record aggregate attendance for a Test series in England is 549,650, for the 1953 series against Australia. Again it was Headingley which produced the top aggregate attendance in the series: 137,915.

On 11 February 1961 a crowd of 90,800 attended the second day's play of the fifth Test between Australia and West Indies at Melbourne. The match receipts for the day were £10,484.

The attendance for Glamorgan's match against Australia at the St Helen's ground, Swansea on August Bank Holiday Monday 1964 was 25,782.

In 1966 the Clark Committee (set up to review English cricket under the chairmanship of David Clark of Kent CCC) reported a steady year-on-year decline in post-war County Championship aggregate attendances. In 1949 the figure stood at 2.2 million, in 1950 it was two million, and in 1951 it had fallen again, to 1.8 million – thought to be the lowest aggregate peacetime attendance since 1919. By 1966 the aggregate number of spectators attending county matches had dropped to 513,578. In that year county clubs also suffered from a fall in membership, down from 250,000 in 1955 to 135,045.

On 3 September 1969 the attendance on the first day of Glamorgan's match against Worcestershire at the club's relatively new ground at Sophia Gardens was 10,500. The following season Glamorgan were posting three-figure attendances for a single day's play at some county matches.

The advent of one-day internationals (ODIs) produced healthy crowds. Some 86,122 people attended the ODI between Australia and the West Indies at Melbourne in 1983–84. The attendance for the 1992 World Cup Final between England and Pakistan at Melbourne was 87,812. In 1993–94 each of India's first ODIs against South Africa and West Indies attracted attendances of 100,000. And the 1996 World Cup semi-final between India and Sri Lanka at Calcutta, which was stopped due to rioting fans, was reportedly watched by 105,000 spectators.

Twenty20 has also had a marked effect on attendances, with many county clubs enjoying their best attendance figures for a number of years. In 2005 derby matches between Lancashire and Yorkshire and Middlesex and Surrey both drew crowds in excess of 10,000.

Attendances at Twenty20 Cup matches in 2008 (taking finals day as a single game) exceeded 525,000. The average attendance was 7,500.

The first Test in England to record match receipts in excess of £2 million was the second Test between England and West Indies at Lord's in 1995, which was watched by a total of 111,219 spectators paying £2,209,321. This series produced then world record receipts of £8,293,637.

The record aggregate attendance for a Test match is 465,000, at Calcutta for India against Pakistan in 1998–99. A crowd of 100,000 was recorded for each of the first four days of play.

Every one of the 502 spectators at the first ODI between Zimbabwe and Kenya at Bulawayo on 25 February 2006 gained free admission. Prior to the game Zimbabwe Cricket discovered that due to rampant inflation, the cost of printing tickets was so expensive it was cheaper to allow spectators in for free.

The first clubs were established in Australia in the late 1820s, the majority of them in the Sydney area.

In March 1856 a representative team from New South Wales played a representative side from Victoria in Melbourne. The game is considered to be the inaugural first-class match in Australia, though the term 'first-class' was not in common usage until the 1890s.

A team led by James Lillywhite, representing England, played a representative team from Australia in 1877. Australia defeated England by 45 runs, in a game recognized as the first ever Test match.

In 1891–92 the Earl of Sheffield was in Australia as the promoter of the England touring team led by W. G. Grace. At the end of the tour Earl Sheffield donated £150 to the New South Wales Cricket Association to fund a trophy for a tournament for the benefit of 'inter-colonial cricket in Australia'.

The Sheffield Shield was first competed for in 1892–93 by New South Wales, Victoria and South Australia. The inaugural winners were Victoria.

The Sheffield Shield is the premier domestic cricket competition in Australia. Six state teams – New South Wales Blues, Queensland Bulls, Southern

Redbacks, Tasmanian Tigers, Victoria Bullrangers and Western Warriors –
play a round-robin series of four-day matches on a home and away basis
with a system of points to be awarded. In 1982–83 it was decided that the two
highest-ranked teams should compete in a five-day final.

New South Wales have won the Sheffield Shield on the most occasions –
45 times. The least successful side is Tasmania (now Tasmanian Tigers), who
first competed in 1977–78 and have won the Shield once, in 2006–07. Arguably
the most famous player to have represented Tasmania is Australia captain
Ricky Ponting.

Having been known for the previous nine years as the Pura Cup, in 2008 the
Sheffield Shield acquired a new sponsor: it is now known as 'The Sheffield
Shield as presented by Weet-Bix'. As you have probably guessed, Weet-Bix is a
breakfast cereal (make of this what you will) made by the Sanitarium Health
Food Company. The 2008–09 winners were Victoria Bullrangers.

Australian cricket has long embraced sponsorship, and unashamedly so. The
domestic Twenty20 competition now bears the wonderful title 'The Kentucky
Fried Chicken Twenty20 Big Bash'.

Whether it is the state opening of Parliament in
Canberra or a new fine-art gallery in some chic
suburb of Sydney, there is no formal event in Australia
that can't be improved by a sausage sizzle.
FRED TRUEMAN

W. G. GRACE: Tell me, Murdoch, how many great players have you played
against now?
BILL MURDOCH (Australia captain): One less than you think.

The Battle of Hastings. In January 1903 Tom Hastings, batting at number 11 for
Victoria against South Australia at Melbourne, scored a century (100). The
last-wicket partnership he shared with Matthew Ellis took Victoria from 261 for 9
to 472 all out.

In February 1904 the MCC/England dismissed Victoria for 15 at Melbourne,
Wilfred Rhodes taking 5 for 6.

The Australian Board of Control (ABC), the governing body for international cricket matches, was formed in 1905 at a meeting of representatives of the New South Wales, Victoria, South Australia and Queensland associations. The omens were not good: South Australia refused to join at first, and Queensland was represented as an 'observer' only. The first meeting took place at Wesley College in Melbourne on 6 May 1905.

The ABC replaced the Australasian Cricket Council, which had been largely ineffective, although it did establish the Sheffield Shield. Prior to the formation of the ABC, tours to England were organized and funded by private groups and individual financers, or by the players themselves. There was no shortage of financial backers as tours, though lengthy, were very lucrative. In time the Australian Board of Control became the Australian Cricket Board, and it is now (since 2003) Cricket Australia.

Diggers and Poms. On 6 September 1909 Australia played J. C. Bamford's XI at Uttoxeter in Staffordshire. The match was drawn. John Bamford was an engineer and industrialist whose family developed the JCB.

Hectic schedule. The Australia team that toured England in 1912 played a triangular series against their hosts and South Africa. The Aussie tour consisted of 36 first-class matches, and they also played two second-class matches; the Test series consisted of a five-Test rubber. The Australian squad, captained by S. E. Gregory, numbered just 15 players.

Who ate all the pies? Warwick Armstrong, the Australia captain of the early 1920s, weighed 20st 3lb.

Of course I was often joshed about my weight. I was once batting with Arthur Mailey. Arthur was at the strike-end when he called out to me, 'Warwick, just move to one side will ya?' 'What's up, can't see the bowler?' I asked. 'See the bowler?' said Arthur. 'I can't see the sightscreen, mate.'
WARWICK ARMSTRONG

Toiled in the field. In December 1926 Victoria achieved a total of 1,107 against New South Wales at Melbourne, a world record total in first-class cricket, eclipsing the previous highest innings total of 1,059, also by Victoria, against Tasmania in Melbourne in 1922–23. Bill Woodfull and Bill Ponsford shared an opening partnership of 375. Woodfull got out on 133, but Ponsford went on to score 352; Jack Ryder scored 295 and 'Stork' Hendry 100. The innings lasted 10 hours 30 minutes, and Victoria won by an innings and 656 runs – just made it then.

If that chap at the back of the grandstand with the brown 'derby' had held his catches I'd have had Victoria out days ago. Very few chances were given, but I think a chap in a tweed coat dropped Jack Ryder near the shilling stand. It was a pity that Ellis got out at 1,107, because I was just striking a length.

ARTHUR MAILEY (reflecting on his 4 for 362 against Victoria)

Cricket a funny game? Four weeks later, New South Wales dismissed Victoria for just 35 and beat them by an innings, which went some way towards revenging their humiliating defeat.

Bowled him over. In 1927 top-order batsman and fast-medium bowler Jack Gregory married the reigning Miss Australia beauty queen.

In January 1930 Don Bradman scored 452 not out for New South Wales in their second innings against Queensland at Sydney, the highest individual score in the history of the Sheffield Shield. In the first innings, Bradman had been dismissed for 3.

As well as playing for Tasmania and Australia, bowler Ted McDonald also played 217 matches for Lancashire. He was an all-round sportsman who also played rugby and football when in Lancashire. McDonald was tragically killed in a road accident in Bolton in 1937.

In 1938–39 Don Bradman scored six centuries in successive innings: 118 v. K. E. Riggs XI, 143 v. New South Wales, 225 v. Queensland, 107 v. Victoria, 186 v. Queensland and 135 not out v. New South Wales, the latter five all for South Australia.

And it was good knock Vienna. In December 1946 Sam Loxton made his first-class debut for Victoria against Queensland, having only been selected because five regular members of the Victoria team were on Test duty. Loxton scored 232 not out, an outstanding achievement for a player making his first appearance in first-class cricket, particularly as Loxton knocked himself out with his own bat while attempting a hook when he was on 183.

Bill O'Reilly's googly was harder to spot than a soda fountain in the bush.
COLIN McCOOL

The Australia team led by Don Bradman that toured England in 1948 were undefeated in 31 first-class matches and three second-class matches. The Test match series comprised five matches, of which Australia won four and lost one.

Playing for New South Wales against South Australia at Sydney in November 1955, Keith Miller took 7 for 12 (eight-ball overs). South Australia were dismissed for 27, the lowest total in a Sheffield Shield match.

The first Test to be televised in Australia was the Brisbane Test against England in December 1958. Viewers were no doubt on the edge of their seats and riveted to their TV sets as Trevor Bailey entertained a capacity Brisbane crowd. Bailey reached his fifty after being at the crease for a little under six hours (357 minutes) – the slowest half century in the history of first-class cricket. Bailey went on to score 68 in seven hours 38 minutes (458 minutes), in the process, as a result of one of his rare run-making strokes, contriving to run out Tom Graveney. During Bailey's obdurate innings, it was reported that one Australian spectator asked, 'Does this guy Bailey ever score?' 'Dunno,' replied his friend. 'I've only been watching him play for the past five years.'

EAMON ANDREWS (TV presenter): You were rarely selected by England for tours of South Africa, India and Pakistan, yet you invariably went to Australia and the West Indies. Why was that?
FRED TRUEMAN: They only picked me for the tough ones.

Ian Meckiff was called for throwing while bowling for Australia against South Africa at Brisbane in 1963.

PETE 'PECK' ANDREWS (Brisbane radio sports journalist): Ian, in light of past accusations, aren't you a little worried Australian bowlers are going to get a reputation for throwing?
IAN MECKIFF: Why? When was the last time it happened?
ANDREWS: Jones against England, 1898.

Ken Barrington (Surrey) appeared to have a liking for the Adelaide Oval. While touring with MCC/England in 1962–63, Barrington scored 104, 52, 52 not out, 63 and 132 not out there, and on the same ground in 1965–66 his scores were 69, 51, 63, 60 and 102.

The only time your hands are together is in church on a Sunday.

FRED TRUEMAN (frustrated at Reverend David Sheppard spilling another chance off his bowling at Adelaide, 1962–63 tour)

The first one-day international took place between Australia and England in 1971.

Right-arm medium-pace bowler of the seventies Max Walker also played Aussie rules football for top club Hawthorn. Following his retirement he wrote several humorous books on cricket, worked in TV and radio and was a popular after-dinner speaker cum stand-up.

Aussie rules football, it's a game suited to padded cells that we Aussies play in the open air.

MAX WALKER

In November 1977, Paul Hibbert scored 100 for Victoria against India at Melbourne; his century did not include a boundary. During the India innings, Chetan Chauhan scored 157 which included only two boundaries.

It was in the Perth Test between Australia and England in December 1979 that the scorebook recorded the famous entry 'Lillee caught Willey bowled Dilley, 19'. Earlier, Dennis Lillee had thrown a wobbler after England skipper Mike Brearley objected to the Australian tail-ender's use of an aluminium bat. Brearley was of the mind the bat scarred the match ball, a view upheld by the umpires, which resulted in Lillee casting the metal bat aside – and no doubt also a lucrative sponsorship deal.

Are you aware, sir, that the last time I saw anything like that on a top lip, the whole herd had to be destroyed?
ERIC MORECAMBE (on being introduced to moustachioed Dennis Lillee)

In 1986–87 England enjoyed triple success in Australia, winning the Ashes, the one-day series and the World Series Cup Final. The team was captained by Mike Gatting.

MIKE GATTING (at the Melbourne Test, 1986): You should have kept your legs together.
STEVE WAUGH: So should your mother, she shudda just had your brothers.
GATTING: At least I'm the best cricketer in our family.

This means Waugh. In 1990–91, Steve and Mark Waugh shared an unbroken fifth-wicket partnership of 464 for New South Wales against Western Australia at Perth, the highest ever partnership in Australian first-class cricket. Mark Waugh scored 229 and Steve hit 216 (both not out), the first time brothers had each scored a double century in the same innings.

 Waugh! What is he good for? Absolutely nothing!
ENGLAND FAN'S BANNER (1993 series v. Australia)

Between 1992 and 2006, Ricky Ponting scored eight double centuries while playing for Tasmania and Australia, equalling the record set by Zaheer Abbas (Gloucestershire and Pakistan, 1976–82).

 Hey, Tufnell, can we borrow your brain? We're building an idiot.
BARRACKER ON HILL AT SYDNEY

The first decade of the new millennium saw the breaking up of yet another all-conquering Australia team, one which contained truly great players whose number included:

Steve Waugh, fraternal twin of Mark, both of whom served Australia with great distinction. Steve played in 168 Tests (average 51.06) and 325 ODIs (average 32.90), captained Australia to a world record 16 successive Test victories and scored 150 or more in an innings against every Test-playing nation.

Adam Gilchrist, who holds the world records for the most dismissals by a wicket-keeper in ODIs (417 caught and 55 stumpings) and by an Australian wicket-keeper in Tests (397 catches and 37 stumpings). An aggressive left-handed bastman, he is the only player to have hit 100 sixes in Test cricket, and he scored 17 Test centuries and 16 ODI centuries – a world record for a wicket-keeper. He also holds the unique record of having scored 50 or more in three successive World Cup Finals (1999, 2003 and 2007).

Justin Langer, a world-class left-handed batsman who, along with Matthew Hayden, formed one of the most successful opening partnerships of all time. Langer could be obdurate when required. Against Pakistan in Hobart in 1999, Australia found themselves 126 for 5 when chasing a winning total of 369. Langer, joined at the crease by Adam Gilchrist, guided Australia to victory, his century, which took him 388 minutes, the longest ever scored by an Australian in Test cricket.

Matthew Hayden, a powerful, swashbuckling opening batsman who holds the record for the highest score made by an Australian in both Test and ODI cricket: 380 and 181 not out respectively. A keen cook, he often made meals for his fellow players when on tour. In 2004 his book *The Matthew Hayden Cookbook* was a number one best seller in Australia, a success he followed with the imaginatively titled *The Matthew Hayden Cookbook Number Two*. In 2009 he signed for Chennai SuperKings in the IPL for a reported $375,000.

Glenn McGrath, regarded by many as the greatest fast-medium pace bowler of all time, who holds the world record for the highest number of Test wickets by a fast bowler and is fourth in the all-time list (behind Anil Kumble, Shane Warne and Muttiah Muralitharan, all spinners). He gained a reputation for 'psyching' opponents before a match. Prior to the Frank Worrell Test against the West Indies he told the press he would dismiss Sherwin Campbell for his 299th Test wicket and follow that by immediately dismissing Brian Lara first ball for his 300th. In the event this happened, and he then dismissed Jimmy Adams with his next ball to complete a hat-trick. When asked by the press to comment on his prediction turning into three successive wickets, McGrath replied, tongue in cheek, 'It just goes to show, I can't be right all the time.'

Shane Warne, arguably the greatest leg-spin bowler of all time, who represented Australia in 145 Tests in which he took 708 wickets, and 194 ODIs (293 wickets). He took 10 wickets in a Test on 10 occasions and only

Muttiah Muralitharan has taken more Test wickets in a career. In 2000 he was named one of the five 'Wisden Greats of the 20th Century'. A myth has grown among some English supporters that his dismissal of Mike Gatting in 1993 with what has been dubbed 'The Ball of the Century' was his first Test wicket. Warne's first Test wicket was in fact that of India's Ravi Shastri (caught by Dean Jones) a year earlier. For a player who would go on to be widely acclaimed as the greatest leg-spin bowler in the history of the game, Warne's Test debut against India was inauspicious to say the least: having taken the wicket of Shastri, he then went on to record figures of 1 for 150.

On 29 February 2009 David Warne became the first man since 1877 to make his debut for Australia without having any experience of first-class cricket. Warne debuted for Australia in the first Twenty20 international against South Africa and hit 89 off 43 balls.

 No one loves cricket more than an Aussie, or any sport for that matter Aussies are basically just British sports fans with something to shout about.
DENNIS LILLEE

M. C. C. A.

Minor Counties v. Australians
AT ASHBROOKE, SUNDERLAND
ON THURSDAY & FRIDAY, 4th & 5th AUGUST, 1977
Hours of Play: 1st Day 11-30 a.m. to 6-30 p.m.

MEMBERS' PAVILION ENCLOSURE
Ground Admission and Reserved Seat (Under Balcony)

Row ....A....

THURSDAY

COMPLIMENTARY
Reserved Seat No. ..25..

Entrance — Rear of Pavilion

J. Iley, Secretary, Durham C.C.C.

THE PROFESSIONAL CRICKETERS ASSOCIATION PLAYER OF THE YEAR

The Professional Cricketers Association (PCA) was founded in 1967.

The PCA Player of the Year award was first presented in 1970. It is highly prized by recipients who see it as recognition of their achievements by fellow professionals.

The PCA Player of the Year award takes place annually at a dinner held at the Albert Hall. Sadly, no player by the name of Albert Hall has yet won.

1970 was the only occasion when two players tied for the award: Mike Procter (Gloucestershire) and Jack Bond (Lancashire).

Only two players have ever won the award in successive years: John Lever (Essex) in 1978 and 1979, and Andrew Flintoff (Lancashire) in 2004 and 2005.

Mike Procter, Peter Lee and Courtney Walsh have also won the award twice but not in successive years, Procter in 1970 (shared with Jack Bond) and 1977, Lee in 1973 and 1976, Walsh in 1986 and 1992.

Only one player has won the award on three occasions, Sir Richard Hadlee (Nottinghamshire and New Zealand), in 1981, 1984 and 1987.

PCA Player of the Year Award Winners

1970	Mike Procter (Gloucestershire) and Jack Bond (Lancashire)
1971	Lance Gibbs (Warwickshire)
1972	Andy Roberts (Hampshire)
1973	Peter Lee (Lancashire)
1974	Barry Stead (Nottinghamshire)
1975	Zaheer Abbas (Gloucestershire)
1976	Peter Lee (Lancashire)
1977	Mike Procter (Gloucestershire)
1978	John Lever (Essex)
1979	John Lever (Essex)
1980	Robin Jackman (Surrey)
1981	Richard Hadlee (Nottinghamshire)
1982	Malcolm Marshall (Hampshire)
1983	Ken McEwan (Essex)
1984	Richard Hadlee (Nottinghamshire)
1985	Neal Radford (Worcestershire)
1986	Courtney Walsh (Gloucestershire)
1987	Richard Hadlee (Nottinghamshire)
1988	Graeme Hick (Worcestershire)
1989	Jimmy Cook (Somerset)
1990	Graham Gooch (Essex)
1991	Waqar Younis (Surrey)
1992	Courtney Walsh (Gloucestershire)
1993	Steve Watkin (Gloucestershire)
1994	Brian Lara (Warwickshire)
1995	Dominic Cork (Derbyshire)
1996	Phil Simmons (Leicestershire)
1997	Steven James (Glamorgan)
1998	Mal Loye (Northamptonshire)
1999	Stuart Law (Essex)
2000	Marcus Trescothick (Somerset)
2001	Dave Fulton (Kent)
2002	Michael Vaughan (Yorkshire)
2003	Mushtaq Ahmed (Sussex)
2004	Andrew Flintoff (Lancashire)

2005   Andrew Flintoff (Lancashire)
2006   Mark Ramprakash (Surrey)
2007   Ottis Gibson (Durham)
2008   Martin van Jaarsveld (Kent)

No Middlesex player has ever won the award.

Notable players who never won the PCA Player of the Year award: Ian Botham,
Geoff Boycott, Mike Brearley, Mike Gatting, David Gower, Gordon Greenidge,
Mike Hendrick, Ray Illingworth, Imran Khan, Allan Knott, Alan Lamb, Derek
Randall, Viv Richards, Bob Taylor, Sachin Tendulkar.

THE CRICKET WRITERS CLUB YOUNG PLAYER OF THE YEAR AWARD

The Cricket Writers Club (CWC) was formed in June 1947.

The idea for the CWC had its roots in the Empire Cricket Writers Club,
which had been formed in 1946. It was on the 1946–47 England tour of
Australia that members of the Empire club and other notable cricket correspondents formed the CWC and dated its origins back to the earlier
formation of the Empire club.

Among the founders of the CWC were E. W. Swanton, Charles Bray and Bruce
Harris.

Membership of the Cricket Writers Club is restricted to recognized cricket
correspondents of newspapers, periodicals, TV and radio. Current membership exceeds 200.

The actor Trevor Howard was once a member of the Cricket Writers Club.
Howard had written one piece on cricket for the *Daily Mail* and badgered the
club to allow him to become a member. It was destined, however, to be only a
brief encounter.

The CWC Young Cricketer of the Year award was the brainchild of the club's
first treasurer, Archie Ledbrooke, who along with Don Davies, the cricket and
football correspondent for the *Manchester Guardian*, tragically died in the
Munich air disaster of 1958.

The award is restricted to players from England and Wales who are under the age of 23 and who qualify to play for England.

The CWC award was first presented in 1950. Roy Tattersall (Lancashire) has the honour of being the first recipient. Curiously, Tattersall was presented with his award by Sir Stanley Rous of the Football Association.

In 1986, for the first time, the vote ended in a dead heat between Ashley Metcalfe (Nottinghamshire) and James Whitaker (Leicestershire). Oddly, Metcalfe was one of the few recipients not to go on and represent England in a Test match, and Whitaker played in only one Test for England.

CWC Young Player of the Year Award Winners

1950	Roy Tattersall (Lancashire)
1951	Peter May (Cambridge/Surrey)
1952	Fred Trueman (Yorkshire)
1953	Colin Cowdrey (Kent)
1954	Peter Loader (Surrey)
1955	Ken Barrington (Surrey)
1956	Brian Taylor (Essex)
1957	Micky Stewart (Surrey)
1958	Colin Ingleby-Mackenzie (Hampshire)
1959	Geoff Pullar (Lancashire)
1960	David Allen (Gloucestershire)
1961	Peter Parfitt (Middlesex)
1962	Phil Sharpe (Yorkshire)
1963	Geoff Boycott (Yorkshire)
1964	Mike Brearley (Cambridge/Middlesex)
1965	Alan Knott (Kent)
1966	Derek Underwood (Kent)
1967	Tony Greig (Sussex)
1968	Bob Cottam (Hampshire)
1969	Alan Ward (Derbyshire)
1970	Chris Old (Yorkshire)
1971	John Whitehouse (Warwickshire)
1972	Dudley Owen-Thomas (Cambridge/Surrey)
1973	Mike Hendrick (Derbyshire)
1974	Phil Edmonds (Essex)
1975	Andrew Kennedy (Lancashire)

1976   Geoff Miller (Derbyshire)
1977   Ian Botham (Somerset)
1978   David Gower (Leicestershire)
1979   Paul Parker (Sussex)
1980   Graham Dilley (Kent)
1981   Mike Gatting (Middlesex)
1982   Norman Cowans (Middlesex)
1983   Neil Foster (Essex)
1984   Rob Bailey (Northamptonshire)
1985   David Lawrence (Warwickshire)
1986   Ashley Metcalfe (Nottinghamshire) and James Whitaker (Leicestershire)
1987   Richard Blakey (Yorkshire)
1988   Matthew Maynard (Glamorgan)
1989   Nasser Hussain (Essex)
1990   Mike Atherton (Cambridge/Lancashire)
1991   Mark Ramprakash (Middlesex)
1992   Ian Salisbury (Northamptonshire)
1993   Mark Lathwell (Somerset)
1994   John Crawley (Hampshire)
1995   Andrew Symonds (Gloucestershire)
1996   Chris Silverwood (Middlesex)
1997   Ben Hollioake (Surrey)
1998   Andrew Flintoff (Lancashire)
1999   Alex Tudor (Surrey)
2000   Paul Franks (Nottinghamshire)
2001   Owais Shah (Middlesex)
2002   Rikki Clarke (Derbyshire)
2003   James Anderson (Lancashire)
2004   Ian Bell (Warwickshire)
2005   Alastair Cook (Essex)
2006   Stuart Broad (Nottinghamshire)
2007   Adil Rashid (Yorkshire)
2008   Ravi Bopara (Essex)

NB Andrew Symonds was born in Birmingham in 1975. Following a successful debut season with Gloucestershire he was selected for the England A tour of Pakistan but pulled out in order to maintain his qualification for Australia, the country to which his parents had emigrated when he was three months old.

And thanks to the magic of television, I have just heard in my headphones that Essex's Phil Edmonds has been voted Young Cricketer of the Year.
DAVID COLEMAN

WISDEN CRICKETERS OF THE YEAR

Wisden currently chooses five cricketers for the honour of Wisden Cricketers of the Year – those who have had the greatest influence on the previous English season. No player is allowed to be a Wisden Cricketer of the Year twice.

The inaugural award was made in 1889, making the Wisden Cricketers of the Year the oldest individual cricket award in the world. The first award honoured 'Six Great Bowlers of the Year'. The following year (1890) the award was made to 'Nine Great Batsmen of the Year'. In 1891 it was the turn of wicket-keepers, though only five of them.

In 1896 W. G. Grace had the honour of being the first sole recipient of the award.

Since 1897, with a handful of exceptions, the award has been made to five players.

In 1913 the award was given solely to John Wisden, the founder of *Wisden Cricketers' Almanack*. The award was posthumous as Wisden had died 29 years earlier and was made to commemorate the jubilee edition of the *Almanack*.

The award was not made in 1916 and 1917 due to the First World War and the suspension of cricket. In 1918 and 1919 the award was made to schoolboy cricketers (public school, of course).

One of the winners in 1918 was schoolboy Harry Calder, who holds a unique position in the history of the award as he is the only recipient who never played first-class cricket. Calder died in 1995, 77 years after he won the award, which is the longest a recipient has lived following presentation of the award.

In 1920 the award resumed with the naming of five players: Andy Ducat, Patsy Hendren, Adrian Gore, Lionel Hedges and Norman Partridge.

In 1921 Plum Warner had the honour of being a sole recipient. He had been among the winners of 1904 but received the honour for a second time to commemorate his final season in first-class cricket, in which he had led Middlesex to the County Championship.

In 1926 Jack Hobbs became the third sole recipient of the award. Hobbs had previously been among the award winners in 1909 but was selected a second time in recognition of his having broken W. G. Grace's record of 126 first-class centuries.

 A snick by Jack Hobbs is a sort of disturbance of a cosmic orderliness.
NEVILLE CARDUS

From 1941 to 1946 the award was suspended, as was cricket, due to the Second World War. The first post-war winners, in 1947, were Alec Bedser, Laurie Fishlock, Vinoo Mankad, Peter Smith and Cyril Washbrook.

In 1951 four West Indies cricketers received the award: Sonny Ramadhin, Alf Valentine, Everton Weekes and Frank Worrell (along with Godfrey Evans).

In 1962 all five award winners were Australian: Bill Alley, Richie Benaud, Alan Davidson, Bill Lawry and Norman O'Neill.

From 2000 to 2003 it was decided the award should be based on players' impact on cricket worldwide, but this decision was reversed in 2004 with the inception of the Wisden Leading Cricketer in the World award.

In 2009 Claire Taylor, captain of England Women, became the first female recipient of the award. The other four recipients were James Anderson, Dale Benkenstein, Mark Boucher and Neil McKenzie.

Gloucestershire's match against Northamptonshire at Moreton-in-the-Marsh on 9 June 1991 was the shortest Sunday League match on record. It lasted just one ball. Gloucestershire's Alan Walker bowled the first ball of the game only for the skies to open and for the pitch to be flooded by a downpour. The ball was played back to Walker who fielded his own delivery just as the rain fell – thus Walker achieved the distinction of playing in a Sunday League match and being the only player to have touched the ball. Tongue in cheek, or perhaps not, Walker asked when he was to receive his Man of the Match award. The request fell on deaf ears.

Cricket balls comprise a core of cork layered with tightly wound string and covered with a leather casing that has a raised seam.

The covering of a ball is normally made out of four pieces of leather, each not dissimilar in size to the peel of a quartered medium-size apple, albeit one hemisphere is rotated by 90 degrees with respect to the other.

The seam of the ball is made of string, stitched into the leather casing. Traditionally this involves a total of six rows of stitches. The two joins between the leather pieces are left unstitched.

The regulation ball for men's cricket must weigh between 155.9 and 163 grams (5.5 to 5.75 ounces). The balls used in women's and junior cricket are slightly smaller.

Traditionally, cricket balls are dyed red. Red balls are used in first-class and Test matches. White balls came into being when day-night games played under floodlights were introduced as they proved more visible at night under lights.

A white ball was first used on 22 November 1979 in the Day-Night World Series in Sydney.

First-class one-day matches use white balls even when play does not extend into night.

Experiments have also taken place using orange, yellow and pink cricket balls. Orange and yellow balls did not fare well and were deemed unsuitable for first-class cricket because they wear differently to standard red cricket balls. The white ball was, of course, given the green light for one-day matches, though many players maintain it swings a lot more during the first half of an innings than the traditional red ball, and that it also deteriorates faster. A pink cricket ball was first used on 22 April 2008 for a match between the MCC and Scotland at Lord's. Initial findings seemed to indicate that the pink ball retained visibility longer than a white ball.

In 1965 Lance Gibbs (West Indies), batting for Whitburn CC against Sunderland at Ashbrooke in the Durham Senior League, hit the ball into a catching cradle positioned near the nets. The ball bounced into the air and on its second descent hit the stumps set up by a group of boys playing their own game of cricket.

Cricket balls are not cheap. In 2008 the average retail price of the ball used in English first-class cricket was £70.

When is a new ball due? In Tests, the captain of the fielding side has the option to take a new ball after 80 overs – theoretically, five hours and 20 minutes of play.

Prior to a new ball being introduced, a ball may only be changed if it is damaged or lost, or if the ball is illegally modified by a player.

In first-class one-day matches there is a mandatory change of ball at the start of the 35th over of each innings. However, the change will not involve a new ball but a 'clean, used ball'.

In local league amateur cricket, clubs often use cricket balls that have been called upon previously, or balls of inferior quality to those used in the professional game, hence the changes in the condition of match balls experienced in first-class cricket are not replicated. Added to which, some local amateur parks teams play on rubber or matting wickets, which also affects the ball.

When I was a kid, in the summer we played cricket on an old rec near my home in Liverpool. The rec was pitted with stones and bricks and had no grass whatsoever. We had an old bat, the rubber of which had long since perished, so it was just the wooden handle wrapped in string. The ball we used had long since lost its leather casing, it was just a bald ball of cork. We had no pads, and wearing short trousers when facing bowling was an adventure in itself. Due to the surface being pitted with stones, the cork ball bounced up at all manner of angles which concentrated the batsman's mind wonderfully. We all became adept with the bat, for no other reason than a deep-seated desire to protect our bare legs from severe bruising or worse.

TOMMY SMITH (Liverpool FC)

With use in a match the surface of a ball becomes rough. Bowlers polish a ball whenever they can, but invariably will buff only one side of the ball in order to create 'swing' as it travels through the air. Bowlers may apply saliva or sweat to the ball as they polish it, but any other substance is illegal.

In order to generate plenty of saliva to apply to the ball, some bowlers will chew gum. Bill Alley of Somerset preferred to suck a boiled sweet.

In 1992 Pakistan became the first international team to come under scrutiny for ball tampering. They were accused of tampering with the ball to obtain larger amounts of reverse swing. The fall-out to these allegations saw Pakistan captain Imran Khan sue Ian Botham for slander and libel in court. Imran Khan was awarded damages of £400,000.

Ian Botham? I wouldn't have needed a ball to get him out. I could have bowled him out with a cabbage with its outer leaves on.

CEC PEPPER

In 1994 England captain Mike Atherton (Lancashire) was accused of ball tampering during the Test against South Africa at Lord's. Television cameras appeared to catch Atherton reaching into the pocket of his trousers and rubbing dirt into the match ball. Atherton claimed he carried dirt and dust in his pocket with which to dry his hands. He was summoned before the match referee and fined £2,000 for failing to inform the said official about the dirt in his pocket.

Athers to Athers, dust to dust.
THE *SUN*

And when you rub the ball on rump or belly,
Remember what it looks like on the telly.
A. P. HERBERT

In 2000 Waqar Younis (Pakistan) became the first player to be suspended for ball tampering.

It was hair-raising stuff. The most infamous instance of alleged ball tampering occurred in August 2006 in the Test between England and Pakistan. The Pakistan team refused to take to the field for the evening session after being accused of ball tampering by umpire Darrell Hair. Umpires Hair and Billy Doctrove awarded England five penalty runs and a replacement ball was selected by England batsman Paul Collingwood. When Pakistan refused to appear after the tea interval the umpires removed the bails and awarded England the match by forfeiture. This resulted in more heated discussion, then some 25 minutes later Pakistan, led by captain Inzamam, took to the field. The umpires, however, refused to retract their decision and also refused to return to the field. The fall-out resulted in umpire Hair being removed from the ICC list, though he was later reinstated. The farce continued into 2008, when the ICC, having reviewed the incident, declared the match a draw and ordered this to be noted in official records – as if it mattered to anyone by then.

The seam of the ball is used to produce different trajectories as the ball moves through the air, or, in the case of seam bowling, sideways movement as it comes off the pitch.

Ray Lindwall knew how to move the ball about, and he was amazingly accurate when bowling. Of the 225 Test wickets taken by Lindwall in his career, almost half, 42.5 per cent, were clean bowled. Dennis Lillee was also noted for his accuracy, but of his 355 Test wickets only 12.5 per cent were clean bowled. Still, I suppose it doesn't matter how you get them out, just as long as you do.
RICHIE BENAUD

A new cricket ball is harder than a used one. Older balls tend to spin more as the roughness grips the pitch more when the ball bounces. Uneven wear on older balls can also produce reverse swing.

To make the ball swing, a bowler has to create a pressure difference between the two sides of the ball. The air pressure depends on the flow of air over each side of the ball; swing is created when a bowler disrupts the flow of air over one side of the ball. Normal swing can be achieved by keeping one side of the ball polished and smooth, and delivering the ball with the polished side forward, and the seam angled in the direction of the required swing. The outswinging delivery moves away from the right-handed batsman, the in-swinger moves in towards him. Reverse swing occurs when the rough side of the ball is to the fore and the ball is bowled at speed, albeit the seam is orientated in the same way as for an outswinger. One of the finest exponents of swing bowling was Ian Botham.

Instances of players having died as a result of being hit by a cricket ball are fortunately rare: George Summers (Nottinghamshire, 1870, at Lord's); Abdul Aziz (Karachi, Quaid-e-Azam final, 1959); Raman Lamba in a club match in Bangladesh (1998); and Ian Folley (Whitehaven CC in 1993).

Injuries from being hit by a cricket ball are common – unwelcome, of course, but considered a hazard of the game. In 2006 Kevin Pietersen fractured a rib after being struck by a delivery from Glenn McGrath during a one-day international between England and Australia.

Glenn Turner looks a bit shaky and unsteady after being dealt that painful blow to what I can only describe as 'the box'. Manfully, he is to carry on. One ball left.

BRIAN JOHNSTON

In November 2004 a diamond-encrusted cricket ball was produced by a jewellery manufacturer in Sri Lanka. It weighed 53.83 carats and contained a seam of pure gold weighing 125 grams.

Not all cricket leagues use conventional cricket balls. The Tennis Ball Cricket Federation of San Francisco has a thriving league and holds an annual TCA Knock-out Tournament with each innings comprising 15 overs – bowled with a 'tennisy'.

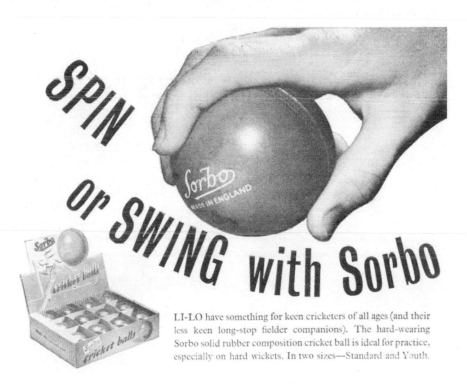

SPIN or SWING with Sorbo

Sorbo

MADE IN ENGLAND

LI-LO have something for keen cricketers of all ages (and their less keen long-stop fielder companions). The hard-wearing Sorbo solid rubber composition cricket ball is ideal for practice, especially on hard wickets. In two sizes—Standard and Youth.

Bangladesh

Bangladesh staged first-class matches even when it was part of Pakistan. In January 1955 Pakistan played India at the Bangabandhu stadium in Dhaka. Pakistan played Tests there and other first-class matches were staged at the stadium up to Bangladesh's declaration of independence in 1971. The stadium no longer hosts cricket. It is now the 'home' of the Bangladesh international football team.

The MA Aziz stadium was another leading venue for first-class cricket but was not used by Bangladesh for Tests until 2001.

In 1979, as an ICC 'associate member', Bangladesh played in the ICC Trophy series in England – their first official participation in international cricket.

In 1986 Bangladesh played their first one-day international against Pakistan in the Asia Cup.

In 1997 Bangladesh won the ICC Trophy. Given they are no longer eligible for this competition having gained full ICC membership, it will stand as their first and only success in the ICC Trophy.

Bangladesh's first-class era as an independent nation began with a game against England 'A' in Chittagong in October 1999. The match ended in a draw.

It's a good pub quiz question: at which ground did Bangladesh win their first ever World Cup match? In 1999 Bangladesh qualified for the World Cup for the first time, and they caused something of a shock when they beat Pakistan by 62 runs in a group match at Northampton's County Ground.

Test status was granted in June 2000. Bangladesh made their Test debut later that year against India in Dhaka, but suffered a nine-wicket defeat.

In April 2001 Bangladesh embarked on their first overseas Test tour, to Zimbabwe, but lost both Tests. This was followed by Test defeats in Pakistan and Sri Lanka.

Later in 2001 Bangladesh hosted their first Test series at home, against Zimbabwe. It was in the first Test at Dhaka that Bangladesh achieved their first result, a draw, albeit helped by the fact that the final two days were washed out.

Bangladesh continued to suffer defeats in Tests, but in September 2003 came very close to their first victory, losing to Pakistan by one wicket.

In December 2004 Bangladesh played their 100th one-day international and celebrated the occasion by defeating India – only the third victory over a Test-playing country.

In 2004 Mohammad Ashraful achieved the highest individual score in a Test match for Bangladesh, 158 not out against India. He also holds the record for the most centuries for Bangladesh and is the youngest player to have scored a Test century, v. Sri Lanka in September 2001.

In January 2005 Bangladesh achieved their first ever victory in a Test match, after 35 attempts, when Zimbabwe were defeated by 226 runs at Chittagong. They also recorded their highest Test score in that match: 488 all out. Enamul Haque junior took 6 for 45 in Zimbabwe's second innings. The second Test ended in a draw, which gave the team its first ever Test series success and triggered jubilant scenes across the country. One over-excited supporter in a village on the outskirts of Khulna fired rifle shots into the air in celebration. He was nudged by another celebrating fan and shot himself in the shoulder, causing him to drop the gun, which on impact with the ground fired off another shot which tore through the tyre of an approaching police car, there to restore order to the street.

It was during the same Zimbabwe tour that Bangladesh also achieved their first one-day international series win: after being 2–0 down they stormed back to win 3–2. It is not known whether 'rifle-man' thought it fit to celebrate on this occasion. Probably not.

On 18 June 2005 Bangladesh secured what remains their greatest victory to date, defeating Australia in the NatWest series in Cardiff. Australia scored 249 for 5 off their 50 overs; Bangladesh achieved the total required for victory with four balls to spare: Aftab Ahmed hit a six off the first ball of the final over, then a single off the second to nail the win. Mohammad Ashraful scored a century off 101 balls, his first in one-day internationals. Just days earlier Mike Gatting had described Bangladesh as not being good enough for Test or one-day international cricket.

In March 2006 Bangladesh won all four one-day internationals against Kenya, achieving in the process their highest total in an ODI: 301 for 7. The following month they came very close to their first Test victory over Australia, after establishing a first-innings lead of 158. Bangladesh were left to rue dropped catches when Australia recovered to win by three wickets.

In 2006 Shakib Al Hasan scored 134 not out against Canada – the highest individual score by a Bangladesh player in an ODI.

In the 2007 World Cup Bangladesh progressed to the Super 8 round following victories over India and Bermuda.

Habibul Bashar was the first player to represent Bangladesh in 50 Tests. He also holds the record for the highest aggregate of runs in Tests – 3,026, at an average of 30.87, which is also a Bangladeshi record – and the most catches in the field (22). Bashar's bowling in one-day internationals is a different matter: in February 2008 he had a career average of 142.00.

Mohammed Rafique has taken more Test wickets than any other Bangladesh bowler – 102 (average 40.76) – and was the first to take 100 wickets in Tests and ODIs.

Bangladesh still come in for criticism for having been elevated to Test status and not being able to produce good results. In response, the Bangladesh Cricket Board point to their thriving youth policy and the fact that it took New Zealand many years to develop into a formidable Test team.

On 9 October 2008 Bangladesh secured their first ODI victory over New Zealand by seven wickets in Mirpur, the highest winning margin by a Bangladesh team in ODI cricket. The victory was all the more creditable as it was Bangladesh's first international match since the exodus of several top players to the Indian Cricket League.

India, who strongly supported Bangladesh's bid for Test status in 2000, is the only ICC full member not to have invited Bangladesh to tour their country.

There are five major venues in the country, based in the cities of Dhaka, Narajanganj, Chittagong, Bogra and Khulna.

Bangladesh has been designated to stage the opening ceremony of the 2011 World Cup.

In April 2009, the Bangladesh government indefinitely suspended home international cricket as it could no longer guarantee the security and safety of visiting teams and their supporters following a failed military coup.

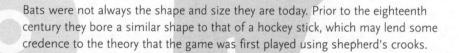

Bats were not always the shape and size they are today. Prior to the eighteenth century they bore a similar shape to that of a hockey stick, which may lend some credence to the theory that the game was first played using shepherd's crooks.

In the early days of the game there were no laws governing the width and size of a cricket bat. On 23 September 1771, during a match between Hambledon and Chertsey, Thomas White (of Reigate) came in to bat for Chertsey with a home-made bat as wide as the wicket. This resulted in protests from the Hambledon players, one of whom produced a knife and proceeded to shave the bat down to acceptable proportions while White stood angrily by. News of this incident soon spread, and a 'law' was introduced (by those who ruled cricket at the time – Hambledon) which limited the maximum width of all bats to 4.5 inches (9.27cm).

Current laws stipulate the bat must not be more than 38 inches (96.52cm) long and the blade no more than 4.25 inches (10.79cm) wide. There is no standard weight for the bat, though a typical weight would be 2lb 8oz to 3lb (1.1 to 1.4kg).

The oldest bat in existence is dated 1729. It is made in one piece of willow and measures 40.5 inches (102.86cm) in length. The bat is on display in the Sandham room at the Oval.

The bat is traditionally made of English willow, specifically cricket-bat willow, and treated with a protective film or linseed oil. English willow is the ideal wood for a cricket bat because it is soft and fibrous with a honeycomb cell structure which when put through the manufacturing process emerges very tough and shock resistant, affording greater strike qualities. For all its toughness it is light in weight.

During the manufacturing process a wooden spring design is incorporated where the handle meets the blade.

The back of the bat forms a V-shaped ridge to allow for improved air flow in the follow-through. It also provides greater strength to the bat as a whole.

Bats are still hand-made by a few specialist manufacturers (mostly for top players) but in the main are machine-made.

Each bat manufacturer may have its own grading system for bats, but usually manufacturers work to five such grades. Top Grade is the very best quality, bats made of finest English willow where the wood grain displays no marks or dis-colouration and is unbleached. This grade of bat is used in first-class cricket and international matches. The lowest grade is usually Grade Five. These bats are also made of English willow but the wood may be bleached and may contain imperfections.

Standard (not used in first-class cricket) and Junior bats are often made of Kashmir willow.

 It is easier to choose a bat than pick a wife. A bat has a watermark of quality – the grain. The one basic flaw in the otherwise perfect constitution of women is that you can't detect the knots in the grain until it is too late.
MICHAEL PARKINSON (and I suppose the same applies to us men)

The majority of professional and top club players do not use a new bat immediately in a match; first they subject it to a 'knocking-in' process. This is 'running in' the bat, and it involves hitting the bat with a cricket ball or a special 'knocking-in bat mallet'. This process will compact the fibres within the bat and protect the bat from splintering or even snapping. Top bat manufacturers such as Gray-Nicholls, Puma and Kookaburra Sport all recommend 'knocking-in' and advise this should be done for three to six hours. Once the knocking-in process has been completed, the bat is not only tougher and more durable, it becomes more controllable and manipulative of the ball and provides the batsman with more power.

Bats can now be purchased 'pre-knocked'. This saves time but adds to the price of the bat.

In general, the chief danger is in buying too heavy a bat. With two or three exceptions, the finest batsmen – Bradman, McCabe, Harvey, Washbrook, Hobbs, Ranjitsinhji among them – have used light bats, which enabled them to get maximum quickness from their wrists. If you choose a heavy bat, you will become slow, and in batting, slowness is the most fatal of all the faults.
WALLY HAMMOND (giving advice to young cricketers)

We are all familiar with the bat terms 'handle', 'shoulder' and 'blade', but do you know what the curved base of a bat is called? Answer: the toe.

On 12 April 1922, during a match at Auckland in New Zealand, a Tri-Tree Point batsman, going for the two runs his side needed for victory, hit the ball hard. The ball split in two as it left the bat. A fielder picked up one half of the ball and threw down the wicket as the batsman was attempting a second run. The umpire gave not out, ruling that when the ball left the bat and split in two it was immediately 'dead'.

In 1975 it was reported that one Mrs D. Driscoll, a nurse at Hortham Hospital in Almondsbury, appeared before the court and was fined £75 for striking a mentally ill patient across the buttocks with the ward's cricket bat. The ward's cricket bat?

In the 1920s, as kids we played cricket in the summer on the cobblestones in the back streets of Hanley. The ball was simply a ball of cork and the first bat we had was custom made, by my father, out of an old coalhouse door. When you went for a big hit with that bat, the feeling that went through your arms was like the spring sensation that goes through you when you hit your funny bone. Some years ago I was telling this to a reporter from the Daily Mail and he asked, 'What about the sweet spot?' I told him the only sweet spot I knew was the one I had for Enid Machin.
STANLEY MATTHEWS

In April 1991 Keith Arthurton, playing for the West Indian Board XI against Australia, was the subject of an umpires' inspection. He was found to be using a bat that was too wide by some 11 millimetres and was ordered to change it. How keen-eyed do you have to be to spot that?

Australia's Ricky Ponting once used a bat with a carbon composite 'meat' (the protruding area of wood out the back face). The bat's manufacturer, Kookaburra, had to re-design the bat in accordance with a directive received from the ICC.

The laws of 2008 stipulate that the blade of the bat must be made entirely of wood. A number of bats now have lightweight carbon handles so that more weight can be used for the blade. In 2008 these bats were the Gray-Nicholls Fusion, Matrix and Powerblow, and the Puma Stealth, all of which adhere to current laws regarding bats.

Top-edged and made a spectacle of himself. In November 1984 Australian Prime Minister Bob Hawke was playing for Australia Parliament XI against the Press when a delivery struck the top of his bat, ricocheted into his face and broke his spectacles, resulting in two black eyes.

In December 1991 India's Mohammad Azharuddin missed the Perth Test against Australia because he tore a groin muscle when attempting to lift a cricket bag overburdened with bats, pads and cricket kit.

The bat, the young fellow in Hobb's assured me, was a beautiful bat. Having scrutinized it carefully, I was forced to pronounce it extremely dull. 'Dull?' said the young man. 'Dull,' I repeated firmly. 'If you think I am going, at my time of life, to buy a bat with only a few words on it you are very much mistaken. I don't suppose you have a bat with the words "What a rotten wicket-keeper" stamped in large letters on the back of it?'

HERBERT FARJEON

10

I played against Australia many times. The only time an Australian batsman walks is when his car runs out of petrol.
FRED TRUEMAN

11

Literally run off his feet. In July 1869 R. Iddison scored 112 runs in a single innings against Cambridgeshire at Hunslet without scoring a boundary.

What is the longest distance a ball has travelled after being hit by a batsman? The answer is 36 miles. In the 1880s George Ulyett, playing for Yorkshire in the Roses match against Lancashire at Old Trafford, hit a ball through the carriage window of a passing train. The ball was eventually recovered in Bradford, some 36 miles away.

In 1893 Arthur Shrewsbury (Nottinghamshire) became the first player to score 1,000 runs in Test matches when he made a century against Australia at Lord's.

Those were the Deyes. Not all Yorkshire batsmen lay claim to greatness. In 1907 George Deyes scored a total of three runs in 14 consecutive innings for Yorkshire. His scores were 0, 0, 0 not out, 1, 1 not out, 0, 0, 0, 0, 1 not out, 0, 0, 0 and 0. In August at Hove (yes, he was still being selected), Deyes scored 12 against Sussex before withering on the vine – Joseph Vine, who bowled him. This proved to be not only Deyes' final innings for Yorkshire but his last in first-class cricket, for his attempts to secure employment with another county proved fruitless.

> ## Unfortunately, he made another of those noughts with which the cricketing public is rapidly becoming familiar.
> R. C. ROBERTSON-GLASGOW

By Hove, that's going it some. In 1911 E. Alletson, playing for Nottinghamshire against Sussex at Hove, scored 189 runs out of 227 in 90 minutes, the last 89 runs being scored (or rather hammered) in 15 minutes and the last 139 in only 30 minutes. With W. Riley, Alletson added 152 for the last wicket. Alletson's share was 142.

Value for money. In 1934 Kent declared at 803 for 4 against Essex at Brentwood, 623 of those runs having been scored on the first day for which admission to general seating for adults was one shilling (5p).

In 1934 Wally Hammond (Gloucestershire) scored 302 not out against Glamorgan. Five years later, on 1 June 1939, Hammond scored 302 again, and once more against Glamorgan. It remains the highest score to have been made twice by an individual batsman in a career.

Wally Hammond topped the County Championship batting averages for seven successive seasons, 1933 to 1939. In 1946, the first official season following the suspension of cricket during the war, he added a record eighth successive season.

Woolley remark. In 1935 the *Daily Sketch* had the temerity to suggest that, as he was now approaching 49 years of age, Frank Woolley's best days as a batsman were behind him. That season Woolley scored over 2,000 runs for Kent and continued to play – and score runs – for the club until 1938.

Until recently it was tradition for the touring side to play their first match against Worcestershire at New Road. Don Bradman is on record as saying New Road was one of his favourite venues. Little wonder, then, that on succeeding tours the great Australian batsman opened with at least a century against Worcestershire: 206 in 1934, 258 in 1938, and 107 in 1948.

What does Sir Don Bradman have in common with W. G. Grace, Jack Hobbs, Herbert Sutcliffe and Kumar Shri Ranjitsinhji? All five batting legends succeeded in going through their respective careers without bagging a pair (0 in each innings of a match).

Batsmanship is an art which consists in some measure of relatively indefinable things, such as judgement and timing.
VICTOR TRUMPER

Don Bradman scored in excess of 200 in an innings on no fewer than 37 occasions. Wally Hammond (Gloucestershire) scored 200 in an innings on 36 occasions and Patsy Hendren (Middlesex) performed this feat 22 times.

The Aussies were very good at getting England selectors to play what they referred to as 'patsies' in preference to a player they knew would cause them problems. When talking to MCC selectors, Don Bradman would wax lyrical about the merits of Doug Wright, telling them he was the finest spin bowler he'd ever come across and just the sight of Wright's name on the team sheet had Australian players worried. So the MCC selectors kept picking Doug Wright, and Don Bradman kept knocking double hundreds off him.
FRED TRUEMAN

Sir Donald Bradman
Would have been a very glad man
If his Test average had been .06 more
Than 99.94
T. N. E. SMITH

Not a great judge of leg-breaks. In June 1946 Peter Judge of Glamorgan suffered a pair not only in successive innings but in successive balls. Playing against India on 11 June, Judge was bowled by leg-break bowler Chandra Sarwate, which brought the Glamorgan innings to a close. India enforced the follow-on, and with little time left Glamorgan decided to open their second innings with the two batsmen who had ended their first, Judge and John Clay. Judge faced the first ball of the second innings only to be bowled again by Sarwate.

By his own admission, Eric Hollies (Warwickshire and England) was 'no batsman'. During his career with Warwickshire, Hollies took 2,201 first-class wickets but averaged only 4.95 with the bat. He was one of that rare breed of cricketers who took more wickets in his career than he scored runs.

Not so good Evans. During the winter tour of 1946–47, Godfrey Evans (Essex) batted for an hour and 37 minutes against Australia in the Adelaide Test without scoring a run.

Surrey captain Errol Holmes played against the MCC in both 1947 and 1948 and suffered the ignominy of a pair on both occasions. What's more, he faced just six balls in those four innings.

In June 1949 Len Hutton (Yorkshire and England) suffered the embarrassment of three successive ducks, but still managed to score 1,294 runs that month.

In 1949 Godfrey Evans (Essex), playing for the Players against the Gentlemen at Lord's, ran six runs as the result of a single shot. This feat was repeated in a Test match by Mike Atherton when playing for England against Pakistan in 1992.

As Horner sat in a corner. Norman Horner, playing for Warwickshire against Oxford University in the 1950s, scored four runs while sitting in the pavilion during the tea interval. One of the umpires was convinced Horner had connected with a ball he had signalled as four byes. The scorer was summoned and asked to alter his book and add four runs to Horner's score.

Worcestershire's Peter Jackson retired from first-class cricket in 1950. During his career with Worcestershire he scored 2,044 runs but never hit a fifty.

In June 1955 a batsman for Wallasey Grammar School XI hit a shot and watched as the ball went down a chimney. It crashed against the fire grate before rolling across a classroom floor to the amazement and no doubt pleasure of teacher and pupils.

In 1961 Bill Alley scored 3,019 runs for Somerset, the 28th and last player to have scored 3,000 runs in the course of a County Championship season. So he was not unique in this, but Alley never dropped a catch when in the field. He was also a fine right-arm fast-medium bowler who during 1960 bowled 93 consecutive balls for Somerset without conceding a run.

PETER WEST: Tony, you appeared to be struck on the head when you were batting. Has it affected you in any way?
TONY NICHOLSON (Yorkshire): No, not at all, I haven't.

 I tell young aspiring batsmen the ideal stance is with feet nine inches apart, left shoulder leading and hiding the right shoulder from the bowler should he be right-handed. He must feel comfortable and able to move his feet very quickly. He must have a good vision of the ball with the face fully turned to the bowler and both eyes level with the ground, so that all defence can be reduced to a quick movement of the feet forward or back, and a very strong top hand. A quick movement of the feet because you are only going to defend against a good length ball, and either the front foot is thrust out on to the pitch of the ball to scotch spin, swing, or lift, or the back foot is pushed back toward the wicket to give you as much time as possible to see any irregularity off the pitch. In either case the head should move on to the line of the ball thus ensuring that the bat will be in the perpendicular position. Then, the top hand must take over, steering the bat down the line of the ball, down out of harm's way, the fingers of the right hand doing no more than helping guide the bat along the line and supporting the demands of the left hand. To the good length, or half volley side of a good length ball, you have to push the front foot to as near the pitch of the ball, with head in line, eye glued to the ball; let the left hand lead the bat through and at the moment of impact you should find the chin, the left wrist and left toe in perpendicular line. I have given this advice to countless youngsters, but very few seem to remember it.

COLIN COWDREY (for all that, excellent advice)

Nervous nineties. On 12 March 1968 at Auckland, India's Rusi Surti was on 99 against New Zealand when he survived an lbw appeal and was then dropped twice. Surti never took advantage of this good fortune. Still on 99, he was offered another chance and was caught by Mark Burgess.

We're all crazeee now. In 1969 Worcestershire lost a wicket with only three minutes of play remaining against Leicestershire at Grace Road. Uncharacteristically, Doug Slade was promoted in the order and sent in as nightwatchman. Slade had been with the club for 11 years, and he surprised everyone by making his maiden century. During his unprecedented innings of 125 he had the distinction of sharing a fourth-wicket partnership of 133 with Tom Graveney.

Couldn't bank on Lloyd. In 1974 David Lloyd (Lancashire) scored 214 not out for England against India at Edgbaston – his only score over 50 in Tests.

Didn't dine out on this story. Playing for Surrey against Middlesex in 1977, Monte Lynch achieved a pair before the lunch interval. Out for nought in the first innings, when Surrey followed on Lynch was promoted in the order, only to be out for a duck again.

Also in 1977, on 30 June, Glenn Turner scored 141 not out in Worcestershire's total of 169 against Glamorgan at Swansea.

Glenn can Turner corner. By 1979 Glenn Turner had scored a century against every Championship county (including his own club, Worcestershire, when playing for New Zealand) bar one, Lancashire, against whom he had previously made 99 before being run out. In that 1979 season, at lunch against Lancashire at Southport, he was stranded on 99 not out, but achieved his hundred after the break to record the first ever 'full house' against every first-class county, a feat equalled by Viv Richards in 1981.

Double double, toil and no trouble. During 1981 Javed Miandad twice scored 200 not out for Glamorgan – the highest score made twice by a batsman during a county season.

No running, but runs galore. On 29 July 1982 Graeme Fowler strained a thigh muscle when playing for Lancashire against Warwickshire at Southport. Fowler was called upon to bat but, unable to run, was aided by a series of runners. He made 126 in Lancashire's first innings and 128 not out in the second innings. He is the only batsman to have scored centuries in each innings of a first-class match with the aid of runners. With more than a hint of humour, on each occasion when Fowler reached his century the respective runner also raised his bat in acknowledgement of applause from the crowd.

Not single. In December 1986 John Emburey (Middlesex) scored 48 for England against Tasmania at Hobart, all the runs coming from boundaries.

Singh when you're winning. In 1989 W. V. Raman and A. K. Singh both scored triple centuries for Tamil Nadu against Goa at Panjim. Raman scored 313 and Singh was 302 not out – the only instance in first-class cricket of two batsmen scoring triple centuries in the same innings.

I can't really say I'm batting badly. I'm not out there long enough to be batting badly.
GREG CHAPPELL

Graham Gooch (Essex) bagged a pair on his Test debut in 1975, but more than repaid the faith placed in him. In 1990 he made 333 and 123 against India at Lord's – the only instance of a triple century and a century by the same batsman in a first-class match.

When batting I would set targets for myself. My first target was not to be out for a duck, then to make it to

50. That done I would set myself to make 75. If I managed that, my next target was to make a hundred. To compartmentalize like that was a great help to me. I didn't feel so much pressure as each target was not overly ambitious, but collectively the end result could be very good.

GRAHAM GOOCH

Robinson makes mark in the game. In his first three innings of the 1990 season Mark Robinson scored 1 not out, 0 not out and 1 for Northamptonshire, and from 4 May through to 13 September failed to get off the mark in 12 consecutive innings, of which seven were not out – a world record in first-class cricket for the number of consecutive innings without scoring. Robinson ended a remarkable season in some style, however, making 1 not out in Northamptonshire's final match of the campaign, against Leicestershire. His three runs for the season at an average of 0.50 were somewhat balanced by the fact that he took 38 wickets, which meant he took over ten times (12.67) as many wickets as he scored runs – another record in English first-class cricket.

No country Hick. In July 1990 Worcestershire's Graeme Hick scored a total of 645 runs across five innings before eventually being out. His successive scores were 171 not out, 69 not out, 252 not out, 100 not out and 53.

In 1990 Graham Gooch (Essex) became the first player to score 1,000 runs in Test cricket in a single season, scoring a total of 1,058 in the series against New Zealand and India. Against India at Lord's, Gooch scored 333 and 121, a total of 456 runs – the highest aggregate score by an England player in a Test match.

Accepted chance to Shine. In August 1992 Hampshire's Kevin Shine was dismissed in successive balls by Northamptonshire's Curtly Ambrose at Bournemouth but given not out on both occasions. Shine was caught off the bowling of Ambrose, only for the Northants and West Indies paceman to be no-balled. Shine was clean bowled by Ambrose's following delivery, also adjudged to be a no-ball.

Lara's theme. On 6 June 1994 Warwickshire's Brian Lara hit 501 not out against Durham at Edgbaston. Lara batted for seven hours and 54 minutes, faced 427 deliveries, hit 10 sixes and 72 fours, and became the first batsman to score 500 runs in a single first-class innings as Warwickshire declared on 810 for 4. The 72 fours scored by Lara is also a record for an individual player in a single innings.

Following Lara's monumental feat, the cricket reporter of the *Sunderland Echo* was asked by his sports editor to obtain a quote from Durham's Wayne Larkins. A little later the reporter rang his newspaper and asked his editor, 'Regarding Larkins, shall I leave out the swear words?' 'Of course,' said the editor. 'Then he never spoke,' the reporter replied.

None but the brave deserves the four.
JOHN ARLOTT

During England's winter tour of South Africa in 2004–05, Steve Harmison created English cricket history when he scored 42 at Cape Town – the first number 11 to top-score for England in an innings in a Test match.

The Benson & Hedges Cup was a one-day competition for county clubs which ran from 1972 to 2002 – the longest-running major sponsorship deal in English first-class cricket.

The B&H Cup began as a 55-over-a-side game but was later reduced in 1976 to 50 overs per team.

The competition comprised four groups. In 1972 these were the (then) 17 County Championship clubs, Minor Counties North, Minor Counties South, and Cambridge University, who for the first two years alternated with Oxford University. In 1976 players from Oxford and Cambridge joined players from other universities as a Combined Universities team. The winners and runners-up in each group took part in the quarter-finals.

In 1976 the Minor Counties teams were divided into East and West. When Scotland were admitted to the competition in 1980, the Minor Counties were reduced to one representative team.

The inaugural competition in 1972 was won by Leicestershire, who beat Yorkshire in the final at Lord's. As winners, Leicestershire received £2,500, Yorkshire £1,000.

Hampshire's Gordon Greenidge and D. K. Turner shared an unbroken second-innings partnership of 285 against Minor Counties South at Amersham in 1973 – the highest ever partnership in the B&H Cup.

In the 1974 final Leicestershire's Ken Higgs achieved a hat-trick against Surrey, taking the wickets of Alan Butcher, Pat Pocock and Arnold Long in successive balls, but still ended on the losing side.

In 1976 at Taunton, Somerset's Vic Marks took five catches against the Combined Universities.

Malcolm Nash scored a century in 62 minutes for Glamorgan against Hampshire at Swansea in 1976 – the fastest hundred in the competition's history.

A remarkable catch by Yardley, especially as the ball quite literally rolled along the ground towards him.
MIKE DENNESS

In 1978 at Ipswich, Middlesex's Wayne Daniel took 7 for 12 against Minor Counties East – the best bowling figures in the competition.

Didn't come up smelling of roses. On 24 May 1979 Somerset captain Brian Rose declared after one over with Somerset 1 for 0. Opponents Worcestershire scored the required two runs to win the match in 10 balls. Rose had declared to protect Somerset's run-rate so they could qualify for the quarter-finals along with Worcestershire. He had done nothing against the Laws of Cricket or the rules of the B&H competition, but the Test and County Cricket Board were far from happy with the situation. So the TCCB did what the Football Association does when they wish to punish an individual or a club that has not violated any law or rule: they hit Somerset with that woolliest of charges 'bringing the game into disrepute' and disqualified them from the competition.

In 1982 at Taunton, Somerset's Derek Taylor took eight catches when playing against the Combined Universities – the most dismissals by a wicket-keeper in a single match in the B&H Cup.

It's a pity Bernard Hedges isn't playing these days. He could almost have lent his name to this competition.
BRIAN JOHNSTON

Graham Gooch will forever hold the record for the highest individual innings in the B&H Cup. He scored 198 not out for Essex against Sussex at Hove in 1982.

In 1982 Somerset became the first county to win the competition in successive seasons (1981 and 1982).

In the 1984 final Lancashire beat Warwickshire by six wickets. Lancashire's Paul Allott took 3 for 15, Steve Jefferies 3 for 28, and Alvin Kallicharran kept Warwickshire in the hunt with a superb 70. Peter May, adjudicator for the much-valued Gold Award (man of the match), named Lancashire captain John Abrahams, who was out for a duck and did not bowl.

In 1989 a Combined Universities XI that featured Mike Atherton, Nasser Hussain, Steve James and Martin Speight reached the quarter-finals – the first non-first-class team to do so. Having beaten county champions Worcestershire, the Combined Universities lost by three runs to Somerset in the quarter-finals. The Combined Universities XI contained five players from Durham University – two more than from the Oxbridge universities – among them James Boiling.

In 1991 Hampshire were dismissed for 50 by Yorkshire at Headingley – the lowest total in the history of the B&H Cup.

Durham, having become a first-class county, joined the competition in 1992. When Ireland were admitted in 1994 the B&H Cup became a straight knock-out competition.

In 1992 at Chelmsford, Essex scored 388 for 7 against Scotland – the highest ever total in the competition. Essex won by 272 runs.

In 1996 Warwickshire's Shaun Pollock took four wickets in four successive balls against Leicestershire at Edgbaston.

In 1997 Ireland caused a major shock when they defeated Middlesex.

The demise of the Benson & Hedges Cup in 2002 was in the main due to two factors: the ban on tobacco advertising, which deprived the competition of its sponsor, and the advent of the Twenty20 Cup, which was first held the following year.

The last final, held in 2002, was umpired by John Hampshire and Barry Dudleston, who had been on opposing sides (Yorkshire and Leicestershire respectively) in the very first final of 1972.

How the sponsorship money had grown. The winners of the 2002 final, Warwickshire, received £52,000, the beaten finalists, Essex, £26,000.

There's a four-letter word they never use in the Warwickshire dressing room – defeat.
PHIL TUFNELL

Benson & Hedges Winners

1972	Leicestershire	1988	Hampshire
1973	Kent	1989	Nottinghamshire
1974	Surrey	1990	Lancashire
1975	Leicestershire	1991	Worcestershire
1976	Kent	1992	Hampshire
1977	Gloucestershire	1993	Derbyshire
1978	Kent	1994	Warwickshire
1979	Essex	1995	Lancashire
1980	Northamptonshire	1996	Lancashire
1981	Somerset	1997	Surrey
1982	Somerset	1998	Essex
1983	Middlesex	1999	Gloucestershire
1984	Lancashire	2000	Gloucestershire
1985	Leicestershire	2001	Surrey
1986	Middlesex	2002	Warwickshire
1987	Yorkshire		

BBC governors have again stated BBC Television will never resort to advertising as this would interrupt the Corporation's coverage of such major sporting events as the Benson & Hedges Cup, the NatWest Trophy and the John Player Sunday League.
RAZZMATAZZ (ITV, 1981)

13

There are nine principal ways a batsman may be given out: bowled, caught, stumped, run out, hit wicket, leg before wicket (lbw), handled the ball, hit the ball twice, and obstructed the field. Throughout the history of cricket, however, there are numerous examples of batsmen getting their marching orders in other ways, or as a result of variations of the above.

In 1847 J. Berry, playing for Bradford and Dalton CC against Sheffield, was given out 'Absent without leave . . . 0'.

Not out, but out. Players rarely walk nowadays, but for many years honesty prevailed when a batsman knew he had connected with the ball, even when umpires and the opposition were unsure. During a game between Surrey and the MCC at the Oval in 1870, James Southerton walked back to the pavilion convinced he had nicked a ball that had been caught by the MCC wicket-keeper. Neither umpire, however, was of the same mind. MCC players and both umpires attempted to persuade Southerton to return to the crease but to no avail, which led to the scorebook detailing the following: 'J. M. Southerton . . . retired thinking he was caught'.

Pocket that – owzat! George Bennett was the first county batsman to be given out for handling the ball. Playing for Kent against Sussex at Hove in 1872, Bennett had not got off the mark when he removed a ball that had become lodged in his trouser pocket. Sussex appealed to the umpire, who gave Bennett out. This happened before the introduction of Law 33(b) in 1899, which presumed such a ball to be 'dead'.

F. W. Wright, batting for Oxford University against the Gentlemen of the Midland Counties, broke his bat as he played the ball. A large splinter hit him on the head and dropped on to the wicket, removing the bails.

Gardeners' question time. During the Test series between England and Australia in 1882, Bill Murdoch and S. P. Jones ran what was a comfortable single. England wicket-keeper Arthur Lyttelton fielded the ball himself and quickly returned it to W. G. Grace at the bowler's end. Jones was safely home, however, and, believing the ball to be dead, stepped out of his crease to do a little gardening and was promptly run out by the quick-thinking Grace.

Duff move. On 21 August 1902 Kent were entertaining Australia at Canterbury. Australia's Reg Duff almost played on to a delivery, and with the ball behind the wicket attempted a quick single. Kent wicket-keeper Huish, thinking quickly, kicked the ball towards the stumps. The ball missed the stumps, carried on down the pitch, hit the wicket at the striker's end and ran out Duff, who hadn't made his ground.

Timely dismissal. The match between Somerset and Sussex at Taunton in May 1920 ended in a tie (Somerset 243 and 103, Sussex 242 and 104) in extraordinary circumstances. With the scores level, Sussex's last man, H. J. Heygate, was given out 'failed to arrive at the wicket on time'. Heygate was suffering from acute rheumatism and had not expected to bat. With the match tied he valiantly agreed to go out to the middle, but it took so long for him to put on his pads, Somerset appealed, and the umpire raised a finger and pulled the stumps.

On 26 August 1921 Leicestershire wicket-keeper Tom Sidwell was given out 'absent, thought lost on the Tube' against Surrey at the Oval. Sidwell had been batting the previous evening – his overnight score was 1 not out – but the following morning didn't join his team-mates on the trip from their hotel to the Oval. While making his own way to the ground he became hopelessly lost and missed the start of play.

Also in 1921, at Headingley, England's Andy Ducat (Surrey) broke the shoulder of his bat when playing a ball from Australia's Ted McDonald. The ball carried through to the slips for a straightforward catch while a large splinter from the broken bat dislodged the bails. It was Ducat's only appearance in a Test for England and he is the only batsman to have been out twice from a single delivery (albeit only 'caught' was recorded in the scorebook).

The batsman who caught himself. In 1939, during a match between Teddington CC and the Surrey Vagrants, Teddington batsman F. R. Parker attempted a defensive shot which resulted in the ball hitting his bat and spooning into the air above his head. Parker caught the ball and returned it to the bowler amid appeals from the Vagrants and was given out, 'handled the ball'.

His appearance on the field of play was slightly delayed by an argument with a member who seemed to be intoxicated, followed by another with the last step down but one. This may have served to disturb his concentration, as Jugg was caught off the back of his bat at third-man when trying to glide to long-leg his first ball, which chanced to be a full-pitcher.
R. C. ROBERTSON-GLASGOW

Pulled the wool over his eyes. During a match between Surrey and Hampshire on 31 August 1946 at Kingston-upon-Thames, Hampshire's R. N. Exton, facing Jim Laker, drove the ball hard towards Alf Glover at short leg. Glover immediately took evasive action, turning his back on the ball and quickly pulling his sweater over the back of his head. The ball kept low and wedged between Glover's thighs, where it remained. The umpire gave Exton out, 'caught Glover'.

V. Merchant of Denis. In 1946, during the final Test between England and India at the Oval, while executing a shot India's V. M. Merchant left his ground. Denis Compton, also a footballer of note for Arsenal and England, took the opportunity to display some of his football skills. He stubbed the toe of his boot against the rolling ball and, as the ball flicked into the air, kicked it on to the wicket to run out Merchant.

It's behind you! In July 1948 M. P. Donnelly was bowled from behind the stumps at the striker's end and given out while playing for Warwickshire against Middlesex at Lord's. Donnelly, who played Test cricket for New Zealand, was hit on the foot by a delivery from Middlesex's J. A. Young. The ball ballooned in the air, over his head and the wicket, hit a piece of the pitch gouged by a bowler's footmark, bounced back and hit the stumps.

A. E. H. Rutter was batting for Wiltshire against Kent Second XI at Trowbridge in 1948 when he advanced down the wicket, played and missed. On hearing the wickets tumble and a chorus of appeals, Rutter, thinking he had been stumped, headed for the pavilion. As he sat in the dressing room, the Wiltshire captain entered to tell him the Kent wicket-keeper, Derek Ufton (who also played football for Charlton Athletic), had whipped off the bails without the ball in his gloves, and that the umpire had seen this and given him not out. Rutter was told he could return to the middle and continue his innings. Just as he was about to set foot on the field midway between the wickets, he suddenly heard his team-mates calling for him to stop as the ball might still be in play. He was told to walk along the boundary until in line with the crease so that he could not be stumped or run out, then to walk out to the pitch. He was bowled without adding to his score.

Must have felt a right nob. On 28 January 1948 South Australia's Geoff Noblett was batting when Western Australia's L. O'Dwyer bowled a wide. Rather than accepting the extra run for his team, Noblett attempted to play the ball, and in so doing trod on his wicket.

1948 proved something of a summer for bizarre dismissals. Playing for England against Australia, Denis Compton was on 148 when, while attempting to play a shot off Keith Miller, his cap fell off his head on to the wicket. He was given out, hit wicket.

Denis Compton is far from being the only player to have been given out when his cap fell off his head on to the stumps. Other batsmen who have suffered a similar fate include Don Kenyon (Worcestershire), against Nottinghamshire, 1949; Joe Solomon (West Indies), against Australia, 1961 (the lucky bowler was Richie Benaud); and Ashok Mankad (India), against England, ironically at Headingley, 1974.

Mayday! On 11 May 1957 at the Oval, Surrey's Peter May was batting at the Vauxhall End against Glamorgan when he hit the ball towards Bernard Hedges, who at first appeared to take the catch. On seeing the ball enter Hedges' hands, May immediately turned towards the pavilion. Hedges, however, spilled the catch. On seeing May walk, Hedges picked up the ball and threw it in to Wilf Wooler, who whipped off the bails. The Oval pavilion was out of the batsman's ground from the Vauxhall End. If May had been batting at the other end he would have been in his ground as he walked back to the pavilion and thus could not have been run out.

A similar instance to the May 'run-out' occurred at Taunton in May 1978. Having edged, Gloucestershire's Alan Tait glanced behind him and, seeing the ball travelling towards the cupped hands of Somerset's Ian Botham, thought his dismissal was inevitable. Botham spilled the catch but ran out Tait who by then was heading for the pavilion.

In 1957, during a match between Eton Ramblers CC and Eton Mission at Eton Manor, a Mission batsman edged the ball to the Ramblers' wicket-keeper. The ball bounced off the wicket-keeper's gloves and wedged itself between the middle and off stumps, dislodging the off bail. The Ramblers appealed. As the ball had not touched the ground when the wicket-keeper retrieved it from between the stumps, the Mission batsman was given out, caught by the wicket-keeper.

Chin up. On 17 May 1961 Tom Pugh, playing for Gloucestershire against Northamptonshire at Peterborough, was the victim of a most unfortunate dismissal. A fiery delivery from David Larter rapped him on the pad, from where the ball ricocheted to hit him under the chin. Pugh broke his jaw in two places and was given out lbw, though Northamptonshire maintained it was 'jaw before wicket'.

Close fielding. On 25 July 1962 at Bristol, Gloucestershire's Martin Young drove the ball to Yorkshire's Brian Close fielding at a very close short leg. Even Close's reactions were not quick enough. He quickly turned, but the ball struck him on the side of his head and arced to first slip where it was caught by Phil Sharpe. Typically, Close was unperturbed by the incident, and seemingly unhurt. Doug Padgett, showing concern for Close, said, 'Thank heavens you're OK. Think what would have happened if it had hit you between the eyes.' Close replied, 'Well, hopefully he'd have been caught at cover.'

Sledging is nothing new. The Yorkshire team of the 1950s and 1960s, in particular the 'Holy Trinity' of Brian Close, Fred Trueman and Ray Illingworth, were renowned for verbally baiting opposing batsmen, sometimes incessantly. During a match at New Road, Close continually goaded Worcestershire's Derek Richardson. When Richardson was eventually dismissed, as he was about to walk up the pavilion steps a member who had missed his dismissal asked, 'How were you out?' 'Bowled Trueman, talked Close,' replied Richardson.

Brian Close was also known among his Yorkshire team-mates for his self-belief. On occasion, following his dismissal for a duck, Close, fuming, entered the Yorkshire dressing room and announced, 'Bloody umpire! He gave me the wrong guard!'

No doubt provoked a Pithey comment. On 10 July 1962 David Pithey, playing for Oxford University against the MCC, was stumped when he left the crease on hearing a noise which made him think he'd been bowled when in fact he hadn't. Suspiciously, there followed a lot of giggling among the MCC slip-fielders.

During a match between Old Bedans CC and Newcastle-upon-Tyne Medical School at Seaburn Camp, Sunderland in 1969, Old Bedans' Dave Colley was in the process of executing a forward defensive stroke when he suddenly jumped in the air as the result of being stung by a bee, and was bowled.

To dismiss this lad, Mike Denness, you don't have to bowl fast, you just have to run up fast.
BRIAN CLOSE (1974)

It doesn't always pay to be helpful. During the second Test between Australia and Pakistan at Perth on 29 March 1979, Australia's Andrew Hilditch was at the non-striker's end when he bent down to pick up a rolling ball, handed it to bowler Sarfraz Narwaz, and was given out 'handled the ball'.

Got the Hump. During a John Player Sunday League match between Sussex and Warwickshire in 1980, Warwickshire's Geoff Humpage attempted to field a strong straight drive but failed to get his hand to the ball. The ball struck Humpage on the leg, ricocheted off at an angle and hit the stumps at the bowler's end to run out non-strike batsman Colin Wells, who was backing up.

And a catch to boot. In 1985 there was little over an hour remaining of the fifth Test at Edgbaston between England and Australia with the series tied at 1–1. Australia were hopeful of holding out for a draw when Wayne Phillips sliced a delivery from Phil Edmonds that hit the boot of Allan Lamb. The ball ballooned into the air where it was caught by a leaping David Gower. After consultation, umpires Shepherd and Constant ruled Phillips to have been caught. Australia then lost their remaining five wickets for 29 runs to give England victory and the Ashes.

On 21 March 1992 New Zealand's Colin Harris was stumped by the Pakistan wicket-keeper Moin Khan when he left his ground and played and missed a ball that was a wide.

You have to hand it to Gooch. During the Old Trafford Test between England and Australia in 1993, Graham Gooch, on 133, prodded down a ball from Merv Hughes. The ball bounced off the pitch and was heading towards the stumps when Gooch fanned it away with a glove. Umpire Dickie Bird ruled Gooch out 'handled the ball'.

In 2001, against India at Bangalore, England's Michael Vaughan became only the second English batsman (after Graham Gooch) to be dismissed for handling the ball. Vaughan played and missed a ball from Sarandeep Singh. The ball became trapped beneath his boot and bat and, despite there being no danger of it hitting the wicket, he brushed it aside with a glove. India appealed and Vaughan was on his way.

There have been 55 instances in first-class cricket of batsmen being dismissed for having handled the ball. In addition to Graham Gooch and Michael Vaughan, notable names include Steve Waugh (Australia v. India) and K. M. Krikken (India v. Derbyshire at Derby).

There have been 21 instances in first-class cricket of batsmen being dismissed for having obstructed the field. The last player in English first-class cricket to be given out 'obstructed the field' was Warwickshire's Billy Ibadulla, against Hampshire at Coventry in 1963.

Only four batsmen have been timed out in first-class cricket. The most recent instance of this in England was Andrew Harris, playing for Nottinghamshire against Durham UCCE at Trent Bridge in 2003.

In 2005–06 at Melbourne, Australia's Andrew Symonds, having hit 66 off 61 balls against Sri Lanka, hit a hard straight drive off the bowling of Jehan Mubarak. The ball travelled at such speed, Andrew Clarke, at the non-striker's end, had no time to avoid it. The ball hit the hopping Clarke on the ankle (producing even more hopping), from where it carried all the way to Tillekeratne Dilshan at wide mid-on, who gratefully accepted the catch.

In 2005–06 at Faisalabad, Pakistan's Inzamam-ul-Haq hit a full toss from Steve Harmison straight back to the England bowler. Harmison managed to get a hand to the bouncing ball and immediately threw it straight back at the Pakistan batsman. Inzamam took evasive action and ducked. The ball hit his wicket and, as his foot had lifted from the crease, he was run out. Needless to say, Inzamam was not a happy man.

Trescothick the head master. During the same series, but at Multan, Pakistan's Salman Butt slashed at a ball from Shaun Udal (making his England debut at the age of 36). The ball shot through to the slips where it hit Marcus Trescothick on the forehead, whereupon wicket-keeper Geraint Jones flung himself low across the ground to take the catch. It was Udal's first ever Test wicket.

The first Test between New Zealand and Sri Lanka at Christchurch in December 2006 was at various times subjected to sun, rain, sleet and hail, but the most notable event was the bizarre dismissal of Muttiah Muralitharan. After running a single that gave Kumar Sangakkara his century, non-strike batsman Muralitharan walked down the wicket to proffer his congratulations to his team-mate as the ball arrived into the gloves of New Zealand wicket-keeper Brendan McCullum from fielder Chris Martin. McCullum broke the wicket. With Muralitharan out of his crease and the ball still 'live', umpire Brian Jerling accepted the appeals of the home players for 'run out'.

Given cricket is played worldwide but is only a major sport in a relatively limited number of countries, the game has spawned an incredible number of books. Arguably, cricket can boast the finest writing of any sport, though in the past the sheer quality of cricket writing had much to do with social standing and the educational and occupational opportunities afforded to those who chose to write about the game. In essence, it was not until after the Second World War that cricket writing became 'an open book'.

It would be impossible to list all books and magazines devoted to cricket. The following are some notables, past and present.

WISDEN CRICKETERS' ALMANACK

On 15 July 1850 John Wisden, playing for the North against the South at Lord's, in a single innings took all ten South wickets, every batsman bowled. At the time he had just entered business selling cricket equipment in Leamington. Legend has it some years later a friend of Wisden suggested there ought to be a book detailing cricket records such as the one he had achieved against the South, a book which might also contain the cricket season's results and statistics. Wisden thought this an admirable idea, and a possible money-spinner, so he founded the *Cricketers' Almanack* which to this day carries his name.

Wisden is the longest-running sports annual in history and arguably the most famous sports annual in the world, quite simply an indispensable source of reference (and entertainment) for the lover of cricket.

The first edition of 1864 comprised 112 pages and sold for a shilling (5p). Curiously, in addition to cricket it included the winners of the Oaks and the dates of battles of the English Civil War.

Wisden has had only 15 editors in over 140 years: W. H. Crockford and W. H. Knight (1864–69), W. H. Knight (1870–79), G. H. West (1880–86), Charles Pardon (1887–90), Sydney Pardon (1891–1925), C. Stewart Caine (1926–33), Sydney J. Southerton (1934–35), Wilfred Brookes (1936–39), Haddon Whitaker (1940–43), Hubert Preston (1944–51), Norman Preston (1952–80), John Woodcock (1981–86), Graeme Wright (1987–92 and 2001–02), Matthew Engel (1993–2000 and 2004–07), Tim de Lisle (2003) and Scyld Berry (2008–09). Matthew Engel edited 12 editions before taking a sabbatical in 2008, the 2008 and 2009 editions being edited by Scyld Berry.

Just about every great cricket writer has contributed to *Wisden* at some point in his career, including John Arlott, Charles Bray, Neville Cardus, Sir Learie Constantine, Jack Fingleton, R. C. Robertson-Glasgow, Christopher Martin-Jenkins, Ian Peebles, E. W. Swanton and A. A. Thomson.

Wisden is considered the 'bible' of cricket, though it has never used this term to describe itself. Current editions contain over 1,500 pages. Among the contents are English Cricket (the most comprehensive and detailed coverage there is of the game in England, including scorecards for every first-class match played the previous summer and summaries of Minor Counties, Second XI, University, League and School cricket); Overseas Cricket (full coverage of all international cricket and summaries of domestic first-class cricket in all countries); Records (the essential source for key statistics relating to the game; an even more comprehensive date of records can be found online at *Wisden*'s associate website Cricinfo); Comment (some 100 pages of informed articles on cricket, including the introductory Notes by the Editor, which is invariably agenda-setting); Review (including the esteemed obituary section and curious and odd-ball events in cricket from the past year); Awards (Cricketer of the Year awards date back to 1889 and enjoy great status among players and supporters alike); and History and Laws of the game and Fixtures for the forthcoming season.

Up to 1938 the jacket of the book appeared in various colours – yellow, salmon pink and buff. The 1938 edition (the 75th) appeared in a distinctive bright yellow cover which has continued to this day.

The cover of the 1938 edition was the first to feature the woodcut of two Victorian cricketers by Eric Ravilious.

E. W. Swanton was taken prisoner by the Japanese during the Second World War. At the time he had with him the 1939 edition of *Wisden*. Swanton loaned his copy to fellow POWs and so popular was it the book had to be reserved and borrowed for no longer than 12 hours. It was so well thumbed it began to fall apart but, like Swanton, it survived the ordeal and is now in the MCC museum at Lord's.

In 1944 a bomb fell on the Wisden factory at Mortlake in south-west London destroying all records – but all important cricket records were, of course, preserved in the many editions of the book.

The 1965 edition carried an obituary for the Lord's cat, Peter.

The first Test of 1877, between Australia and England, was not carried in *Wisden* for 100 years. The match was finally referred to during coverage of the Centenary Test of 1977. (Coincidentally, Australia won both matches by 45 runs.)

In 2000 *Wisden* asked a panel consisting of 100 cricketers and authoritative voices on the game to vote for their five cricketers of the twentieth century. The chosen five were Sir Donald Bradman, Sir Garfield Sobers, Sir Jack Hobbs, Sir Viv Richards and Shane Warne. The only player to receive votes from every member of the panel was Don Bradman. So he finally achieved the 100 average that eluded him as a player.

In 2003 *Wisden* broke with tradition and dropped the woodcut, featuring a photograph of a player (Michael Vaughan) on its cover for the very first time.

Since 2006, a larger format of *Wisden* has been published in response to comments by those readers who find the print size of the standard edition difficult to read, albeit this print size is that of many standard books.

The only downside to *Wisden* is the price. Understandably, such a voluminous tome is going to be expensive, but even the price of the paperback is now beyond those on a tight budget.

PLAYFAIR CRICKET ANNUAL

For those who cannot afford *Wisden*, this pocket-battleship of a cricket annual is essential reading and retails at a price which is within most budgets (the cost of the 2009 edition was £6.99).

The annuals were originally published by Raceform, which produced various horse racing titles as well as the *Playfair Football Annual* and *Playfair Rugby Annual*.

It is widely believed the term 'Playfair' originates from a desire to engender fair play in all sport. It is also believed the idea was inspired by the name of Sir Nigel Playfair who, though he had no connection with Raceform, was a well-known actor and keen sports fan.

The annual first hit the bookshelves in 1948 and was edited for the first six years of its existence by writer/broadcaster Peter West. The foreword for the first edition was written by C. B. Fry.

From 1948 to 1962 the annual was of a larger size, 4.75 inches (12cm) by 7.25 inches (18cm), and was quite different in style. In 1963, following a takeover by Dickens Press, it adopted the now familiar pocket-size. It is now published by Headline.

From 1954 to 1985 the annual was edited by Gordon Ross, from 1986 to 2009 by one of the game's most loved figures, Bill Frindall.

A typical contemporary edition contains Previous Season – first-class results, tables, averages, touring teams and university details, statistical highlights, awards; Current Season – details of tours by England teams, a guide to tourists, a guide to county clubs with pen pictures/career records of every player, averages, records, umpires register; Career Records and Scores in Tests and ODIs; All-time First-Class Records; Minor Counties, Women's Cricket; Fixtures; Guide to Benefits; County Caps awarded in previous season; Duckworth-Lewis method, and more.

The *Playfair Cricket Annual* is hugely popular with cricket fans, particularly those who cannot afford *Wisden*. Former editor Bill Frindall's common-sense approach to cricket matters did, however unwittingly, gain him a reputation as the 'voice' of the 'ordinary' supporter. For example, Frindall ignored the ICC decision to afford Test match status to a match between Australia and an ICC World XI (part of the ICC Super Series), describing the decision as 'witless'.

OTHER BOOKS

ABC Cricket Book, published annually by the Australian Broadcast Corporation. First published in 1934, it is Australia's longest-running cricket book and is considered a definitive guide to Australian cricket.

The Art of Cricket, by Sir Donald Bradman, first published in 1958 and subjected to many a reprint. Heralded as one of the best coaching manuals ever penned, it also contains fascinating Bradman ruminations on the pitch, declarations, temperament and mental strength, and what to do should you win the toss.

Beyond a Boundary, by C. L. R. James. Memoir of Trinidadian cricketer which mixes experiences and thoughts on the game with social commentary. Contains the line 'What do they know of cricket who only cricket know?' – seemingly a parody of Rudyard Kipling's 'What do they know of England who only England know?'

The Art of Captaincy, by Mike Brearley, published in 1985, often referred to as a 'treatise on captaincy'. The only book devoted to the various challenges of cricket captaincy.

The much-loved and much-missed Brian Johnston wrote over 20 books on cricket, such as *A Delicious Slice of Johnners*, *The Wit of Cricket*, *Views from the Boundary* (with Peter Baxter) and *An Evening With Johnners*. It is thought no other author has written as many books on cricket as Johnston.

Cricket autobiographies have always been popular with readers, long before those of footballers. Popular titles of recent years include *My Autobiography* by Harold 'Dickie' Bird, *Botham* by Ian Botham, *The Autobiography* by David Gower, *As It Was* by Fred Trueman and *Being Freddie* by Andrew Flintoff.

Dickie Bird called his book My Autobiography. It's an autobiography, who else's could it be? Victoria Beckham's was called Learning to Fly. Sounds like a training manual. I bet that confused a few would-be terrorists.

FRED TRUEMAN (*As It Was*)

MAGAZINES

The Cricketer, founded in 1921 by Plum Warner, who edited the magazine until 1963 after which editors included E. W. Swanton and Christopher Martin-Jenkins. In 2003, following a merger with Wisden, the magazine was relaunched bearing the name *The Wisden Cricketer*.

Wisden Cricket Monthly ran from June 1979 to September 2003. The driving force of the first edition was David Frith. Occasionally ran with inflammatory articles. In 1987 Surrey CCC banned the magazine from shops at the Oval following an article headlined 'Bloodbath in Birmingham' – a reference to crowd trouble during the ODI between England and Pakistan at Edgbaston. In 2003 it merged with *The Cricketer* to form *The Wisden Cricketer*.

The Wisden Cricketer, see above re. merger. The magazine provides comprehensive coverage of the game and detailed reports and analysis of Test matches and ODIs from around the world as well as coverage of county and minor cricket, with considered and humorous articles – essential and entertaining reading for followers of cricket.

Spin, a UK-based monthly magazine, first published in 2005 and edited by Duncan Steer. *Spin* is rapidly growing in popularity and offers a comprehensive coverage of international and domestic cricket, together with interviews with players, officials and commentators and, unusually for a cricket magazine, comedy and satire on the game.

All Out Cricket, a monthly magazine published jointly by the Professional Cricketers Association and Trinorth publishing company. Launched in April 2004, *All Out Cricket* is available at all first-class clubs as well as leading book and magazine retailers such as WHSmith. Though varied in content, the magazine focuses on insightful features and interviews with players. It is edited by former England 'A' international Andy Afford and cricket publisher Matt Thacker.

Cricket Spotlight, a top-selling cricket magazine of the 1950s and 1960s, albeit only published annually, prior to the commencement of each new domestic season. Published by Mercury Press (Northampton) and for many years edited by Robert Baker, each edition featured comprehensive coverage of every first-class county's performance in the previous season, together with team photographs of every county team, the tourists and leading Minor Counties. The team photographs gave *Spotlight* an advantage over all other cricket magazines: schoolboys could now put a face to every player whose name they were familiar with via the county scoreboards which appeared daily in local evening newspapers. Advertisements for manufacturers of cricket equipment and related goods peppered the magazine. Among the most regular were the Cork Manufacturing Company, makers of Chingford cricket balls – 'kinder to the bat'; Gunn and Moore bats; Concrete Cricket Pitches – 'Play cricket with confidence on precast concrete pitches, ideal for parks cricket'; Meltonian Whitener – 'Cricket's famous 12th man'; Morley Cricket Socks – 'Help you run faster between wickets'; and the 'Wombwell Cricket Lovers Society' whose motto was 'My song shall be cricket and cricket my theme' (the society invited new members to apply, proudly proclaiming 'BOTH sexes welcome').

14 LITERARY CONNECTIONS

Lord Byron was an enthusiastic cricketer and played for Harrow against Eton in 1805.

H. G. Wells's father Joseph played for Kent in the 1860s.

Spencer Austen-Leigh, who played for Sussex in the 1860s, was the great nephew of Jane Austen.

Sir Arthur Conan Doyle played for the MCC and various London-based clubs including Writers CC, who also included in their ranks J. M. Barrie.

In February 1881 a Buenos Aires publisher produced a book on cricket in Spanish entitled *La Tranca* (*The Wicket*).

In 1900 the Dulwich College First XI included P. G. Wodehouse, and Westminster School First XI boasted A. A. Milne in their ranks.

In 1906 Rugby School played Marlborough at Lord's. Included in the Rugby team was budding poet Rupert Brooke.

The only Nobel Prize for Literature winner to have played first-class cricket is Samuel Beckett, who played for Dublin University against Northamptonshire in 1925 and 1926. Beckett scored 18 and 12 in the first match against Northamptonshire and 4 and 1 in the second, which must be some sort of record in that his top score came in his first innings and thereafter his scores in his first-class career decreased with each innings.

Underarm tactics play results in riotous assembly. In 2004–05 a new play entitled *The Underarm* written by David Greary and Justin Gregory opened at the Centrepoint Theatre in Palmerston North, New Zealand. The play, which tells the story of Trevor Chappell's infamous underarm delivery of 25 years earlier, was interrupted on several occasions by the audience barracking the actors playing the Australians and by some members of the audience throwing empty beer cans at the Aussies.

15

'B' is for bowler, bowling and . . . In January 1883 all 20 Australian wickets in the Melbourne Test fell to England bowlers whose surname began with a 'B': W. Bates (14 wickets), R. G. Barlow and W. Barnes.

This feat was equalled on two other occasions in Tests, most famously in July 1956 at Old Trafford, when Jim Laker took 19 Australian wickets, and the other was taken by Tony Lock. In July 1983 at Headingley all 20 England wickets fell to New Zealand bowlers whose surname began with the letter 'C': B. L. Cairns, E. J. Chatfield and J. V. Coney.

In 1880 Nottinghamshire's Alf Shaw took 186 wickets for 1,589 runs at an average of just 8.54 – the lowest average recorded by a bowler taking in excess of 100 wickets in a season.

Not all right, Jack. Australian Test bowler of the 1890s Jack Harry often bowled alternatively right-handed and left-handed to flummox batsmen. Should he have wanted to, he could also have reversed his Christian name and surname and got away with it.

Biggs hitter. In July 1897 Johnny Biggs conceded what remains the most runs off one bowler in a County Championship match. Playing for Lancashire against Sussex at Old Trafford, he took 2 for 174 and 2 for 132 – a total of 306 runs conceded (for four wickets). Biggs achieved another notable record in this match: he bowled 630 balls, the most by an individual bowler in the course of a County Championship match.

In the match between Worcestershire and Warwickshire at Dudley in June 1914, Frank Field came on to bowl for Warwickshire with the Worcestershire second-innings score at 85 for 4 and took the remaining six wickets in eight overs and four balls (seven maidens) at a cost of only two runs. What's more, in taking those six wickets Field received no assistance from his team-mates: three batsmen were bowled, two caught and bowled, and one lbw.

On 28 August 1914 at Weston-super-Mare, Yorkshire's Alonzo Drake bowled unchanged in both innings against Somerset, having done the same in Yorkshire's previous match. In the second innings Drake took all 10 Somerset wickets in only 42 deliveries.

Blythe Spirit. The record for the most wickets taken for the least runs in a County Championship match is held by Colin Blythe. Playing for Kent against Northamptonshire at Canterbury on 1 June 1907, Blythe achieved match figures of 17 wickets for 48 runs. In Northamptonshire's first innings, Blythe took 10 for 30. Northants were dismissed for only 60 and asked to follow on. In their second innings they were skittled out for a mere 39, Blythe taking 7 for 18. What was equally remarkable was Blythe took all 17 wickets in a single day's play.

Seeking bail. Bowling for Worcestershire against Lancashire at Old Trafford in June 1911, Robert Burrows sent a bail a distance of 67 yards and six inches, to the boundary – thought to be the longest a bail has travelled after being removed by a bowler's delivery.

Legendary Australian bowler Jack Gregory was subjected to a baptism of fire in English cricket in 1919. Playing for the Australian Imperial Forces team against Surrey at the Oval, the home side wanted 287 to save the follow-on and were 26 for 5 when John Crawford came in at number eight. Crawford scored 144 not out in two hours and at one point, with a mighty hit, drove a ball from Gregory into the pavilion which shattered a window, cracking and splintering his bat in the process.

Playing for Gloucestershire against Yorkshire at Bristol in August 1922, Charlie Parker hit the stumps with five successive balls but only succeeded in taking four wickets. The second dismissal was ruled as being off a no-ball. That notwithstanding, Parker remains the only bowler in English first-class cricket to have hit the stumps five times with successive deliveries.

Charlie Parker also jazzed up the record books in August 1923, recording the most expensive bowling figures in a County Championship match when he took 6 for 231 against Somerset at Bristol.

In December 1926 when playing for New South Wales against Victoria in Melbourne, Arthur Mailey conceded 362 runs off his bowling in a single innings. Mailey did take four wickets but Victoria went on to score a world record total of 1,107. A month later, when New South Wales exacted revenge, dismissing Victoria for a miserly 35, Mailey took 4 for 12.

Giant achievement by Tich made him freeman of the county. Kent's A. P. 'Tich' Freeman is the only bowler to have taken in excess of 300 first-class wickets in a single English first-class season. Freeman, a leg-spinner, achieved this feat in 1928, taking a record 304 wickets at an average of 18.5. To offer further proof of his prowess as a bowler, Freeman went on to take 200 wickets in each of the following seven seasons.

Tich Freeman, however, was not done with breaking and making records. He is also the only bowler to have taken all 10 wickets in a first-class match on three occasions. What's more, he achieved this feat in successive seasons, v. Lancashire at Maidstone in 1929 (10 for 131), v. Essex at Southend in 1930 (10 for 53), and v. Lancashire at Old Trafford in 1931 (10 for 79).

Tich Freeman proved himself a mere mortal in September 1934, however. Playing for Kent against the MCC at Folkestone, he conceded the most runs by a bowler in an English first-class cricket match – 331. He returned first-innings figures of 6 for 199 and a second-innings 2 for 132.

Tich Freeman was as short and stubby as a hedge fence.
HERBERT SUTCLIFFE

Wilfred Rhodes (Yorkshire) holds the record as the greatest wicket-taker in the history of English cricket. Between 1898 and 1930 he took a total of 4,184 wickets, a record that included 100 wickets in a single season on 23 occasions. No player has ever bowled more deliveries in first-class cricket than Rhodes – 184,890. Rhodes was so successful a bowler, he took more wickets during his career than he scored runs.

In 1931 Charlie Parker was at it again, not exactly breaking a record but equalling one, as set by Jack Hearne (1896, Middlesex): the earliest date in a season in which a bowler achieved 100 wickets in the County Championship – 12 June.

Had them all in Notts. On 12 July 1932 Hedley Verity (Yorkshire) took all 10 Nottinghamshire wickets at Headingley for only 10 runs. His haul included seven wickets in only 15 deliveries. Verity's figures read 19.4–16–10–10.

The England tour of Australia in 1932–33 resulted in arguably the most infamous bowling controversy in the history of the game – 'Bodyline bowling'. Bodyline was a tactic devised by England captain Douglas Jardine in order to combat the batting prowess of Australia's Don Bradman, though it was used against all recognized Australian batsmen. It called for England bowlers to aim at the body of an Australian batsman in the hope of creating deflections that would carry to a ring of fielders behind square leg. The main exponents of the tactic were Harold Larwood, Bill Voce (both Nottinghamshire) and Bill Bowes (Yorkshire). The Australians were outraged by Bodyline, which they saw as unsporting and a deliberate attempt to injure batsmen; needless to say, Jardine did not agree. England won the series 4–1 and thus the Ashes, but few friends. So inflammatory was the Bodyline tactic, the matter was debated at diplomatic level, and when England returned from Australia the Laws of Cricket were changed to prevent such a tactic ever being used again.

MAURICE LEYLAND (to W. A. S. Oldfield of Australia after he'd swung at and seemingly missed a ball from Larwood): You never touched it.
OLDFIELD: Maybe, but I'm going all the same.

What must you do? In 1933 Charles Marriott (Oxford University, Lancashire) returned match figures of 11 for 96 for England against the West Indies at the Oval. It was Marriott's first appearance in a Test match. He was never selected again.

The feat of taking 250 wickets in a season has been achieved on only 12 occasions in first-class cricket. A. P. 'Tich' Freeman was the last bowler to accomplish this feat, in 1933.

Gubby Allen (Middlesex) bowled the first over of the 1934 third Test between England and Australia at Old Trafford, which comprised 18 deliveries. His opening fusillade included 11 no-balls and a wide.

Playing for Derbyshire against Warwickshire on 17 July 1937, Bill Copson, affectionately known as 'Cop', playing his first match in over a month, took five wickets in six balls and ended with bowling figures of 8 for 11 in 8.2 overs as Warwickshire collapsed to 28 all out. Cop's sensational spell of bowling resulted in his name subsequently being widely adopted to emphasize something surprising or unpleasant happening to someone, as in 'cop that'. Copson, an excellent right-hand batsman and right-arm medium-fast bowler, was Wisden Cricketer of the Year in 1937.

He might have done better if he had chucked the ball. The highest number of runs conceded by a bowler in a single innings of a first-class match in England is 298. The luckless bowler was 'Chuck' Fleetwood-Smith, playing for Australia against England at the Oval in 1938, when a Len Hutton-inspired England hammered the Aussie bowling to make 903 for 7 declared (those were the days).

In March 1945, in the final of the Ranji Trophy in Bombay, Holkar's C. S. Nayudu bowled 152.5 overs (917 balls) and conceded 428 runs against Bombay, who scored 462 in their first innings and 764 in their second – a world record for the most balls bowled and most runs conceded by a bowler in a first-class match. For the record, Holkar made 360 and 492 in reply, with Denis Compton scoring 249 not out.

What a delivery that was! McCullum dispatched the bails to all four corners of the hemisphere.
RADIO SPORT NEW ZEALAND

Playing for Warwickshire against Nottinghamshire at Edgbaston in 1946, Eric Hollies took all 10 Nottinghamshire wickets without the assistance of his team-mates. Leg-spinner Hollies clean-bowled seven Nottinghamshire batsmen and the other three were given out lbw.

Got 'out of jail' but not out on bail. In 1947 A. R. Morris, batting for New South Wales against Victoria, was bowled middle-stump but not given out by the umpires. The reason: the bails had not been dislodged. The temperature was 116 degrees, and the heat was so intense it had melted the varnish on the bails and glued them to the stumps. As rules stipulate the bails must be removed in order for a batsman to be given out when bowled, stumped or run out, the only decision the umpires could give was 'not out'.

In July 1956, when playing for England against Australia in the fourth Test at Old Trafford, Jim Laker famously recorded figures of 10 for 53 (51.2–23–53–10), this after having taken 9 for 37 (16.4–4–37–9) in the tourist's first innings. Laker's match figures of 19 wickets for 90 runs is unparalleled in Test cricket. In all, Laker took 49 wickets in the series. Perhaps equally amazing, given modern-day celebrations by bowlers, is the press photograph of Laker leaving the field after performing this unique feat: he is casually strolling, with a thoughtful look on his face, sweater draped over his left shoulder as if returning to the pavilion from net practice. Less well known is the fact that this was the second time Laker had done this to the Aussies that summer. Two months earlier, on 16 May, when playing for Surrey against the tourists, Laker had recorded figures of 10 for 88 in a single innings.

Dot, dot, dot but no dash, dash, dash. At Durban in January 1957 H. J. Tayfield (South Africa) bowled 137 successive deliveries without conceding a run against England.

England bowled very well. We've had the main course, now it's time for the hors d'oeuvres and cheese.
DAVID LLOYD

In 1957 West Indies spinner Sonny Ramadhin bowled a record 588 deliveries at Edgbaston during England's second innings. Ramadhin bowled a marathon 98 overs in a single innings – a Test record. In England's first innings he had taken 7 for 49, and the total number of balls he bowled in the match, 774, is also a record in English first-class cricket.

Lock retains key record. The last bowler to take in excess of 200 wickets during a County Championship season was Tony Lock (Surrey) in 1957. Lock took a total of 212 wickets at an average of just 12 runs per wicket.

Under-age but no under-achiever. In 1963 spinner Derek Underwood took 101 wickets at an average of 21.12 in his maiden season in county cricket with Kent. Underwood was only 17 years old, and remains the youngest player to have achieved a century of wickets in a first-class domestic season – and the last to achieve this feat in a debut season.

Underwood continued to perplex batsmen with his left-arm slow bowling. In 1966 he took 157 first-class wickets at an average of 13.8 – the last bowler to have taken in excess of 150 wickets in the course of a County Championship season.

Derek Underwood had the face of a choirboy, the demeanour of a civil servant and the ruthlessness of a rat catcher.
GEOFF BOYCOTT

Shack attack. Derek Shackleton (Hampshire) was nothing if not consistent. For 20 consecutive seasons, 1948 to 1968, Shackleton took 100 wickets in every campaign.

It's his second finger, technically his third.
CHRISTOPHER MARTIN-JENKINS

Worthy of more than a pat on the back. One of the most sensational and dramatic spells of bowling occurred during the match between Surrey and Sussex at Eastbourne on 15 August 1972. Sussex, needing 205 for victory, were 187 for 1 with only three overs remaining when Pat Pocock was called upon to bowl. Pocock took three wickets, and Sussex suddenly found themselves on 189 for 4. The penultimate over was bowled by Robin Jackman, during which Sussex added a further 11 runs without loss. As Pocock began the final over Sussex were 200 for 4, needing just six runs for victory. Unbelievably, five Sussex wickets fell during this final over with the addition of only two runs, which meant the match ended in a draw. Pocock's ball-by-ball analysis for this final over reads as follows: Prideaux, caught, 200 for 5; Griffith, caught, 200 for 6; Morley, stumped, 200 for 7; Spencer, one run, 201 for 7; Buss, bowled, 201 for 8; Joshi, run out going for second run, 202 for 9. Pocock had taken 0 for 63 prior to these last two overs; he finished with figures of 7 for 67. Sussex's extraordinary collapse saw them lose eight wickets in only 18 deliveries, going from 187 for 1 to 202 for 9. The five wickets that fell in Pocock's final over is a record for the number of wickets to fall in a single over of a first-class game. Pocock's final two overs also produced two other bowling world records: six wickets in nine balls, and seven wickets in 11 balls. Pocock's devastating spell of bowling was so sensational and record-breaking, the fact it also included a hat-trick was almost overlooked.

Now Botham, with the chance to put everything that's gone before him behind him.
TONY COSIER

Mike Brearley doesn't have to stick with the bowling of Old and Dilley. He has other irons in the fire, but at the moment seems happy to keep them close to his chest.
TREVOR BAILEY

On 1 February 1981 New Zealand needed six runs for victory off the last ball of the Third Final Match of the Benson & Hedges World Series Cup (too weighty a title by half) against Australia with the series tied at one-all. Australia captain Greg Chappell gave instructions to his brother Trevor to bowl underarm to ensure New Zealand's Brian McKechnie did not hit a six to win the match and the series. Trevor Chappell bowled the underarm delivery and McKechnie could do nothing more than play back to the bowler. Australia triumphed amid much controversy. The delivery was within the laws of the game, but the Chappells were widely criticized as many believed their action was not in keeping with the spirit of cricket. It was arguably a turning point in the game, the time when people fully realized that in top-flight cricket winning was everything and a team had to win at all costs.

And Greg Chappell instructed his brother, Trevor, to bowl the last ball underground.
RICHARD KAUFMAN, New Zealand cricket commentator

Out of this world. In 1982 West Indies fast bowler Malcolm Marshall took 134 wickets in 22 county matches for Hampshire – the highest aggregate of wickets taken since the reduction in the number of County Championship matches in 1969. In reporting Marshall's accomplishment the *Guardian* noted, 'The highest aggregate for first-class wickets in a single season for almost twenty years has been achieved by Hampshire spaceman Malcolm Marshall'.

When Middlesex spinner Fred Titmus retired from first-class cricket in 1982, he became one of only three bowlers to have achieved in excess of 80,000 dot balls in the course of a first-class career. The others are Wilfred Rhodes (Yorkshire) and Charlie Parker (Gloucestershire).

 The first time you face a googly, you're going to be in trouble if you've never faced one before.
E. W. SWANTON (BBC Radio)

Also in 1982, at Coventry, Warwickshire's Gladstone Small bowled an 18-ball over against Middlesex – a record for first-class cricket. Small's big over included 11 no-balls and a wide.

 Once, playing for Somerset in Derby, I queued for tea during the tea interval. The lady serving tea took one look at me, nudged her friend and said, 'My word you're a big lad, how tall are you?' 'I'm six foot eight,' I replied. 'Oooh,' she cooed, nudging her friend again, 'and are you all in proportion?' 'No, ma'am,' I replied. 'If I was I'd be twelve feet six.'
JOEL GARNER

CHRISTOPHER MARTIN-JENKINS: As a batsman, what would your tactics be if you were up against Shane Warne?
GEOFF BOYCOTT: Get a quick single and observe him from the other end.

Wide of the mark start. In 2002 Steve Harmison (Durham) bowled seven consecutive wides in the first match of England's tour of Australia against the ACB Chairman's XI at Lilac Hill.

Harmison's form continued to be erratic, and he was something of a controversial choice for England's tour of the West Indies in 2003–04, but came good, taking 7 for 12 to help dismiss the West Indies for their lowest ever Test score – 47.

The obvious replacement for the injured Steve Harmison isn't obvious at the moment.
JONATHAN AGNEW (BBC Radio)

The feat of a bowler taking all 10 wickets in a single innings has been performed 79 times in first-class cricket. A. P. 'Tich' Freeman accomplished this feat three times (1929, 1930 and 1931), and three bowlers have accomplished the feat twice: V. E. Walker (1859), Hedley Verity (1931 and 1932) and Jim Laker (1956). The last bowler to take 10 wickets in a single innings of a County Championship match was Ottis Gibson, for Durham against Hampshire on 22 July 2007. Gibson became the 79th player to achieve this feat and the first in county cricket since Richard Johnson in 1994. Gibson's bowling card read as follows:

Michael Carberry, c. Harmison b. Gibson, 4
John Crawley, c. Mustard b. Gibson, 6
Michael Brown, not out, 56
Michael Lumb, lbw Gibson, 16
Chris Benham, b. Gibson, 2
Nick Pothas, c. and b. Gibson, 0
Dimitri Mascarenhas, c. Mustard b. Gibson, 8
Shane Warne, lbw Gibson, 1
Shaun Udal, c. Mustard b. Gibson 4
David Griffiths, c. Mustard, b. Gibson, 2
Jamie Bruce, b. Gibson, 0

Gibson finished with figures of 10 for 47 – not bad for someone approaching 39 years of age.

Anil Kumble was the last bowler to take all 10 wickets in a single innings of a Test match when playing for India against Pakistan at Delhi in 1998–99.

Since 1969, when the number of County Championship matches was reduced, the feat of taking 100 wickets in a season has been accomplished 50 times.

What do bowlers Maurice Tate, Geoff Arnold and Ryan Sidebottom have in common? They are the only England bowlers to have taken a wicket with the first ball of a Test match: Tate v. Australia at Headingley in 1926, Arnold v. New Zealand at Christchurch in 1974–75, and Sidebottom v. West Indies at Riverside in 2007.

15

LORD'S GROUND

ENGLAND v. AUSTRALIA

THURSDAY, FRIDAY, SATURDAY, MONDAY & TUESDAY.
JUNE 25, 26, 27, 29, 30, 1953 (5-day Match)

AUSTRALIA

		First Innings		Second Innings
1	A. R. Morris	st Evans b Bedser	38	
2	G. B. Hole	c Compton b Wardle	13	c Evans b Statham 3
3	A. L. Hassett	c Bailey b Bedser	104	
4	R. N. Harvey	b W. Bedser	59	
5	K. R. Miller	lbw Wardle	25	
6	R. Benaud		0	
7	A. K. Davidson	c Brown b Bedser	76	
8	G. R. Langley	c Watson b Bedser	4	
9	R. R. Lindwall	b Brown	18	
10	D. Ring	lbw Wardle	5	
11	W. A. Johnston	not out	3	
		B 4, l-b 4, w , n-b	8	B .l-b . w . n-b
		Total	346	Total

FALL OF THE WICKETS

1. 65 2. 190 3. 225 4. 229 5. 240 6. 7. 8. 9. 10. 346
1. 3 2. 3. 4. 5. 6. 7. 8. 9. 10.

ANALYSIS OF BOWLING 1st Innings 2nd Innings

Name	O.	M.	R.	W.	Wd.	N-b	O.	M.	R.	W.	Wd.	N-b

ENGLAND

		First Innings		Second Innings
+1	Hutton, L.	c Hole b Johnston	145	
2	Kenyon, D.		3	
3	Graveney, T. W.	b Lindwall	78	
4	Compton, D. C. S.	c Hole b Lindwall	57	
5	Watson, W.	c Lindwall b Johnston	4	
6	T. E. Bailey	c Hole b Benaud	22	
7	F. R. Brown	c Langley b Lindwall	22	
8	Evans, T. G.	b Lindwall	0	
9	Wardle, J. H.	b Davidson	23	
10	Bedser, A. V.	b Lindwall	17	
11	Statham, J. B.	not out		
		B .l-b . w . n-b		B .l-b . w . n-b
		Total		Total

FALL OF THE WICKETS

1. 9 2. 177 3. 279 4. 291 5. 301 6. 328 7. 328 8. 332 9. 341 10. 372
1. 2. 3. 4. 5. 6. 7. 8. 9. 10.

ANALYSIS OF BOWLING 1st Innings 2nd Innings

Name	O.	M.	R.	W.	Wd.	N-b	O.	M.	R.	W.	Wd.	N-b

Umpires—F. S. Lee & H. G. Baldwin   Scorers—W. Mavins & W. Ferguson

+ Captain   * Wicket-keeper

Play begins at 11.30 each day   Stumps drawn at 6.30 each day

Spectators are requested not to enter or leave their seats during the progress of an over

This card does not necessarily include the fall of the last wicket

AUSTRALIA WON THE TOSS

England played their first Test match in 1877 and have had more captains than any other international cricket team.

In the nineteenth century, captains of touring teams were chosen by the promoters of the tour. James Lillywhite, Alfred Shaw and Arthur Shrewsbury were all professional promoters — and captains of England.

Amateur tours abroad, such as those under Lord Harris and Lord Hawke, played teams whose captains were selected by those who administered the club at which the match was to be played. This invariably resulted in the choice of the local favourite as skipper.

The first man to captain England was James Lillywhite, in the 1876–77 Test series against Australia. He was captain for two Tests. England won one and lost one.

The first man to captain England against a team other than Australia was Walter Read, on the 1891–92 tour of South Africa. One Test was played, and England were triumphant.

C. Aubrey Smith (Sussex) has the distinction of having captained England in the only Test he ever played, against South Africa in 1888–89.

In 1902–03 the MCC assumed responsibility for organizing international tours. The preference was to appoint an amateur as captain of England as opposed to a professional.

When Plum Warner (Middlesex) was appointed England captain for the 1903–04 tour of Australia it was a controversial appointment as he had never played in a Test match; the popular choice was A. C. MacLaren. Warner, however, came up trumps: England defeated Australia 3–2. On his return he was awarded a place on the MCC committee, and in 1908 he succeeded Gregor MacGregor as captain of Middlesex.

The esteemed all-rounder Johnny Douglas (Essex) – international cricketer, boxing champion and amateur footballer – captained England prior to the First World War (v. Australia 1911–12 and South Africa 1913–14) and also after the war (v. Australia 1920–21, the home series of 1921, and v. South Africa in 1924). He died tragically along with his father in 1930, both drowned when the steamships *Oberon* and *Arcturus* collided in the Kattegat.

Arthur and Harold Gilligan were the first brothers to captain England, Arthur (Sussex) against South Africa at Edgbaston in 1924 and for the 1924–25 tour of Australia, and Harold in the 1929–30 series in New Zealand.

In the first Test of the 1924 series against South Africa at Edgbaston, Arthur Gilligan made a dream start as captain. South Africa were bowled out for just 30 in their first innings with the newly appointed England skipper returning bowling figures of 6 for 7. One shudders to think what the media would make of such a debut by an England captain should such a thing occur today. In 1924 headlines were somewhat more reserved. The *Daily Sketch* ran with 'New Captain Helps England Gain Upper Hand'.

Douglas Jardine is synonymous with the infamous 1932–33 Bodyline tour of Australia but was also captain of England in three Tests against New Zealand in 1931, one Test against India in 1932 and one against New Zealand in 1932–33, two Tests against the West Indies in 1933, and three Tests against India in 1933–34.

 Poor Harold Larwood. After Bodyline he was blamed and never picked for England again. Bloody Jardine,

of course, whose idea Bodyline was and who, as skipper, implemented it, carried on captaining England on overseas tours, for no other reason than to maintain the hierarchical position of his class.
FRED TRUEMAN

The first father and son to captain England. Frank Mann (Middlesex) was captain for the 1922–23 series against Australia, while son George (also Middlesex) skippered England on the 1948–49 tour of South Africa and in the 1949 series against New Zealand. The accomplishment of the Manns was later matched by Colin Cowdrey (Kent) and his son Chris.

 I was very proud to be appointed England captain against the West Indies in 1988. I went out for the tossing of the coin wearing my whites and England blazer. Viv Richards came out wearing a Bob Marley T-shirt, surfing shorts and flip-flops. After tossing the coin, etiquette dictated I, as England captain, should read our team sheet to the opposing captain. I got no further than four names when Viv said, 'Play who you want, man. Ain't gonna make any difference.'
CHRIS COWDREY

The first professional to captain England was Len Hutton (Yorkshire), in the home series against India in 1952.

David Sheppard is the only Church of England bishop ever to have captained England, in two Tests against Pakistan in 1954.

Peter May (Surrey) captained England in 41 Tests, his first against South Africa in 1955 and his last against Australia in 1961. Under May's captaincy England won 20, drew 11 and lost 10.

In 1958 Yorkshire appointed Ronnie Burnet as captain. Initially a controversial choice as he was 39 years old and had not played a single game for the Yorkshire First XI, having spent all his time with the club in the Second XI, in 1959 Burnett led Yorkshire to their first County Championship success since 1946.

The West Indies went out to win every game we played. We were gutted when we lost. The only man who was allowed to say 'There is nothing wrong with defeat' was our skipper Gary Sobers' chiropodist.
LANCE GIBBS

As captain of England, Tom Graveney (Worcestershire) can claim to have never lost a Test against Australia or any other nation. Graveney was skipper for but one Test, against Australia in 1968, which ended in a draw.

I remember Tom Graveney being introduced to Her Majesty the Queen during the tea interval of a Test. Unfortunately, the Queen misheard his name and, much to the delight of the rest of us, kept referring to him as Mr Gravy.
FRED TRUEMAN

Between 1977 and 1981, England enjoyed a successful spell under the captaincy of Mike Brearley (Middlesex). Of the 31 Tests in which Brearley was captain, England won 18, drew nine and lost just four.

I was privileged to play for two great captains, Mike Brearley with England and Brian Close at Somerset. Brearley was a highly intelligent skipper, a great tactician; Brian Close was an inspirational leader who never asked a player to do what he didn't do himself. Only problem was, Closey did some insane things which none of us had the guts, or too much sense, to do.
IAN BOTHAM

Clive Lloyd continually offered encouragement and instructions to his players in the field. His voice came in gusts, like linnets in the pauses of the wind.
JOHN ARLOTT

In 1980 Worcestershire boasted three captains in the space of three days. Norman Gifford skippered the team in the Benson & Hedges Cup match against Essex on 27 June. The following day, a Saturday, Glenn Turner was captain for the County Championship match against Northamptonshire, only for Ted Hemsley to lead the side out for the Sunday League match against Northants.

Tim Munton is the only captain of a County Championship club never to have made an appearance as captain for the team. Munton was appointed captain of Warwickshire for 1987 but sustained an injury that resulted in him missing the entire season. The following year Brian Lara was appointed Warwickshire captain.

David Gower's tenure as captain of England never replicated the success he enjoyed as a batsman. Gower skippered England in 32 Tests of which England won only five. Nine were drawn, and 18 ended in defeat.

It's difficult to be more laid back than David Gower without actually being comatose.
FRANCES EDMONDS (wife of Phil, Middlesex and England)

Yes, the words 'laid back' fit snugly around Gower's blond curls as a halo.
PETER HAYTER (cricket correspondent)

England's longest-serving captain in terms of Tests is Michael Atherton (Lancashire), who captained his country in 54 Test matches. England won 13, drew 20 and lost 21.

From 2003 to 2008, Michael Vaughan (Yorkshire) skippered England in 48 Tests and under his captaincy England won 26, drew 13 and lost nine. Vaughan's crowning moment was the Ashes victory of 2005.

Who would have guessed that, a month into the new football season, Beckham, Rooney and company would have been reduced to a sideshow? They are talking about Vaughan, Freddie, Tres and Hoggy as if they have known them all their lives.
MAX DAVIDSON, cricket writer

Middlesex was formed in 1864, yet up to 2008 has had only 28 captains. The first was V. E. Walker, the current skipper is Shaun Udal.

Sussex was formed in 1839 and up to 2008 has appointed 42 captains only six of which were born in Sussex. The Sussex-born captains are C. H. Smith (born Henfield), 1864–74; C. L. A. Smith (Henfield), 1906–09; James Langridge (Newick), 1950–52; Robin Marlar (Eastbourne), 1955–59; Jim Parks (Haywards Heath), 1967–68; and Alan Wells (Newhaven), 1992–96.

On 7 January 2009 Kevin Pietersen resigned as England captain following a series of disagreements with coach Peter Moores. Pietersen was reported as saying he 'did not have the full support of the England team for his ideas as captain'. The following day Peter Moores was sacked as England coach.

PETER WEST: You were besieged by dozens of autograph hunters, all wanting the signature of the Surrey captain, how do you feel about that? One's signature can often reveal much about a person's character.
KEN BARRINGTON: And sometimes even his name.

> There is nothing in cricket more calculated to raise a
> laugh than the sight of some determined and serious
> man under a spiralling catch.
> PETER ROEBUCK

Right on the money. In the Varsity match of 1870, Cambridge University's
J. W. Dale dropped what appeared an easy catch. He felt he should offer an
explanation for his uncharacteristic faux pas and informed Cambridge captain
W. B. Money, 'Sorry, chaps, and to you in particular, W. B., I was too busy looking at
rather a cracker of a young lady alighting from a drag.' 'Perfectly understandable,
old boy,' replied Money. The spilled chance proved not too costly: Cambridge
beat Oxford by two runs.

The record number of catches taken by a fielder in a Test series is 15, by Jack
Gregory for Australia in the 1920–21 series against England.

In August 1928 Wally Hammond took a record 10 catches during
Gloucestershire's County Championship match against Surrey at Cheltenham.
Hammond held four catches in Surrey's first innings and six in their second. To
round off a perfect time of it, he also scored a century in each innings for
Gloucestershire. Hammond ended 1928 with 78 catches – still the record for the
most catches in the field by a player in a single season.

Four years later, in 1932, Hammond took eight catches for Gloucestershire in the match against Worcestershire at Cheltenham.

Hammond was also the first fielder to hold 100 catches in Test cricket.

The most catches taken by a player in the field during the course of a first-class career in England is 1,018, by Frank Woolley (Kent, 1906–38). No other fielder has achieved in excess of 1,000 catches in the field. The closest to Woolley are W. G. Grace (Gloucestershire) with 887, Tony Lock (Surrey) with 830, Wally Hammond (Gloucestershire) with 819 and Brian Close (Yorkshire and Somerset) with 813.

The most catches taken by an individual player in the field in a single innings of a County Championship match is seven. This was first achieved by Micky Stewart for Surrey against Northamptonshire at Northampton in 1957, and equalled by Tony Brown for Gloucestershire against Nottinghamshire at Trent Bridge in July 1966. Stewart held six catches at backward short leg and one when fielding in the gully. Four of Brown's catches came off the off-break bowling of David Allen. The accomplishments of both Stewart and Brown were the inspiration for the 1974 poem 'Seven in an Innings' by Cheshire poet Tony Steinbeck.

Micky Stewart's seven catches against Northamptonshire helped him achieve a total of 77 catches in 1957 – one short of Wally Hammond's record for the most catches taken in a season.

The record number of catches by a fielder in a Test match is seven, first accomplished by Greg Chappell for Australia against England at Perth in 1974–75.

Rarely slipped up. In 1959 John Langridge took 66 catches in the slips for Sussex – the most catches in a County Championship season by a slip fielder other than a wicket-keeper.

In 1961 Glamorgan's Peter Walker took 73 catches in the field, the third highest in the history of the County Championship. In 1970 Walker took eight catches for Glamorgan in their match against Derbyshire at Swansea.

In June 1963 at Lord's, every player in the Middlesex team against Essex took at least one catch but no Middlesex player took a catch in both innings.

In 1964 Worcestershire wicket-keeper Roy Booth took a record 88 catches behind the stumps.

In July 1966 at Folkestone, Kent's Alan Ealham took five catches against Gloucestershire, all off the bowling of Derek Underwood.

At last the ball came down. To Mr Hodge it seemed a long time before the invention of Sir Isaac Newton finally triumphed.
A. G. MACDONELL (*England, Their England*)

The record number of catches taken by a fielder in a season since the reduction of County Championship matches in 1969 is 49, by Chris Tavaré for Kent in 1970.

The run-rate has dropped because Chris Tavaré has quite literally dropped anchor.
TREVOR BAILEY (BBC Radio)

In a match between Yorkshire and Nottinghamshire, Yorkshire's Jackie Hampshire hit Nottinghamshire's Bob White with a straight drive towards the sightscreen where Derek Randall was fielding. As the ball approached him, Randall stepped forward and, audaciously, put his hands behind his back, bent forward and took the catch.

In 2005 Graeme Hick took eight catches for Worcestershire in the match against Essex at Chelmsford.

Burns Night in the Highlands. In May 2005, during the game between Northern Counties (Scotland) and Ross County, Simon Harrison of Northern Counties set himself to take a catch but missed the ball, which ignited a box of matches in his trouser pocket. Harrison received treatment for minor burns, but the scorching was so widespread his cricket trousers were beyond repair.

On 6 April 2009 Rahul Dravid set a new record for the number of catches taken in Tests by an outfield player. In the third Test between India and New Zealand Tim McIntosh became his 102nd victim, which passed the previous record set by Mark Waugh (Australia).

I remember once catching John Langridge of Sussex off what was a mighty hit. I was at mid-on but the ball was travelling so fast I couldn't pick it out. I instinctively flung out a hand and the ball just stuck to my fingers. Ten minutes later I looked down at my fingers and they were the size of bananas.

MAURICE HALLAM (Leicestershire)

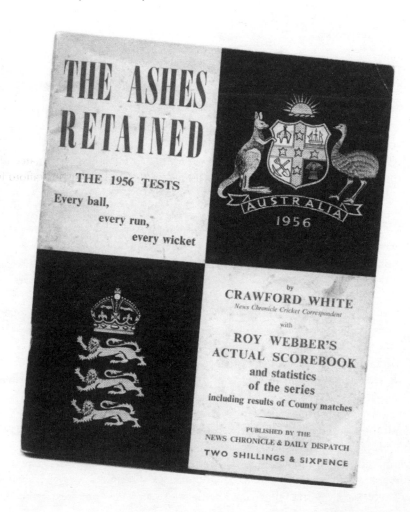

The first player to score a century and take a hat-trick in a first-class match in England was George Giffen, for Australia against Lancashire at Old Trafford in 1884.

The first English player to accomplish this feat was W. E. Roller, for Surrey against Sussex at the Oval in 1885. Roller has the unique distinction of having scored a double century as well as taking a hat-trick in this match (6 for 44).

In 1890 K. S. Prince Ranjitsinhji achieved the remarkable feat of scoring three centuries in a single day: 128 for Cassandra against Saffron Walden, 132 for the Basinettes, and 150 for Long Vacation Students (was it ever thus) XI, all at Cambridge. Perhaps equally remarkable is the fact Ranjitsinhji managed to play in three different matches in a single day. Surely he must have participated only in part in at least one.

In 1896 Ranjitsinhji was at it again, scoring two centuries in a single day for Sussex against Yorkshire at Brighton.

In 1901 C. B. Fry, in appearances for both Sussex and Rest of England, scored six successive centuries – the record for the most hundreds in successive innings.

In 1931–32, playing for Blackheath against Lithgow in New South Wales, Don Bradman scored a century in only three (eight-ball) overs. At one stage during his innings he and Oliver Wendell-Bill added 102 in three overs, of which Bradman scored 100. Bradman's final total was 256.

In 1938 Wally Hammond scored a record 13 centuries in the County Championship for Gloucestershire. During his career with Gloucestershire he also scored a double century on 22 occasions – also a record for the competition.

Mike Procter is the only player to score a century and take a hat-trick in a match twice. Procter did so for Gloucestershire against Essex at Westcliff-on-Sea in 1972, and against Leicestershire at Bristol in 1979.

The last player to score a century and take a hat-trick in first-class cricket in the UK was Kevan James, for Hampshire against India at Southampton in 1996. James enhanced his prowess as a bowler by taking four wickets in four balls.

Only two players have scored a century and taken 10 wickets in an innings in a first-class match: V. E. Walker, for England against Surrey at the Oval in 1859, and W. G. Grace, for the MCC against Oxford University at The Parks in 1886.

Only two players have scored a century in each innings and taken 10 wickets in the same match: Bernard Bosanquet (father of ITN newsreader Reginald), for Middlesex against Sussex at Lord's in 1905 (103 and 100 not out, and 3 for 75 and 8 for 53), and Franklyn Stephenson, for Nottinghamshire against Yorkshire at Trent Bridge in 1988 (111 and 117, and 4 for 105 and 7 for 117).

Yorkshire's George Hirst is the only player to score a century in each innings and also take five wickets in each innings of a match. He accomplished the feat against Somerset at Bath in 1906, scoring 111 and 117 not out and achieving bowling figures of 6 for 70 and 5 for 45.

The only player to score a double century and take in excess of 15 wickets in the same match is George Giffen, for South Australia and Victoria at Adelaide in 1891–92. Giffen scored 217 and took 16 wickets, 9 for 96 and 7 for 70.

Between 1976 and 1981, Zaheer Abbas, playing for Gloucestershire and Pakistan, made a double hundred and a century in a single match on four occasions.

On 21 December 1968 Ian Chappell scored a century for Australia against the West Indies unaware he had reached a milestone in Test cricket: the 1,000th batsman to score a Test century.

Geoff Boycott eat your heart out. In August 1974 Keith Fletcher (Essex) scored a century for England in the third Test against Pakistan at the Oval. It wasn't the sort of innings to have the crowd on their feet, however: Fletcher was at the wicket for seven hours and 38 minutes before finally hitting the run that gave him his century. His was the slowest century in English first-class cricket.

Pushing the boundaries. In September 2006, when playing for Essex against Leicestershire at Grace Road, Mark Pettini became the first ever batsman in the history of first-class cricket to score a century entirely from boundaries. Pettini scored his historic century during Essex's second innings, his undefeated 114 comprising 12 fours and 11 sixes. With the exception of one four, all of Pettini's runs came off the bowling of Leicestershire's Darren Robinson, and his century was achieved in only 24 minutes and off just 27 balls.

On 2 August 2008, playing for Surrey against Yorkshire at Headingley, Mark Ramprakash became the 25th batsman to score 100 hundreds. Ramprakash reached the landmark off 196 balls, hitting nine fours and one six, and went on to reach 113 not out. (Coincidentally, Ramprakash also scored his maiden first-class century against Yorkshire, in July 1989.) He also became the second batsman to reach the landmark of 100 hundreds on the Headingley ground, the first being Geoff Boycott, while playing for England against Australia in 1977.

 Now, the next question has nothing at all to do with music, or sport. At which ground did Geoff Boycott score his one hundredth hundred?
CLASSIC FM

In 2009 against the West Indies, Ravi Bopara became only the fifth England batsman to score three successive Test centuries, following in the footsteps of Herbert Sutcliffe, Denis Compton, Geoffrey Boycott and Graham Gooch. Even more remarkable was the fact that two years earlier in Sri Lanka, Bopara had made three successive ducks.

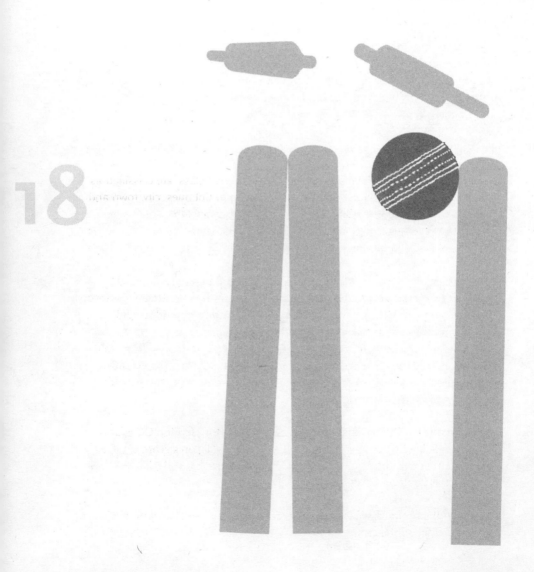

In essence, all matches that are not deemed to be 'first class' are classified as 'minor cricket'. Minor cricket encompasses the Minor Counties, city, town and village clubs, universities (Cambridge and Oxford excepted, of course), the armed forces, colleges, schools, teams of a religious nature, candering (nomadic) clubs, in fact any team which does not by definition enjoy first-class status.

Most clubs play at the weekend, though there are numerous leagues whose matches take place in the evening in mid-week. Whatever the format, the Laws of Cricket are universally observed.

Matches are limited by overs or, in some cases, time. Matches played at the weekend normally consist of 60 overs per innings, mid-week evening matches normally 20 overs per innings.

In August 1879 Thomas Fison scored 264 not out for Hendon CC against Highgate School without scoring a single boundary. Fison's score could have been even higher: the official scorebook recorded that he 'retired to catch a train to the Continent'.

In 1893 Arthur Coningham was reprimanded by his club and Lancashire officials after he set fire to the outfield while fielding in a match between Blackpool and

District and the touring Australians at Blackpool. What on earth was he thinking? Equally, what did he find to set fire to?

I played many matches for the Authors, mainly at Esher. The matches were organized by E. W. Hornrung of 'Raffles' fame and our side regularly featured Arthur Conan Doyle, J. M. Barrie and A. E. W. Mason, who often brought his typewriter along to games so he could work whilst awaiting to bat. Against the Artists CC, we sat outside the Pavilion listening to Mason's typewriter click-clacking in the dressing room, prompting Horace Bleakley to remark, 'One has to give it to Mason, he's hard at it with the writing even when playing cricket.' When the seventh wicket fell the typewriter was still intermittently clacking and I was sent to call upon Mason to take to the middle. On entering the dressing room I was astounded to see a magpie bouncing up and down on the typewriter keys and no Mason in sight. It transpired at the commencement of our innings Mason had fallen in with a group of locals and taken off to the nearby pub for refreshment.
ALBERT KINROSS

Went for a duck. In the 1920s 'Buns' Thornton (founder of the Scarborough Cricket Festival, and who also played for Cambridge University, Kent and Middlesex) was playing for United North XI against Bingley and District when he lofted a ball towards the unfenced side of the ground that backed on to a river. Bingley's cover point, hopeful of taking the catch, took to his toes and, not taking his eyes off the ball, disappeared over the bank and into the river, as did the ball.

On tune. On 6 May 1922, in a Howden and District League match, Jennings Tune of Cliffe CC took all 10 Eastrington wickets for no runs.

Stout performance. On 8 September 1925 Percy Chapman scored all the first 150 runs posted by Mackeson's Brewery CC against Eltham Police (Kent) and went on to score 183 in Mackeson's final total of 201. The second highest score in the Mackeson total that day was 11, in extras.

Grave circumstances. During the match between Spalding CC and the Indian Students in 1926, Spalding batsman the Reverend Lancelot Smith had to abort his innings when he was called upon to conduct a funeral, stepping in for a vicar who had suddenly taken ill.

There are lies, damned lies and . . . When Kettering Town CC played G. S. Robertson's Nottinghamshire XI at Kettering in August 1927, W. Cawston was called upon to open the bowling for the home side. Cawston's over lasted 17 balls, included 10 wides and a no-ball, yet the opposition failed to score a single run off any of his legitimate deliveries. Following this opening debacle, Cawston was not asked to bowl another over, but had the satisfaction of seeing a respectable bowling analysis in the scorebook of 1–1–0–0.

Let's face it, he was so very near. In 1939, in a match between St Albans Second XI and Radlett Second XI at St Albans' Clarence Park, the Radlett bowler F. Green had taken 9 for 1 when he bowled to the St Albans number 11. The ball reared up and hit the St Albans man in the face, and he had to retire hurt.

For many years Darlington CC's ground and the home of Darlington AFC were all part of the same site at Feethams, the respective grounds backing on to each other. On 30 August 1947 at 3.30 p.m. a Darlington batsman hit the ball out of the ground and into the football ground. The teams waited for the ball to be thrown back by a spectator at the football match and a ball duly arrived over the wall – the match ball being used in the game between Darlington and Crewe Alexandra.

Worked up a good appetite. At the Oval in 1948, H. J. J. Malcolm scored 203 not out before lunch for Stoics against HMS *Dolphin*.

In July 1955 Gerald Luckhurst scored six consecutive centuries for Gore Court CC (Kent) and F. Day's XI without ever being out in any of those innings.

In 1957 members of Yoxall CC in Staffordshire must have heard many an old tale from team-mate Fred Lester. He was 87, thought to be the oldest cricketer to play regularly at an organized level. Sadly, 1957 turned out to be Fred's last season for the club, for he died not long after. Still, he'd had a good innings.

Writer and broadcaster Michael Parkinson, Geoffrey Boycott and Dickie Bird played in the same team for Barnsley CC.

And sixes to boot for Wellington. In 1962–63 in New Zealand, John Reid scored 296 for Wellington CC against Northern Districts, a total that included 15 sixes.

Webb trapped them. On 11 August 1963 at Woodford Green, the first six Southgate County Old Boys wickets fell to catches taken by Whitbread Sports and Social Club slip fielder K. Webb.

Beyond our Ken. In 1971 Ken Lewsey, Saltwood CC's batsman at the non-striker's end, was run out after calling for a fourth run off the first ball of the match against Evington.

Disappointingly, there is only a small crowd here to watch this game. In fact I would say there were more cars than there are people.
BRIAN JOHNSTON

In a match at Falkirk CC in 1976 the ball was lost down a rabbit hole and never recovered.

In July 1977 Tim McVey scored 101 not out in a morning match for his school, Penrith Queen Elizabeth Grammar School, and in the afternoon scored 108 for Penrith Third XI against Gamblesby CC.

In 1978, at one stage during their match against Abbots Langley CC, West Herts were 60 without loss, all their runs having been scored by Richard Simons.

In 1978 Mark Lockett, playing for Charfield CC, took three catches in the field off three successive balls bowled by team-mate Dave Bennett.

Purple patch Hayes. Also in 1978, D. L. Hayes scored a fifty all in boundaries and off only nine balls for Quidnuncs CC against the Royal Navy at Portsmouth.

Gimme five! In 1979 Barnes Green CC, with five wickets in hand, needed four runs off the last five balls to win the match against Ockley, only for the Ockley bowler, Roddy Cowles, to take five wickets in five balls.

It's all bye the bye. In 1979 Cawood CC won their York Senior League match against Dringhouses without any of their batsmen hitting the ball. Cawood had dismissed Dringhouses for only 4, and the first ball of the Cawood innings went for four byes.

Join a throng, Ross. Playing for Stanmore CC in 1980, Ross Chiese took five Radlett wickets in a single over without achieving a hat-trick. His over proceeded as follows: wicket, wicket, dot ball, wicket, no-ball, wicket, wicket. On achieving this feat Ross was immediately engulfed by players and spectators offering their congratulations.

Maxwell's full house. In May 1985 Ken Maxwell, playing for Marchington CC against Trentside, took all 10 Trentside wickets while conceding only one run. Maxwell's 10-wicket haul was achieved in 14 balls and included seven Trentside wickets in seven successive deliveries.

End to End Stuff! On 16 June 1985, during a match between Hambledon and Petersfield CC, a Hambledon bowler bowled from both ends and finished by taking all 10 Petersfield wickets for one run. The bowler who intermittently operated from both ends was Martin Stereo.

Shere brilliance. On 1 September 1985 Shere CC bowler Lionel Jones took 10 for 58 against Hove Montefiore CC. In Shere's following match, on 7 September, Jones surpassed himself and his best ever bowling figures by taking 10 for 15 against Motspur Park. Jones was 47 years old at the time.

He took some ribbing for this. During the winter of 1985–86, Martyn Goulding of Torquay CC was practising his batting skills against a bowling machine with the machine set to 'fast' when a delivery hit and broke a bone in his foot. In considerable pain, Goulding fell to the ground, only for the machine to continue bowling at the helpless batsman, who was peppered with deliveries that caused multiple bruising and two broken ribs.

It's what it's all about. On 23 August 1986 Ken Hudson and Dean King found themselves batting together for Alexandra Park CC Third XI against Hanwell Third XI. Ken Hudson was 78 years old and Dean King 15 – an age difference of 63 years.

Ealing comedy. On 10 May 1987 Kurt Jansen of Northolt CC hit 41 against Ealing CC off an over which included two no-balls. Jansen's whirlwind batting resulted in him hitting six sixes, a four and a single.

Chipped in with winning runs. On 22 June 1988 David Cox scored nine runs off the last ball of the match to give Chipping Sodbury CC victory over Patchway.

The last batsman, Albeit Carefully, survived to lunch.
HAWKES BAY GAZETTE

On 31 July 1988 Duncan Falconer scored 206 not out in Ewell CC's total of 228 against Dorking.

The 1986 Central Electricity Generating Board North West Region Cup Final was contested by the beaten semi-finalists Pennine (Preston) and Padiham because the winning semi-finalists refused to play each other – or perhaps they were just fed up with having to say such a long-winded and drawn-out tournament title.

Not so fine leg. On 10 July 1989 John Holden was shot in the leg with an air-rifle while fielding near the boundary for Linden Park CC against Leigh.

Jack Hyams played cricket at senior club level from 1934 to 1990 for, among others, the RAF, Stoics, the Forty Club and London Counties. In that time he scored over 112,000 runs including 168 centuries, notching up at least one hundred in each of the 56 years he played cricket.

In 1989 occasional bowler Jed Bowers took the last wicket in a match for Trevose CC (Cornwall) but was not required to bowl again that year. In 1990 Bowers was asked to bowl for the first time that year, took the last wicket in a match with his first delivery, but was never called upon by Trevose to bowl again that season. In 1991 Bowers was again called upon to bowl and took a wicket with his first ball. A hat-trick – and it only took three years.

The final of the Beaconsfield Festival tournament at Beaconsfield CC in June 1992 was abandoned after a car went of out control and zig-zagged across part of the pitch before careering into the crowd, injuring a number of spectators, fortunately none seriously. The car was 'driven' by Tom Orford, the 86-year-old president of Beaconsfield, who had been invited to make the presentation to the winners.

Honley on terrns. Also in June 1992, during the Huddersfield League Division Two match between Honley CC and Meltham, Honley's Simon Walker hit six sixes and a four off an over from Meltham's James Moulson that included a no-ball.

The final two Longton wickets were taken by leg-spanner Steve Hilsdon.
EVENING SENTINEL (Stoke)

Milford Hall 2nds match was postponed due to pain.
STAFFORDSHIRE NEWSLETTER

Hambledon CC still exists, albeit not the Hambledon club famous for its organization of cricket matches in the eighteenth century. The current Hambledon CC play at Ridge Meadow, just off the road to Broadhalfpenny Down, about half a mile from Hambledon village. The club is currently rebuilding following a fire that destroyed the clubhouse on 8 September 2007, almost 211 years to the day since the original Hambledon club folded. In the 1990s some bright spark from Fuller's brewery stripped cricket's most famous pub, the Bat and Ball at Hambledon in Hampshire, of all its historic cricket memorabilia and converted the pub into a sham Mexican-style pub cum restaurant. In July 2006 the pub was taken over by Tony and Jane Drinkwater (you couldn't make it up) and new management at Fuller's reinstated the historic cricket artefacts.

Never crossed the white line because he had to run one. Ceri Hughes withdrew from Llangennech CC's match against Port Talbot in May 2006 because he received a last-minute call to be a linesman (referee's assistant) at the FA Cup Final at the Millennium Stadium.

Gutted. In 2006 Mark Pilgrim of Billingborough CC (Lincolnshire) was bowled by 16-year-old Mark Stanway of Market Deeping. Stanway's delivery came at such speed it smacked one of the bails over 50 yards on to the pavilion roof, where it then rolled back down and lodged in the guttering.

All's well that ends well. On 2 June 2006 Alok Patra of Poleneight CC in Bengal had to be rescued by emergency services after chasing a ball to the boundary and disappearing down an old well whose depth was estimated at over 40 feet.

Sham of the big hitters of Shamley. Shamley Green CC (Surrey) can no longer award sixes for balls that land on the property of Mr Mike Burgess, whose home overlooks the Shamley village green ground. Mr Burgess was moved to act following a claim that as many as 24 tiles had been broken by balls hit for six. Shamley have been playing on the village green since 1840. Mr Burgess moved into his home in 2005.

Grandfather 'etched' in 'font' memory. In 2006 Etchingham and Fontridge CC in Sussex played its first match since 1939, when the club disbanded due to the outbreak of war. Somewhat fittingly, the first ball for the re-formed E and F was bowled by Matt Neve, whose grandfather had bowled the final ball of E and F's final match in 1939.

In September 2006 Winterbourne Bassett CC (Wiltshire) received official notification that after 23 years the club had been evicted from their home ground by an Austrian count. Landlord Count Konrad Goss-Saurau took the action after the club, somewhat understandably, refused to support his application to build houses on the ground.

On 20 April 2009 England paceman Ryan Sidebottom appeared for Leek in their North Staffordshire and South Cheshire League match against Leycett CC. Sidebottom was returning from injury, needed match practice, and his appearance for Leek was part of his programme to rebuild his fitness. He returned figures of 6 for 34 and scored 64.

Comical music duo Flanders and Swann once recorded a song the lyrics of which simply comprised a long list of country railway stations closed by Dr Beeching (what a catastrophic and short-sighted policy that was). An updated tribute version was recently performed by the appropriately named musician Ken Bolam, the lyrics of which comprised minor English cricket clubs, and an extract of which runs as follows:

Addingham, Beckwithshaw, Burley-in-Wharfedale,
Long Itchington, Ramsbottom, Bangor-on-Dee,
Horsforth, Buttershaw, Marton cum Grafton,
Twiddlesworth, Wilnecote, Hopton-on-Sea.
May the batsmen be bolder
May the sun melt the roller
At Cockington Corinthians, Mullion and Haimes,
Mortimer Common, Borrowash, Bolsover,
Lofthouse and Middlesmoor, Exeter St James.

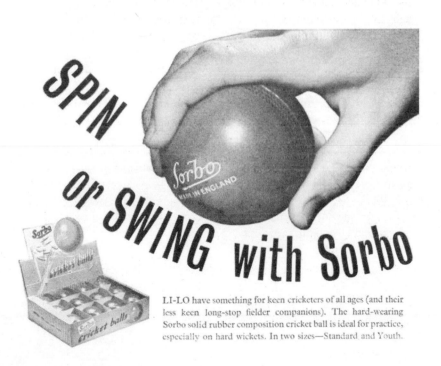

SPIN or SWING with Sorbo

LI-LO have something for keen cricketers of all ages (and their less keen long-stop fielder companions). The hard-wearing Sorbo solid rubber composition cricket ball is ideal for practice, especially on hard wickets. In two sizes—Standard and Youth.

Coaching

Unlike football, for example, coaching has been an integral part of cricket since the nineteenth century. Technically, cricket is arguably the most demanding of sports, hence coaching has been a part of the game since its earliest days.

The MCC held the first of its Easter Coaching Classes at Lord's in 1902.

 Coaching has long since been essential to the development of the young cricketer. During my playing career I learned a lot about the game and, since retirement, I'm continuing to learn.
SIR DONALD BRADMAN

When Sir Jack Hobbs scored his 100th century, K. S. Ranjitsinhji sent Hobbs a silver souvenir inscribed 'From a humble student of the game'. Hobbs sent a letter of thanks to the England and India batsman which included the line 'We are all humble students of the game and will continue to be so'.

 I never had so much as an hour's coaching in my life.
JACK HOBBS

Cricket is a science – the study of a lifetime – in which you may exhaust yourself but never your subject.
SIR FREDERICK TOONE (Yorkshire CCC)

The MCC Coaching Manual has long been a bible of cricket coaching. Regularly updated, it is still read today. Written and compiled by Harry Altham, it first appeared in 1952. It was superseded by the *MCC MasterClass* book, which in turn was superseded in 1994 by *The New MCC Coaching Book*, which is still available today. The original by Altham is still mentioned idiomatically by players and supporters alike, particularly with reference to an unorthodox stroke, as in 'You'll not find that one in the *MCC Coaching Manual*'.

I suppose the first coaching tip I ever received was when I was around 13 years of age. I was playing league cricket around Manchester and taking plenty of wickets. One day a chap, who must have been in his late seventies, said to me, 'You're going to have to change if you want to make it as a professional bowler, lad.' 'How do you mean?' I asked. 'Because you're always trying to bowl the batsman out.' That completely changed my thinking about bowling.
BRIAN STATHAM

Throughout the twentieth century all county clubs held winter coaching classes for promising young players. The classes were held by old pros many of whom possessed no official coaching qualifications but who could pass on considerable experience, technique and expertise.

As a lad in the late 1940s I attended Yorkshire's winter coaching sessions which were held in what was a large shed at Headingley. There were four principal coaches, Cyril Turner, Bill Bowes, Maurice Leyland and Arthur Mitchell, each one a first-class coach. Arthur Mitchell was, to my mind, the best, but he was a dour man who I can never recall smiling. If Arthur had ever gone riding with the four horsemen of the Apocalypse, his presence wouldn't noticeably have enlivened the party.

FRED TRUEMAN

 I joined the Surrey staff in 1938 and that was when my real cricket education began. A coach taught me how to hold the ball correctly; to my amazement, up to that point I hadn't been. One day he showed me the correct grip for a leg-cutter to be bowled on a dry wicket taking spin. 'Second finger almost round the seam,' he said, and showed me. 'Second finger does most of the work and you hold the ball more tightly than for swing bowling. Now for a leg-cutter bowled on a soft wicket,' he went on to tell me, 'your fingers are in the same position as those of a normal leg-spin bowler, but it's your second and third fingers that do all the work.' It was a revelation to me. I never forgot that, or the myriad of other things I was to be taught.

ALEC BEDSER

One of the most popular of all coaching books, even to this day, is *The Art of Cricket* by Sir Donald Bradman. First published in 1958, so popular has the book proved it has been reprinted numerous times over the years. It is widely regarded as one of the best coaching manuals ever written on the various techniques and tactics of batting, bowling, wicket-keeping, fielding, even the importance of winning the pre-match tossing of the coin.

 There is no bowling secret I know of to achieve pace off the pitch. Tate had it because he had magnificent shoulders and wrists, and he co-ordinated everything to give the ball real punch at delivery. It was power and timing, and it was taught to him.

SIR DONALD BRADMAN

Today, the ECB runs a successful National Coaching Scheme which comprises various levels of qualification. Up to and including Level Three of the scheme is managed by the ECB County Coaching Education Office based at Edgbaston; Level Four and above is part of the ECB's Elite Coaching Development Scheme. The principal awards are the ECB Coaching Assistant Award, ECB Coaching Award, ECB Head Coach Award, ECB Master Coach Award and ECB Coaching Fellowship Award.

All county clubs employ coaches at various levels. The coaching at minor clubs is undertaken, but not wholly so, by the professional employed for that particular season.

Former players who are now top coaches include Geoff Arnold, John Bracewell, Greg Chappell, Kapil Dev, John Emburey, Desmond Haynes, Geoff Lawson, Dennis Lillee, Rodney Marsh, Mushtaq Mohammed, Javed Miandad, Andy Pick, Ian Redpath, Jack Russell, Graham Thorpe and Fred Titmus.

Mentally, cricket develops the ability to think, to reason out a problem, and to act quickly.
SIR DONALD BRADMAN

Sly young Fox. Oxford University batsman Dan Fox prepared for 2004 practising shots while immersed in a swimming pool. One of the reasons for this was he believed such routines would strengthen his arms. Fox made a century on his debut in the Varsity match – obviously a stroke player not out of his depth, especially when playing shots into the deep.

The medium-pace tango? Following Darren Gough's success in winning the BBC's *Strictly Come Dancing* in 2005, Essex introduced dance-steps as part of the players' pre-season training programme. Skipper Ronnie Irani said, 'I think it could benefit us greatly. Goughie lost a stone and built up so much leg strength because of his dancing.'

Coincidences

On 2 January 1902 Australia's Clem Hill was out for 99 against England – the first player to be dismissed for 99 in a Test match. He vowed to make amends by scoring a century in the following Test at Adelaide. He was out for 98 in the first innings and 97 in the second.

In 1905 England captain Stanley Jackson won the toss five times out of five during the Test series against Australia. Jackson and Australia captain Joe Darling had been born on the same day, 21 November 1870 – the only time this has happened in Test match history.

Australia's Warren Bardsley was born in 1909, in the Bardsley district of Warren, New South Wales.

In the Varsity match of 1919 F. W. Gilligan played for Oxford University whereas his brother, A. E. R Gilligan, was in the Cambridge team. In the first innings A.E.R was stumped by his sibling. In the same match, J. H. Naumann, playing for Cambridge, was bowled by his brother, F. C. G. Naumann of Oxford.

On 20 June 1931 L. A. J. Sadler, playing his first match for the RA Signal Corps, was dismissed in both innings by Oliver Battock (Datchet CC). Thirty years later, on 3 September 1961, Sadler (then a Major) played his final match for the RA Signal Corps and was dismissed in both innings by the same Oliver Battock.

In the meeting between Yorkshire and Surrey in 1937, Yorkshire wicket-keeper H. Crick and his Surrey counterpart E. W. J. Brooks had words when the former believed he had dismissed the latter by taking a catch, only for Brooks to maintain he had not connected with the ball – a view shared by the umpires. The pair remained at loggerheads after the game, and thereafter their relationship remained 'competitive' whenever they encountered each other, presumably even unto the day they both passed away, 10 February 1960.

On 14 June 1938 T. L. Brierley scored 116 for Glamorgan against Lancashire at Old Trafford, his career-best score. Following the Second World War, Brierley joined Lancashire and against his former club Glamorgan at Liverpool he equalled his career-best score of 116.

In June 1967 Brian Crump and Ray Bailey sat next to each other when Northamptonshire travelled to Cardiff to play Glamorgan. Crump and Bailey found themselves room-mates at the team's hotel and, amazingly, the pair were the only bowlers used by Northants in the entire match. Crump returned first-innings figures of 5 for 45, whereas Bailey took 5 for 64. In Glamorgan's second innings Crump took 7 for 29 and Bailey 3 for 31 to help Northants to a 132-run victory.

Never got his eye in. In June 1966, during a match between Sunderland Corporation Transport and Sunderland GPO in the Wearside Half-Holiday League, Transport's Harold King was bowled for a duck by the GPO's Norman Archer.

At sixes and sevens. On 6 September 1990, during Yorkshire's match against The Yorkshiremen at Scarborough, Steven Rhodes hit a mighty six. Having cleared the boundary, the ball struck a spectator, who fortunately proved none the worse for the experience. Seven minutes later Rhodes hit another mighty six. The ball sailed into the crowd and hit the same spectator, who was at the time ferrying drinks to friends.

Creepy Crawleys? On 2 July 1992 John Crawley of Cambridge University scored a century (106) in the Varsity match against Oxford University at Lord's. On the same day, John's brother Mark scored a century for Nottinghamshire against Kent at Maidstone.

Through the glass darkly. In 1987 BBC radio commentator Edward Bevan was showered with shards of glass when Courtney Walsh smashed the ball through the window of the BBC Wales commentary box during Glamorgan's match against Gloucestershire at Cardiff. Nineteen years later, on 10 July 2006, Bevan was commentating for BBC Radio Wales on the Twenty20 match between the same two clubs when a hefty shot from Glamorgan's Richard Grant smashed the same window in the same commentary box and again Bevan was showered with glass.

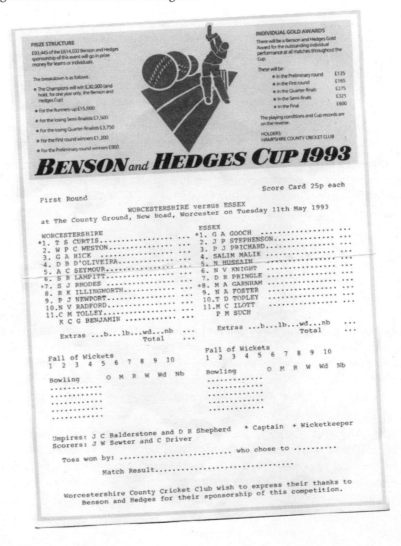

Corporate hospitality is now an invaluable source of revenue for England and county clubs. For some, being invited to attend a match in a corporate hospitality suite or tent may be their first experience of a cricket match. With this in mind, the following may provide a useful guide to the County Championship sides.

22

DERBYSHIRE: used to wear baggy caps like the Australians in the hope it would make them play like Australia. It didn't. With the exception of the Twenty20 Cup and Pro40 League, which they have never won, Derbyshire has won each of the other major competitions just once. Last time they won the County Championship, King Edward VIII abdicated, but perhaps not for that reason. When top players become formerly top players they often end up at Derbyshire.

DURHAM: only admitted to the County Championship in 1992 and after enduring a miserable 10 years or so are now full of themselves. Won their first trophy, the Friends Provident Trophy, in 2007 and followed this by winning the County Championship in 2008. Prior to this Durham made up for their initial lack of success by continually telling people how their Riverside ground is now a Test ground and what a wonderful academy they have; and, while other county clubs suffer meagre attendances for Championship matches, how once, though no fixture was scheduled, they had over 2,000 turn up at Riverside just on the off chance there might be a game on; and that everything would be a cakewalk for them if not for the fact England and England 'A' are now reaping the benefits of all the years of hard work they put in coaching young players since childhood.

ESSEX: enjoyed unprecedented success in the 1980s and early 1990s when they won the County Championship six times, mainly due to the run-making of Graham Gooch and the ability of their bowlers to bowl out the opposition very cheaply at Chelmsford – curiously, a feat Essex bowlers were not able to replicate once the Chelmsford groundsman retired. They like the Pro40 game and won Division One in both 2005 and 2006, even though the team does not have any pros who are over 40. They do, however, have a player called Danish, who is actually Pakistani.

GLAMORGAN: the only first-class county club not in England, it carries the flag for Wales, and much more besides. Gary Sobers once hit six sixes off one over bowled by Glamorgan's Malcolm Nash, which always features in those TV list programmes with titles like *One Hundred Great Sporting Moments*, though it is doubtful whether Glamorgan supporters see this as a 'great sporting moment'. There is an Alexander Wharf in what was Cardiff Docks, and, coincidentally, the Glamorgan team has one too.

GLOUCESTERSHIRE: formed in 1871, and the county for whom W. G. Grace and his brothers played before lending their name to the departmental store in BBC TV's *Are You Being Served?* They have never won the County Championship, which suggests that for all the great players who have graced Gloucestershire sides over the years they might have just been playing for themselves. Since 2000 Gloucestershire have become something of a specialist one-day team, winning several trophies – understandable, really, as in the County Championship Gloucestershire rarely bat for more than a day.

HAMPSHIRE: here's a fact to drop into conversation: the last time Hampshire won the County Championship (1973) there was not a single commercial radio station in the UK. Once boasted Shane Warne, the best spin bowler of all time and cricket's original peroxide blond. Also Kevin Pietersen, who plays so rarely for Hampshire now, when he does turn out he has to be introduced to his team-mates.

KENT: once had a rule that no one was allowed to play for the team unless they bore the surname Cowdrey. Like Hampshire, Kent have not won the County Championship since the 1970s, and, again like Hampshire, they don't look like doing so for a good many years. Kent did, however, win the Twenty20 Cup in 2007 which suggests they might be an 'up like a rocket but down like a stick' team.

LANCASHIRE: think Jack Dee and Clement Freud. Historically scored massive totals but by then there was no time for the opposition to bat. They have not won the County Championship since famous Lancastrian son George Formby first played his ukulele. Did very well in the 1970s in one-day competitions, when they would do anything to win, even play in the pouring rain.

LEICESTERSHIRE: enjoyed a golden period in the 1970s under the captaincy of Ray Illingworth, who joined not only Leicestershire but the ever-growing list of players to have been badly treated by Yorkshire. The seventies team also included the young David Gower, a batsman of sublime, effortless strokes and hair like Harpo Marx. Just when cricket fans in general were beginning to forget that Leicestershire existed, they won the Twenty20 Cup (2004 and 2006), but have since returned to their favoured shadows. Hotly competitive with Derbyshire for players who are former top players.

MIDDLESEX: can swagger and swank, and invariably do, because their home ground is Lord's. Middlesex have provided more England captains than is good for them, or England. In post-war Britain they boasted the nation's favourite sporting star in Denis Compton, who would score a double century before lunch before nipping off to score a hat-trick for Arsenal, then be back at Lord's for the afternoon session. Tradition plays a very big part in cricket. Traditionally, other counties loved to beat Middlesex – and tradition dictates they still do.

NORTHAMPTONSHIRE: another club which has never won the County Championship and which for many years never even won a match. In 1992 Northamptonshire won the NatWest Trophy, but since then, like that trophy itself, they appear to have gone west. Star player is Monty Panesar, beloved of lovers of spin. Talking of spinning, in 2007 they had on their books David Jacobs and Mark 'Trevor' Nelson.

NOTTINGHAMSHIRE: can boast some of the greatest names of cricket – Larwood, Voce, the Gunns, Sobers, Hadlee. After decades of underachievement, in 2005 Nottinghamshire threw off the reputation of being a side always near the bottom and won the County Championship, which is ironic, given their star player is Sidebottom.

SOMERSET: have never won the County Championship, have never looked like winning it, and don't look as if they will soon. Famous for having produced Ian Botham, arguably England's greatest cricketer, certainly the most entertaining. These days the accent is on youth and players with a West Country accent. Historically the Taunton wicket has been known to favour batsmen, particularly those of the opposition.

SURREY: dominated the County Championship in the 1950s to such an extent, should you ever be asked in a quiz who won the title in such and such year in the fifties, just say Surrey. Started to have flashbacks when they won the title three years out of four between 1999 and 2002, the Pro40 League in 2003, and later the Twenty20 Cup. But that is all it proved to be, a flashback.

SUSSEX: used to offer the impression of being a real family club with members of the Cox, Oakes, Parks, Langridge, Buss and Wells families all playing for the club and quite often in the same teams. As one member recently remarked, 'This is still very much a family club. In every room I go into there's a bloody argument going on.'

WARWICKSHIRE: in 1994 everyone was jealous of Warwickshire because they won the 'treble' of County Championship, Sunday League and Benson & Hedges Cup. All the rest could find to say was, 'But you didn't win the NatWest Trophy, did you?', which they did the following year. Appears to be a rather well-off county club – another thing that sticks in the craw of many.

WORCESTERSHIRE: club with the most pompous description of its club badge – 'Shield Argent a Fess between three Pears Sable' – which is not even good grammar. Traditionally the first match played by any international touring team was always against Worcestershire, a tradition which ended a few years back when touring teams became fed up of bailing out their dressing room when the nearby River Severn overflowed its banks, which it often does, even at the so-called height of summer.

YORKSHIRE: used to have a rule that no one could play for Yorkshire unless they had been born within the county itself. For decades the tiresome fact (but a fact all the same) was tripped out that England had never won a Test match without a Yorkshireman in the side. Then Yorkshire relaxed its rules on eligibility and England started losing irrespective of who played in their side. The most successful county of all in terms of County Championships won: the 1950s apart, they seemed to win every year up to 1968, since when there has been a lot of in-fighting, grumbling and general discontentment, and few trophies. No one has ever seen a rose that looks like the white rose depicted on their club badge – are they sure the artist got it right?

Matches between county teams first took place in the eighteenth century. The earliest known match was Kent against Surrey at Dartford Brent on 29 June 1709.

For most of the nineteenth century inter-county matches continued to be played on an ad hoc basis. In the early 1800s it is doubtful such teams were truly representative of counties. Individual clubs often played matches claiming to be their county team. Through the first half of the nineteenth century teams did become more representative of the county, and some claimed to be 'Champion County of England', but there was no accepted method of determining this and only four of the clubs in today's County Championship were formed prior to 1863.

As county clubs were formed, they played one another in what is now termed the 'unofficial' County Championship.

In 1864 overarm bowling was legalized.

Rules governing playing qualifications for county teams were laid down by the counties in 1873. Prior to this it was common for a player to play for two county teams, the county of his birth and his county of residence.

On 10 December 1889 representatives of eight county clubs – Gloucestershire, Kent, Lancashire, Middlesex, Nottinghamshire, Surrey, Sussex and Yorkshire – met at Lord's and agreed to form an official County Championship. In 1890 the County Championship was officially constituted. It is from this date that authorized records of matches began. The competition initially featured the eight county teams that had instigated the Championship the previous year. Each team was scheduled to play 14 matches on a home and away basis, but it didn't always work out that way.

The inaugural winners of the County Championship, in 1890, were Surrey. The final places were based on the number of wins minus the number of defeats; only later was a structured points system introduced. Surrey went on to win the Championship in each of its first three seasons.

In the inaugural season, Sussex had the dubious honour of being the first club to finish bottom of the table, in so doing also becoming the first team not to draw a single match in the course of a season. Of Sussex's 12 matches they won one and lost 11.

In 1891, Somerset joined. They were followed in 1895 by Derbyshire, Essex, Hampshire, Leicestershire and Warwickshire. The rules were changed so each team had to play at least 16 matches a season. Until the Second World War, counties played differing numbers of matches. The points system had to be modified so the ratio of points to completed matches (games minus draws) decided final places.

In 1894 Surrey were crowned champions for a fourth time and managed to become the first team to win the Championship without drawing a match, though one match was tied.

In 1899 Worcestershire was admitted to the Championship.

In 1900 Yorkshire became the first club to go through an entire season undefeated. They played 28 matches, won 16 and drew 12.

Northamptonshire joined the County Championship in 1905.

In 1910 the system of determining final places was again modified. The places were based on ratio of matches won to matches played. From 1911 to

1967 a variety of systems were used which generally relied on points for a win and for first-innings leads in games left unfinished.

On 12 August 1912 Kent wrapped up the title with victory over Gloucestershire at Cheltenham – the earliest stage in a season the title had ever been won.

In 1919 the County Championship experimented with two-day matches. It proved 'unsuccessful and unpopular amongst clubs and players alike'. It seems what supporters thought of this didn't come into it.

After the experiment of two-day matches in 1919, all County Championship matches were to be of three-day duration until 1988, albeit between 1982 and 1992 some matches were scheduled as four-day games.

In 1921 Glamorgan were admitted to the County Championship.

Buckinghamshire were invited to join in 1921 but declined because the county's playing facilities were not up to the required standard, and it seems they had neither the wherewithal nor the desire to upgrade them.

On 26 August 1924 Yorkshire lost to Surrey at the Oval but did not lose another game until defeat by Warwickshire at Hull on 24 May 1927. It was a run of 70 County Championship matches without defeat – 41 wins, 28 draws and one match abandoned due to rain.

The mainstays of this great Yorkshire team were George Hirst and Wilfred Rhodes, who both batted right-handed but bowled with their left. Each took over 2,000 wickets and scored in excess of 20,000 runs during their respective careers (Hirst 1891 to 1921, Rhodes 1898 to 1930).

When Wilfred Rhodes retired after playing his last County Championship game for Yorkshire in 1930 he had 762 Championship matches to his name – a record.

 It was not without great sadness and emotion that, in our dressing room, I announced my retirement to my Yorkshire team-mates. Those lads I had sweated blood for, for whom I had given my all, and they to me. I knew my life would be all the poorer for not having their daily friendship and camaraderie. I felt my announcement was a bombshell to them because, for a few moments, not one spoke. It was Barber who was the first to break the silence. 'I'll give you ten bob for your pads,' he said.

WILFRED RHODES

In 1925 Glamorgan lost 20 of their 26 matches – the most by any team in the history of the Championship. Of Glamorgan's other six matches they won one and drew five.

Victories like World Cups. On 14 May 1935 Northamptonshire defeated Somerset at Taunton but had to wait four years for their next victory in the Championship, against Leicestershire at Northampton on 29 May 1939. Following that victory and the suspension of the Championship due to war, Northamptonshire's next win came in 1946. So, Northants enjoyed only one County Championship win in 11 years.

When Phil Mead played his final match for Hampshire in 1936 he had some statistics to contemplate. Having made his first appearance in the County Championship in 1906, he had clocked up 665 matches, scored 46,268 runs – including 2,843 in 1928, and 132 centuries – and scored 1,000 runs in a season 26 times and 2,000 runs in a season nine times.

A. P. 'Tich' Freeman also played his final match in 1936, for Kent, and he too had some outstanding statistics to contemplate, not least 3,151 Championship wickets (1914–36), most wickets in a single season (252 in 1933), and 200 wickets in a season on six occasions.

No way Torbay. In 1948 Devon applied to join the County Championship but their application was rejected.

In 1949 the Championship title was shared for the very first time, by Middlesex and Yorkshire. Curiously, this happened again the following year, when Lancashire and Surrey shared the title.

In 1951 the County Championship pennant was introduced for the very first time by champions Warwickshire.

Seven-up. From 1952 to 1958 inclusive Surrey won seven consecutive County Championship titles – a record for the competition.

In Surrey's title-winning season of 1955 they won 23 and lost five of their 28 matches – a rare occurrence of a team having an outright result in every match played.

In 1961 Nottinghamshire equalled Glamorgan's 1925 record for the most defeats in a single season (20). The 1961 season comprised 28 matches (two more than in 1925) and Nottinghamshire won four and drew four.

In 1967 Nottinghamshire were undefeated in 24 of their 28 matches yet failed to win a game, having drawn 24 times.

In 1968 Derek Shackleton (Hampshire) accomplished the feat of taking 200 wickets in a season for the 18th time.

Very Suttle. Between 1954 and 1969, Ken Suttle made 423 consecutive appearances for Sussex in the County Championship.

In 1974 Lancashire did not lose a single match, yet only finished eighth in the Championship table.

Sch . . . you know who. In 1977 the County Championship was sponsored for the very first time by Schweppes.

In 1977 the title was shared for only the third time in its history, on this occasion by Kent and Middlesex.

How the mighty had fallen. In 1983 Surrey suffered the ignominy of the lowest post-war total in the Championship when they were dismissed for 14 by Essex at Chelmsford.

Between 1982 and 1992 some fixtures were scheduled as four-day games in a trial period to ascertain 'the practicality and popularity of such matches'. It appears there was no rush to discover the outcome – a trial period of 10 years?

In 1992 Durham were admitted to the Championship, the first change to club format since the admission of Glamorgan in 1921.

From 1993 onwards all matches were scheduled as four-day games.

In 2001 the County Championship underwent a major change when it was divided into two divisions. The 18 clubs were allocated to either Division One or Two on the basis of their final places the previous season. Thus promotion and relegation came into being for the very first time. From 2001 up to and including 2005, the bottom three clubs in Division One were relegated and the top three in Division Two promoted. At the end of 2006 this was reduced to two clubs either way.

Promotion and relegation affected a lesser-spotted ritual of the County Championship, that of denoting a team's final position in the previous season in brackets, following the name of the club in its current position in the County Championship table. The ritual is still, however, in place. A team's position in the previous season is still denoted in brackets but only applies if the team is still in the same division. Promoted and relegated teams are simply denoted thus: (-).

In 2005 Surrey were deducted eight points for 'ball tampering'. It proved costly: the reduction resulted in Surrey being relegated to Division Two.

In 2006 Surrey's Mark Ramprakash scored a total of 537 runs in matches against Northamptonshire – the highest number of runs made by an individual batsman against another team in a single season since W. G. Grace (Gloucestershire) scored 547 off Sussex bowling in 1896.

In 2007 Glamorgan were deducted eight Championship points for an unprepared wicket at Swansea.

In terms of titles won, Yorkshire are the most successful, having won the County Championship 30 times (and one shared).

Only three counties have never won the County Championship: Gloucestershire, Northamptonshire and Somerset.

Since the 1960s concerns have been expressed about the viability and future of the County Championship, particularly in recent years with the introduction of Twenty20, and top players rarely making appearances for their county due to central contracts/England commitments. In July 2008, however, the ECB announced the current County Championship format would continue until 'at least 2013'.

The County Championship has enjoyed six major sponsorships: Schweppes (1977–83), Britannic Assurance (1984–98), AXA Healthcare (1999–2000), Cricinfo (2001), Frizzell (2002–05) and Liverpool Victoria (since 2006).

Quick (and very précised) guide to how the current points system works:

WIN – 14 points for a win plus any first-innings points awarded
DRAW – each team awarded four points plus any first-innings points awarded
TIE – each team awarded seven points plus any first-innings points awarded
ABANDONED MATCH – if a ball has not been bowled, each team is awarded four points
LOSE – bonus points for batting/bowling

The actual awarding of points is a detailed business, particularly with regard to the awarding of first-innings points. Suffice to say a team can be given a maximum of five first-innings batting points, a fielding team a maximum of three bowling points, but only from the first 130 overs. Just be thankful the Duckworth-Lewis method only applies to one-day matches.

Sensational debut! Twelve players have scored a double century on their first-class debut. Their totals, in descending order:

260	A. A. Muzumdar, for Bombay against Haryana at Faridabad, 1993–94
240	W. F. E. Marx, for Transvaal against Griqualand at Johannesburg, 1920–21
232 not out	Sam Loxton, for Victoria against Queensland at Melbourne, 1946–47
230	G. R. Viswanath, for Mysore against Andhra at Vijayawada, 1967–68
227	T. Marsden, for Sheffield and Leicester against Nottingham at Sheffield, 1826
215 not out	Hubert Doggart, for Cambridge University against Lancashire at Fenners, 1948
210 not out	David Sales, for Northamptonshire against Worcestershire at Kidderminster, 1996
209 not out	A. 'Andy' Pandey, for Madhya Pradesh against Uttar Pradesh at Bhulai, 1995–96
207	N. F. Calloway, for New South Wales against Queensland at Sydney, 1914–15
202	J. Hallebone, for Victoria against Tasmania at Melbourne, 1951–52

200 not out   A. Maynard, for Trinidad against MCC/England at Port of Spain, 1934–35
200 not out   Michael Powell, for Glamorgan against Oxford University at The Parks, 1997

N. F. Calloway's double century was his only innings in first-class cricket. He was killed in action in France in 1917.

Hubert Doggart's 215 not out is the highest score by a batsman making his debut in English first-class cricket.

Northants got a bargain in Sales. David Sales was out for a duck in his first innings on his first-class debut but quickly overcame that disappointment to make his 210 not out in the second innings. Sales is the only player ever to have been out for a duck and then to make a double hundred on his first-class debut.

Fifteen batsmen have scored a century on their Test debut for England:

W. G. Grace, 152, against Australia at the Oval, 1880
Kumar Shri Ranjitsinhji, 154 not out, against Australia at Old Trafford, 1896
Pelham Warner, 132 not out, against South Africa at Johannesburg, 1898–99
Reginald 'Tip' Foster, 287, against Australia at Sydney, 1903–04
George Gunn, 119, against Australia at Sydney, 1907–08
Nawab of Pataudi Sr, 102, against Australia at Sydney, 1932–33
Bryan Valentine, 136, against India at Bombay, 1933–34
Paul Gibb, 106, against South Africa at Johannesburg, 1938–39
Billy Griffith, 140, against West Indies at Port of Spain, 1947–48
Peter May, 138, against South Africa at Headingley, 1951
Arthur Milton, 104 not out, against New Zealand at Headingley, 1958
Jackie Hampshire, 107, against West Indies at Lord's, 1969
Frank Hayes, 106 not out, against West Indies at the Oval, 1973
Graham Thorpe, 114 not out, against Australia at Trent Bridge, 1993
Andrew Strauss, 112, against New Zealand at Lord's, 2004

Only two batsmen have scored a century in each innings on their Test debut: Lawrence Rowe, 214 and 100 not out, for the West Indies against New Zealand at Kingston in 1971–72; and Yasir Hameed, 175 and 105, for Pakistan against Bangladesh at Karachi in 2003.

Nervous nineties tested them. Three players have been dismissed for 99 on their Test debut: Arthur Chipperfield, for Australia against England at Trent Bridge in 1934; Robert Christiani, for West Indies against England at Bridgetown in 1947–48; and Asim Kamal, for Pakistan against South Africa at Lahore in 2003–04.

Age is all in the mind. In 1930 George Brook took 132 wickets in his debut season for Worcestershire having joined the club from Kidderminster in the Birmingham League. When first approached by Worcestershire and asked his age, Brook told club officials he was 33; he was in fact 41. Brook thus became the oldest bowler to achieve 100 wickets in his debut season – and good on him.

The most wickets taken by a bowler in his first season in first-class cricket is 154, by Wilfred Rhodes (aged 20), for Yorkshire in 1898.

Fred Trueman came within a whisker of taking all 10 wickets in an innings and creating cricket history on his debut match at Lord's in 1949. Playing for Yorkshire against the Minor Counties, Trueman took 8 for 70 in the Minor Counties second innings.

 Against the Minor Counties I finished an over by taking successive wickets and had figures of 8 for 70. Skipper Norman Yardley and the rest of the team tried to engineer it so I would take 10 wickets on my Lord's debut and, hopefully, achieve a hat-trick into the bargain. Alan Mason was bowling at the other end and he sportingly said, 'I'll bowl wide of the off-stump to help you out, Fred.' Alan did just that, but the Minor Counties tail-enders were so bad he got them both out with successive balls that they dragged on to their wicket. When we were coming off the pitch Norman Yardley came up and put a comforting arm around my shoulder and said, 'Don't be disappointed, Fred. I'll tell you what, when we go to the bar, you can still get a round in for the team.'
FRED TRUEMAN

Stephen Moreton of Oxford University has the distinction of having bowled the most expensive debut over in first-class cricket. Playing for Oxford University against Gloucestershire at The Parks, Moreton was called upon to bowl his maiden over in first-class cricket against Craig Spearman (New Zealand), who hit the debutant for 34 runs. The sequence was 6, 6, 6, 6, 4 and 6.

In June 1990 against Oxford University at The Parks, Jason Gallian took a wicket with his first ball in first-class cricket on his first appearance for Lancashire.

Footballer Jimmy Greaves has the distinction of having scored on his debut for every team he ever played for, from school through to England's full international team. The opposite is true of the great Len Hutton. Hutton was out for a duck in his first school match, in his first first-class match, in his first innings for Yorkshire Second XI, and in his first innings for both the Yorkshire first team and England.

The club is based at the County Ground in Derby, previously known as the Racecourse Ground. The capacity is 9,000.

In addition to the County Ground, Derbyshire also play matches at Buxton and Chesterfield (Queens Park). In the past Derbyshire have also staged matches at Burton, Blackwell, Darley Dale, Heanor, Ilkeston, Wirksworth and even Abbeydale Park in Sheffield (Yorkshire territory); and, more recently, one-day games at Trent College (Long Eaton – 1975–79), Cheadle (Staffordshire – 1973–87), Knypersely in Staffordshire (1985–90), Repton School (1988) and Checkley (Staffordshire – 1991–93).

The number one is significant regarding honours: Derbyshire have only won the County Championship on one occasion (1936), the NatWest Trophy once (1981), the Sunday League once (1990) and the Benson & Hedges Cup once (1993).

The club badge features a rose topped by a crown.

The earliest reference to cricket being played in the county is a report of a match between Wirksworth and Sheffield cricket clubs at Brampton Moor (Chesterfield) in September 1757.

Derbyshire County Cricket Club was formed at a meeting in the Guildhall in Derby on 4 November 1870. The club played their first match on 26/27 May 1871 against Lancashire at Old Trafford, under the jurisdiction of what was then an unofficial County Championship League.

Prior to the 1888 season, following several seasons of poor results, Derbyshire were demoted from first-class status, only to be awarded it again in 1894. The following season they were re-admitted to the County Championship.

In 1876 W. Mycroft recorded match figures of 17 wickets for 103 runs against Hampshire at Southampton. This remains a club record.

Derbyshire's lowest score as a team is 16, against Nottinghamshire at Nottingham in 1879.

In 1897 Derbyshire failed to win a single county match, though they did achieve a number of draws. In 1920 they suffered the ignominy of losing every single game they played.

Thomas left in no doubt. On 9 July 1921 W. Bestwick bowled A. E. Thomas of Northamptonshire in some style. Bestwick's delivery sent a bail hurtling a distance of just over 50 yards and also broke one of the stumps.

When Derbyshire won the County Championship in 1936, four players scored in excess of 1,000 runs – 'Aldo' Alderman, Dennis Smith, Les Townsend and Stan Worthington – while Bill Copson and Alf Pope each took in excess of 100 wickets. The Championship team also included Charlie Elliott, who went on to become a renowned Test umpire.

The best figures recorded by a Derbyshire bowler in a single innings are those of W. Bestwick who took 10 for 40 against Glamorgan at Cardiff in 1921.

Bill Copson showed no interest whatsoever in cricket until his late teens. He became a miner, and during the General Strike of 1926 was persuaded by fellow striking miners to participate in an ad hoc cricket match on a recreation ground near Morton Colliery. It was the first time he had ever played the game. Copson proved so adept at bowling, the following season he was a regular in the Morton CW team from where he graduated to Clay Cross in the Derbyshire League. In 1931 he took all 10 wickets against Staveley for five runs which earned him a trial with Derbyshire. In the trial against a Nottinghamshire XI he took eight wickets for 10 runs. The following season Copson made his first-class debut for Derbyshire against Surrey at the Oval and with his very first ball took the wicket of Andy Sandham. As he later said, 'If it hadn't been for the General Strike I would never have discovered I had a talent for cricket and bowling in particular. It was pure serendipity.'

In 1935 Copson was widely regarded as Derbyshire's best bowler and one of the finest in the country, but leg-spinner Tom Mitchell proved the most lethal, taking 168 wickets at an average of 19.55 – to this day a club record.

Since 1945 the club has experienced more downs than ups and has finished bottom of the County Championship a record 14 times, though it has over the years boasted such notable bowlers as Les Jackson, Harold Rhodes, Alan Ward, Mike Hendrick, Geoff Miller, Michael Holding, Devon Malcolm and Dominic Cork.

Who can forget Malcolm Devon?
TED DEXTER

FRED TRUEMAN (on the BBC's *Test Match Special*): There is an upside and downside to Mike Hendrick.
BRIAN JOHNSTON: Which is?
TRUEMAN: The upside is, he is one of the most economical bowlers in the world today.
JOHNSTON: And the downside?
TRUEMAN: From where we're sitting he bears an uncanny resemblance to Jeremy Beadle.

Les Jackson played for Derbyshire from 1947 to 1963 and in that time took a club record 1,670 wickets (at an average of 17.11). When Jackson retired from cricket he became a driver for the National Coal Board in Mansfield, then chauffeur to one of the NCB directors (Derbyshire region).

Why Les Jackson was never chosen more often for England is a mystery to me. Quite simply, any number of bowlers chosen ahead of him for England in the 1950s were only half the bowler he was.
FRED TRUEMAN

In 1958 at the Ind Coope ground, Burton upon Trent, Derbyshire skittled out Hampshire for just 23 runs – a club record for the lowest score recorded by first-class opposition.

In 1959 Donald Carr set a new club record for the most runs scored by an individual in a single County Championship season – 2,165.

Donald Carr combined his role as captain with that of club secretary (1959–62) before accepting a secretarial post with the MCC in 1962. In 1963, while still serving in an administrative capacity with the MCC, Carr returned to 'help out' Derbyshire who were suffering from a series of injuries to players, and in his first innings scored a century against Sussex. In the same season he also played in Derbyshire's first ever Gillette Cup match against Hampshire, which Derbyshire won off the last ball of the game. Carr managed England on the winter tours to South Africa (1964–65), India/Pakistan (1972–73) and the West Indies (1973–74) and was one of the principal administrators of the TCCB from its inauguration in 1968.

In a Derbyshire career that spanned the years 1950–1969, D. C. Morgan took 563 catches in the field – a club record.

In 1982 P. N. Kirsten scored eight centuries – a Derbyshire record for the number of centuries scored by an individual player in the course of a season.

Bob Taylor (1961–84) was also England's regular wicket-keeper in the 1970s and widely regarded as one of the best in the world. During his career behind the stumps for Derbyshire Taylor amassed 1,304 dismissals – 1,157 caught and 147 stumpings.

Bob Taylor, on 90, ten short of the mythical figure of 100.
TREVOR BAILEY (BBC Radio)

In a NatWest Trophy match against Cornwall in 1986, Derbyshire scored 365 for 3 – a club record score for a limited-overs match.

In 1993 John Morris and Dominic Cork shared a fifth-wicket partnership of 302 against Gloucestershire at Cheltenham. Morris is the current Derbyshire coach.

302! Disbelieving Derbyshire fans just can't believe it.
BBC RADIO DERBY COMMENTATOR

In 1997 Kim Barnett and Tim Tweats shared a second-wicket partnership of 417 against Yorkshire at Derby – a club record for the highest partnership for any wicket.

The most runs scored by a single player in the course of his career with the county is 23,854, by Kim Barnett. Only one other player has scored in excess of 20,000 runs for Derbyshire, Denis Smith (20,516). Barnett also holds the club record for the highest number of centuries – 53.

Derbyshire recorded their highest ever score, 801 for 8 declared, against Somerset at Taunton in 2007. The game was also significant for the fact that four players scored centuries – a club record for a single match: Simon Katich (221), Ian Harvey (153), James Pipe (106) and Ant Botha (101).

In 2008 Derbyshire boasted the player with the longest name in county cricket, Sri Lanka-born Denagamage Proboth Mahela De Silva Jayawardene.

Former Derbyshire all-rounder Geoff Miller is the current chief selector of the England team.

Well, Derbyshire are dead in the water, unless they manage to pull something out of the fire.
GEOFF MILLER

Most appropriately named player – Peter Bowler.

The club's limited-overs team is the Derbyshire Phantoms.

Worth a visit for . . . the supporters book shop situated in the County Ground. It contains hundreds of second-hand books including *Wisdens* and many cricket books that are rare and long since out of print. It is also one of the friendliest and most sociable shops you will ever visit.

Contemporary reports state that three players were killed in a fracas that broke out during a match between Kent and Essex at Tilbury in 1776.

George Summers was killed while playing for Nottinghamshire against the MCC at Lord's in 1870, when he was struck on the temple by a delivery from J. Platts.

Play was abandoned during the match between Lancashire and Gloucestershire on 25 July 1884 due to the 'death of a woman'. The woman in question was Martha Grace, mother of two of the Gloucestershire team, the legendary W. G. and his older brother E. M. As a mark of respect and out of sympathy to the Grace brothers, play was brought to a premature close.

The two world wars deprived any number of players of the best years of their cricket careers and tragically cost many their lives. Among the top players who lost their lives in the Great War were Colin Blythe (Kent), killed at Passchendaele; Tibby Cotter (Australia), who had had the temerity to hit W. G. Grace with a full-toss on his first tour of England, killed at Beersheba while serving with the 4th Light Horse Brigade; and Percy Jeeves (Warwickshire), killed during the Battle of the Somme. (P. G. Wodehouse, a great lover of cricket, named Bertie Wooster's valet Jeeves in honour of Percy Jeeves, his cricketing hero.)

When the Great War brought its wholesale slaughter of junior officers and men, the duties of the compilers of Wisden's obituary pages became at once shocking and overwhelming. In the absence of any first-class cricket Wisden for four years was little more than a catalogue of death. The appalling statistic is, over 1,500 cricketers lost their lives on the Western Front alone. The Wisden staff had the sad and onerous task of bestowing upon each and every one a sort of immortality through their pages, and if some of the fallen received an immortality which bore no relationship to what they had done on the field of play, then we are, all of us, in understanding.
BENNY GREEN

Former Nottinghamshire and England wicket-keeper William Whysall died in November 1930 at the age of only 43 as the result of a fall on a dance floor while performing the Military Two-Step. Whysall injured his elbow, septicaemia set in, and despite a blood transfusion, he passed away.

Legendary West Indies bowler of the 1930s Donald Eligon died at the age of only 28 after contracting blood poisoning caused by a protruding nail in his cricket boot.

In 1936 two top county players died in separate motoring accidents that occurred within days of each other. Reg Northway (Northamptonshire) was killed on 26 August, D. A. Page (Gloucestershire) seven days later, on 2 September.

Two spectators, Norman Elliott and Alice Dumma, were killed when struck by lightning while attending a Northumberland match at Jesmond on 26 August 1939.

Andy Ducat, who played for Surrey and was a dual international at both cricket and football (his clubs included Arsenal and Aston Villa), collapsed and died of a suspected heart attack while batting for the Surrey Home Guard against Sussex Home Guard at Lord's on 23 July 1942.

In August 1942 Corporal A. Harris was killed while playing for the Army against Kent Police at Folkestone. An enemy Focke-Wulf fighter bomber flying over Folkestone released a bomb which landed a short distance from the pitch. Corporal Harris was fielding at the time and was killed by the subsequent explosion. A number of other players suffered various injuries, including Lieutenant George Wood, who was thrown into the air by the blast but fortunately suffered nothing more serious than an ankle sprain and concussion.

Among the top players to lose their lives during the Second World War were Ken Farnes (Essex), killed during a flying training exercise while serving with the RAF; Maurice Turnbull (Glamorgan), killed during the Normandy invasion; and Hedley Verity (Yorkshire), a captain in the Green Howards who died of his wounds while interned in an Italian POW camp.

Former Australian tour manager Thomas Burge died at his home in Brisbane on 7 January 1957 of a heart attack while listening to a radio commentary of a match in which his son, Peter, was batting and survived an lbw appeal.

When playing for Karachi against Pakistan Combined Services in 1959, Abdul Aziz was struck over the heart by an off-break ball from Dildwar Awan. Aziz collapsed when preparing to face Awan's next ball and died of a heart attack en route to hospital. A week earlier Abdul Aziz had been the non-strike batsman when Hanif Mohammed was run out on 499, the highest score in first-class cricket by an individual batsman until surpassed by Brian Lara (501) in 1994.

During the 1968 tour of the West Indies, England's Freddie Titmus (Middlesex) lost four toes in an accident with a speedboat propeller while swimming in the Caribbean. The injury did not prevent the courageous Titmus from later continuing his career as a player.

A spectator was found dead in his seat at the end of the 1975 Gillette Cup Final between Lancashire and Middlesex at Lord's, which Lancashire won by seven wickets. The deceased man was discovered at around 6.30 p.m. with an almost full pint of beer at his feet. It was later determined the spectator had passed away at approximately noon.

Wilf Slack (Middlesex) suffered a heart attack and died while batting in a match in Gambia in January 1989. The Arden Field Cricket Ground in

Finchley where Middlesex Second XI play their home matches was re-named the Wilf Slack Ground as a lasting tribute to the former England player.

In 1989 national newspapers reported that a defendant appeared before the Old Bailey and was given a two-year suspended sentence for attempting to throttle his fiancée with his MCC tie during an argument between the pair following the 1989 NatWest Trophy Final (won by Warwickshire). On the face of it, the fact it was an MCC tie appears irrelevant to the case. From an editor's point of view, however, given the incident took place after the final which was what had sparked the argument, it made darn good copy and sadly took precedence over the key element of the story.

While playing for Whitehaven CC in Cumberland in 1993, Ian Folley (Lancashire and Derbyshire) was accidentally hit above the eye. He continued to participate in the field but later in the day, when feeling unwell, was taken to hospital and, while under anaesthetic, suffered a heart attack and died.

In 1997 two players died from stab wounds and six were taken to hospital for treatment when a fight broke out between players at the end of a match between Falevau and Sauano in Western Samoa. The match had been staged to raise funds for a local church.

In February 1998 former India Test cricketer Raman Lamba died as a result of being hit on the temple by a ball while fielding at short leg for his club, Abanhiad, against Mohammedan at Bangabandhu. Lamba was able to walk from the field and at first his injury was considered not to be serious. But he suffered an internal haemorrhage and his condition deteriorated dramatically over the next 24 hours. Three days after sustaining the injury, Lamba died in Dhaka hospital.

Pakistan coach Bob Woolmer died in Jamaica on 18 March 2007 a matter of hours after Pakistan had been eliminated from the 2007 World Cup following defeat to Ireland. Days later the Jamaican police announced they were conducting a murder inquiry into the death of the former Warwickshire and England batsman. Three months after that it was announced Woolmer had died from 'natural causes'. The inquest into his death recorded an open verdict.

Durham

Durham's headquarters is at the Riverside Ground, a relatively new arena which enjoys a spectacular location overlooked by Lumley Castle, has a capacity of 15,000 and has been granted Test status.

In addition to Riverside, Durham has also played home matches at the following venues: Feethams, Darlington; Grangefield Road, Stockton; The Racecourse, Durham; Park Drive, Hartlepool; Ropery Lane, Chester-le-Street; and Eastwood Gardens, Gateshead.

The club badge bears the coat of arms of the county of Durham.

Being a relatively new first-class county, Durham's trophy successes have been few.

In 2007 they won the Friends Provident Trophy, the county's first major success. In the same year Durham also won the Pro40/National League Division Two. Then, in 2008, they topped them both by winning the County Championship for the first time.

The earliest reference to organized cricket in the county is a match between the Earl of Northumberland's XI and the Duke of Cleveland's XI at Raby Castle on 5 August 1751. The game is commemorated in a traditional Durham folk song that contains the lines:

> Durham city has been dull so long
> No bustle at all to show,
> But now the rage of all the throng
> Is a cricketing to go.

Cricket may well have been all 'the rage' but it would be a long time before 'the throng' enjoyed County Championship cricket. Durham is the youngest first-class county. They began the process of applying to become a first-class county in 1989 and became one on 6 December 1991 – the first county to be granted such status since 1921. Their first season in the County Championship was 1992, their first match against Leicestershire.

The first recorded representative match in Durham took place in 1848 between a Bishopwearmouth representative team and an All England side at Sunderland. To avoid a mismatch, Bishopwearmouth were allowed to name a team consisting of 22 players. The home side's distinct numerical advantage had little effect against an experienced All England team who scored 129 and 143 in their two innings, whereas Bishopwearmouth XXII were dismissed for 56 and 59 respectively.

The first official team to carry the name 'Durham County' played their first match in 1876 against the MCC. Two years later a Durham County representative side played their first match against a touring side, Australia. Durham caused something of a sensation by winning by 71 runs. Australia's captain, D. W. Gregory, was in little doubt as to why his team fared so badly. 'All proceeded well upon the first day of play,' Gregory explained, 'then, in the evening and well into the night, our genial hosts plied us with ale, beers and porter to such excess it was to be to the detriment of our play the following day.' (Nothing new there then.)

In 1880 Durham met the touring Australians again. They were not to be sidetracked as the 1878 tourists had been. Durham lost to Australia by an innings and 38 runs, Fred Spofforth, one of the first right-arm medium-fast bowlers, returning match figures of 17 for 66.

Durham County Cricket Club was officially formed on 23 May 1882.

Durham CCC's first official match took place at Ashbrooke, Sunderland on 12/13 June 1882 and resulted in a four-wicket victory over Northumberland.

Durham were a formidable force in Minor Counties cricket, winning the Minor Counties Championship a record seven times between 1901 and 1984. They also shared the title twice.

Throughout the 1950s, 1960 and 1970s, Sunderland's Ashbrooke ground was a regular venue for the annual match between the Minor Counties and the tourists.

In 1959, making his debut for the county at the age of 17, Colin Milburn (later Northamptonshire and England) scored 101 against tourists India at Sunderland.

In a Gillette Cup match at Chester-le-Street in 1968, Durham dismissed Worcestershire for 98 but lost the match. In the history of the competition Worcestershire's 98 is the record lowest score for a team that batted first yet won the tie.

Between 1976 and 1982 Durham remained unbeaten (65 matches) – a Minor Counties record that exists to this day.

Durham was the first Minor County to defeat a first-class county in the Gillette Cup when they beat Yorkshire in 1972.

Throughout the 1990s and into the new millennium Durham struggled to make an impact in first-class cricket. Hope sprang eternal for all connected with the club, however, as they waited for their vibrant youth/academy policy to bear fruit. In the interim Durham relied heavily on signing players of vast experience, such as Ian Botham, Wayne Larkins, John Morris and Australian David Boon.

Durham cricket suffers from the fact it has only two seasons, June and winter.
DAVID BOON

Wayne Larkins holds the record for the most runs scored in a first-class season by a Durham batsman – 1,536 (average 37.46), in 1992.

In 1994 Durham bowling was laid to waste at Edgbaston by Warwickshire, who made 810 for 4 declared – the highest total conceded by Durham in a single innings.

Durham's Riverside ground was opened for business on 18 May 1995 for a County Championship match against Warwickshire.

In 1995 right-hand fast-medium bowler Alan Walker returned match figures of 14 for 177 against Essex at Chelmsford – a club record.

In 1996 Durham were dismissed by Middlesex for 67 at Lord's – the lowest total inflicted upon the county in the Championship.

Also in 1996 Stewart Hutton and Michael Roseberry shared an unbroken opening partnership of 334 against Oxford University at Oxford – to this day the highest partnership for the county.

Between 1997 and 2001 wicket-keeper Martin Speight totalled 194 dismissals (189 caught, five stumped) – the current club record aggregate.

In 2002 Durham made 645 for 6 declared against Middlesex at Lord's – the county's highest total in first-class cricket.

Durham's Riverside staged its first international match, the second Test between England and Zimbabwe, in 2003 (5–7 June). Riverside now regularly hosts Test matches.

In 2003, at Chester-le-Street, Durham dismissed Somerset for 56 – a club record for the lowest score inflicted upon an opposing county side. Also in 2003 Martin Love scored 273 against Hampshire at Riverside – a club record highest innings.

Durham enjoyed their first success of note in 2005, gaining promotion to Division One of the County Championship and the one-day National Cricket League.

In 2005 Paul Collingwood scored six centuries – a club record for an individual player in a single season.

In 2006 Dale Benkenstein and Ottis Gibson shared a seventh-wicket partnership of 315 against Yorkshire at Headingley – a club record partnership against another first-class county.

Durham has a lot of things going for it. Not the least of which is, it isn't Yorkshire.
IAN BOTHAM

Jon Lewis had a lot in store. The most runs scored in the course of a career with Durham is 7,854 (average 31.41), by Jonathan Lewis (1997–2006).

Only one Durham player has taken 10 wickets in a single innings: Ottis Gibson, 10 for 47 against Hampshire at Chester-le-Street in 2007.

Gibson also holds the record for the most wickets taken in a single County Championship season – 80, at an average of 20.75, in 2007.

Catch me if you can. Between 1996 and 2007 Paul Collingwood held 117 catches in the field. No other Durham player can boast such a record. It is all the more remarkable given that due to England commitments in recent years Collingwood's appearances for Durham have been spasmodic.

Ottis gives Durham a lift. In 2007 Durham enjoyed their first major trophy success, defeating Hampshire by 125 runs at Lord's. In their 50 overs Durham made 312 for 5 – a record for the most runs scored in a 50-over cup final – and dismissed Hampshire for 187 (41 overs). Ottis Gibson, approaching his 39th birthday, was named man of the match, having made 15 not out and returned bowling figures of 3 for 24 off eight overs.

The youth policy here at Durham is fantastic. We have such strength in depth, when players are called up for England, we have such quality in reserve it doesn't weaken the first team in the least. In fact, I'd go as far as to say Durham's second XI would beat several county sides.
LIAM PLUNKETT (2008)

In 2008 the Durham middle order had a distinctly culinary taste to it: it included Mustard and Onions.

On 7 July 2008 Durham's Twenty20 Cup quarter-final against Yorkshire at Riverside was postponed minutes before it was due to start (5.10 p.m.) when it emerged Yorkshire had fielded an ineligible player, 17-year-old spinner Azeem Rafiq, in a previous Twenty20 match, against Nottinghamshire. It would appear that along with Yorkshire, Durham, an innocent party, also suffered from the decision to postpone the game as a five-figure crowd was inside Riverside to watch the tie. Having been removed from the tournament, Yorkshire subsequently won an appeal against the decision and were awarded their win against Nottinghamshire, only then to have the two points they won deducted for breach of rules. As a consequence of this, Nottinghamshire lost the two points they had been subsequently awarded, which meant Glamorgan, as one of the second best third-placed sides, faced Durham in the quarter-final. As one Durham supporter put it, 'As farragos go it will take some beating.'

Durham secured their first ever County Championship success on the final day of 2008. Come that final day the title was going to go to either Durham or Nottinghamshire. Notts faltered against Hampshire at Trent Bridge, losing by 203 runs; Durham kept their nerve, beating Kent by an innings and 71 runs at Canterbury. Steve Harmison took the final three Kent wickets while bowling with a broken wrist.

Geoff Cook [head coach] has been the heart and soul of the club. I've just come in to enjoy the end product after a lot of hard work.
DALE BENKENSTEIN (Durham captain, on his team's County Championship success)

Most appropriately named player – William 'Billy' Box

Durham's limited-overs team is the Durham Dynamos.

Worth a visit for . . . the experience of Riverside, a state-of-the-art ground overlooked by an ancient castle and surrounded by stunning scenery. Riverside affords easy access and parking and attracts good attendances whatever the game, so there is always an 'atmosphere', helped by arguably the cheapest beer prices to be found on any county ground. What's not to like?

There are, of course, numerous instances of teams winning a match in minor cricket without losing a wicket; in all probability it happens every week in matches of a single innings per team. Teams winning a two-innings-per-team match in first-class cricket without losing a wicket, however, are rare. It has happened on only four occasions. The first occasion was in the County Championship in 1956: Lancashire 166 for 0 declared and 66 for 0 defeated Leicestershire by 10 wickets at Old Trafford. In 1957–58, Karachi A (277 for 0 declared) defeated Sind A by an innings and 77 runs at Karachi. In 1960–61, Railways (236 for 0 declared and 16 for 0) defeated Jammu and Kashmir by 10 wickets at Srinagar. And in 1977–78, Karnataka (410 for 0 declared) defeated Kerala by an innings and 186 runs at Chikmagalur.

In 1884 at Aston, the match between England XI and Australians was completed on the first day and after just 419 balls: England 82 and 26, Australians 76 and 33 for 6.

The County Championship match between Somerset and Middlesex at Lord's in 1899 was completed in 350 balls: Somerset 35 and 44, Middlesex 86 – the shortest first-class match in terms of balls delivered.

In a rain-affected match at Bradford in 1931 Northamptonshire scored 4 for 0 declared in their first innings. In reply Yorkshire too declared on 4 without loss. In their second innings Northamptonshire scored 86. Yorkshire secured victory by scoring 88 for 5 in their second innings. The match comprised a total of 435 balls.

The County Championship match between Derbyshire and Northamptonshire at Northampton in 1992 was completed in 425 balls. Derbyshire scored 180 for 6 declared and forfeited their second innings, while Northamptonshire forfeited their first innings and in their second scored 181 for 2.

Lancashire's County Championship match against Glamorgan at Liverpool in 1997 was completed in 445 balls. Glamorgan scored 272 for 1 declared in their first innings and forfeited their second; Lancashire forfeited their first innings and in their second were dismissed for 51.

Since the Second World War, five County Championship matches have been completed on the first day of play: Derbyshire against Somerset at Chesterfield, 11 June 1947; Lancashire against Sussex at Old Trafford, 12 July 1950; Surrey against Warwickshire at the Oval, 16 May 1953; Somerset against Lancashire at Bath, 6 June 1953; Kent against Worcestershire at Tunbridge Wells, 15 June 1960.

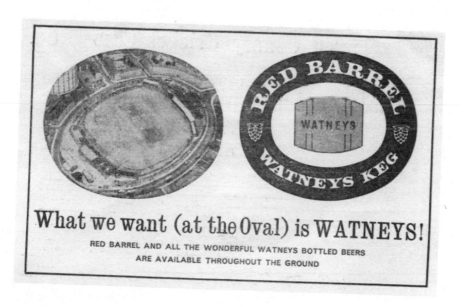

The England and Wales Cricket Board (Bwrdd Criced Cymru a Lloegr), also known simply as the ECB, is the governing body for cricket in England and Wales.

The ECB was formed on 1 January 1997. The Board combined the roles of the National Cricket Association and the Cricket Council.

The headquarters are at Lord's.

The ECB is a limited company by guarantee. This enables the Board to maximize its funding of cricket in England and Wales rather than be duty bound to make a return for investors. The Board is governed by representatives of the 38 first-class counties and Minor Counties and the MCC.

One of the main roles of the ECB is the development of the England team. The chairman of the England selectors, David Graveney, is employed by the Board, as are all England coaches. The Board also employs players who have been selected for England on central contracts.

Another remit of the Board is the development of young cricket talent in England and Wales. The ECB National Academy is based at Loughborough University.

The ECB is responsible for the financial direction and commercial development of cricket. Its revenue encompasses ticket sales for Tests and one-day internationals in England and Wales and shares in revenues from overseas tours and international tournaments.

The Board is also responsible for generating income from broadcasting rights and sponsorship, primarily for the England team.

The Board also pays a number of costs relating to the domestic first-class cricket programme, such as umpires' salaries and the cost of erecting temporary floodlights at county matches.

The Board administers the four major domestic cricket competitions: the Liverpool Victoria County Championship, the Friends Provident Trophy, the NatWest Pro40 and the Twenty20 Cup.

The Board encourages the playing of cricket at all levels. Should you want to play cricket they will help you find a club by putting you in touch with the ECB's cricket development manager and staff in your county. Alternatively, log on to the ECB's 'Play Cricket' network of websites where there are nigh on 5,000 clubs listed along with details of geographical position and club contacts.

The Board also offers funding to ECB-affiliated clubs with junior sections to assist with the development of facilities at grounds. The funds are available in two forms: a grant aid facility or an interest-free loan in the way of a partnership up to a maximum of £50,000 with the club concerned contributing a minimum of 25 per cent to the overall cost of the project, which may be anything from development of the pavilion to a new sightscreen or nets.

England

England's always expecting. No wonder they call her the Mother Country.
FRED TRUEMAN

In the eighteenth and early nineteenth centuries many teams laid claim to representing England. The earliest known 'All England' team played Kent, who themselves laid claim to being the best team in all of England, on 9 July 1730. It is recorded that 'All England' lost by 'very few notches'.

In 1846 William Clarke formed the 'All England XI' (just to keep things simple). Between 1857 and 1866 this team competed on an annual basis against a 'United All-England XI'. Irrespective of which team they represented, it is generally agreed these matches did involve the best players in England at the time.

The first overseas tour by a representative England team was in September 1859, the destination was North America. The first man to captain an England team overseas was George Parr and the team comprised 12 players, six each from 'All England XI' and 'United All-England XI' – so a very good chance of getting a game, then.

The inaugural tour of Australia took place in 1861–62, as England was not keen to tour North America again due to the American Civil War.

The 1863–64 tour, which encompassed New Zealand, was the first to be organized by the MCC.

Most England tour matches prior to 1877 were played 'against odds', that is the opposing team was allowed to have more than 11 players, often as many as 22.

Get the banners out for that man. On 21 September 1876 James Lillywhite and an England team set sail on the P&O steamship *Poona* bound for Australia – a journey of eight weeks. It was on this tour, on 15 March 1877, that England took the field at Melbourne to play a combined Australian XI in what is regarded as the first Test match.

The first Test match in England took place between England and Australia in 1880. England won the series 1–0. It is generally accepted that this England team was the first to be fully representative of English players of the time. It included W. G. Grace (Gloucestershire).

In August 1884 at the Oval all 11 England players bowled against Australia in a single innings. Wicket-keeper Alfred Lyttelton had two spells of bowling while still wearing his pads. In his second spell, Lyttelton took 4 for 19, with W. G. Grace keeping wicket and taking a catch off Lyttelton's bowling.

In 1884–85 the England team remained unchanged throughout the five-match series against Australia – the only time this has ever happened with an England side in a five-match Test series.

Spectators short-changed but saw history in the making. The third Test between England and Australia at Old Trafford in 1888 is still the shortest in the history of Test cricket. The match ended before lunch (taken then at two p.m.) on the second day. The total duration of the match, which England won, was six hours and 34 minutes.

In 1889 England played their first Test match against South Africa at Port Elizabeth. Thus South Africa became the third Test-playing nation.

In December 1894 at Sydney, England, 261 runs short of Australia's first-innings total, were asked to follow on by Australia but won the match by 10 runs – the first instance of a team following on and going on to win a Test match.

In February 1895, during the fourth Test against Australia at Sydney, Johnny Briggs (Lancashire) became the first England bowler to take 100 Test wickets.

In March 1895 Jack Brown (Yorkshire) scored 50 in 28 minutes for England against Australia at Melbourne. He went on to score 140.

In 1905–06 England lost their first series against South Africa, 4–1.

In 1912 a nine-Test triangular tournament took place between England, Australia and South Africa. The English summer proved to be a very wet one (nothing new there then) which hampered proceedings considerably. The public did not attend in the numbers expected, partly because of the 'stop-start' nature of the matches due to the weather, and partly because spectators saw the event as a dilution of the gravitas of international cricket (no lessons learned from this then). The *Daily Sketch* wrote, 'Nine Tests provide a surfeit of cricket, and contests between Australia and South Africa are not a great attraction to the British public. There is also the cost of attending games for which admission prices for this tournament have risen considerably. Whilst many a manual worker might extend to attending one Test match, at these new prices, nine is overly taxing of the budgets of even the professional classes.'

England's first Test match after the First World War did not take place until 1920–21, against Australia. Though Australia too had lost many players in the war, England suffered most. They lost the series 5–0 – England's first 'whitewash' in a series.

By 1926 English cricket had largely recovered from the ravages of the First World War and this showed when a strong Australia team were defeated in the Ashes series. The side went on to win the 1928–29 series in Australia, 4–1.

The 1930 Test series in England was won by Australia, not least due to the batting of the young Don Bradman, who scored 254 at Lord's, 334 at Headingley and 232 at the Oval. It was in response to Bradman in particular that for the following series against Australia in Australia, England captain Douglas Jardine (Surrey) developed the fast leg theory, or Bodyline, tactic.

England's tour of India in 1933–34 saw the first ever Test on the subcontinent.

In June 1934 England defeated Australia at Lord's for the first time since 1896. The England hero was Yorkshire spinner Hedley Verity, who took 14 Australian wickets in a single day's play (25 June).

England lost the 1934 Ashes series and, due to the Second World War, it would be 19 years before the Ashes were regained.

Worked up an appetite. On 20 August 1935 Leslie Ames, on an overnight score of 25 in the Test against South Africa at the Oval, added another 123 runs before lunch to take his score to 148 not out.

The highest individual innings by an England batsman in a Test is 364, by Len Hutton (Yorkshire) against Australia at the Oval in 1938. Hutton's innings helped England achieve their highest ever total in a Test (903 for 7 declared) and the largest ever victory by any team in a Test (England won by an innings and 579 runs). During Hutton's time at the crease (797 minutes), England scored 770 runs.

England's last tour before the outbreak of the Second World War was to the West Indies.

Understandably, English cricket suffered as a result of the war and the post-war years saw Australia twice defeat England and the West Indies secure their first series win over England (2–0).

On 4 December 1950 at Brisbane, Australia declared their second innings on 32 for 7 when only 192 runs ahead of England. The match was played on what was described as a 'crank of a pitch'. Australia won by 70 runs.

On 19 July 1952 at Old Trafford, England dismissed India twice (58 and 82) in one day to win the match.

On 26 June 1953, during the Test against Australia at Lord's, Alec Bedser (Surrey) became the first England bowler to take 200 Test wickets.

England won the Ashes in 1953 and embarked upon another 'golden' period, not losing a Test series for over five years.

Sonny daze. In June 1957 at Edgbaston, during their second innings against West Indies, England batsmen faced 588 balls from Sonny Ramadhin – the most balls delivered by an individual bowler in a single innings of a Test match.

The record batting partnership for England is 411, compiled by Colin Cowdrey (Kent) and Peter May (Surrey) against the West Indies at Edgbaston in 1957.

Against the West Indies at Lord's in 1963, Colin Cowdrey (Kent), who earlier in the match had sustained a broken arm, returned to bat with his arm in plaster. There were only two balls of the match remaining when Cowdrey took his place at the non-striker's end. David Allen (Gloucestershire) was taking no chances. He successfully defended the remaining two deliveries to earn England a draw and spare Cowdrey the ordeal of batting in a Test with one arm.

In July 1965 at Headingley, John Edrich (Surrey) hit 57 boundaries (five sixes and 52 fours) when making 310 not out against New Zealand.

On 25 August 1973 play was stopped in the Test match between England and the West Indies at Lord's due to 'a bomb scare'. Fortunately the suspected terrorist bomb proved nothing of the sort.

In July 1975 Graham Gooch became the first player with a moustache to play for England in a Test match since Peter Smith of Essex against New Zealand in March 1947.

In 1975 England hosted the inaugural World Cup, and reached the semi-finals.

England boasted a formidable team in the late 1970s and early 1980s. Under captain Mike Brearley, players such as Ian Botham, Geoff Boycott, Graham Gooch, David Gower and Bob Willis became household names.

In his element. In 1977 Geoff Boycott achieved the unique distinction for an England player of batting on every day of the five-day Test match against Australia at Trent Bridge.

England were runners-up in the 1979 World Cup, which they also hosted.

The 1981 series against what could be termed a 'weakened' Australian team due to the loss of players to Kerry Packer's World Series was one of the most memorable between the countries. England looked set for defeat in the third Test at Headingley but Ian Botham rallied to score 149 and the following day England's bowlers, particularly Bob Willis, performed heroics. England won by 18 runs after having to follow on – only the second time in the history of Test series between England and Australia that a team asked to follow on ended up winning the match, the only previous occasion having been in 1894.

 We didn't have much time to celebrate, most of us had NatWest Trophy matches the next day. It was only when I turned on my car radio and listened to the news that the significance of what we had done hit me. I thought, 'That's me they're talking about.'
BOB WILLIS

Fast bowler Bob Willis's career as an England player spanned January 1971 to July 1984 in which time he batted on 128 occasions for England and was not out 55 times.

When in his early twenties, Bob Willis (Warwickshire) officially added 'Dylan' to his name, in honour of his hero, the singer-songwriter Bob Dylan.

In July 1982, against India at the Oval, Ian Botham reached a double century in 268 minutes off 220 balls on his way to making 208.

Andy Lloyd (Warwickshire) enjoys the distinction of being the only England player never to have been dismissed while representing his country. Lloyd played just the one Test match, the first Test against the West Indies at Edgbaston in 1984. During England's first innings Lloyd was 10 not out when he was hit on the head by a wicked delivery from Malcolm Marshall. Lloyd was helped from the field and taken to hospital. He did not play first-class cricket again that year and was never again selected for England.

In 1986–87 England retained the Ashes in Australia but then embarked upon nigh on a decade of what were at worst woeful, at best little more than adequate performances in Test series. With the likes of Ian Botham, David Gower and Allan Lamb at the end of their careers, in the 1990s England never found suitable replacements. The decline of England as an international team in that decade played no small part in the ECB taking over from the MCC as the governing body and creating central contracts which ensured the availability of players over the demands of their county clubs.

England were runners-up in the 1987 World Cup, again beaten by Australia.

In 1990 Graham Gooch (Essex) became the first player to score 1,000 runs in Test cricket in a single season, scoring a total of 1,058 in the series against New Zealand and India. Against India at Lord's, Gooch scored 333 and 121, a total of 456 runs – the highest aggregate score by an England player in a Test match.

Despite failures in Test series, throughout the 1990s England enjoyed relative success in ODIs, defeating Australia, West Indies and South Africa to reach the final of the 1992 World Cup. But they finished runners-up for the third time in the history of the competition and have still to win the trophy!

When England defeated South Africa in the 1998 Test series, it was their first success in a series since retaining the Ashes in 1986–87.

England hosted the 1999 World Cup, but were eliminated in the first round. That same summer, England lost the home Test series to New Zealand 2–1, which resulted in the ignominy of being ranked as the worst Test-playing nation.

The appointment of Duncan Fletcher as coach and Nasser Hussain as captain saw a revitalization of fortunes. England won four consecutive Test series, including the first series win against the West Indies for 32 years.

In 2004 England's victory against South Africa at Port Elizabeth was their eighth successive victory in Test matches – England's best sequence of results for 75 years (since 1929).

In 2005 a new generation of exciting young players such as Andrew Flintoff and Kevin Pietersen under the captaincy of Michael Vaughan (Yorkshire) defeated Australia 2–1 to regain the Ashes for the first time since 1986–87.

In the wake of England's victory over Australia, as is the wont nowadays, the celebrations were overdone to the point of embarrassment – almost as if

England had never defeated Australia in a series before. The victorious England team were paraded around the streets of London on an open-top bus, and players were later honoured with MBEs.

Of course I'm delighted England beat Australia, and I'm happy for the players. But parading them through the streets of London is a slight on every England team and player that has defeated Australia in the past. Those who have organized this nonsense have no sense of the history of English cricket. When England lose the series out in Australia, which they will, they should put everyone involved in this farrago on the same bus and drive it back over the same route through London in reverse gear.
CALLER TO BBC FIVELIVE

Following the 2005 victory over Australia, England were denied the services of key players such as Andrew Flintoff, Ashley Giles, Simon Jones and captain Michael Vaughan due to injuries. Yet another generation of promising players were given an opportunity to show their mettle at Test level, such as Monty Panesar, Ian Bell and Alastair Cook.

Alastair Cook's playing cricket for England? I wondered why his Letters from America wasn't on the radio any more.
PAUL BOARDMAN

In 2006–07 England lost all five Tests against Australia – the first Ashes whitewash for 86 years.

England were unimpressive in the 2007 World Cup, losing heavily to Australia, New Zealand and South Africa. Coach Duncan Fletcher resigned and was succeeded by Peter Moores, who had enjoyed considerable success with Sussex.

In 2007 England defeated the West Indies 3–0 in the Test series but lost 1–0 to India.

During the second Test between England and India at Trent Bridge in 2007, India batsman Zaheer Khan reported to the umpires that jelly beans had been thrown at his wicket, presumably in an attempt to divert his attention from the task of batting. The identity of the perpetrator of this act has never bean discovered.

In 2008 England defeated New Zealand but lost the Test series to South Africa. Following the five-wicket defeat to South Africa in the third Test, which gave the tourists victory in the series, England captain Michael Vaughan tendered his resignation. Kevin Pietersen assumed the captaincy and led England to victory in the fourth and final Test, and also in the ODI series.

After the series defeat against South Africa in 2008, England had played 877 Test matches in their history, of which 305 had been won.

England toured India in November and December 2008, playing two Test matches and seven ODIs, giving rise to concerns that ODIs now take precedence over Test matches. In February and March 2009, however, England's tour of the West Indies comprised four Test matches (extended while on tour to five) and five ODIs.

Swanning around town. On 13 December 2008 Graeme Swann took two wickets in the first over of his England Test debut against India at Chennai. He dismissed Gautam Gambhir and Rahul Dravid, both lbw.

On 29 February 2009 Andrew Strauss and Alastair Cook set a new England record for an opening stand in the West Indies when they put on 212 on the opening day of the Barbados Test. Strauss scored 142 and Cook was dismissed on 94.

In 2009 the West Indies accepted an invitation to replace Zimbabwe prior to England's hosting of the ICC Twenty20 World Cup and the Ashes series against Australia – the first time two Test series and a World Cup have been staged in England in the course of a single summer.

England's most capped player is Alec Stewart (Surrey), who played in 133 Test matches for his country. Stewart has also taken more catches in the field for England than any other player – 277.

In addition to Alec Stewart, seven other players have played 100 Tests or more for England: Graham Gooch (Essex), 118; David Gower (Leicestershire), 117; Mike Atherton (Lancashire), 115; Colin Cowdrey (Kent), 114; Geoff Boycott (Yorkshire), 108; Ian Botham (Somerset), 102; and Graham Thorpe (Surrey), 100.

Graham Gooch (Essex) holds the record for the most aggregate runs for England – 8,900.

The best career Test batting average for England is 60.73, by Herbert Sutcliffe (Yorkshire).

Three players jointly hold the record for the most centuries scored for England, at 22: Wally Hammond (Gloucestershire), Colin Cowdrey (Kent) and Geoff Boycott (Yorkshire).

The record number of wickets taken by a bowler in an England career is 383, by Ian Botham (Somerset, later Worcestershire and Durham).

The best bowling average for England is 10.75, by George Lohmann (Surrey).

England Test venues are Lord's, the Oval, Trent Bridge, Edgbaston, Old Trafford, Headingley, Riverside and Sophia Gardens (Cardiff). England also play ODIs at the Rose Bowl (Southampton) and Bristol.

The origin of the word 'wicket' lies in its standard definition, 'small gate'. One theory as to the origins of the wicket concerns shepherds on the downs of southern England taking a wicket-gate from sheep pens and using it to play a form of cricket.

Likewise, there is a popular theory as to how the term 'stumps' came into being. In the days when England was largely covered in woodland, tree cutters took to bowling at the stump of a tree when playing a game of 'crecket' ('crecket' meaning 'small stick or bat').

The wicket is 28 inches (71.12 centimetres) in height. Historically, wickets had only two stumps and were, in the days of underarm bowling, smaller in height.

In the 1980s Honley CC kept a parrot in their clubhouse. It was given an old stump on which to sharpen its beak.

Umpires can agree to dispense with bails if conditions are too windy for the bails to remain on the stumps. If one bail is off, removing the remaining bail or striking or pulling any of the three stumps out of the ground is sufficient to put the wicket down. The decision as to whether the wicket has been put down is one for the umpire concerned.

In 1901 Essex experimented with rubber bails in a match at Leyton.

In September 1902, during a match between Eleven Players of England and the touring Australians at Harrogate, so blustery were the conditions, clay was used to keep the bails on the stumps.

In 1957, during a match at Victoria College (Jersey), college batsman Ian Field attempted a shot off the back foot, totally misjudged it, and hit the off stump with such force it was sent a distance of 11 yards towards extra cover. That's the way to do it.

Bowlers removing the off and leg stumps and leaving the middle stump standing is not uncommon. One of the most celebrated instances of this was when England's Mike Hendrick bowled India's Madan Lal in 1974.

In 1969–70 John Inverarity, playing for Western Australia against Southern Australia in Adelaide, had his middle stump removed when a ball from Greg Chappell was deflected in the air by a passing swallow. The bird was killed. Inverarity began to walk but was called back by the umpire and went on to make 89.

Batsmen's gloves are considered to be an extension of the bat.

If a fielder uses any part of his clothing to field the ball he may be penalized five penalty runs, which go to the opposition. As instances of fielders stopping a ball near the boundary with their boot, or the ball hitting a fielder on the leg and thus his trousers when diving to prevent a boundary, are commonplace, umpires invariably apply common sense where this rule is concerned.

In the 1950s teams would play three-day matches home and away one after the other. No sooner was a match over at, say, Headingley than we would quickly pack everything into the skip and rush to the station to catch a train to wherever we were due to play the following day. Often the same clothing was used for two, maybe three matches. One day I asked Johnnie

Wardle how it was decided we should be issued with clean socks. 'We players decide,' he told me. 'At the end of one match, throw your socks against the dressing room wall. If they stick, you can send them to be washed. If they don't stick, you can get another match out of them.'

FRED TRUEMAN

Cricket-bags, they say, are getting bigger. Little wonder. The modern-day player may include in his bag shirt, trousers, long-sleeve jumper (possibly also a short-sleeve one too), cap (of any variety), spiked shoes, helmet, pads, thigh guard, arm guard, chest guard, elbow guard, box, batting gloves and bat.

I sat and watched a young Mike Atherton bat for Lancashire and thought, 'He's a strong, well-built, muscular lad.' After one match I called into the Lancashire dressing room to offer my congratulations to him on what was a wonderful performance with the bat. Athers took off his pads, a thigh guard, chest guard and elbow guard, I couldn't believe it. He was like a waif.

BRIAN STATHAM

Once an essential item of any cricketer's equipment was whitener, used on boots and pads. The most popular whitener was Meltonian, available in both bottle and tube form. According to the advertising copy of the 1950s, 'Guaranteed smartness of play at the wicket will be matched by smartness of appearance.'

The MCC museum at Lord's (the world's oldest sporting museum) features among its wide range of exhibits an extensive display of bats, caps and cricket clothing used by some of the greatest players of all time, such as W. G. Grace, Victor Trumper, Jack Hobbs, Don Bradman, Glenn McGrath and Shane Warne. The MCC has been collecting cricketing artefacts since 1864, and as the collection is now so vast, displays may change from time to time, but there is always a range of clothing and equipment as used by the greats of the game. A visit to the MCC museum is included in the Lord's Tour. Alternatively, it can be visited on any match day if you hold a ticket for the game.

Sunday cricket; multi-coloured pyjamas, two-tone umpires, white balls with black seams. There is nothing like traditional English sport.
DAVID HUNN (cricket writer)

Paintings of cricket matches and players of the eighteenth century depict players wearing a variety of similar versions of the traditional cricket cap.

In the late nineteenth and for the first half of the twentieth centuries the wearing of caps at all levels of cricket was popular. Caps came in all colours, some in multi-coloured circlets, the colours those of the club or school for which the cap was designed.

There was nothing that could induce me to get up a real head of steam than a batsman walking to the crease wearing a cap with multi-coloured circles, particularly if he was holding up his trousers 'Grace fashion', with his club tie.
FRED TRUEMAN

Caps are not commonly worn by players in matches today but are still favoured by many, not least because of what the cap may represent, such as recognition by club or country.

Players who represent first-class and Test match sides are invariably presented with a cap to mark their debut. There are exceptions, such as Worcestershire, who now award debutants with club colours.

The cap is numbered according to how many players have represented that team before them. For example, Sachin Tendulkar has a cap numbered 187, which means he was the 187th Indian to represent his country at Test level. As in international football, caps can be awarded to a player following each occasion on which he represents his country.

It had always been my dream to be awarded a Yorkshire cap. I would dream of how happy and proud I would feel at the ceremony. That it would be a momentous moment in my life. On 13 August 1951, that day finally came. We were playing at Bradford when Norman Yardley told me and Bob Appleyard to report to the club office. Bob and I duly presented ourselves, wondering why we had been summoned. Norman looked up, pointed to two caps lying on a side table and said, 'Your caps are there.'
FRED TRUEMAN

Arguably the best known and certainly most easily identifiable cap is that worn by the Australian team – the famous baggy green cap.

The traditional dress of the Australian cricketer is the baggy green cap on the head and the chip on the shoulder. Both are ritualistically assumed.
SIMON BARNES

It has become the vogue for players to wear baseball-style caps rather than the traditional cricket cap. India, Pakistan, New Zealand and Bangladesh teams invariably prefer the baseball cap.

Whether the caps are of the traditional or baseball variety, the colours of the caps of international teams have remained unaltered: Australia – dark green; England – navy blue; India – light blue; New Zealand – black; Pakistan – green; Sri Lanka – dark blue; South Africa – dark green; West Indies – maroon.

In the early 1990s three London cricketers, Prakesh Patel, Ramesh B. Patel and Ramesh Amin, had the idea of forming their own club. They sought the help of three cricketing friends, Pirthipal Singh and Minhas and Pravin Jilka, and in 1993 formed the 3 Caps Cricket Club, based at Ley's ground in Dagenham. The name derives from the fact the original three were known to prefer to wear caps when playing.

The helmet may be a relatively new innovation but many were the instances of players using towels, scarves or padding in their caps to protect their heads when batting. Patsy Hendren (Middlesex) was one of the first to use a self-designed protective hat, in the 1930s. Mike Brearley was another player who wore his own design.

Graham Yallop was the first player to wear a helmet in a Test match, when playing for Australia against West Indies at Bridgetown on 17 March 1978. Helmets began to be widely worn thereafter – but only in matches!

Helmets are compulsory in Under-19 cricket for all batsmen and any fielder within 15 yards of the bat.

Though Brian Close would no doubt have had none of it, fielders positioned very close to the batsman in first-class cricket often wear a helmet and shin guards.

In 2004 Fred Trueman took the great Australian bowler of the 1940s Sam Loxton along to the Test match at Headingley during which Fred introduced Sam to a bowler who had recently announced his retirement from Test cricket but was still playing county cricket. During the course of their conversation, Loxton asked the recently retired England bowler, 'What's all this with players wearing helmets nowadays?' Somewhat ungraciously, the former England player retorted, 'I know what you're going to tell me: "I never wore a helmet when I played cricket in my day!"' To which Loxton replied, 'Never wore a helmet when I played cricket? I never wore a helmet at Tobruk!'

Batsman with no pads or gloves. In September 2005, during the match between Glamorgan and Hampshire at Sophia Gardens, Hampshire's John McLean came out to bat, arriving at the non-striker's end minus his gloves and pads. When umpires Michael Harris and Peter Hartley took McLean to task, he explained he knew Hampshire were set to declare after the next ball and it didn't seem worth getting padded up. Messrs Harris and Hartley were not amused.

Didn't box clever. In 2006 Ben Foster, an employee at the Eden Project in Cornwall, claimed to have invented the world's first eco-friendly cricket box. Mr Foster's attempt to demonstrate his invention to the press by batting against Charlie Shreck, however, was sadly curtailed when he was hit in the face by a ball from the Nottinghamshire fast bowler and taken to hospital for treatment.

The only known instance of a fielder wearing a trilby hat in a first-class match occurred during the Roses match between Lancashire and Yorkshire at Old Trafford on 11 August 2006. During the final over of the drawn match, Lancashire's Mal Loye, with the sun in his eyes, donned a black trilby loaned to him by a spectator.

31

The headquarters of Essex County Cricket Club is the Ford County Ground, New Whittle Street, Chelmsford.

Billericay, Colchester, Ilford, Leyton and Southend have also been venues for Essex cricket.

The Essex badge is one of the most easily recognized of all county club badges: three seaxes (sabres) above a scroll bearing the county name.

Essex has won the County Championship six times, in 1979, 1983, 1984, 1986, 1991 and 1992. Other major honours: NatWest/Friends Provident Trophy winners 1985, 1997 and 2008; Benson & Hedges Cup winners 1979 and 1998; Sunday League/Pro 40 winners 1981, 1984, 1985, 2005 and 2006.

It is widely believed cricket was first played in the county as early as the sixteenth century. The earliest record of an 'official' match is that between Chingford and Mr Edward Stead's XI in 1724. Chingford had, however, played matches in previous years for which there are no known records. The 1724 match gained notoriety as Chingford refused to continue playing when it appeared Stead's XI was in a position from which they could not lose the game. The matter was referred to court and the presiding judge, Lord Chief Justice Pratt, ordered Chingford to play out the remainder of the game so that 'all wagers can be fulfilled'. The remainder of the match was eventually completed at Dartford Brent in 1726, Stead's XI emerging victorious.

The earliest known reference to an Essex team dates back to July 1732 when an Essex and Hertfordshire representative XI played London Cricket Club.

Essex CCC was formed on 14 January 1876 at the Shire Hall in Brentwood. The club, however, was not afforded first-class status until 1894.

Essex played their inaugural first-class match on 14–16 May 1894 against Leicestershire at Leyton. The match also marked Leicestershire's debut as a first-class county.

Essex did not have the best of starts as a first-class county, failing to win a single match in their first season (1894). Still, in 1895 Essex was admitted to the County Championship.

Essex made their debut in the County Championship in 1895 against Warwickshire (also making their debut) at Edgbaston. James Burns made 114 to become the first Essex player to score a century in the County Championship; he was soon followed by G. F. Higgins, who also made a century. The pair shared a fourth-wicket stand of 205.

The inaugural season in the County Championship proved memorable in more ways than one. Playing against Leicestershire at Leyton, H. Pickett became the first Essex bowler to achieve 10 wickets in a single innings. Pickett's 10 for 32 remains a club record. Weeks later, Walter Mead returned match bowling figures of 17 for 119 against Hampshire at Southampton. Again, this remains a club record.

In 1901 Essex were dismissed for 30 by Yorkshire at Leyton – the lowest total recorded by an Essex team in a single innings.

In 1904 Percy Perrin scored an unbeaten 343 in the first innings against Derbyshire at Chesterfield – the highest individual score recorded by an Essex player. Unwittingly, Perrin's 343 also created a County Championship record that exists to this day – the highest score made by an individual player who ended the match on the losing side. Derbyshire replied to Essex's first-innings total of 597 by scoring 548, then dismissed Essex for only 97 in the second innings and knocked off the winning runs for the loss of one wicket to win by nine wickets.

In 1928 Essex endured a miserable season, on what was then uncovered pitches. Their bowlers conceded an average of 40 runs per wicket – the highest of any Essex team in the County Championship.

Jack's all right. In 1929 Jack O'Connor scored a club record nine centuries in the County Championship, a feat he himself equalled in 1934, and which was also equalled by Doug Insole in 1955.

In the 1930s one of the team's regular bowlers was the curiously named Hopper Read.

In 1947 T. P. B. Smith took 172 County Championship wickets at an average of 27.13. He holds the club record for the most wickets taken in a career – 1,610 (average 26.6), between 1929 and 1951. Smith took nine wickets in a single innings on four occasions in successive seasons – twice in 1947 and twice in 1948.

On 15 May 1948 at Southend, Essex had the distinction of being the only team that summer (county or England) to dismiss Don Bradman's touring Australians in a single day's play. It was costly, though: Australia were all out for 721 (in 348 minutes of play) with four Australian batsmen scoring centuries (Bradman 187, Brown 153, Loxton 120 and Saggers 104) – some day's cricket that was. Essex were dismissed for 83 and 187 respectively to give the tourists victory by an innings and 451 runs. The match attracted a sell-out crowd of 16,000 for each day of play – a record for the county.

With friends like these . . . S. W. Montgomery did not enjoy the best of write-ups in the Essex CCC handbook for the 1949 season, being described thus: 'an unusual type of batsman in that he is rather lacking in strokes'.

In May 1949 Essex suffered the ignominy of two Cambridge University batsmen both making double centuries against the county. The undergraduates in question were John Dewes and Hubert Doggart who enjoyed a partnership of 429.

The star of the post-Second World War Essex team was all-rounder Trevor Bailey, a medium-fast bowler of some note and, generally, an obdurate batsman (once, when playing for England against South Africa in 1955, he went one hour and 19 minutes without adding to his score). Bailey achieved the double of 1,000 runs and 100 wickets in a season on eight occasions, and in 1959 became the first county player for 22 years to score 2,000 runs and take in excess of 100 wickets. His Essex career spanned the years 1945 to 1967, during which time he scored 28,642 runs (average 33.42) which included 28 centuries. His career tally of wickets was 2,082 (average 23.13). He also played 61 Tests for England between 1949 and 1959. Bailey later became a member of BBC Radio's *Test Match Special* commentary team.

 Seeing Trevor Bailey prepare for a session in the field was like a lecture in anatomy.
RAY EAST

In the 1940s and 1950s Essex occasionally played matches at Southchurch Park in Southend, a pitch which had gained a reputation for being something of a 'batsman's nightmare' and which moved cricket writer and broadcaster John Arlott to compose the following lines:

32

> Umpire or fieldsman or scoreboard clerk,
> Bowler, spectator – Oh! Pause! – and hark!
> Above the crowd's cheers and the stray dog's bark
> To cricket-field birdsong – perhaps the lark
> Or thrush or the magpie or piebald mark.
> But batsmen, oh batsmen, be deaf to the dark,
> Ill-omened, cold-fear-breeding, run-killing, stark
> Quack, quack of the ducks down at Southchurch Park.

In 1973 wicket-keeper Brian Taylor wrote himself into the county's record books by recording his 1,231st dismissal.

Essex had to wait 84 years for their first major trophy, the County Championship in 1979, a season during which they also won the Benson & Hedges Cup.

In what was a period of unprecedented success in the 1980s, the Essex team was captained by Keith Fletcher, who holds the club record for catches taken – 519. The team also included Graham Gooch, Ken McEwan, John Lever, Ray East, Derek Pringle and Neil Foster.

I can't bat, I can't bowl and I play for Essex. So I must
have a shout for the England team.
RAY EAST

In 1983 Essex created a new club record for the lowest score achieved by the
opposition when they dismissed Surrey for a paltry 14 at Chelmsford.

In 1988 Essex made 386 for 5 against Wiltshire at Chelmsford in the NatWest
Trophy – a club record score in one-day cricket.

In 1988, for the first time in the county's history, Essex provided four players
for the England team. John Childs, Neil Foster, Graham Gooch and Derek
Pringle all played against the West Indies in the fifth Test at the Oval. This
accomplishment was repeated twice in 1993 when Graham Gooch, Nasser
Hussain, Mark Ilott and Peter Such played for England in two Tests against
Australia.

In 1990 Essex scored 761 for 6 declared against Leicestershire at Chelmsford –
the highest total in the county's history. Graham Gooch and Paul Prichard
shared a second-wicket partnership of 403 – the highest partnership achieved by
an Essex pair.

Not ones to rest on their laurels, four years later, in 1994, Gooch and
Prichard shared an opening partnership of 316 against Kent, also at
Chelmsford – a club record first-wicket partnership.

Graham Gooch holds three further club records of note: most runs in a single
season (2,559, average 67.34, in 1984); most runs scored in an Essex career
(30,701, average 51.77, in a career spanning from 1973 to 1997); and most
centuries (94).

In the 1990s Nasser Hussain matched both Keith Fletcher and Graham
Gooch in becoming the third post-war Essex skipper also to captain England.

In 2006 Essex was the only county against which Mark Ramprakash (Surrey) did
not score a fifty.

Also in 2006 Essex Second XI achieved what England could not: they beat
the tourists Sri Lanka in a one-day match.

In 2008 Essex won the Friends Provident Trophy by defeating Kent in the final.

Most appropriately named player – Roger Luckin (1960s).

The club's limited-overs team is the Essex Eagles.

Worth a visit for . . . the Southend Festival, usually held at the end of July. A week-long festival of cricket geared to families, which normally includes a four-day county match, a limited-overs game, an opportunity to meet Essex players, all manner of cricket-related activities for all ages, bookstalls and a supporters shop. Concessions are available for family groups, and many children are offered free tickets via their school. In 2008 the admission for the first day of the festival for senior citizens was 'ten bob', the advertising copy reading, 'If you don't know how much this is, you won't qualify for this concessionary price.'

The first line of defence during the war should have been a line of those officious cricket stewards, you know the type. If Hitler had tried to invade these shores he would have been met by a short, stout man in a white coat sporting a steward's badge who would have told him, 'Fuhrer? I don't care who you are, you can't come in here unless you're a member or have an official pass.'
RAY EAST

If there is any sport truly worthy of the epithet 'family game' it is surely cricket. Arguably, cricket has witnessed more family connections in the way of players than any other sport, with fathers and sons, siblings and, in some cases, whole families representing the same team.

They were mustard. In the mid-nineteenth century the Colman family (of mustard fame) fielded an entire team of family members in several matches played in the Norfolk area.

England served by Grace Brothers. W. G. Grace and brothers Edward and Fred played in the first Test match played in England, against Australia in 1880.

The record number of players from the same family to have played in an international match is four. Brothers Charles, Daniel, George and Robert Charles played for the USA against Canada in 1880.

Alfred Lyttelton, enterprising batsman and outstanding wicket-keeper for England, had five brothers who also played first-class cricket, including Edward, who also played football for England.

Testing time for the Hearne brothers. In 1891 brothers Alec and George Hearne played together for England against South Africa whose team included their brother Frank.

Prior to the First World War One the Northamptonshire opening batsmen were W. H. and J. S. Denton, who were not only brothers but identical twins. In 1914, when Northants played Somerset, the Somerset team also included identical twins in Dudley and Sydney Rippon, and they also opened the batting.

'Branscombe wasn't half in form.'

'What, F. P. Branscombe?'

'No, no, F. P.'s gone to Pyjong. M. J. – you know, M. J. of Wadham.'

'Never came across M. J. I know his brothers, B. T. and L. V. Useful man, L. V. He must be getting on now.'

'Oh, not so very. Let me see, he was up the same year as Hartington.'

'J. K. or D. F.?'

HERBERT FARJEON

In June 1922 W. G. Quaife (Gentlemen) and his son Bernard (Player) found themselves batting together for Warwickshire against the Derbyshire bowling of Billy Bestwick (Player) and his son R. S. (Gentlemen). The match proved a real family occasion as the Smart brothers, Jack and Cyril, were also playing.

No (Lee) way. In June 1933, in the match between Middlesex and Somerset at Lord's, Middlesex's H. W. Lee was caught by his brother, Somerset's F. S. Lee, off the bowling of his other brother, J. W. Lee.

Oh brother, where art thou? In June 1939 Sussex fielded three pairs of brothers against Warwickshire: James and John Langridge, Jim and Harry Parks and Charles and Jack Oakes. The Sussex team also included two players with the surname Cornford, but, oddly, given the sibling nature of the Sussex team for this match, the Cornfords were unrelated.

Sussex boasts a long lineage of players who were related. In the mid-sixties the Sussex team included brothers Tony and Michael Buss; two players whose fathers played for Sussex, Richard Langridge (son of James Langridge) and Jim Parks (son of J. H. Parks); and the Nawab of Pataudi was the son of Nawab of Pataudi Senior who played for Oxford University, Worcestershire and captained the India team that toured England in 1946.

In 1947 members of the Edrich family, which included Bill (Middlesex), formed an entire team that played several charity matches in the home counties.

It's there in blue and white. In December 1961, in the match between Karachi Whites and Karachi Blues, the Whites team included brothers Hanif, Mushtaq and Raess Mohammad, who found themselves up against their other two brothers, Sadiq and Wazir, who were playing for the Blues.

Ron and Dean Headley are unique in cricket, the first father and son to play Test cricket for two different countries, West Indies and England respectively. Ron's dad, George, also played for the West Indies and therefore headed the first family to produce three generations of Test cricketers. The feat was subsequently matched by the Khans: Jahangir (who played Test cricket for India), his son Majid and grandson Bazid (both of whom represented Pakistan).

Sir Len Hutton's son, Richard, also played for Yorkshire and England.

David Graveney, formerly of Gloucestershire and Durham and now an England selector, is the son of Tom, of Gloucestershire, Worcestershire and England.

Australia's Chappell brothers, Greg, Ian and Trevor, are the grandsons of Australian Test cricketer Victor Richardson.

In the 1980s brothers Robin and Chris Smith played for Hampshire.

The Crowe brothers, Martin and Jeff, played Test cricket together for New Zealand in the 1980s.

The Cowdreys are one of English cricket's most famous family dynasties. Colin captained both Kent and England; his son Chris did likewise, while Colin's other son, Graham, also gave sterling service to Kent. Chris's son, Fabian, displayed the family cricketing genes in 2005, scoring two centuries for Caldicott School.

In 1984, at Huish Champflower in Somerset, an entire team comprising members of the Buckingham family of Somerset played a team comprising members of the Maltravers family.

Australia Test cricketer Paul Sheahan's great grandfather is William Cooper, who also played for Australia (1881–84).

Though their respective Test careers did not entirely coincide, twins Mark and Steve Waugh played together in the same Australia team for 12 years (1990–2002).

Hamish and James Marshall played together for New Zealand against Australia in the third Test at Auckland in March 2005. The Marshalls are the first set of identical twins to play Test cricket.

Brothers Andrew and Grant Flower played for Zimbabwe. In 2009 Andy Flower's career blossomed further when he was appointed coach to the England team.

In August 2005 Phil Rutland took five wickets for Trowbridge 'B' against Bathford Second XI (Wiltshire). The other five Bathford wickets fell to Phil's son, David.

James Joyce proud of his Dubliners. On 13 June 2006 James Joyce proudly watched as his two sons Ed and Dominick opened the batting for England and Ireland respectively in the ODI at Stormont, Belfast – the first instance of brothers opening the batting for opposing teams in an official international match.

Modi operandi. On 13 August 2006, during the second ODI against Bangladesh at Nairobi, Kenya's Hitesh Modi was given out lbw by umpire Subhash Modi, the father of the Kenyan batsman. In the first match between the two teams umpire Modi had also given his son out caught bat and pad following an appeal by the Bangladeshi fielders.

Also in 2006, Lancaster Bombers (Northern League) signed Chris Flintoff, brother of Andrew.

In 2009 Derbyshire had three players with family connections in cricket, each relating to Nottinghamshire. Dan Birch is the son of former Nottinghamshire player J. D. Birch; Nayan Doshi is the son of Dilip Doshi (formerly of Nottinghamshire, Warwickshire and India); and Akhil Patel is the brother of Samit Patel (Nottinghamshire).

Carl Greenidge (Gloucestershire) is the son of Gordon Greenidge (Hampshire and West Indies), while team-mate Kadir Ali has a brother and cousin who both play for Worcestershire, Moeen Ali and Kabir Ali.

On several occasions in 2008 Steve Harmison and brother Ben found themselves bowling in tandem for Durham, whose team was captained by Dale Benkenstein. Dale's father, M. M. Benkenstein, played for Rhodesia in the 1970s, and his twin brothers B. R. and B. B. played together for Natal in the 1990s.

Meet the Butchers. In 2009 Surrey's coach was Alan R. Butcher and their captain Alan's son, Mark. Alan's other son, G. P. Butcher, also played for Surrey, and Glamorgan (1994–2001). Alan's brother I. P. played for Leicestershire and Gloucestershire (1980–90), and his other brother, M. S., had one season with Surrey (1982).

M. C. C. A.

Minor Counties v. Australians

AT ASHBROOKE, SUNDERLAND

ON THURSDAY & FRIDAY, 4th & 5th AUGUST, 1977
Hours of Play: 1st Day 11-30 a.m. to 6-30 p.m.

MEMBERS' PAVILION ENCLOSURE
Ground Admission and Reserved Seat   (Under Balcony)

THURSDAY
Row ...A....

COMPLIMENTARY
Reserved Seat No. .25..

Entrance   Rear of Pavilion

J. Iley, Secretary, Durham C.C.C.

When's the game going to begin?
GROUCHO MARX (after an hour of watching a match at Lord's)

 I've watched cricket. It's the slowest game on earth, or any other planet.
ROBIN WILLIAMS

Cricket, slow? Don't you believe it . . .

In 1938 James Smith scored a fifty in 11 minutes for Middlesex against Gloucestershire at Bristol – the fastest fifty in first-class cricket. Smith had previously scored one for Middlesex in 14 minutes against Kent at Maidstone in 1935.

The second fastest fifty in English first-class cricket was also scored by a Middlesex batsman, Francis Mann, in 14 minutes against Nottinghamshire at Lord's in 1921.

Clive Inman scored a fifty in eight minutes for Leicestershire against Nottinghamshire at Trent Bridge in 1965, but this does not appear as the fastest fifty in official records as it was scored in contrived circumstances, off full-tosses to expedite a declaration.

The fastest fifty in a Test match was scored by John Brown in 28 minutes for England against Australia at Melbourne in 1894–95.

The fastest fifty in a Test match since 1900 was scored by Salim Durani in 29 minutes for India against England at Kanpur in 1963–64.

Gloucestershire's Gilbert Jessop was renowned for his hard hitting and for achieving high scores in a short time. In 1891 he scored a century in 40 minutes for Gloucestershire against Yorkshire at Harrogate, and a century in 42 minutes for the Gentlemen of the South against the Players of the South at Hastings in 1907. Jessop also scored the fastest century by an England player in a Test, in 75 minutes against Australia at the Oval in 1902.

The hospital that overlooks Cheltenham has a chipped brick under one of the eaves which has never been repaired. The broken brick is a memorial to Gilbert Jessop, who did the damage with one of his mighty hits.
ARTHUR MILTON

The fastest Test century by an England batsman is that of Gilbert Jessop, who scored 100 off 76 balls (59 minutes, 40 seconds) against Australia at the Oval in 1902.

The fastest century in first-class cricket was scored by Percy Fender in 35 minutes for Surrey against Northamptonshire at Northampton in 1920.

Greg Chappell scored a century in 21 minutes for Lancashire against Glamorgan at Old Trafford in 1993, but, as with Inman's fifty for Leicestershire, this was achieved off a mixture of full-tosses and long-hops deliberately bowled to expedite a declaration, so does not qualify.

In 1921–22 Australia's Jack Gregory scored the fastest century in Test cricket, in 70 minutes against South Africa at Johannesburg.

The fastest Test century in terms of balls received was scored by Viv Richards, who hit 100 off 56 balls for the West Indies against England at St John's in 1985–86.

The fastest double century was scored by Ravi Shastri, in less than two hours, for Bombay against Baroda at Bombay in 1984–85.

The fastest double century in the County Championship was scored by Gilbert Jessop in 120 minutes for Gloucestershire against Sussex at Hove in 1903; Jessop went on to score 286. Two years later (1905) Jessop scored a double century for Gloucestershire against Somerset at Bristol in 130 minutes.

Spectators would come specifically to watch Jessop bat.
F. S. ASHLEY-COOPER (yes, and we know why now)

The fastest double century in Test cricket was scored by Don Bradman in 214 minutes for Australia against England at Headingley in 1930.

The fastest double century for England in a Test match was scored in 240 minutes by Wally Hammond against New Zealand at Auckland in 1932–33. Hammond went on to set the record for the fastest ever triple century in Test cricket, in 288 minutes, meaning the third century of Hammond's innings was accomplished in just 48 minutes.

In 2001–02 Nathan Astle scored a double century in 217 minutes for New Zealand against England at Christchurch.

The fastest triple century was scored by Denis Compton in 181 minutes for the MCC/England against North Eastern Transvaal at Benoni in 1948–49.

If you go in with two fast bowlers and one breaks down, well, you're left two short.
BOB MASSIE (Australia)

In 1975 the *Sydney Herald* hired a machine to assess how quickly Dennis Lillee and Jeff Thomson could bowl and set it up on a practice strip. Lillee's fastest delivery on the day was recorded at 96.5mph; Thomson was even faster at 98.9mph.

Lillee bowled seven overs, no maidens, no wickets for 35, and I think that is a true reflection of his bowling figures too.
ALAN McGILVRAY (BBC Radio)

Dennis Lillee was one of the financial backers of the hit movie *Crocodile Dundee*.

In 2003 Shoaib Akhtar bowled a ball that was recorded travelling at 100mph when playing for Pakistan against England. It was the first officially timed 100mph delivery in Test cricket in England, albeit seasoned players and supporters were of the opinion such a speed was attained and possibly surpassed by Australia's Jeff Thomson in 1975.

In 2005 Durham's Steve Harmison was estimated to have bowled at 97mph. That same summer he was fined £100 by Harrogate magistrates for having matched his bowling speed in his car when driving on the A1(M) in North Yorkshire.

Cricket has not featured as the main theme in movies as frequently as sports such as football, golf, motor racing, boxing, baseball and American football, but it has, on occasion, served as an inspiration to screenwriters. Here are two films with cricket as a central theme:

The Final Test (UK, 1953) – screenplay by Terence Rattigan from his own play. Jack Warner as Sam Palmer, a professional batsman who has done well enough out of cricket to give his son a private education. To the father's chagrin the son shows no interest in the game and would rather visit pompous arty poet Robert Morley than watch his dad play cricket, even in his final Test against Australia. There is a nod towards Noel Coward's *This Happy Breed*. The poet turns out to be a cricket fanatic, all pass their 'test' of character, so all ends well. There are cameos from Alec Bedser, Denis Compton, Jim Laker and Cyril Washbrook, who play Warner's team-mates. Curiously, the part of the one named cricketer, Len Hutton, is played by actor Frank Jarvis. There is footage of an actual match at the Oval and a scene in which an American senator has cricket explained to him by Richard Wattis. What more could you want?

Playing Away (UK, 1987) – screenplay by Caryl Phillips. The action centres around the annual cricket match between the Suffolk village of Sneddington and Brixton. Willie Boy (Norman Beaton), the Brixton captain, dreams of returning to

Jamaica and his experiences in Sneddington help him make up his mind. Most of the cultural exchanges are stereotypical, such as Brixton introducing Sneddington players to 'weed', and a bit of inter-racial fancying. The finale, in which Brixton win the match but Sneddington are so bitter they do not lay on the normal end-of-match buffet, is unworthy and unbelievable. Cricket teams from whichever community simply don't behave and treat one another the way they do in this story, so the film lacks credibility.

As one might expect, Bollywood has taken cricket as a main theme for numerous movies, the most recent being *Stumped* (2003), *Wondrous Oblivion* (2003), *Iqbal* (2005), *Chennai 600028* (2007), *Jannat* (2008) and *Victory* (2008).

Films which have featured cricket scenes:

The Lady Vanishes (1938) – directed by Alfred Hitchcock. Though the film does not actually feature a game of cricket it does contain arguably the most famous reference to the game. Charters and Caldicott (Basil Radford and Naughton Wayne), travellers in pre-war Tyrol, play archetypal cricket-obsessed Englishmen more interested in debating field placings and obtaining the score from the Old Trafford Test than being concerned at the fact their hotel and, later, train are awash with Nazi spies. They do, however, come good in the end. So popular were these cricket-obsessed Englishmen abroad characters, Radford and Wayne reprised them in several other movies, such as *Night Train to Munich* and *It's Not Cricket*, which again does not feature cricket other than references to the game by Radford and Wayne's characters Bright and Early, though by then it was more a case of dull and too late.

The Common Touch (1941) – homely fable proposing socialist utopia of fair play and freedom once the war is over, featuring Bernard Miles. It opens with a cricket match as a symbol of England and the English sense of fair play.

The Browning Version (1951) – Terence Rattigan's second screenplay to feature a cricket match (he must have been a fan of cricket), on this occasion a game at a public school.

The Titfield Thunderbolt (1952) – Ealing comedy in colour. Locals band together to save their local branch line from the axe by British Railways. A village cricket match is in progress when the old (very old) steam train passes and sounds its whistle. Cut to a camera shot from behind the wicket. The batsman's attention is drawn to the passing train and he is bowled. Keen-eyed observers will notice the bails being pulled from the stumps by a wire.

Three Men in a Boat (1956) – the film adaptation of Jerome K. Jerome's mannered, eccentric novel features a mannered, eccentric cricket match towards the end.

How I Won the War (1967) – anti-war comedy during which British soldiers are sent behind enemy lines to set up a cricket pitch to impress a visiting VIP. Among those detailed to mark out the pitch are Michael Crawford and John Lennon. I repeat, John Lennon is sent to mark out a cricket pitch.

Carry On . . . Follow That Camel (1967) – given the period setting, appropriately topped and tailed by glorious scenes of Edwardian cricket, and featuring *Boy's Own* Fry-like hero Bertram Oliphant-West (Jim Dale), the film proudly boasts among its reviews the line – 'It's rubbish, but at least it's English rubbish'.

The Go-Between (1970) – glorious adaptation of L. P. Hartley's novel which begins, as does the book, with one of the best first lines of any novel/film: 'The past is a foreign country: they do things differently there.' Features cricket match between the family who own Brandham Hall and locals from the village. Rude man of the open Alan Bates literally knocks them for six, until caught by the film's protagonist, the young Leo.

The Shout (1978) – starts with a cricket match. Bees buzz, elderly fans recline in deckchairs by the boundary, two scorers (in blazers) sit in a tin hut, it's an idyllic English scene – oh, and the teams and all the spectators are from a local mental hospital. Alan Bates gets to play cricket again.

Hope and Glory (1987) – London in the Blitz, and another nod to *This Happy Breed* in which Ian Bannen instructs his son on how to bowl a googly.

Maurice (1987) – adaptation of E. M. Forster's novel about a gay man in Edwardian England features a cricket match set in 'Brideshead country'.

King Ralph (1991) – John Goodman plays a Las Vegas entertainer and all-round loser who succeeds to the 'throne of England' and is introduced to English eccentricities such as cricket.

The Crying Game (1992) – features scene of a cricket match in which we are treated to the sight of Forrest Whitaker in whites offering the best impression of a bowler you are going to get – from Forrest Whitaker.

The Beach (2000) – Leonardo DiCaprio finds a map detailing the location of a backpackers' Holy Grail, a virgin beach in the Gulf of Thailand populated by a commune living at one with nature and playing the occasional game of cricket – as they do.

Vertical Limit (2000) – a brother and sister in an adventure on K2. Brief scene of a local hillside village cricket match makes a mountain out of a molehill.

Seducing Dr Lewis (2002) – Canadian movie. A doctor caught taking illegal drugs is sent to a remote island off the Canadian coast and sets about teaching the locals to play cricket, forming them into two teams. Cricket is totally alien to the islanders but they go for it.

Master and Commander (2003) – based on the Patrick O'Brien novels. Features a scene in which a British ship of the early nineteenth century anchors off the Galapagos Islands and the crew wind down with a game of cricket. Superb film and accurate representation of cricket equipment of that period – hockey-stick-shaped bats, etc.

Other movies in which a cricket scene is featured include *Bend it like Beckham* (2002), *Finding Neverland* (2004), *Syriana* (2005), *The Chronicles of Narnia* (2005) and *A Good Year* (2006).

Arguably cricket's most famous connection with the movies is C. Aubrey Smith, who in addition to playing for Sussex and captaining England against South Africa in his only Test appearance went on to appear in over 60 movies in Hollywood, including *Dr Jekyll and Mr Hyde*, *Waterloo Bridge*, *The White Cliffs of Dover* and *Little Women*. Smith formed the Hollywood Cricket Club (still thriving today) which, in addition to Smith, featured David Niven, Laurence Olivier and Boris Karloff.

During one Hollywood CC match, C. Aubrey Smith dropped a catch off the bowling of David Niven which Smith described as 'one a child would have taken at midnight with no moon'. Chagrined at spilling the catch, Smith asked his butler to bring him his spectacles. (His butler was in attendance?

That's Hollywood for you.) A little later, Smith was fielding in the slips and Niven was again bowling. The batsman edged, but again Smith spilled what was a straightforward catch. Annoyed at having another chance go a-begging, Niven glowered at Smith, who removed his spectacles, examined them, turned to Niven and said, 'Darned fool butler, he brought me my reading glasses!'

C. Aubrey Smith was indeed a major Hollywood film star. When visiting London in the summer he could often be seen at Lord's or the Oval. On one of these occasions an MCC member spotted Smith and remarked to a fellow member, 'That chap's face is jolly familiar, where have I seen him before?' To which his fellow member replied, 'Played a few games for Sussex.'

Finally, forgive this one, but one can't refer to cricket in the movies without mentioning the character whose name is the word 'cricket' – Jiminy Cricket (*Pinocchio*, 1940).

35

The first batsman to score ten first-class centuries in a season was W. G. Grace (Gloucestershire), in 1871.

W. G. Grace was also the first batsman to score 2,000 runs in a first-class season (2,739 in 1871).

The first bowler to take 100 wickets in his debut season in first-class cricket was George Harrison (aged 21), for Yorkshire in 1883.

The first bowler to take 10 wickets in an innings in the County Championship (since formation in 1890) was Tom Richardson (10 for 45), for Surrey against Essex at the Oval in 1894.

Tom Richardson was also the first bowler to take in excess of 250 wickets in a first-class season – 252 in 1895, from five-ball overs.

The first bowler to take in excess of 250 wickets in a season off six-ball overs was Wilfred Rhodes (261), for Yorkshire in 1900. Rhodes was also the first bowler to take 100 wickets in a first-class season 20 times (23).

The first batsman to be given out twice for having obstructed the field was Tom Straw of Worcestershire, in 1899 and again in 1901. Oddly, both instances were against Warwickshire.

The first West Indies team to tour England (but not to play Tests) arrived in 1900. It was not, however, the West Indies' first overseas tour: in 1886 a team had toured the USA and Canada.

The first bowler to accomplish the feat of a hat-trick on his debut in the County Championship was H. Sedgwick, against Worcestershire at Hull, in what proved to be his only season with Yorkshire (1909).

The first player to score a century and take a hat-trick in a County Championship match was William Burns, for Worcestershire against Gloucestershire at Worcester in 1913. (W. E. Roller accomplished this feat, scoring a double century for Surrey against Sussex at the Oval, but in 1885, prior to the official formation of the County Championship.)

The first professional cricketer to play in spectacles was Albert Barbery, a fast-medium bowler with Warwickshire prior to the First World War, who later served Leamington CC with much distinction. His career was curtailed by a serious injury sustained during the First World War.

The first batsman to score two double centuries in the same County Championship match was Arthur Fagg (244 and 202 not out), for Kent against Essex at Colchester in 1938.

The first batsman to average over 100 runs in an English season (of completed innings) was Don Bradman (115.60 in 1938).

The first English batsman to average over 100 in a season was Geoff Boycott (Yorkshire), with 102.53 in 1979.

The first County Championship match known to have attracted a form of sponsorship was the game between Essex and Northamptonshire at Clacton-on-Sea, 29–31 August 1948. The sponsors were a form of local builders and contractors, Cockram, Smith and Company. The sponsorship involved the company's name appearing on scorecards, and a board was erected at the pavilion gate which proudly proclaimed 'Cockram, Smith and Co. are proud to support Essex CCC v. Northants – proud to be on Admiralty and War Office Lists'.

The first County Championship match to end in a tie since the law was rewritten in 1948 (stating a tie to be when the scores are level and all wickets down in the fourth innings) was Hampshire against Kent at Southampton in 1950.

The first wicket-keeper since the formation of the County Championship to take in excess of 10 dismissals in a county match was Arthur Long (11), for Surrey against Sussex at Hove in 1964.

The first player to score six successive centuries since 1946 was Mike Procter (Gloucestershire/South Africa), in 1970–71.

The first and to date only player to have scored 5,000 runs and taken 100 wickets and 100 catches in both Test matches and ODIs is Carl Hooper (West Indies).

The first player to score in excess of 12,000 runs in Test matches was Sachin Tendulkar. Tendulkar set the new record while playing for India against Australia. On 17 October 2008, on the first day of the second Test in Mohali, Tendulkar passed the record previously held by Brian Lara (West Indies) of 11,953 Test match runs, then passed the 12,000 mark off the bowling of Peter Siddle on his way to making 88. Tendulkar already held the record for the most centuries in Test cricket – 39 in 151 Tests.

ENGLAND v AUSTRALIA at MANCHESTER		HOW OUT	BOWLER	TOTAL	
BATSMEN	2nd innings of AUSTRALIA				
1 C.C. McDONALD		c Oakman	Laker	89	341
2 J.W. BURKE		c Lock	Laker	33	106
3 R.N. HARVEY	0/	c Cowdrey	Laker	0	2
4 I.D. CRAIG		lbw	Laker	38	263
5 K. MACKAY	0/	c Oakman	Laker	0	8
6 K.R. MILLER	0/	b	Laker	0	17
7 R.G. ARCHER	0/	c Oakman	Laker	0	3
8 R BENAUD		b	Laker	18	107
9 R.R. LINDWALL		c Lock	Laker	8	144
10 I.W. JOHNSON		not out		1	27
11 L. MADDOCKS		lbw	Laker	2	8
WIDES				EXTRAS	16
BYES				TOTAL	205
LEG BYES					
NO BALLS					
FALL OF WICKETS 1 28	2 55	3 114	4 124	5 130	6 130 7 181 8 198 9 203 10 205

The Friends Provident Trophy competition began life as the Gillette Cup in 1963.

The Gillette Cup was the first one-day competition in England and Wales. In its early days it came in for much criticism from those who believed one-day cricket was too frivolous and not a true test of cricket skills.

The competition was launched to combat falling attendances at County Championship matches. It was a straight knock-out competition which initially did not involve Minor Counties teams.

In 1963 matches consisted of 65 overs per team. This was reduced to 60 overs in 1964.

As there was an uneven number of County Championship teams (17), the 1963 competition began with a preliminary round match between Lancashire and Leicestershire at Old Trafford – the two clubs that had occupied the bottom two places in the County Championship the previous season.

Peter Marner was the first player to score a century (121) in the competition, for Lancashire (304 for 9) in that preliminary tie against Leicestershire in 1963. Marner became the first winner of the Gillette Man of the Match award, for which he received a medal and a cheque for £50. Maurice Hallam also scored a century (106), for Leicestershire, and was given a special award for 'The Spirit in Which He Played the Game'.

Lancashire's match against Leicestershire was not only the first ever Gillette Cup tie, due to rain it was the first cup match to move into a second (reserve) day.

 Sussex worked out one-day cricket quicker than anyone else, and that was down to skipper Ted Dexter who decided on our tactics. Sussex's first Gillette Cup tie was against Kent at Tunbridge Wells. We scored over 300 and were surprised to see them still playing the game as they would a County Championship match, with slips, gully and what have you. We defended from the start, one slip and everyone back, and won quite easily. Our secretary then received a letter from the Kent chairman saying it had been a disgusting performance by the Sussex team.
JIM PARKS (Sussex)

In round two of the 1963 competition, the Sussex–Yorkshire tie drew to the Hove ground a then competition record attendance of 15,007. Sussex won by 22 runs.

In the first 1963 semi-final Lancashire were dismissed by Worcestershire for 59 and the tie was over by two o'clock.

Sussex were the first winners of the Gillette Cup, beating Worcestershire by 14 runs in the final at Lord's before a crowd of 21,234.

The 1963 Man of the Match award for the final was won by Worcestershire's Norman Gifford. It was judged by Frank Woolley and Herbert Sutcliffe. The trophy, the winners and losers medals and the Man of the Match award were presented by Lord Nugent, president of the MCC, during incessant rain.

In 1964 five Minor Counties teams were invited to participate for the first time: Cambridgeshire, Cheshire, Durham, Hertfordshire and Wiltshire. To accommodate these teams the competition comprised a first round of six matches, a second round of eight matches, a third round, semi-finals and a final.

In the 1964 final Sussex beat Warwickshire by eight wickets, thus becoming the first county to win the Gillette Cup twice and the first to win in two successive seasons.

In 1972 Lancashire defeated Warwickshire by four wickets to become the first county to win the cup in three successive seasons (1970, 1971 and 1972).

Due to inclement weather the 1977 semi-final between Middlesex and Somerset spanned six days.

The last Gillette Cup Final took place in 1980. Middlesex beat Surrey by seven wickets.

In 1981 the competition got a new sponsor and was renamed the NatWest Trophy.

The first NatWest Trophy Final, between Derbyshire and Northamptonshire, ended in a tie, both teams having scored 235. Derbyshire were declared the winners by virtue of having lost fewer wickets (six).

In 1985 Ireland were dismissed for 39 by Sussex at Hove – the lowest total in the history of the competition.

In the 1985 final at Lord's, Essex (280 for 2) defeated Nottinghamshire by one run – the smallest winning margin in a final.

Due to bad weather the 1987 final was reduced to 50 overs per team, and it became the first final to move into the reserve day. Nottinghamshire beat Northamptonshire by three wickets.

Derbyshire's Michael Holding took 8 for 21 against Sussex at Hove in 1988 – the competition's best ever bowling figures.

The tie between Devon and Somerset at Torquay in 1990 produced the competition's fastest century in terms of balls received. Somerset's Graham Rose reached 100 in just 36 balls.

Warwickshire's total of 322 for 5 in the 1993 final against Sussex is the highest total in a final. Warwickshire won by five wickets.

The record partnership in a tie involving two first-class county teams is 309 (unbroken), shared by Worcestershire's Tim Curtis and Tom Moody for the third wicket against Surrey at the Oval in 1994.

In the 1996 final Essex were dismissed for 57 by Lancashire – the lowest total by any team in a final. Lancashire had batted first and scored 186, so they won by 129 runs.

In 1997 at Bristol, Anthony Wright and Nick Trainor shared a first-wicket partnership of 311 for Gloucestershire against Scotland – a record partnership for the competition.

In 1999 the number of overs was reduced to 50 per side, as this would give cricketers more experience of playing in matches that consisted of the same number of overs as ODIs.

In 2001 the competition engaged its third sponsor and became the C&G Trophy.

In 2001 Worcestershire's David Pipe created a new record for dismissals by a wicket-keeper in a single tie – eight, all caught, against Hertfordshire at Hertford.

In 2002 Surrey's Alistair Brown set a new record for the highest individual innings in the competition when he scored 268 against Glamorgan at the Oval. Brown faced 160 balls and his total included 30 fours and 12 sixes. To commemorate his achievement there is now a 268 bar at the Oval. Surrey's total of 438 for 5 was a record for the competition. Spectators certainly got their money's worth that day: in reply, Glamorgan scored 429. The aggregate score of 867 is also a record for the competition.

The most wickets taken by a bowler in the history of the competition is 88, by Allan Donald during spells with Warwickshire and Worcestershire (1987–2002).

In 2006 the Minor Counties were omitted and the competition took on a new format. The first-class counties, Ireland and Scotland were divided into two leagues, North Conference and South Conference, each consisting of 10 teams. The two league winners contested the final at Lord's.

In Scotland's C&G Trophy match against Lancashire at Edinburgh in 2006, the home side's Ian Stanger bowled one over, a maiden, but returned bowling figures of 1–1–6–0. Stanger's maiden was followed by a single delivery, adjudged a no-ball (worth two runs to the opposition), which Luke Sutton hit for four runs, and which gave victory to Lancashire.

Following the end of C&G's sponsorship of the competition in 2006, for a short period the competition was known as the ECB Trophy as no new sponsorship deal had been agreed.

Sponsor number four came along in 2007, and the competition became the Friends Provident Trophy.

The 2007 competition underwent another change of format: the winners and runners-up of the North and South Conferences now contested semi-finals.

In 2007 Surrey scored 496 for 4 against Gloucestershire at the Oval – a new record highest total for the competition.

In 2007 Durham won the trophy for the first time, defeating Hampshire by 125 runs.

In 2008 quarter-finals were introduced to the competition, with eight teams, four from each regional division of Midlands, North, South-East and South-West, qualifying for the quarter-final stage.

In 2008 Essex won the competition for the third time, defeating Kent in the final.

Three players have scored eight centuries in the competition. The joint holders of the record are Robin Smith (Hampshire, 1985–2003), Nick Knight (Essex and Warwickshire, 1992–2006), and Graeme Hick (Worcestershire, 1986–2007).

Graeme Hick has also scored the most runs in the competition – 3,416.

On 3 May 2009 at Riverside, Surrey were 265 for 4 needing two runs to defeat Durham with two balls remaining. Ian Blackwell then dismissed Grant Elliott and John Betts with successive balls to secure victory for Durham by one run.

Gillette/NatWest/C&G/Friends Provident Trophy Winners

1963	Sussex	1986	Sussex
1964	Sussex	1987	Nottinghamshire
1965	Yorkshire	1988	Middlesex
1966	Warwickshire	1989	Warwickshire
1967	Kent	1990	Lancashire
1968	Warwickshire	1991	Hampshire
1969	Yorkshire	1992	Northamptonshire
1970	Lancashire	1993	Warwickshire
1971	Lancashire	1994	Worcestershire
1972	Lancashire	1995	Warwickshire
1973	Gloucestershire	1996	Lancashire
1974	Kent	1997	Essex
1975	Lancashire	1998	Lancashire
1976	Northamptonshire	1999	Gloucestershire
1977	Middlesex	2000	Gloucestershire
1978	Sussex	2001	Somerset
1979	Somerset	2002	Yorkshire
1980	Middlesex	2003	Gloucestershire
1981	Derbyshire	2004	Gloucestershire
1982	Surrey	2005	Hampshire
1983	Somerset	2006	Sussex
1984	Middlesex	2007	Durham
1985	Essex	2008	Essex

Wins by County

7	Lancashire
5	Gloucestershire, Sussex and Warwickshire
4	Middlesex
3	Essex, Somerset, Yorkshire
2	Hampshire, Kent, Northamptonshire
1	Derbyshire, Durham, Nottinghamshire, Surrey, Worcestershire

Glamorgan and Leicestershire are the only two County Championship clubs not to have won the trophy.

Gentlemen & Players

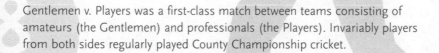

Gentlemen v. Players was a first-class match between teams consisting of amateurs (the Gentlemen) and professionals (the Players). Invariably players from both sides regularly played County Championship cricket.

There were variations on the theme of Gentlemen v. Players, such as Gentlemen of the South v. Players of the North, Gentlemen of Nottinghamshire v. Players of Nottinghamshire and so on, but Gentlemen v. Players was the most prestigious. The last 'variation' match took place in 1920 between the Gentlemen of the South and the Players of the South.

In County Championship and even international cricket, Gentlemen and Players of the same team often had separate dressing rooms and would even take to the field via separate gates.

The terms Gentlemen and Players were used to distinguish between players who earned a living from cricket and those who did not (because they enjoyed a living by other means) and served to further cement the class structure not only in cricket but English society. For much of its history English cricket was administered and run by establishment figures in the MCC at Lord's. Until relatively recently no working person, or woman, was a member of the MCC. That said, it is doubtful whether many spectators who attended these matches saw them as a 'battle' between the classes, more an opportunity to see some of the best players in the game pitting their cricket skills against one another.

Financially, Gentlemen v. Players matches were farcical from the start, and continued to be so. The Players received a good fee for participating in the fixture, but each of the Gentlemen, though unpaid, invariably received more than a Player's fee in the form of expenses. This was not only true of Gentlemen v. Players but also England matches, a situation which continued into the late 1950s, particularly on overseas Test tours.

The first two Gentlemen v. Players matches took place in 1806, but the fixture did not take place again until 1819 (not classified first-class). Thereafter it was more or less an annual event until the last match in 1962.

In the early history of the fixture the Gentlemen teams were often weak compared to the Players. To even things up, the Players XI would often take on a numerically superior Gentlemen team. In 1829 at Lord's the Gentlemen enjoyed one of their highest margins of victory over the Players in terms of runs, 193, but their team consisted of 12 men. In 1837 the Gentlemen had 16 men in their side.

The Gentlemen team became truly competitive during the era of W. G. Grace, whose performances resulted in long-awaited success for the Gentlemen over the Players. Even so, the fixture continued to confirm the view that Gentlemen tended to be batsmen first and foremost, hence there were few outstanding bowling performances on the part of the Gentlemen, as opposed to the Players, who enjoyed the services of some superb bowlers, among them the great Wilfred Rhodes.

W. G. Grace scored 15 centuries for the Gentlemen. He also had the distinction of representing the Players at the age of 16.

Other Gentlemen who represented the team while still at school (very grand fee-paying schools) before invariably going up to Oxbridge were C. F. Buller, Alfred Lubbock, R. A. Mitchell and A. J. Webbe. Archie MacLaren played for the Gentlemen while at Harrow School prior to joining Lancashire. Reg Spooner also represented the Gentlemen while still at school prior to joining Lancashire.

On all but a handful of occasions, the fixture was a three-day game.

The match was usually played at Lord's. Other popular venues were the Oval and Scarborough.

In 1823 the Players enjoyed their highest winning margin in terms of runs, defeating the Gentlemen by 345 runs at Lord's.

In 1829 at Lord's the Players made a first-innings total of 24 – their lowest ever.

William Lillywhite, known as 'Nonpareil', is credited with being largely responsible for the development of round-arm bowling and has the distinction of having played for both Gentlemen and Players. Playing for the Gentlemen in 1829, he took 14 wickets in the match at Lord's – the most by any Gentlemen bowler in a single match. In 1837, playing for the Players, he did even better, taking 18 wickets in the match at Lord's – the biggest haul of wickets in a single match in the history of the fixture. William Lillywhite was the uncle of James Lillywhite junior, England's first Test captain.

In 1837 at Lord's, the Gentlemen were dismissed for 24 – their lowest ever total.

The smallest margin of victory occurred at Hove in 1881, the Players winning by one run.

In 1872 at the Oval, the Gentlemen beat the Players by nine wickets, a feat they repeated at Prince's cricket ground in 1877.

In 1879 at the Oval, the Gentlemen won by an innings and 126 runs – their largest margin of victory.

During the match of 1881, A. N. Hornby became the first batsman to attempt the reverse sweep shot, which he had been developing in net practice. Hadn't quite perfected it though: he was bowled.

In 1900 R. E. Foster scored 102 not out in his first innings and 136 in his second – the first man to score two centuries in a single match between the teams.

In 1903 at Lord's, C. B. Fry scored 232 not out – the highest individual total for the Gentlemen in the history of the fixture.

In 1904 the Gentlemen recorded their highest total in a single innings – 578. It was in this match that J. King scored 104 and 109 not out – the first Player to score a century in each innings.

At Scarborough in 1925 Jack Hobbs scored 266 not out – the highest ever individual score by a Player.

The best ever bowling figures in a single innings were achieved by A. S. Kennedy – 10 for 37 for the Players at the Oval in 1927.

In 1934 at the Oval, the Players enjoyed their largest margin of victory, by an innings and 305 runs. It was also in this match that the Players achieved their highest ever total: 651 for 7 declared.

In 1952 at Lord's, Len Hutton of the Players took five catches in a single innings.

The final Gentlemen v. Players fixture took place at Scarborough in 1962. Fred Trueman captained the Players.

In all, 274 matches were played. The Players won 125, the Gentlemen 68, with 80 drawn and one, in 1883, ending in a tie.

The Players defeated the Gentlemen by 10 wickets on seven occasions.

In the late 1950s and up to the final fixture of 1962, the Players received a fee of £56 for playing in the game, plus expenses. The cheque was paid by the MCC direct to the Player's county club.

I thought the fee for playing was £22. It was only during the final fixture in 1962 that Brian Statham and Geoff Pullar told me it was £56. Turned out Yorkshire had only paid me £22 because they'd deducted £34 to pay the player who had replaced me in the Yorkshire side when I was away representing the Players against the Gentlemen. I raised the roof in that Yorkshire committee room but they were having none of it, so I referred the matter to the MCC who found Yorkshire 'guilty of malpractice regarding the payment of professional fees'. The MCC ruled that Yorkshire had not only to pay me the full fee of £56 for the final Gentlemen v. Players match, but all the fees they had deducted from me from previous games. I was never popular with that Yorkshire committee prior to this so, after having had their knuckles rapped by the MCC and the case splashed across the newspapers, you can imagine what they thought of me after this.

FRED TRUEMAN

By the early 1960s the Gentlemen v. Players fixture had become an anachronism. In November 1962 the MCC met to discuss a recommendation from the Advisory County Cricket Committee and approved the motion that the distinction between amateurs and professionals be abolished. All first-class players became, in theory at least, professional.

In 1962 there were only 50 amateur players playing in the County Championship, albeit 12 of them as captains. In 1963 the number dropped to 33. Come the start of 1966 there were no former amateurs in county teams.

I was a miner but showed enough talent at cricket to be taken on the Lord's groundstaff. In those days Lord's would send their groundstaff to play for various teams on an ad hoc basis. As a member of the groundstaff I was told to seek out the respective captain, report for duty and, as he was invariably a Gentleman, to call him 'sir'. I'd introduce myself by saying, 'I'm Jim Sims, sir, from Lord's groundstaff.' I was nearly always asked to bat as a tail-ender and only occasionally asked to bowl. I got fed up with it all, so one day I changed tack. I casually strolled up to the captain of this club and said, 'Morning, sir,

Morton-Sims from Lord's, no less. Spiffing weather for cricket.' The captain said, 'I'll say! Jolly good stuff, Morton-Sims, how would you like to open the batting?'

JIM SIMS (who went on to play for England)

So, with this abolish-the-amateur decision of the M.C.C. advisory committee . . . the last link with cricket's squire and peasant tradition is shattered.

FRANK ROSTRON (*Daily Express*)

A game without Gentlemen? Where will we find our future leaders?

E. W. SWANTON

Glamorgan

Glamorgan County Cricket Club (Criced Morgannwg) is the only first-class club in Wales.

The county headquarters is the SWALEC Stadium, Sophia Gardens, Cardiff. The ground has a capacity of 17,500.

For many years Glamorgan's principal home was Cardiff Arms Park, which had staged the first match in 1889 and the first County Championship match in 1921. The club switched to Sophia Gardens in 1967. This ground was extensively redeveloped in 2006–07 to Test match standard. The Arms Park is now part of the rugby ground which is the current home of Cardiff Blues.

Glamorgan have also played matches at Swansea and Ebbw Vale, Colwyn Bay and Cresselly, despite the latter two respectively being in Denbighshire and Pembrokeshire.

The club's badge is a golden daffodil.

Glamorgan has won the County Championship three times, in 1948, 1969 and 1997. They were Sunday/Pro40 League champions in 1993, 2002 and 2004.

And Glamorgan are the 1969 county champions. A
unique occasion, really, a repeat of 1948.
JIM LAKER (BBC Radio)

The earliest known reference to cricket in the county is a match at Swansea in
1780, though it is believed cricket, in one form or another, has been played in the
county since the late seventeenth century.

The county club was formed at a council of over 30 representatives of leading
Welsh clubs that took place at the Angel Hotel in Cardiff on 6 July 1888 –
curiously, the day county councils came into being in Great Britain.

Glamorgan's first game took place in August 1888, a challenge match against
Llnynpia CC. Between 1889 and 1896 the county club played friendlies and
challenge matches against teams representing other counties and touring sides,
though none of these teams enjoyed first-class status.

In 1897 Glamorgan gained admission to the Minor Counties Championship.

The club applied for first-class status and membership of the County Championship
in 1919 and were eventually accepted in 1921, increasing membership of the
championship to 17 teams.

Glamorgan's debut in the County Championship was against Sussex at
Cardiff Arms Park on 18–20 May 1921, a game they won by 23 runs.
Following this encouraging start, Glamorgan contrived to win only one more
match and ended the season bottom of the league.

In 1924 Lancashire dismissed Glamorgan for 22 at Liverpool – the county's
lowest score in first-class cricket.

Magic bowling. In 1936 Jack Mercer became the first Glamorgan bowler to
take 10 wickets in a single innings, returning figures of 10 for 51 against
Worcestershire at Worcester. He was a member of the Magic Circle and
regularly performed in variety shows. When he retired as a player he became
the official scorer at Northamptonshire.

Didn't potter about. The following year (1937), J. C. Clay returned match figures
of 17 for 212 against Worcestershire at Swansea – to this day a club record.

When Glamorgan won their first County Championship in 1948, captain Wilf Wooller maintained the key to his side's success was 'exacting standards in the field, which enabled us to beat teams who were much stronger than us in terms of batting or bowling'.

Between 1950 and 1972 Don Shepherd took 2,174 wickets – the most wickets taken by a Glamorgan bowler in the course of a career with the county.

The county's most prolific batsman is Alan Jones, who in a career spanning the years 1957 to 1983 scored a total of 34,056 runs at an average of 33.05.

There'll be another one along in a minute. On 18 June 1958 W. E. Jones was bowled by Anthony 'Tony' Buss of Sussex with what was only his second delivery in first-class cricket. The headline ran 'Jones First Player to Miss A. Buss'.

In 1965 Glamorgan dismissed Leicestershire for 33 at Ebbw Vale.

Glamorgan's most successful wicket-keeper in terms of dismissals is E. W. Jones (1961–83) whose career tally of 933 included 840 catches and 93 stumpings.

The skipper of Glamorgan's Championship team of 1969 was Tony Lewis, who went on to enjoy a highly successful career as a cricket commentator and broadcaster with the BBC.

The Test match in Brisbane begins in ten minutes – that's British standard time of course.
TONY LEWIS

The record for highest number of runs scored in a single season by a Glamorgan batsman is held by Hugh Morris, who in 1990 amassed 2,276 of them (average 55.51). Morris's total included 10 centuries – a club record for the number of hundreds scored by an individual player in a single season.

In 1993 Viv Richards and Adrian Dale shared an unbeaten fourth-wicket stand of 425 against Middlesex at Cardiff – a record for the county.

Playing against Viv Richards is physically and mentally soul-destroying.
GEOFF BOYCOTT

In 2000 Glamorgan scored a club record highest total of 718 for 3 declared against Sussex at Colwyn Bay. Stephen James hit 309 not out – the highest score by an individual player in the county's history.

Glamorgan staged its first Test match when England played Australia at Sophia Gardens on 8 July 2009 – the first ever home England Test match not to have been played on 'home soil'.

Most appropriately named player – E. Carless (he was), 1934–36.

The club's limited-overs team is the Glamorgan Dragons.

Worth a visit for . . . the Heritage Gallery situated within the National Cricket Centre at the SWALEC Stadium. Video footage of former Glamorgan greats such as Don Shepherd, Tony Lewis, Viv Richards and Matthew Maynard, photographs and memorabilia. In addition to charting the history of Glamorgan, displays tell of the importance of cricket in the urban and rural communities of Wales.

Gloucestershire

Gloucestershire HQ is the County Cricket Ground, Nevil Road, Bristol. It has a capacity of 8,000 but can, with temporary seating, accommodate 15,000.

Gloucestershire play the majority of their home matches at the County Cricket Ground but also at the College Ground, Cheltenham and King's School, Gloucester. Usually, matches at these two grounds coincide with festivals held at the two venues.

The club badge features a sailing ship passing a turreted coastal fortress, which is the coat of arms of the city and county of Bristol.

Gloucestershire have never won the County Championship, though they were 'Champion County' in 1874, 1876 and 1877, and also shared the title in 1873.

Gloucestershire have won the Gillette/NatWest/C&G Trophy five times, in 1973, 1999, 2000, 2003 and 2004. The club's honours also include the Benson & Hedges Cup (1977, 1999 and 2000), and they were Pro40/Sunday League winners in 2000.

A form of cricket, locally referred to as 'Stow-ball', was played in the county in Tudor times. The earliest reference to an organized event is a match between two Gloucester parishes that took place on 22 September 1729.

The club was officially formed in 1871, though it had played its inaugural first-class match the previous year, against Surrey at Durdham Down near Bristol on 3 and 4 June, when members of what was then the unofficial County Championship.

The Grace family was synonymous with the club in its early days. Dr H. M. Grace played a significant role in the formation of the club, but it was his son William Gilbert who was to become a legend of cricket. W. G.'s elder brother, Edward, also played for the county and, like his younger sibling, was also a doctor by profession. Edward Grace also served for a time as the coroner for West Gloucesterhire. Gloucestershire was also well served by another of the Grace brothers, George Frederick, who tragically died at the age of 30 from severe congestion of the lungs following a severe cold.

W. G. Grace bestrode Gloucestershire and English cricket for 40 years, and it can be claimed he elevated cricket from rural leisure pursuit to national sport. W. G.'s physical appearance during his career changed from that of a lithe, athletic young man to that of a bearded, portly gent (he appeared in his last Test for England at the age of 50). Between 1865 and 1908 W. G. scored a total of 54,896 runs (average 39.55), dwarfing the efforts of his contemporaries. His career with the bat included 26 centuries with a top score of 344 not out. He also proved himself more than useful as a bowler, taking 2,876 wickets (average 17.92). Between 1880 and 1899 he represented England in 22 Tests (13 as captain), scoring 1,089 runs (average 32.29) and taking nine wickets (average 26.22). In August 1866 he scored 224 not out – at the time the highest individual score in English cricket – for England against Surrey at the Oval but missed the second day's play to run in the first National Olympic Association meeting at Crystal Palace, where he won the 440-yard hurdle race.

In 1896 Gloucestershire fell from 'Grace' when dismissed for only 17 runs by Australia at Cheltenham.

Give us a break. In the 1890s Gloucestershire boasted a player by the name of S. A. P. Kitcat, who in 1896 at Bristol shared a ninth-wicket stand of 193 with W. G. Grace against Sussex. It remains a club record.

He'll dine out on this story. On 24 July 1900 Gilbert Jessop hit a century (104) before lunch in Gloucestershire's first innings against Yorkshire at Bradford (Park Avenue). In Gloucestershire's second innings Jessop hit another century (139) before lunch – the only player to have scored a century before lunch in both innings of a first-class match. It was said the bar would empty when Jessop came to the crease, and little wonder: he hit a century in an hour or less on no fewer than 11 occasions.

In 1906 E. G. Dennett took 10 for 40 against Essex at Bristol, which remains the best bowling figures of any Gloucestershire player.

In their early years Gloucestershire struggled as a County Championship side, but during the inter-war years enjoyed relative success, finishing runners-up in both 1930 and 1931 – to date their highest placing, which they have achieved 16 times in total. This relative success had much to do with the 'twin' spin attack of Charlie Parker and Tom Goddard.

Playing against Essex at Gloucestershire in 1925, Charlie Parker returned match figures of 17 for 56 – a club record that exists to this day.

Between 1903 and 1935 Charlie Parker took a club record 3,170 wickets at an average of 19.43.

Nowadays bowlers have bowling coaches, personal fitness coaches, physios and nutritionists to monitor diet. Charlie Parker was a great bowler and all he needed was room service.
FRED TRUEMAN

The sauce of it. In 1933 Wally Hammond made 2,860 runs – the highest number of runs scored by an individual for Gloucestershire in the course of a season.

Hammond played for Gloucestershire from 1920 to 1951 and in that time scored a club record aggregate of 33,664 runs (average 57.05), which also includes a club record 113 centuries. He topped the English first-class averages for eight successive seasons, 1933 to 1939 and 1946, a feat which has never been matched. During 1938 Hammond hit 13 centuries – again, still a club record. He is widely regarded as the best English batsman of his generation. In 84 Tests he scored 7,249 runs (average 58.45), passing Jack Hobbs's record of 5,410 in 1937. His 36 career double centuries is bettered only by Donald Bradman. Hammond's batting record for Gloucestershire could have been even greater but for the Second World War. Also for the fact that when he joined the club in 1920 the then club rules prevented him from playing regularly in the side due to the fact he was born in Kent.

In the post-war years Gloucestershire's star player was Tom Graveney (1948–60), who left the county for Worcestershire when he was controversially stripped of the captaincy. Graveney was the first post-war English cricketer to make 100 first-class centuries. In June 2004 he became the first former professional (or 'commoner', as his pal Fred Trueman gleefully described him) to become president of the MCC.

In 1962 Martin Young and Ron Nichols shared a club record partnership (for the first wicket) of 395 against Oxford University at The Parks.

Gloucestershire's most vaunted wicket-keeper is Jack Russell (1981–2004), whose career tally of 1,054 dismissals (950 catches, 104 stumpings) is a club record.

And Gloucestershire have won that game by a solitary nine runs.
FRANK BOUGH (BBC TV)

Chris Taylor made his Gloucestershire debut against Middlesex at Lord's in 2000, and scored 104 – the first player to score a century at Lord's in a Championship match on his first-class debut.

Opponents were on a wing and a prayer. In 2003 Gloucestershire created a club record score in a limited-overs game of 401 for 7 in the C&G Trophy against Buckinghamshire at Wing.

In 2004 Gloucestershire achieved their record score in first-class cricket, 695 for 9 declared, against Middlesex at Cheltenham. Craig Spearman scored 341 – a club record score for an individual player.

Also in 2004 the club changed its policy regarding the awarding of caps. Players now receive their county cap on the occasion of their first-class debut.

Most appropriately named player(s) – H. W. Game (1880s) and A. E. Dipper.

The club's limited-overs team is the Gloucestershire Gladiators.

Worth a visit for . . . If fixtures fall right in early September, the chance to see county cricket, Championship football (Bristol City) and Division One rugby union (Bristol) in the same provincial city on the same weekend.

The First Ten Grounds to Stage a Test Match

Melbourne Cricket Ground, Melbourne, Australia v. England, 15 March 1877

The Oval, England v. Australia, 6 September 1880

Sydney Cricket Ground, Sydney, Australia v. England, 17 February 1882

Old Trafford, England v. Australia, 11 July 1884

Lord's, England v. Australia, 21 July 1884

Adelaide Oval, Adelaide, Australia v. England, 12 December 1884

St George's Park, Port Elizabeth, South Africa v. England, 12 March 1889

Newlands, Cape Town, South Africa v. England, 25 March 1889

Old Wanderers Ground, Johannesburg, South Africa v. England, 2 March 1896

Trent Bridge, England v. Australia, 1 June 1899.

LORD'S

The ground is named after its founder Thomas Lord and is owned by Marylebone Cricket Club (MCC).

The oldest fixture to take place at Lord's is the annual Eton v. Harrow schools match, first played at Lord's in July 1818, 13 years after the fixture first took place on the Old Ground.

Lord's has more stands than any other English cricket ground (eight): The

Pavilion, Warner Stand, Grand Stand, Compton Stand, Edrich Stand, Mound Stand, Tavern Stand, Allen Stand and, though strictly speaking not a stand, the Investec Media Centre.

Much of Lord's was redeveloped in the late twentieth century. The Media Centre, added in 1998–99, was designed by Future Systems and won The Royal Institute of British Stirling Architects Prize in 1999.

 The new Media Centre at Lord's is a fantastic building, but there is no getting away from it, it looks like Cherie Blair's mouth.
FRED TRUEMAN

The pavilion, with its famous Long Room, was built in 1889–90 to the designs of architect Thomas Verity. It is a listed building and in 2005 was subjected to an £8 million refurbishment.

 Following the final match at Lord's in 1939 two workmen were assigned the task of placing a green beige cloth over the bust of W. G. Grace in some futile attempt to protect it from expected Luftwaffe bombs. On seeing this, one greying old member turned to another and said, 'Did you see that, sir? It's an outrage. This means war!'
NEVILLE CARDUS

One of the most famous features of Lord's is the Father Time weather vane, formerly on the north-west stand and now on the Grand Stand. It was presented to Lord's by architect Sir Herbert Baker in 1926.

The Tavern Stand now stands on the site where the old Tavern pub once stood. The Lord's Taverners were formed in 1950 by a group of actors who used to meet in the pub for a pint to raise money for young people with special needs in order that they may pursue their chosen sport. The old pub was demolished in 1968 but there is a new pub in the ground that bears the old name. The Lord's Taverners have raised over £40 million for charitable and worthy causes.

One of the most distinctive features of Lord's is the slope across the field. The north-west side of the field is some eight feet higher than the south-east, and should you stand at either of these sides, the slope can be readily seen. It causes an appreciable deviation in bounce, making it easier for bowlers from the Pavilion End to move the ball into right-handed batsmen, and to move it away when bowling from the Nursery End.

The first match to take place under floodlights at Lord's was the Pro40 match between Middlesex and Derbyshire in 2007.

Lord's is to be the venue for the archery event in the 2012 Olympic Games.

OLD TRAFFORD

Not to be confused with the football ground of the same name, Old Trafford was established in 1857 and has been the home of Manchester CC since 1856 and Lancashire since the formation of the county club in 1864.

The two famous ends of the ground were known as the Warwick Road End (to the east) and the Stretford End (to the west). The Warwick Road End is now called the Brian Statham End in honour of the great Lancashire and England bowler, and the road leading from this stand to the Metro station is now named Brian Statham Way (every time you say it you then want to sing 'absolutely pouring down with rain, what a terrible day', after 'Blackberry Way' by The Move).

In the days of steam-hauled trains, many was the time a train would slow down when passing the Warwick Road End to allow the driver and fireman a view of a match in progress. When the wind was blowing from the east, there were even instances of engines pausing at signals and spectators being engulfed with smoke.

With the elevation of Sophia Gardens in Cardiff to Test status, Old Trafford has lost its long-held 'accolade' of being the wettest Test venue in the UK.

Old Trafford was never a favourite ground of Don Bradman. He only scored a total of 81 runs in Tests there.

Old Trafford has been witness to much cricket history in the making, not least Jim Laker's 19 wickets in the 1956 Test against Australia. It was also the venue for Shane Warne's 'Ball of the Century' in 1993, which bemused, befuddled and dismissed Mike Gatting.

How anyone can spin a ball the width of Mike Gatting boggles the mind.
MARTIN JOHNSON

Old Trafford holds a rock concert at least once a year. Artistes/bands who have played there include David Bowie, Morrisey, Arctic Monkeys, Oasis, REM, Editors, Feeder, Richard Ashcroft, Razorlight, Foo Fighters, Supergrass, The Strokes, Amy Winehouse, Green Day and The Subways.

A multi-million-pound redevelopment programme is now under way which includes permanent floodlights and a new main scoreboard.

THE OVAL

The Oval was established in 1845. It is the oldest Test venue in the UK and, after the MCG, the second oldest Test venue in the world.

The Oval is owned by the Duchy of Cornwall.

The original contract to turf the Oval in 1845 cost £300. The Oval field was laid with 10,000 squares of turf taken from Tooting Common.

The Oval was the first sporting venue in the world to have floodlights, in 1889, in the form of gas lamps. It also has the largest playing area of any sports stadium in the UK.

The Oval and Bramall Lane, Sheffield, are the only two grounds to have staged both England cricket and football internationals and FA Cup Finals. The Oval has also hosted a rugby union international (England v. Scotland in 1872).

The famous gasometers are only eight years younger than the ground itself, having been erected in 1853.

The current pavilion dates from 1898.

The two famous ends are the Pavilion End and Vauxhall End. The Vauxhall End now boasts the OCS Stand, which is outstanding in every sense of the word. For all that this stand is very much 'state of the art', the Oval still manages to convey a great sense of tradition and history, not least as a result of the superb pavilion.

Between the wars the Oval experimented with having spectators watch Test matches from above the ground in a Zeppelin, but it was not commercially viable – one would think because it did not afford a close view of proceedings.

During the Second World War the Oval was designated as a prisoner of war camp, though it never housed POWs.

Philip Larkin's poem 'MCMXIV' about the First World War makes reference to the Oval.

Surrey CCC hope work will commence in 2009 on a multi-million-pound redevelopment programme which will encompass the Pavilion End and Lock, Laker and May south stands. The plan includes a hotel and a 'pedestrian plaza' (one fears the worst) on the site where the Surrey Tavern stands at the entrance to the ground.

HEADINGLEY

Headingley comprises two separate grounds with the only two-sided stand in the UK. One side of Headingley is the home of Yorkshire CCC; on the other side of the two-sided stand is the ground which is the home of Leeds Rhinos rugby league club and rugby union club Leeds Carnegie.

Originally the entire Headingley complex was owned by Leeds Cricket, Football and Athletic Company, the parent company of both rugby clubs.

It was not until 31 December 2005 that Yorkshire CCC purchased Headingley cricket ground with a loan of £9 million from Leeds City Council. In October 2006 the whole complex came under the joint management of Yorkshire CCC and Leeds Rugby.

In January 2006 a major sponsorship deal was agreed with Leeds Metropolitan University and the name of the ground became Headingley Carnegie Stadium.

Headingley was established as a cricket ground in 1890, and the first Test match took place in 1899.

The most famous end is the Kirkstall Lane End. One of the unusual past features of the ground was the 'Coconut Shy', situated behind the bowler's arm and so called because the rows of seating were so deeply set only the heads of spectators were visible.

Headingley has witnessed many an historic cricket moment. In 1902 Yorkshire dismissed Australia in their second innings for 23, George Hirst and Stanley Jackson each taking five wickets. In 1932 spinner Hedley Verity took 10 for 10 against Nottinghamshire.

In 1952 the Headingley scoreboard became the most photographed in cricket history when it displayed the India score of 0 for 4. England were captained by Len Hutton (Yorkshire), the first professional to captain England. Three of the India wickets fell to another Yorkshireman, Fred Trueman.

Having telephoned his sports desk with the news that India were 0 for 4, the cricket correspondent of the *Yorkshire Evening Post* immediately received a return call from his sports editor to say the score had been relayed the wrong way round. When the reporter insisted India were indeed 0 for 4, the sports editor received the sensational news incredulously.

The attendance for the 1952 Test between England and India was 34,000. Headingley's current capacity is 17,000, though in keeping with other major cricket venues a multi-million-pound redevelopment programme is on the table. Should it be realized it will, among other things, increase capacity to in excess of 20,000.

Arguably the most famous match Headingley has witnessed is the 1981 Test between England and Australia. England followed on 227 runs behind and at one point in their second innings were 135 for 7. They then rallied dramatically, thanks to an unbeaten 149 from Ian Botham, and on the final day Bob Willis (Warwickshire) took 8 for 43 to secure a sensational England victory, by 18 runs.

In 2000 England dismissed West Indies at Headingley for 61, Andrew Caddick (Somerset) taking four wickets in an over.

EDGBASTON

The Edgbaston site was originally a 12-acre plot of land owned by Lord Cathorne, who leased it to Warwickshire. The first match there took place in June 1886 between Warwickshire and the MCC. It ended in a draw when the MCC players left the field early to catch a train back to London.

The first Test match at Edgbaston took place in 1902.

Arguably the most recognizable (and endearing) feature of the ground is the Thwaite Memorial scoreboard, situated at the City End of the ground.

From a spectators' point of view, the Edgbaston pavilion is the most unremarkable of all the pavilions at major English cricket venues. Quite frankly, architecturally it is dull. It looks like the sort of two-tiered structure supported by 'legs' with large glass-panelled windows constructed in the 1960s at one of the less popular English seaside resorts to accommodate a café on the upper level above sheltered seating and public toilets.

All, however, may change. Plans are in place for a £20 million redevelopment.

TRENT BRIDGE

Trent Bridge is situated close to the main bridge over the River Trent and close to the football grounds of Nottingham Forest and Notts County, albeit the football grounds are on opposite sides of the river.

In the 1960s Manchester United were travelling to a match at Nottingham Forest's City Ground when their team coach pulled up in the city centre. The coach driver, on his first trip with the United team, asked a young, fresh-faced policeman for directions to the City Ground. 'It's near Trent Bridge cricket ground,' said the coach driver. The rookie constable informed the driver he did not know the location of either ground, but would ask a more seasoned officer who he was due to link up with within minutes. As the coach idled, United's Denis Law called out, asking why there was a delay. The driver informed Law of the situation, and he responded, 'A Nottingham copper who doesn't know the way to the Forest ground or Trent Bridge? No bloody wonder they never caught Robin Hood!'

The first Test match at Trent Bridge, between England and Australia, took place in 1899.

The Trent Bridge pavilion has been described as 'serene', and so it is. It is a marvellous structure still faithful to its original design and construction of 1899, one of the most renowned landmarks in English cricket.

Another striking feature is the Fox Stand, which boasts an 'aircraft wing' roof. The ground has seen considerable development over the years, and it is ongoing. The superb leisure complex which fans still refer to as the Radcliffe Road End contains the 'Bodyline' gym.

Unfortunately – and this has nothing to do with Nottinghamshire CCC – Trent Bridge is somewhat spoiled by the unsightly tower block that overlooks the ground, constructed on a plot leased to the local council in 1960 and for which some bright spark thought fit to grant planning permission. It's a multi-storey monstrosity.

OTHER VENUES

The Port Elizabeth ground is more of a circle than an oval. It is long and square.
TREVOR BAILEY

The word 'pavilion' is said to originate from an old Arabic (Saracen) word meaning 'large ornate peaked tent'.

Only two grounds have hosted home matches of two County Championship clubs: the Oval, home ground of Surrey, which also played host to Middlesex v. Nottinghamshire in 1939 as Lord's was required for the annual Eton v. Harrow match (which some may see as being indicative of priorities and preference back then); and Abbeydale Park in Sheffield, which hosted Derbyshire matches in 1946 and 1947 and a Yorkshire home match in 1976.

This ground holds about 60,000, but when there are 30,000 in, you get the feeling it is half empty.
RAVI SHASTRI

Baldon Green CC's ground in Oxfordshire is bisected by a road. When the ball is hit in the direction of the pavilion, fielders have to pause at the side of the road to check it is clear before crossing in the hope of preventing a boundary.

At the ground of Welsh club Ynysygerwyn CC there is a tree at one end almost parallel to the wicket which is painted white to act as a sightscreen.

In 1988 South Crofty Tin Mine CC of Cornwall were banned from playing at their Roskear ground by Kerrier District Council following complaints from nearby residents about the number of windows in their homes that had been broken by players hitting sixes.

In the summer of 1988 Northern Premier League football club Leek Town held a single-wicket competition for local cricketers in the centre of their Hamil Park pitch. The winner of the competition was Brian Mellor, who played cricket for Leek in the North Staffs and South Cheshire League and football in the winter for Leek Town. (As one wag asked on seeing a cricket pitch devoid of grass running right to left across the halfway line, 'Have Leek Town signed Ray Wilkins?')

In 1991 a cricket pitch was marked out at the North Pole for a match between teams from nuclear submarines HMS *Tireless* and USS *Pargo*; the pitch itself was made of rope matting. The indefatigable men of HMS *Tireless* ran out the victors, though with the crew of USS *Pargo* not being completely au fait with the Laws of Cricket it could be said the teams were poles apart.

The pitch of Epping Foresters CC is laid over a tunnel roof of the M25.

The Waiyevo ground on the Fijian island of Taveuni is bisected by the International Date Line so it would be theoretically possible for a batsman to hit the ball on a Saturday and for the ball to cross the boundary the following day. Only theoretically possible, as the International Date Line is 'rubberized': should it meet land it is diverted out to sea to avoid terra firma; once land has been bypassed it is re-diverted to resume its meridian route around the globe.

In July 2005 Kent's St Lawrence Ground at Canterbury staged three performances of *Macbeth*.

In April 2005 the Nottinghamshire club Langwith CC had to close their ground and postpone their opening matches of the season when some 200 'travellers' camped on their pitch.

In May 2005 the groundsman of South Llanelli CC was driving a tractor pulling a grass cutter and only narrowly avoided being swallowed into the earth when the ground gave way creating a hole some 24 feet deep. The hole was caused by subsidence following the collapse of an old flywheel pit of a steelworks that had shut down in 1941.

In 2005 Derbyshire resumed playing out matches at Queens Park in Chesterfield. A crowd of over 1,000 attended a Twenty20 match between Derbyshire and host club Queens Park. The ground has a wonderful 'park' setting, the only drawback being the pavilion: situated at one end of the ground behind the bowler's arm it requires an outsize sightscreen which nigh on obliterates the view.

In September 2005 Crathie CC, who play on the royal estate at Balmoral, discovered they had been playing all season on a pitch that was seven feet too long.

Ground is an ugly duckling. In October 2005 the Hampshire League ruled Swan Green CC could not be promoted as their pitch was 'too dangerous'. A spokesman for the Hampshire League told local media (and the *Daily Telegraph*) that several clubs had submitted complaints about the Swan Green ground which had a 20-foot drop from one side to the other, a bumpy outfield and five trees inside the boundary. On learning of this you can hear recreational cricketers saying, 'OK, but what, exactly, was it that they found wrong with the ground?'

On 6 September 2008 some two and a half inches (5.5cm) of rain fell on the ground of Stafford CC in little over 24 hours. The Stafford ground is called Riverway.

On 13 February 2009 the second Test between the West Indies and England at the relatively new Sir Vivian Richards Stadium in Antigua was abandoned after only 10 balls with England 7 for 0 due to an unfit outfield. The umpires and match referee Alan Hurst became concerned the West Indies bowlers might sustain an injury as they struggled to keep their footing during run-ups. The game was abandoned and rearranged as a third Test at Antigua's Recreation Ground starting the following Sunday (15 February), with the series extended to five matches.

Surrey County Cricket Club 6d.

SURREY v. YORKSHIRE

at Kennington Oval, Sat., Mon., Tues., Aug. 14th, 16th, 17th, 1965

SURREY	First Innings		Second Innings
*1 M. J. Stewart	lbw b Taylor	29	N/O 9
2 J. H. Edrich	st Binks, b Close	12	N/O
3 W. A. Smith	c Boycott, b Wilson	39	
4 K. F. Barrington	c Hampshire, b Hutton	54	
5 R. A. E. Tindall	b Hutton	15	
6 S. J. Storey	c Boycott, b Wilson	11	
7 D. Gibson	not out	60	
‡8 A. Long	c Illingworth, b Wilson	0	
10 R. Harman	c Sharpe, b Wilson	5	
9 D. A. Marriott	c Padgett, b Hutton	2	
11 D. A. D. Sydenham	b Waring	12	
	B4 , l-b2 , w , n-b3	9	B , l-b , w , n-b

Total 248 Total

Fall of the wickets 1st: 1—28 2—81 3—97 4—152 5—159 6—173 7—179 8—199 9—216 10—248
2nd: 1— 2— 3— 4— 5— 6— 7— 8— 9— 10—

Bowling Analysis 1st Ins. O. M. R. W. Wd. N.b. 2nd Ins. O. M. R. W. Wd. N.b.
Hutton 28 5 85 3 1
Waring 10 7 17 1
Close 13 4 47 1 ?
Taylor 6 3 20 1
Wilson 26 10 70 4

TEST MATCH AT THE OVAL, ENGLAND v. SOUTH AFRICA, AUG. 26th-31st, AND GILLETTE CUP FINAL AT LORD'S, 4th SEPT., 1965

Please call at the Office or write to the Secretary, S.C.C.C., S.E.11., for information concerning advance bookings.

YORKSHIRE	First Innings		Second Innings
1 G. Boycott		92	
5 K. Taylor		54	
7 P. J. Sharpe		37	
3 D. E. V. Padgett			
4 J. H. Hampshire		4	
*6 D. B. Close		30	
7 R. Illingworth			
8 R. A. Hutton			
‡9 J. G. Binks			
10 J. Waring			
11 D. Wilson			
	1 B , l-b1 , w 7 , n-b 8		B , l-b , w , n-b

Total 251 Dec Total

Fall of the wickets 1st: 1—96 2—97 3—105 4—189 5—190 6— 7— 8— 9— 10—
2nd: 1— 2— 3— 4— 5— 6— 7— 8— 9— 10—

Bowling Analysis 1st Ins. O. M. R. W. Wd. N.b. 2nd Ins. O. M. R. W. Wd. N.b.

Toss won by—YORKS.

*Captain ‡Wkt.-keeper
Umpires—A. E. Fagg & R. S. Lay
Result—
Hours of play—1st day 11.30—6.30. 2nd day 11.30—6.30. 3rd day 11.0 to 5.30 or 6.0. Lunch 1.30 all days

NEW BALL may be taken by the fielding captain after 85 overs.

SUPPORTERS' ASSOC. URGENTLY NEED AGENTS. Apply at the Office by Press Entrance

Hampshire play all their home matches at the Rose Bowl, Botley Road, West End, Southampton. The ground was newly constructed in 2001.

Hampshire's previous HQ was at the County Ground in Northlands Road, Southampton, which had been 'home' since 1885, though the club also occasionally staged matches in Basingstoke, Bournemouth and Portsmouth.

The club badge is a Tudor rose topped by a crown.

Hampshire have twice won the County Championship, in 1961 and 1973. Other notable trophy successes include the NatWest/C&G in 1991 and 2005 and the Benson & Hedges Cup in 1988 and 1992. They were also Sunday League winners in 1975, 1978 and 1986.

A Latin poem by Robert Matthew written in 1647 contains a reference to cricket being played in the county by the pupils of Winchester College. The first known reference to Hampshire dates back to 1729 when a combined Hampshire, Surrey and Sussex XI played Kent. The earliest reference to a Hampshire county representative side is dated June 1766, for a match against Sussex.

Arguably the most famous club in English cricket history is Hambledon, in Hampshire. There is a reference to Hambledon playing in 1756, though it is believed matches were played before that date. The foundation of the club is sadly lost in the mists of time.

To all intents and purposes, Hambledon was a Hampshire county club as it organized Hampshire representative matches. The Hambledon club played a number of other sports but dominated the cricket scene in the eighteenth century until the formation of the Marylebone Cricket Club (MCC) in 1787.

Representative Hampshire teams played friendly, wager and challenge matches in the late eighteenth century up to the mid nineteenth century.

Hampshire County Cricket Club was founded on 12 August 1863. The inaugural first-class match took place against Sussex at the Antelope ground, Southampton, on 7–8 July 1864.

In 1886, after some years of poor results and with the club in a dire financial state, Hampshire relinquished its first-class status, only to be awarded it again in 1895 when readmitted to what was now the official County Championship.

Not so poor after all. In 1899 R. M. Poore and E. G. Wynyard shared a sixth-wicket partnership of 411 against Somerset at Taunton – the club's record partnership.

Fry's 'irkish' delight. In the early twentieth century Hampshire boasted a true renaissance sportsman in C. B. (Charles) Fry. London born, Fry originally played for Sussex (1894–1908), and for Hampshire between 1909 and 1921. Though it is fair to say his greatest days as a cricketer were during his spell with Sussex, Fry captained England in six Tests in 1912 when with Hampshire, and has the distinction of not losing one of those matches. His opponents may have found his sporting prowess irksome, nowhere more so than on the cricket pitch, where Fry scored 30,886 runs (at an average of 50.22), a career tally which included 94 centuries. A first-class honours graduate in Classics at Oxford University, Fry failed to get elected to Parliament though he stood several times as a Liberal. His appearances for Hampshire were limited after the First World War due to his being India's representative at the League of Nations. Following his final game for Hampshire in 1921, he declined an offer to become King of Albania. In later life he captained his own naval training ship, *Mercury*, and worked as an editor for several boys' adventure magazines. One is given to think no adventure story that ever came across his desk could have matched his own.

In the 1920s the fast-medium bowling partnership of Jack Newman and Alec Kennedy formed a formidable attack. Both achieved 100 wickets in a season five times. In 1921 and 1923 they bowled through entire matches unchanged.

In 1922 Alec Kennedy took 190 wickets (average 15.6) – the highest number of wickets taken by a Hampshire bowler in a single season.

Also in 1922, while playing against Nottinghamshire at Trent Bridge, Jack Newman was sent off the field by Hampshire captain the Honourable L. H. Tennyson, 3rd Baron Tennyson, after having kicked down the stumps in frustration at being barracked by supporters. Tennyson later admonished Newman in the dressing room, and on receiving a profuse apology from his bowler replied, 'Good show,' reached into his wallet and gave Newman a pound.

He had anything but a Mare. Bowling against Somerset at Weston-super-Mare in 1927, Jack Newman returned match figures of 16 for 88 – a club record.

In a Hampshire career that spanned the years 1905 to 1936, Phil Mead scored 48,892 runs – more than any other player has ever scored for any single first-class team. Regarding centuries, his career tally includes two Hampshire records: most hundreds in a career (138) and most hundreds in a single season (12 in 1928).

Dick Moore scored 316 against Warwickshire at Bournemouth in 1937 – the highest innings by a Hampshire player. His 316 runs came in only 380 minutes and included 43 fours and three sixes. One of Moore's sixes passed through an open window of the Bournemouth pavilion, across the corridor, through an open door and landed in a cricket bag on the floor of the room opposite.

Colin Ingleby-Mackenzie, who skippered Hampshire to their first County Championship in 1961, was voted 'Best Young Cricketer and Most Promising Youngster of the Year' in 1958 by the Cricket Writers Club even though he was 25 years old at the time and already Hampshire captain.

On 22 August 1963, during the match against Northamptonshire at Southampton, Northants batsman/wicket-keeper Keith Andrew played a shot past mid-on that was fielded by a dog. The dog had run on to the pitch, picked up the ball in its mouth and proceeded to run around until collared by Hampshire players. Following a consultation, the umpires awarded Andrew four runs for the shot.

On 14 July 1964, at one point in their match against Australia Hampshire were 52 without loss. Nothing remarkable about that, except all 52 runs were scored by Michael Barnard, and all off the same bowler, Reg 'Rex' Sellars – the only known instance of this in a first-class match in England.

No Hampshire bowler has ever succeeded in taking all 10 wickets in a single innings. The club record bowling figures are 9 for 25, as returned by Bob Cottam in 1965 in a match against Lancashire at Old Trafford.

In 1965 Hampshire created a sensation by dismissing Yorkshire for 23 at Middlesbrough. The final day of the match was scheduled to be broadcast live on ITV, beginning at two p.m., but by then the match was over.

The most wickets taken by a bowler in a Hampshire career is 2,669 (average 18.23), by Derek Shackleton (1948–69). Alec Kennedy also took in excess of 2,500 wickets.

And we have just heard, although this is not the latest score from Bournemouth, that Hampshire have beaten Nottinghamshire by nine wickets.
PETER WEST (BBC TV)

In 1975 Hampshire achieved their highest score in limited-overs cricket, 371 for 4, against Glamorgan at Southampton in the Gillette Cup.

Between 1980 and 1992 wicket-keeper Bobby Parks achieved a club record 700 dismissals from behind the stumps, of which 630 were catches and 70 stumpings. Playing against Derbyshire at Portsmouth in 1981, Parks took 10 catches in the match.

In the mid-nineties Sir Ian Botham's son Liam played for Hampshire.

Liam Botham, the son of his father.

LEE HURST (on the BBC's *They Think It's All Over*)

In 2005 Hampshire created a new club record for the highest total in a single innings when they made 714 for 5 declared against Nottinghamshire at the Rose Bowl.

The first Noel. In 2005 Oasis played a live concert at the Rose Bowl.

Also in 2005, the Rose Bowl was the venue for England's first ever Twenty20 international, against Australia.

In addition to C. B. Fry and others already mentioned, Hampshire's history is peppered with great players, among them West Indians Roy Marshall, Gordon Greenidge, Malcolm Marshall and Andy Roberts; the South African Barry Richards; Aussies Shane Warne, Simon Katich and Matthew Hayden; former England stars David Gower, John Crawley, Robin Smith and Shaun Udal; and current England stalwart Kevin Pietersen.

Most appropriately named player – W. L. C. Creese.

The club's limited-overs team is the Hampshire Hawks.

Worth a visit for . . . the hog roasts held frequently throughout the season, principally at one-day and Twenty20 matches. For those who are 'veggie' (and even if you're not), the panini stuffed with peppers, various beans and salad is a meal in itself.

In keeping with all county clubs, Hampshire is forever looking at ways to generate extra income. The Rose Bowl hosts the annual 'South Coast Tool Fair' where, according to the club, you can find on display 'the largest selection of hand and power tools to be regimented under one roof in England'. Sounds well drilled to me.

When playing for the All-England XI against Hallam and Staveley at Hyde Park in Sheffield on 8 September 1858, H. H. Stephenson took three wickets with successive balls in the home team's second innings. To mark the achievement he was presented after the match with a hat – hence our term 'hat-trick'.

Fred passes the Test. The first bowler to achieve a hat-trick in a Test match was Frederick Spofforth, for Australia against England at Melbourne in 1879 (the first ever Test match).

The first England bowler to achieve a hat-trick in a Test match was Willie Bates (Yorkshire), against Australia at Melbourne in 1882–83. Bates's career was prematurely ended in tragic circumstances. During the England tour of Australia in 1887, while practising in the nets at Melbourne, a ball struck him in the face which resulted in his sight being severely impaired.

'Ow much does a bowler 'earne? The first England bowler to take a hat-trick on home soil in a Test match was Jack Hearne (Middlesex), against Australia at Headingley in 1899. To mark the achievement he was presented with a cheque for five guineas by a Yorkshire mill owner.

The only bowler to have achieved a hat-trick in both innings of a Test match is James Matthews, for Australia against South Africa in the triangular tournament at Old Trafford in 1912. Remarkably, both hat-tricks were taken on the same day and South African wicket-keeper Tommy Ward was the hat-trick victim on both occasions, thus suffering the ignominy of a king pair.

In 1998–99, Wasim Akram achieved a hat-trick in successive Tests for Pakistan against Sri Lanka, first at Lahore then at Dhaka. The only other player to have achieved two hat-tricks in Tests is Hugh Trimble of Australia, the first in 1902, the second in 1904.

The first England bowler to accomplish a hat-trick on his debut in Test cricket was Maurice Allom, against New Zealand at Christchurch on 10 January 1930. Allom took four wickets in his eighth over.

Divine intervention. On 22 June 1939, in a four-innings match between St Augustine's College and Ashford Church XI, college bowler W. Clarke achieved three hat-tricks in the first innings and two in the second.

In 1947 left-arm bowler E. F. Mellor of Perry Street CC achieved a hat-trick against Axminster. The following season Mellor changed to bowling right-arm and took a hat-trick when playing against Forton CC.

The first England bowler to register a hat-trick in a post-war Test match was Peter Loader (Surrey), against the West Indies at Headingley in 1957.

Two players can lay claim to six hat-tricks in first-class cricket, Thomas Goddard (1922–52) and Gloucestershire team-mate Charlie Parker (1903–35). Goddard was a man of formidable physique, six feet three inches tall with hands so large they were described as being like 'shovels'. Parker was recommended to Gloucestershire in 1903 by none other than W. G. Grace, who had seen him perform in local cricket. His first hat-trick came in 1922, the last in 1930, in between which, in 1924, he became the first bowler to take three hat-tricks in a season.

Albert Trott (Middlesex) is the only bowler to have achieved two hat-tricks in the same innings in a first-class county match. This unique feat happened on 22 May 1907 against Somerset at Lord's. Trott's first hat-trick actually occurred within a spell of four wickets with four consecutive deliveries; he finished with figures of 7 for 20. Trott can also lay claim to another unique feat: he is the only man to have hit a ball over the present pavilion at Lord's, when playing for the MCC against the Australians in 1899.

Only one bowler other than Albert Trott has achieved a double hat-trick in the same innings of a first-class match: J. S. Rao, for Services against Northern Punjab at Amritsar in 1963–64. Equally remarkable is the fact this was only Rao's second first-class match, and on his debut against Jammu and Kashmir at Delhi he had also struck with a hat-trick.

In addition to the aforementioned James Matthews of Australia, four players have recorded a hat-trick twice in the same match albeit not in the same innings: Alfred Shaw for Nottinghamshire against Gloucestershire at Trent Bridge in 1884; Charlie Parker for Gloucestershire against Middlesex at Bristol in 1924; 'Roly' Jenkins for Worcestershire against Surrey at Worcester in 1949; and Amin Lakhani for Combined XI v. India at Multan in 1978–79.

The most hat-tricks achieved by a bowler in the course of a first-class career is seven, by Doug Wright of Kent (1932–57). Wright achieved his hat-tricks – six for Kent and one for the MCC/England against Border during the winter tour of 1938–39 – using a distinctive style: leg-breaks and googlies bowled at medium pace.

Seemingly, for some players a hat-trick is not enough. In the process of registering a hat-trick three bowlers have taken five wickets with six balls: Bill Copson for Derbyshire against Warwickshire in 1937; W. A. Henderson for North East Transvaal against Orange Free State at Bloemfontein in 1937–38; and Pat Pocock for Surrey against Sussex at Eastbourne in 1972.

In 2005 Yasir Arafat also took five wickets in six balls and thus a hat-trick when playing for Rawalpindi against Faisalabad at Rawalpindi; but Arafat's five wickets were spread across two innings, though only interrupted by a no ball.

An Old story of so near yet so far. Yorkshire's Chris Old took four wickets with five balls without registering a hat-trick when bowling for England against Pakistan at Edgbaston in 1978. Having taken two wickets, Old's third ball was adjudged a no-ball, which he followed with another two wickets.

Made Hay while the sun shone. The first bowler to take a hat-trick on his first-class debut was H. Hay, for South Australia against Lord Hawke's XI at Adelaide in 1902–03.

Three bowlers have achieved a hat-trick on their first-class debut in English cricket: H. A. Sedgwick for Yorkshire against Worcestershire at Hull in 1906; W. E. Benskin for Leicestershire against Essex at Southend in 1906; and R. 'Bertie' Wooster for Northamptonshire against Dublin University at Northampton in 1925.

He would, would Harwood. The most recent instance of a bowler achieving a hat-trick on his first-class debut is Shane Harwood for Victoria against Tasmania at Melbourne in 2002–03.

Greswell plays well – at most sports. Somerset's William Greswell (525 wickets at 20.77) left the club in 1909 to take up a position with his family's tea and rubber estates in Ceylon but continued to play first-class cricket, and to register hat-tricks – at various sports. In addition to cricket, Greswell was a fine hockey player who represented both Somerset and the West of England. While in Ceylon he played for Colombo Hockey Club and twice scored a hat-trick. He also played for Colombo CC, took four wickets in four balls against Galle CC, and performed a hat-trick of first-class dismissals on three further occasions. Not content with this, Greswell also scored a hat-trick when captaining the Ceylon Association football team, and he won the Ceylon AAA half-mile championship in three successive years.

Dom and Daz dazzle and dominate. Former Derbyshire, Lancashire and England bowler Dominic Cork accomplished two hat-tricks during his career, as did Yorkshire, Essex and England paceman turned ballroom dancer Darren Gough. Coincidentally, for both bowlers one of their hat-tricks was achieved in a Test match: Cork's came against the West Indies at Old Trafford in 1995, and Gough got his against Australia at Sydney in 1998–99.

Hogged the limelight. In 2003–04 Matthew Hoggard achieved a hat-trick while playing for England against the West Indies at Bridgetown.

The last England player to take a hat-trick in a Test match was Ryan Sidebottom, against New Zealand in March 2008. Sidebottom's was England's 11th hat-trick of a total of 37 achieved in the history of Test cricket.

Their very own ashes. In 1886–87 at Melbourne, the Non-Smokers scored 803 against the Smokers, albeit at the fag-end of the season.

In 1896 at Edgbaston, Yorkshire scored 887 against Warwickshire – the highest total in first-class county cricket in England.

The record highest fourth-innings total in English first-class cricket was also achieved in 1896: 507 for 7 by Cambridge University against the MCC at Lord's. Cambridge won the match, so their 507 is also the highest total a team has achieved to win a match in English first-class cricket.

The highest total achieved in the fourth innings of a County Championship match is 502 for 6, by Middlesex against Nottinghamshire at Trent Bridge in 1925. Middlesex won the match, thus their 502 is also the highest target a county side has reached for victory.

The highest ever total in the fourth innings of a match is 654 for 5, by England against South Africa at Durban in 1938–39. England were set a total of 696 to win the match, so despite their Herculean effort the game ended in a draw.

The highest ever total achieved in the second innings of a match is 770, by New South Wales against South Australia in 1921.

Only one team has scored in excess of 1,000 runs in a single innings, Victoria, and they did it twice: 1,107 against New South Wales in 1926–27, and 1,059 against Tasmania, also at Melbourne, in 1922–23.

The wizards of Oz. The most runs scored in a single day's play is 721, by Australia against Essex at Southend in 1948.

The highest match aggregate in first-class cricket is 2,376 runs (Maharashtra against Bombay at Poona in 1948–49).

England's highest post-war margin of victory in a Test match was achieved at Lord's against India on 20 June 1974. England won by an innings and 285 runs.

On 7 June 1975 at Lord's, England achieved their largest margin of victory in a one-day international with their 202-run victory against India.

On 22 August 1980 at Edgbaston, England scored their highest ever total against Australia in a one-day international – 320 for 8.

In 1990 at the Oval, Lancashire scored 863 against Surrey – the highest post-war total in a single innings in the County Championship.

Taunton is the venue if you want to see runs. On three occasions totals in excess of 800 have been racked up here – more than any other county ground. In 1895 Lancashire scored 801 against Somerset; in 2007 Derbyshire scored 801 for 5 declared against their hosts; also in 2007 Somerset scored 850 for 7 declared against Middlesex.

Apart from the above-mentioned (Yorkshire, Lancashire, Derbyshire and Somerset), a score in excess of 800 runs in a single innings has occurred on only three other occasions in the history of the County Championship: Surrey, 810 for 4 declared v. Somerset at the Oval, 1899; Kent, 803 for 4 declared v. Essex at Brentwood, 1934; Warwickshire, 810 for 4 declared v. Durham at Edgbaston, 1994.

The highest total in a single innings in Test cricket is 952 for 6 declared, by Sri Lanka against India at Colombo in 1997.

On 21 June 2005 England scored their highest ever total in a one-day international – 391 for 4 (50 overs), against Bangladesh at Trent Bridge.

England's highest total on home soil in a Twenty20 international is 193 for 7, against the West Indies at the Oval on 28 June 2007.

England's highest total in a Twenty20 international is 200 for 6, against India at Durban on 19 September 2007.

Five days earlier, on 14 September 2007 at Johannesburg, Sri Lanka achieved the largest ever margin of victory by runs in a Twenty20 international, defeating Kenya by 172 runs.

Top Ten Highest Innings Totals in First-class Cricket

1,107	Victoria against New South Wales at Melbourne, 1926–27
1,059	Victoria against Tasmania at Melbourne, 1922–23
952 for 6 dec.	Sri Lanka against India at Colombo, 1997–98
951 for 7 dec.	Sind against Baluchistan at Karachi, 1973–74
944 for 6 dec.	Hyderabad against Andhra Pradesh at Hyderabad, 1993–94
918	New South Wales against South Australia at Sydney, 1900–01
912 for 8 dec.	Holkar against Mysore at Indore, 1945–46
912 for 6 dec.	Tamil Nadu against Goa at Panjim, 1988–89
910 for 6 dec.	Railways against Dera Ismail Khan at Lahore, 1964–65
903 for 7 dec.	England against Australia at the Oval, 1938

Top Ten Highest Number of Runs in English First-class Career

	County	Career	Runs	Matches	Innings
Jack Hobbs	Surrey	1905–34	61,760	834	1,325
Frank Woolley	Kent	1906–38	58,959	978	1,530
Patsy Hendren	Middlesex	1907–37	57,611	833	1,300
Phillip Mead	Hants	1905–36	55,061	814	1,340
W. G. Grace	Gloucs	1865–1908	54,211	870	1,478
Herbert Sutcliffe	Yorkshire	1919–45	50,670	754	1,098
Wally Hammond	Gloucs	1920–51	50,551	634	1,005
Geoff Boycott	Yorkshire	1962–86	48,426	609	1,014
Tom Graveney	Gloucs/Worcs	1948–72	47,793	732	1,223
Graham Gooch	Essex	1973–2000	44,846	581	990

Top Ten Highest Individual Scores in First-class Innings

501 not out	Brian Lara, for Warwickshire v. Durham at Edgbaston, 1994
499	Hanif Mohammad, for Karachi v. Bahawalpur at Karachi, 1958–59
452 not out	Don Bradman, for New South Wales v. Queensland at Sydney, 1929–30
443 not out	B. B. Nimbalkar, for Maharashtra v. Kathiawar at Poona, 1948–49
437	Bill Ponsford, for Victoria v. Queensland at Melbourne, 1927–28
429	Bill Ponsford, for Victoria v. Tasmania at Melbourne, 1922–23
428	Aftab Baloch, for Sind v. Baluchistan at Karachi, 1973–74
424	Archie MacLaren, for Lancashire v. Somerset at Taunton, 1895
405 not out	Graeme Hick, for Worcestershire v. Somerset at Taunton, 1988
400 not out	Brian Lara, for West Indies v. England at Antigua, 2003–04

Brian Lara features three times in the top twenty highest innings in first-class cricket with scores of 501 (not out), 400 (not out) and 375. He also holds the record of the highest number of fours scored by a batsman in a single innings – 72, for Warwickshire against Durham at Edgbaston in 1994. In the same match he set the record for the highest number of runs scored by an individual batsman in a single day's play in the County Championship – 390 (undefeated).

 When Lara is in this sort of form and scoring runs, he really connects with the ball with that bat of his.
TONY GREIG

 I don't suppose I can call you a lucky bleeder when you've got 375.
ANGUS FRASER (to Lara at Antigua in 1994)

The highest average achieved by a batsman in the course of a County Championship season is 103.54 (2,278 runs), by Mark Ramprakash (Surrey) in 2006.

The highest first-class ground is the Wanderers Ground (Johannesburg) at 6,004 feet above sea level. Gymkhana CC in Nairobi, the foremost ground in Kenya, is 5,501 feet above sea level. The Western Province Ground in South Africa is 5,010 feet above sea level. And, yes, the altitude does affect the way the ball moves through the air, which is thinner.

The highest ground in England is Cartworth Moor CC (near Huddersfield) which is 1,014 feet above sea level.

The highest altitude at which County Championship cricket has been played is 1,005 feet above sea level, when Derbyshire played matches at Buxton.

The International Cricket Council (ICC) is the governing body of world cricket.

It was founded in June 1909 as the Imperial Cricket Conference, the founder members being Australia, England and South Africa. Originally membership was restricted to governing bodies of cricket within the British Empire, where Test cricket was played.

The headquarters of the Imperial Cricket Conference was at Lord's. The offices were situated in the 'Clock Tower' building at the Nursery End.

In 1926 India, New Zealand and the West Indies were elected as full members.

Pakistan was elected as a full member in 1952 following the formation of the country in 1947.

In 1961 South Africa resigned from the ICC due to its government's policy of apartheid, but continued to play Test cricket until 1968, when an ICC ban was imposed following England's refusal to play a Test series in what was known as the 'D'Oliveira Affair'. South Africa's subsequent applications to rejoin were rejected.

In 1965 the name was changed to the International Cricket Conference as the word 'Imperial' had connotations not in keeping with the times. New rules were instituted to allow cricket-playing nations from outside the Commonwealth to become associate members. Associate members were allowed one vote on resolutions while full members were entitled to two votes.

In 1981 Sri Lanka was elected as a full member.

In 1989 the word 'Conference' was replaced by 'Council' to reflect the egalitarian and democratic nature of the organization, and the fact it was cricket's ruling body. The name remains the International Cricket Council.

In 1991 South Africa was re-elected as a full member following internal political changes in the country and an end to apartheid.

In 1992 Zimbabwe was elected as a full member, and in 2000 Bangladesh gained full membership, becoming the 10th Test-playing nation.

In 1993 the ICC ceased to be administered by the MCC and became a self-administering body.

In 2000, amid concerns relating to illegal bookmaking, the ICC set up an Anti-Corruption and Security Unit under the leadership of the former Commissioner of the Metropolitan Police Lord Condon. Among the cases on which the ACSU has reported are those involving former South African captain Hansie Cronje, and former India captain Mohammad Azharuddin and Ajay Jadeja.

In 2001 the ICC established an office in Monaco. This was done purely for financial reasons as the commercial appeal of cricket was now so great the avoidance of excessive tax liability on income generated became desirable.

The downside to the Monaco office was the ICC administrators were still based at Lord's. An appeal was made to the British government to allow the ICC to be given special dispensation from having to pay UK corporation tax on commercial income generated worldwide. The British government refused this request. As a result of this the ICC explored other options for headquarters where the host nation would be more flexible. The United Arab Emirates informed the ICC it would welcome the establishment of the ICC's headquarters in the country and would offer exemptions regarding taxable income on commercial revenue. The ICC's Executive Board voted 11–1 in favour of moving to Dubai, and offices were established in the city in August 2005. A secondary reason for the move was the desire to globally centralize the ICC headquarters and for it to be closer to the emerging centres of cricket power in South Asia.

The ICC does not benefit financially from revenue generated by Test matches, ODIs and Twenty20 internationals; such income is shared by the member nations. In the main the ICC's commercial income comes in the form of sponsorship and media broadcasting rights for the World Cup. The current deal has run from 2007, will continue until 2015, and is worth US$1.6 billion.

To supplement its income the ICC has instigated several tournaments such as 'The Super Series' and the 'Champions Trophy', with varying degrees of success. The upside to such tournaments is they do generate income in the form of sponsorship and broadcasting rights; the downside is many players feel such tournaments are an intrusion on an already overburdened fixture programme, and many cricket supporters simply don't see them as possessing gravitas or importance.

Part of the function of the ICC is to appoint all umpires and referees qualified to officiate in official Test matches, and to impose the ICC Code of Conduct, which lays down professional standards of behaviour and decorum for international cricket. It also monitors playing conditions and reviews aspects of play such as bowling.

In 2008 the ICC opened its Global Cricket Academy (GCA) at Dubai Sports City in Dubai. The academy's director of coaching is Rodney Marsh (Australia). The facilities include 20 turf pitches, outdoor and indoor synthetic practice areas, gymnasiums and indoor pitches with hawkeye technology.

The current chairman is David Morgan (formerly chairman of the ECB). In 2010 he will be succeeded by Sharad Pawar of India.

The ICC has 104 member countries: 10 full members that play official Test cricket, 34 associate members and 60 affiliate members.

The ICC also has five regional bodies whose remit is to organize, promote and develop cricket in their respective part of the world. The five regional bodies are the Asian Cricket Council, European Cricket Council, African Cricket Association, Americas Cricket Association and East Asia-Pacific Cricket Council.

 I have travelled the world and been to most countries. I've walked in countless parks in dozens of major cities throughout the world, but have yet to see a statue to a committee.
STANLEY MATTHEWS

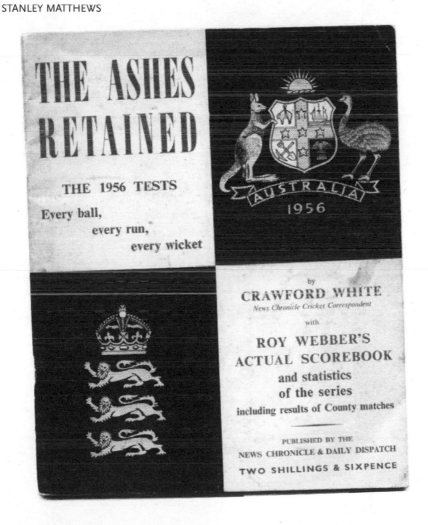

46

Cricket is the national sport in India. As is the case with most cricketing nations, the sport was introduced to the country by the British. The earliest reference to a game is a match between sailors of the East India Trading Company ship *Cambay* in 1721.

The first club formed was Calcutta CC, dating from around 1792, though its membership was restricted to 'Europeans' – and by that we can assume British.

In 1848 the Parsee community in Bombay (now Mumbai) formed the Oriental Cricket Club – the first club formed by Indians.

In 1854 Calcutta CC was the first club outside Britain to publish a cricket book, of scores, entitled *Calcutta Cricket Club Matches 1844–54*. Presumably for what publishers nowadays would term 'a niche market'.

In the 1870s Oriental CC began playing matches against clubs comprising Europeans.

The first tour of India by an English team – an all-amateur side which included G. F. Vernon (Middlesex) and Lord Hawke (Yorkshire) – took place in 1888–89. One of the teams they played was the Oriental Club of Bombay which inflicted on the Englishmen their only defeat.

At the turn of the twentieth century clubs from the Parsee, Hindu, Muslim and European communities of Bombay regularly played against one another. By 1912 they were playing an annual quadrangular tournament.

In the early twentieth century top Indian players such as Kumar Shri Ranjitsinhji and K. S. Duleepsinhji left for Britain and played for the England team. These two players lent their names to the Ranji and Duleep trophies, two of the major domestic tournaments in India. The Ranji Trophy was introduced in 1934–35 to commemorate K. S. Ranjitsinhji (Cambridge University, Sussex and England), who had died the previous year. The winners of the inaugural competition were Bombay. Since 1946 the competition has been India's premier championship.

In 1911 an India team embarked upon its first official tour of England but only played county teams.

In 1926 India was invited to join what was then called the Imperial Cricket Council.

In 1928 India established its first centralized administrative body – the Board of Control for Cricket in India.

India toured England in 1932 and played their first Test (only three days, 25–28 June) against England at Lord's. They lost by 158 runs. The India team was captained by C. K. Nayudu who was also a noted singer.

The first knight to play against England, and in a Test match, was Sir Gajapatairaj Vijaya Ananda for India in the Old Trafford Test in July 1936. Known to team-mates and opponents as 'Vizzy', he received his knighthood between the first and second Tests that year. The only other player to have received a knighthood while still playing first-class cricket is New Zealand's Sir Richard Hadlee.

India continued to improve as a Test nation throughout the 1930s and 1940s but still awaited their first international victory.

In 1948 India played a Test series for the first time as an independent nation, against Australia (Don Bradman's 'Invincibles'). India lost the five-match series 4–0.

In March 1948, in a Ranjit Trophy match between Holkar and Mysore, in scoring 912 for 8 declared Holkar set a world record for the most individual centuries in a single innings – six. The sextet of centurions were B. B. Nimbalkar (172), M. M. Jagdale (164), K. V. Bhandarkar (142), C. K. Nayudu (101), C. T. Sarwate (101) and R. Pratap Singh (100).

1948 proved a very good year with the bat for B. B. Nimbalkar. In December, playing for Maharashtra against Kathiawar at Poona, he scored 443 not out – the highest individual innings in Indian first-class cricket. Nimbalkar is the only batsman to have scored 400 in a first-class innings and never be selected for a Test match.

In 1952 India recorded their first Test victory against England, in Madras. Later in 1952 India won their first Test series, against Pakistan.

The 1960s saw India develop as a Test team. They proved very difficult to beat at home. In the sixties India won two series at home against New Zealand and drew with Australia, England and Pakistan.

In June 1967, in the Edgbaston Test, 'Budhi' Kunderan, normally a wicket-keeper, opened India's batting and bowling against England. His figures were 4–0–13–0. Nothing disgraceful there, but he was not called upon to bowl again during the tour.

Come the 1970s India had a formidable Test team that included two of the world's greatest batsmen, Sunil Gavaskar and Gundappa Viswanath, an outstanding spin quartet in Bishen Bedi, E. A. S. Prasanna, Bhagwat Chandrasekhar and Srinivas Venkataraghavan, and a superb wicket-keeper in Farokh Engineer.

In 1971 India enjoyed back-to-back series wins in England and the West Indies.

In 1976, in the third Test against the West Indies at Port of Spain, India were set a total of 403 and, in the teeth of some hostile bowling, won the match.

Later, in November 1976, India scored 524 for 9 declared against New Zealand with not one India player scoring a century. Mohinder Amarnath top-scored with 70, and all 11 India batsmen reached double figures.

In the 1980s a new generation of great India players made their mark, including Mohammad Azharuddin, Dilip Vengsarkar, Kapil Dev and Ravi Shastri.

In 1983 India won the Cricket World Cup for the first time, defeating favourites West Indies in the final.

In the 1990s Sachin Tendulkar, Anil Kumble and Javagal Srinath emerged as world-class players, yet in that decade India did not win any of its 33 Tests outside the subcontinent, and won only 17 of its 30 Tests at home. India also flattered to deceive in World Cups, being eliminated at home by Sri Lanka in 1996 and failing to reach the semi-finals in 1999.

Andhra second and bad at Secunderabad. In January 1994 Hyderabad scored a total of 944 for 6 declared against Andhra in the Ranji Trophy at Secunderabad – the fifth highest total in all first-class cricket.

In 2000 former India captain Mohammad Azharuddin and fellow batsman Ajay Jadeja were the subject of a match-fixing investigation. The case was found to be proved and Azharuddin was given a life ban and Jadeja was banned for five years.

Later in 2000, India appointed its first foreign coach, John Wright (New Zealand).

During the series against Australia in 2001, in the Kolkata Test, India became only the third team in the history of Test cricket to win a Test match after being asked to follow on.

In December 2006 India played and won their first Twenty20 international. Their opponents were South Africa.

In the 2007 World Cup India suffered a shock result, losing to Bangladesh. Poor performances saw the team fail to reach the Super 8. In contrast, later in 2007, India won the first ever Twenty20 World Cup held in South Africa.

In March 2008, during the first Test against South Africa, India created Test cricket history by becoming the first team to record two 200-plus run partnerships for the first and second wickets in a single innings. Virender Sehwag and Wasim Jaffer shared a first-wicket partnership of 213, then

Sehwag was joined by Rahul Dravid and the pair shared a second-innings partnership of 255.

In October 2008 Gautam Gambhir and V. V. S. Laxman both scored double centuries against Australia.

Sachin Tendulkar is India's most capped player, and leading run scorer and century maker in both Tests and ODIs. In October 2008 he became the first player to score 12,000 runs in Test matches.

Eden Gardens in Kolkata has the largest capacity of any cricket ground in the world. In 2007 the capacity was set at 105,000.

In 2007 India and world cricket was rocked by the formation of the India Cricket League (ICL), a 'private' league running parallel to the existing league administered by the Board of Cricket Control in India (BCCI). The 'breakaway' league was instigated by Zee Telefilms and promoted by Subhash Chandra, who had previously failed in bids for the broadcasting rights to major tournaments (e.g. 2003 World Cup). The formation of the ICL caused a rumpus, and several players were banned by their respective boards of control. The league was funded by a partnership of investors and each of the teams has a financial 'mentor'. The ICL commenced in November 2007 with six teams. Matches of Twenty20 format were played at Panchkula near Chandigarh and drew huge crowds and TV audiences. The prize for the winning team was a million US dollars. A fourth edition of ICL matches took place in October 2008.

The ICL has been overshadowed by the Indian Premier League (IPL), a Twenty20 competition created by the BCCI. Eight franchised teams formed the inaugural IPL in 2008. The winners were Rajasthan Royals who defeated Chennai SuperKings in the final in Mumbai.

The second season of the IPL took place in South Africa in the summer of 2009 as a result of the Indian government stating it could not guarantee the security of players or spectators due to Indian security forces being stretched in their policing of the Indian general elections.

Plans are afoot for the IPL to be expanded on a year-on-year basis so that by 2012–13 it will involve 12 as opposed to eight teams.

The IPL is the richest cricket competition in the world. In 2008 the IPL sold global broadcasting rights to Sony and the Singapore-based World Sports Group in a deal worth $1,026 billion over 10 years.

47

Cricket was introduced to Ireland in the early 1800s. Numerous clubs were formed between 1830 and 1860, many of which are still in existence.

In 1855 an Ireland national team played the Gentlemen of England in Dublin. Three years later an Irish national team played the MCC.

The development of the game was retarded by two factors in the 1880s: the outbreak of land wars when landlords and tenants became alienated, and the Gaelic Athletic Association's ban on the playing of 'foreign' games. If a player played a 'foreign' game such as cricket he would be banned from playing Irish games such as hurling and Gaelic football. The ban, which was not lifted until 1970, did not result in players not playing cricket in Ireland, but for many years it restricted the number of participants.

In 1902 Ireland toured England for the first time. The team played four first-class matches, winning one and losing one with two ending in a draw. After such a promising tour Ireland did not play another first-class match for five years.

In 1908 South Africa and Yorkshire visited Ireland.

In 1928 in Dublin, Ireland defeated the West Indies by 60 runs.

Ireland played annual matches against Scotland on a home and away basis throughout the twentieth century, only interrupted by the two world wars.

At Sion Mills in County Tyrone in 1969, Ireland defeated the West Indies by nine wickets after bowling them out for 25. Among the players in that West Indies team were Clive Lloyd and Clyde Walcott (who came out of retirement to play).

Due to political difficulties, it was not until 1993 that the Irish Cricket Council was elected to the ICC.

In 1994 Ireland competed in the ICC Trophy for the first time but only won three of their seven allotted matches.

In 1997 Ireland reached the semi-finals of the ICC Trophy, losing to Kenya by seven runs. The Ireland team included Leicestershire's Justin Benson.

Ed Joyce (Middlesex) had a batting average of 71.80 in the 2001 ICC Trophy in Canada. His performances with the bat belied what was a poor performance by Ireland in the tournament which saw them defeated by the USA, Canada and Denmark.

In 2005 the Republic of Ireland and Northern Ireland hosted the ICC Trophy. Ireland reached the final but lost to Scotland by 47 runs. The tournament, however, was a tremendous success, matches on both sides of the border enjoying healthy attendances.

Courtesy of being runners-up in the 2005 ICC Trophy, Ireland qualified for the 2007 World Cup.

On 13 June 2006 Ireland played their first official one-day international in Belfast. The opponents were England – the first time Ireland had played the full England side. The match was a 7,500 sell-out. England reached 301 for 7, Ireland replied with 263 for 9 from their allotted 50 overs. Andre Botha top-scored for Ireland with 52.

In August 2006 Ireland recorded their first official ODI victory, defeating Scotland by 85 runs.

In February 2007 Ireland scored 308 against Canada in an ODI in Nairobi, Kenya.

Later that month, on 11 February, Ireland scored 531 for 5 declared against United Arab Emirates in an ICC Intercontinental Cup match at Abu Dhabi – Ireland's highest total in first-class cricket.

2007 was the first time Ireland had participated in the World Cup. They tied with Zimbabwe and in their second match (played on St Patrick's Day) defeated Pakistan by three wickets, thus knocking the fourth-ranked team in the world out of the tournament. Ireland qualified for the Super 8 stage, where they lost to England, South Africa, New Zealand, Sri Lanka and West Indies but enjoyed victory over Bangladesh. The Ireland team received a heroes' welcome in Dublin on returning from the World Cup.

In March 2008 Ireland toured Bangladesh and in July of that year played a tri-series against New Zealand and Scotland in Aberdeen but lost both matches. Compensation came just weeks later when Ireland won their third European Championship title, winning every game, including a seven-wicket victory over Scotland.

In the past Ireland competed in the Benson & Hedges Cup, and currently in the Friends Provident Trophy. Since there is no nationality restriction in county cricket, non-Irish players have competed for Ireland in these matches. South African Hanse Cronje has, for example, represented Ireland in the B&H Cup.

In 2008 Ireland defeated Warwickshire by four wickets in the FP Trophy (Midland Division).

In 2009 Peter Connell took 5 for 19 as Ireland dismissed Worcestershire for 58 – their lowest score in one-day cricket.

Kent's home is the St Lawrence Ground, Canterbury. The present capacity is 15,000, but this will increase if plans for development come to fruition. Kent also play some home matches at Beckenham (The County Cricket Ground) and Tunbridge Wells (Nevill Ground).

The traditional club badge is a rearing white horse on a red background. Somewhat alarmingly, a new badge has emerged which would appear to be the work of some design company. This takes the form of a circle of condensed blue on which is written 'Kent County Cricket Club' in white letters. The words are stacked and the 'K' of Kent enlarged and perpendicular so that it falls to the length of the other words. A line drawing of a cricketer is embossed on the large K. Something that looks rather like a roll of camera film but is probably the seam of a cricket ball runs from the K to the outer circle, but only on the left side of the badge. It looks a mess.

The most famous feature of the St Lawrence Ground is, alas, no more. It was one of only three senior cricket grounds in the world to have a mature tree within the playing area, the other two being the Pietermaritzburg Oval in South Africa and the Amstelveen in Amsterdam, Holland. The original tree at the St Lawrence Ground was a lime, estimated to have been 290 years old. Only four players are known to have cleared it with a scoring shot in first class matches: Arthur Watson (Sussex) in 1925, Learie Constantine (West Indies) in 1928, Jim Smith

(Middlesex) in 1939 and Carl Hooper (Kent) in 1992. In the 1990s the Canterbury lime was diagnosed as having heartwood fungus. It was reduced from 120 feet in height to 90 feet to encourage growth but to little avail. On 7 January 2005 the tree split in two, leaving a seven-foot stump. In 1999 a new tree had been planted by the cricket writer E. W. Swanton, but outside the playing area. On 8 March 2005 the club moved the tree to the original site within the boundary, where it remains. It is currently only some seven feet in height, but growing.

 It's typical of English cricket. A tree gets in the way for 200 years and when it falls down, instead of cheering they plant a new one.
DAVID GILBERT

Kent has won the County Championship on six occasions – 1906, 1909, 1910, 1913, 1970 and 1978 – and were joint winners of the title in 1977. Other honours include the Gillette Cup in 1967 and 1974; the Benson & Hedges Cup in 1973, 1976 and 1978; winners of the Sunday/Pro40 League in 1972, 1973, 1976, 1995 and 2001; and Twenty20 Cup winners in 2007.

Along with Sussex, it can be said Kent is where cricket really started. History books refer to a form of cricket being played on the Weald in Saxon times. The earliest reference to an organized game dates back to 1610 and a match between teams from the Downs and the Weald. Cricket became an established sport during the seventeenth century with games regularly being played between neighbouring villages. The earliest record of a county match is Kent v. Surrey in 1709.

In the eighteenth century a Kent representative side often played an All-England team. In the latter half of the century Kent, possibly along with Surrey, was the only county to realistically challenge the famous Hambledon Cricket Club.

In 1837 Kent was proclaimed 'Champion County of England', a status they enjoyed for a decade and more.

On 6 August 1842 Kent County Cricket Club was officially formed. The inaugural match of the new club took place on 25–27 August against All-England at the White Hart Ground in Bromley. In March 1859 the club was reconstructed and reorganized to create the present Kent CCC.

Prior to the First World War the club enjoyed unprecedented success in the County Championship – four titles in eight seasons. The captain was the wonderfully named Cloudesley Marsham, who succeeded Cuthbert Burnup. (You simply don't get names like those in cricket any more.)

In 1907 Colin Blythe set a club record by taking 10 for 30 against Northamptonshire at Northampton. He recorded match figures of 17 for 48 – also a club record.

Colin Blythe and Frank Woolley, both left-arm spinners, bowled unchanged throughout both innings in Kent's victory over Yorkshire at Maidstone in 1910.

In 1913, at Tunbridge Wells, Kent dismissed Warwickshire for only 16 – the lowest score by first-class opposition against the county.

Also in 1913 the Tunbridge Wells pavilion was burned down by suffragettes who objected to the non-admittance policy towards women, a situation inflamed by a Kent official who reportedly said, 'It is not true that women are banned from the pavilion. Who do you think makes the teas?'

To this day Frank Woolley (1906–38) holds no fewer than seven club records: most runs in a season – 2,894 (average 59.06) in 1928; most runs in a Kent career – 47,868 (average 41.77); most centuries in a single season – 10 in 1928 and 1934; most centuries for Kent – 122; most catches – 773; the highest fifth-wicket stand, with Les Ames – 277, against New Zealand at Canterbury in 1931; and the highest last-wicket partnership, with A. Fielder – 235, against Worcestershire at Stourbridge in 1909. Woolley's career total of 773 catches is also a record for English first-class cricket.

Frank Woolley? He has more records than our local radio station.
FRED TRUEMAN

In 1934 Kent achieved what remains the club's highest score – 803 for 4 declared, against Essex at Brentwood. W. H. Ashdown top-scored with 332 – a club record highest score by an individual batsman. Les Ames scored 202 not out and Frank Woolley 172. The attendance for the first day of play was 3,121 and Kent scored 623 runs on that first day. It is not known what the admission price was, but whatever it was, it was value for money.

Over the years Kent has gained a reputation for producing top-class wicket-keepers, most notably Les Ames, Godfrey Evans, Alan Knott and current furniture minder Geraint Jones.

 Alan Knott is small, pokey, alert as a cat, as alive to possibilities of misadventure as a boy playing French cricket on a bumpy lawn.
JOHN THICKNESSE (cricket writer/broadcaster)

One of Kent's greatest players – and characters – was former skipper Colin Cowdrey. Born into a cricket-mad family, he was purposely named Michael Colin so that he would bear the initials M. C. C. Such was his cricket prowess, particularly as a batsman, he was a regular in the Tonbridge team at the age of 13 and was the youngest schoolboy ever to play in a match at Lord's. Following four years at (and playing for) Oxford University he was immediately selected by England for the 1954–55 winter tour of Australia. Over the next 20 years he surpassed the records of Wally Hammond for the most runs (7,624) and catches (120) for England in Test cricket. Between 1950 and 1976 Cowdrey scored 42,719 runs in first-class cricket (average 42.89) including 107 centuries, and took 638 catches. He was an all-round sportsman. In 1952 he was runner-up in the All-England rackets championship, was awarded a blue at Oxford for tennis, also played golf for Oxford, and occasionally rugby union too. His second wife was the racehorse trainer Lady Herries of Terregles, and his sons Chris and Graham also served Kent with distinction, the former following his dad and becoming captain of England (albeit for just one Test, v. West Indies in 1988). He was awarded the CBE in 1972 and knighted for services to cricket in 1992. He was president of the MCC in 1986–87 and chairman of the ICC for several years until 1993.

Mike Denness (1959–80) captained Kent and became the first Scotsman (born Bellshill, Lanarkshire) to captain England. He was England vice-captain for the winter tour of India in 1972–73 when the captain was a Welshman – Tony Lewis.

No piece on Kent would be complete without mention of Derek Underwood (1963–87), a medium-pace left-arm spinner of mercurial powers. He should have been selected more often than he was for England but it was an age when pace bowling dominated the international scene. In 86 Tests he took 297 wickets at 25.83. His record for Kent is equally impressive: 2,465 wickets at 20.23.

In 1995 Graham Cowdrey and Aravinda de Silva (Sri Lanka) shared a fourth-wicket stand of 368 against Derbyshire at Maidstone – a club record partnership.

On 4 August 2007 Kent won the Twenty20 Cup for the first time, defeating Gloucestershire in a thrilling final. Requiring 147 for victory, Kent needed to score 13 off the last over and did so with three balls to spare. The final was also notable for a hat-trick by Ryan McLaren.

When they were relegated to Division Two in 2008, Kent relinquished their proud record of being the only county never to have played anything but top-flight County Championship cricket.

Most appropriately named player – A. Fielder.

Most county teams adopt alliteration when naming their limited-overs team. Not so Kent, whose team is the Kent Spitfires, after the fighter plane which in the early years of the Second World War fought many a dogfight over the county.

Worth a visit for . . . the chance for you and your mates to form a team, arrange opposition and play a one-day match on the hallowed turf of the St Lawrence Ground. Prices start at £2,500 (share it among yourselves). You'll have use of the dressing rooms and the players' dining room and the club provides everything from scorers, scoreboard operators and umpires to catering. Contact the club's commercial department or chief executive Paul Millmann.

In May 1988 wicket-keeper Steve Marsh went to the aid of team-mate Graham Cowdrey who was having problems with his contact lenses. Cowdrey handed the lenses to Marsh who, to keep them moist, placed them on his tongue – only then to swallow them.

No cricketer who has played for Kenya has ever sported a moustache.

Kenya's first international was in December 1951 against Tanzania in Nairobi.

In 1958 Kenya played a touring side captained by Basil D'Oliveira.

Kenya, Tanzania and Uganda combined to form East Africa, which became an associate member of the ICC in 1966.

In 1967 India became the first Test team to visit Kenya. A three-day match took place in August which ended in a draw.

In 1972 Kenya toured England for the first time. Two years later the MCC played East Africa in Nairobi, as part of East Africa's preparations for the 1975 World Cup. East Africa was one of the two non-Test teams invited to participate in the tournament.

In the 1975 World Cup Kenya were drawn in the same group as England, India and New Zealand but lost all three matches. While in England they also played matches against Somerset, Glamorgan and Wales, and a match against Sri Lanka at Taunton.

In 1981 Kenya broke ranks from the East Africa team and joined the ICC in their own right.

In 1994 the ICC Trophy was hosted in Nairobi. Kenya were beaten in the final by the United Arab Emirates. Kenya's performance in the ICC Trophy brought qualification for the World Cup.

In 1996 Kenya caused one of the biggest upsets in the history of the World Cup when they dismissed the West Indies for just 93 and won by 73 runs. Kenya also acquitted themselves well against Australia, India and Sri Lanka. As a result of these performances they were granted full one-day international status by the ICC.

In October 1997 Kenya achieved their highest ever total in ODIs – 347 for 3, against Bangladesh in Nairobi.

In 1998 England 'A' toured Kenya for the first time. A three-day match was drawn and the only one-day game that was not abandoned due to rain was won by England 'A'.

On 18 May 1999 Kenya scored their highest total against England – 203, at Canterbury.

In 2000 Kenya won the ICC Emerging Nations Tournament in Zimbabwe which involved the host nation, Ireland, Scotland, Denmark and Holland.

In 2002 Kenya toured Sri Lanka. Though they lost all three first-class matches, they caused another major upset by winning the one-day series 2–1.

The 2003 World Cup proved memorable for Kenya. Though the tournament was held in South Africa, Kenya were designated to play Sri Lanka and New Zealand in Kenya. Kenya lost to hosts South Africa but then beat Canada in Cape Town. New Zealand forfeited their match, due to take place in Nairobi, due to safety concerns, but Sri Lanka did visit and were beaten by 53 runs. Kenya became the first non-Test-playing nation to progress beyond the first round of a World Cup and thus qualify for the Super 6 stage.

Since 2003 Kenyan cricket has suffered a series of setbacks and the international team has not reproduced the form, or results, of previous years.

In August 2004 one of Kenya's top players, Maurice Odumbe, was banned when found guilty of match-fixing. Later in 2004 Kenyan cricket suffered when many leading players went on strike. By the end of the dispute Kenyan cricket had no sponsors, the domestic game was in financial straits, and the governing body of Kenyan cricket had stepped down. International cricket virtually ceased.

In 2005, with new administrators in place and the players' dispute resolved, Kenya began the rebuilding process. They reached the final of the 2005 ICC Inter-Continental Cup, but were beaten by Ireland.

In 2006 the Kenya Cricket Association was disbanded and replaced by a new governing body, Kenya Cricket.

On 29 January 2007 Kenya beat Bermuda by 10 wickets – their first and so far only 10-wicket victory.

In 2007 Kenya won a triangular tournament against Scotland and Canada in Mombasa. Kenya achieved their biggest victory margin in a one-day international when they defeated Scotland by 190 runs.

Later in 2007 Kenya participated in what was their fourth World Cup. They beat Canada but lost to England and New Zealand.

Kenya's captain is Steve Tikolo, who is also their highest scorer in ODIs with more than 3,000 runs to his name.

Nairobi and Mombasa are the two principal venues for cricket in the country. While Nairobi boasts ten grounds, Mombasa has only one first-class venue, and its capacity is just 1,000. One of the Nairobi venues, often used for ODIs, was funded by the Aga Khan, and the stadium bears his name.

The ODI between Kenya and Bermuda on 11 November 2006 was the first to be staged at the Mombasa Sports Club, a ground which boasts a large mango tree inside the boundary.

Lancashire's HQ is Old Trafford, Manchester. The current capacity is 19,000. Lancashire also plays at least one match a year at Blackpool (Stanley Park) and Liverpool (Aigburth).

The club has been based at Old Trafford since its formation in 1864 and has played host to England matches since 1884. Plans are afoot for a £30 million redevelopment of the ground.

Lancashire has won the County Championship seven times – in 1897, 1904, 1926, 1927, 1928, 1930 and 1934 – and were also joint champions in 1950. Other successes include Gillette Cup/NatWest Trophy winners on a record seven occasions (1970, 1971, 1972, 1975, 1990, 1996 and 1998); Benson & Hedges Cup winners a record four times (1984, 1990, 1995 and 1996); and Sunday/Pro40 League winners a record-equalling five times (1969, 1970, 1988, 1998 and 1999).

The *Manchester Journal* of 1 September 1781 carries a report of a game held in late August between two local teams from Brinnington Moor – the earliest known reference to cricket in the county.

Manchester Cricket Club was formed in 1816 and assumed representative status for the county at cricket. On 23–25 July 1849 Manchester played a match against

Sheffield at Hyde Park, Sheffield, though handbills referred to this game as 'Yorkshire v. Lancashire' – to all intents and purposes the first 'Roses match'.

In 1857 Manchester CC moved to a site at Old Trafford, the actual ground of which was privately owned. It was here that Lancashire CCC was founded in 1864.

Lancashire's inaugural match took place in 1865 against Middlesex for whom Vyell Walker took all 10 Lancashire wickets in their second innings, but the home team marked their debut with a 62-run victory.

In the late 1860s and early 1870s the Lancashire team was primarily amateur, which led to problems in terms of fulfilling fixtures, as gentlemen players often refused to travel to away games.

Two of the first professionals to play for the county were Alex Watson and Dick Barlow, whose batting was immortalized in Francis Thompson's poem 'At Lord's'.

In 1870 W. Hickton took 10 for 46 against Hampshire at Old Trafford – to this day the best figures by a Lancashire bowler in a single innings.

In the late nineteenth century Lancashire drew healthy crowds to games at Old Trafford. An aggregate crowd (over three days) of 28,212 watched their match against Gloucestershire in 1878. These were heady days for the club. In 1879 Lancashire were joint champions of the 'unofficial' County Championship with Nottinghamshire, though, curiously, *Wisden* refused to acknowledge this and awarded the title solely to Nottinghamshire. Not to be fazed by this, Lancashire became undisputed champions of the 'unofficial' title the following year (1880) but had to make do with being joint champions again in 1881 – coincidentally, again with Nottinghamshire.

In 1885 George Kemp – later to be the Most Honourable 1st Baron of all Rochdale (somehow the stately kudos of that title just falls away) – scored Lancashire's first century in a Roses match.

In 1895 Archie MacLaren scored 424 against Somerset at Taunton – the highest score by an individual player in the history of the club.

In 1898 Lancashire bought Old Trafford and some adjoining land from the owners, the de Trafford family, for the sum of £24,732.

Johnny Tyldesley scored 2,633 runs in 1901, which remains a club record total for a batsman in a single season.

In 1902 the club changed its rules, stipulating that the club's amateur and professional players should take to the field together for games.

In 1913 Harry Dean returned match figures of 17 for 91 against Yorkshire at Liverpool, which also remains a club record.

During the First World War the Old Trafford pavilion was used as a hospital for injured soldiers returning from the Western Front.

In 1921 the club boasted 4,500 members, and over a quarter of a million spectators watched Lancashire's home games that summer.

In 1924 Lancashire dismissed Glamorgan for just 22 at Liverpool – the lowest total inflicted upon first-class opposition.

Make mine a Big Mac. In 1925 Ted McDonald took 198 wickets (average 18.55) in a single season. No Lancashire bowler has ever surpassed this feat.

Hallows be thy name. In 1928 Charlie Hallows scored the existing club record of 11 centuries.

Also in 1928 Ernest Tyldesley and Frank Watson shared a second-wicket stand of 371 against Surrey at Old Trafford – the highest partnership in the history of the club. In a Lancashire career spanning over a quarter of a century (1909–36), Tyldesley scored a total of 34,222 runs – a club record. He also holds the record for the most centuries scored in the course of a Lancashire career – 90.

By Eck. In 1930 Peter Eckersley skippered Lancashire to the County Championship through a season during which the team remained unbeaten.

In 1934, the last occasion on which Lancashire won the County Championship outright, Len Hopwood performed the double of 1,000 runs and 100 wickets. He told the *Manchester Guardian*, 'Luck was with me. This will be a once-in-a-lifetime experience for me, but I shall always have it to look back on.' The following season he did it again.

In 1947 Ken Cranston was appointed captain – a choice that surprised many as Cranston had never played a first-class match of any kind. Cranston was skipper for two seasons and under him Lancashire finished third and fifth respectively in the County Championship. Not a bad choice after all.

In August 1948 Cyril Washbrook's benefit match at Old Trafford attracted, in total, 50,010 spectators. He received the sum of £14,000. Washbrook was appointed captain in 1954 – the first professional to captain Lancashire.

In 1954 Ken Grieves, Geoff Pullar and Alan Wharton all scored in excess of 2,000 runs.

All cut and dried. In 1960, under the captaincy of Bob Barber, three Lancashire bowlers – Tom Greenhough, Ken Higgs and Brian Statham – all took in excess of 100 wickets.

On 23 August 1960 Lancashire's Peter Marner scored 44 against Nottinghamshire at Southport, but he never had to run for his runs: they all came from boundaries.

 Roses matches are very much a private war of attrition. I remember an MCC official once attending a Roses match at Old Trafford. His indiscriminating applause began to annoy the Lancashire members around him. Eventually one jumped up and said, 'Hey you! Keep outta this. This has nowt to do with you.'
FRED TRUEMAN

When Brian Statham retired in 1968 from a Lancashire career that began in 1950 he had taken 1,816 wickets – a current club record.

Jack Bond was appointed captain in 1968, a position he held until 1972. In that time Lancashire won five one-day trophies. The players key to this success were Farokh Engineer (India), Frank 'Purple' Hayes, David Hughes,

Clive Lloyd (West Indies), David Lloyd, Harry Pilling, Jack Simmons, Ken Shuttleworth and Barry Wood. Following his retirement from cricket, Bond took over a pub in Whalley Bridge, the walls of which were adorned with photographs of Lancashire games and personal trophies won. He kept a good pint too.

And Clive Lloyd casually hits him high and away over mid-wicket for four, a stroke of a man knocking a thistle top with a walking stick.

JOHN ARLOTT (*TMS*)

All credit to the Lancashire batting, they've made this semi-final a little bit wide open again.

PETER WEST (BBC TV)

Roses rivalries were often taken to different counties when players moved clubs. In the mid-seventies Yorkshire were playing Leicestershire at Bradford, and included in the Leicestershire team was Ken Higgs, not a native of Lancashire but a bowler who had served the county well for many years. Higgs and Yorkshire's Geoff Boycott engaged in a war of words which, as the game progressed, became more heated, eventually degenerating into a tirade of insults that would have made Bernard Manning blush. Umpire Don Oslear, in his first season on the county circuit, spoke to Leicestershire skipper Ray Illingworth (himself a veteran of many a Roses match when with Yorkshire). Oslear made it clear to Illingworth that the insults directed at Boycott by Higgs must stop. At the end of Higgs's over, Illingworth walked over to the other umpire, Cec Pepper, and said, 'Cec, do me a favour. Ask your mate over there not to interfere in private Roses battles.'

And the Lancashire fieldsmen are scattered in the wilderness like missionaries.

JOHN ARLOTT

In 1990 Lancashire became the first county to win both the NatWest Trophy and Benson & Hedges Cup in the same season, a feat the club repeated in 1996.

In 2001 skipper Mike Atherton (who also captained England) announced his retirement. Lancashire Supporters Club asked its members for ideas for a suitable gesture as a send-off, and one supporter suggested spooning two ounces of soil into his trouser pocket.

In 2003 Mark Chilton, Carl Hooper, Stuart Law and Malachy Loye all scored in excess of 1,000 runs.

Lancashire's most vaunted current player is Andrew Flintoff, though in keeping with all England contracted players his appearances for his county side are very limited.

It appears the premature excitement about Andrew Flintoff playing for Lancashire on Wednesday may have been a little premature.
BBC RADIO LANCASHIRE

Lancashire's chief executive is Jim Cumbes, who in addition to keeping wicket for Worcestershire was also a top-notch goalkeeper with Aston Villa.

Lancashire is at the forefront in terms of commercial activities which have brought in much-needed finance. The club has its own TV station. Supporters can take advantage of travel offers to away games, wallpapers for PCs and mobile phones, and an E-card which sends via email news of the club and its activities. The club is big on attracting young supporters who can gain entry to many top matches, including County Championship and Pro40 games, for only a pound (Kids for a Quid).

Most appropriately named player – Geoff Pullar.

The club's limited-overs team is the Lancashire Lightnings.

Worth a visit for . . . the Lancashire CCC museum at Old Trafford which charts the history of cricket in general as well as the club and contains fascinating photographs, memorabilia, artefacts and historical documents. Worth combining with a visit to the Manchester United museum at Old Trafford some 15 minutes' walk away.

 If Cyril Washbrook was alive today he'd be turning in his grave.
E. W. SWANTON (cricket writer and broadcaster)

51

IAN BOTHAM (following a ball that struck Allan Border on the toe): Can you walk?
BORDER: I think so.
BOTHAM: Then get back to the pavilion, you're lbw.

Leg Before Wicket is Law 36 of the Laws of Cricket. It was devised in 1774.

The law states a batsman may be given out if a bowler delivers a ball, not being a
no-ball, and . . .

The ball, if it is not intercepted full pitch, pitches in line between wicket and
wicket or on the off side of the striker's wicket and . . .

The ball not having previously touched his bat, the striker intercepts the ball,
either full pitch or after pitching, with any part of his person, and . . .

The point of impact, even if above the level of the bails, either is between
wicket and wicket, or . . .

Is either between wicket and wicket or outside the line of the off-stump, if the
striker has made no genuine attempt to play the ball with his bat, and . . .

But for the interception, the ball would have hit the wicket.

The law also encompasses 'Interception of the ball' and 'Off side of wicket'.
And to think some not au fait with cricket have trouble understanding this.

W. G. Grace enjoyed some mighty scores but some were courtesy of the fact
he sometimes disputed an umpire's decision and no one had the courage to

stand up to him. During one London County match at Crystal Palace, umpire Joe Filliston gave Grace out lbw. 'Nonsense!' barked Grace, and remained at the crease. He was notorious for not accepting decisions from umpires, or appeals from bowlers, on one occasion telling a bowler who had appealed for lbw, 'Not out! People have come to see me bat, not see you bowl!'

Grace was once fielding in a match for Gloucestershire when the last ball of the day struck the batsman's pads. Nobody appealed for lbw. During the evening the batsman told Grace how lucky he was that there had been no appeal, because he was sure he was out. The following morning, before the first ball was bowled, Grace shouted, 'How's that!' The batsman was given out lbw from the last ball of the previous day's play. Present laws prevent this happening today.

Yorkshire's Horace Fisher was the first bowler to register a hat-trick of lbw victims. Playing against Somerset at Sheffield's Bramall Lane on 17 August 1932, Fisher dismissed Mitchell-Innes and Andrews lbw then trapped Walter Luckes in similar fashion, prompting umpire Alec Skelding to raise his eyes, and one finger, to the heavens and say, 'As God's my judge, that's out too – and, I believe, some sort of record.'

 It used to be very difficult for a bowler to get a decision from an umpire when on tour in Australia. I once had Peter Burge L.B.W. when he was on single figures but the umpire didn't give the decision. Burge went on to make fifty or so when he got an edge. I appealed, as did the England players. We were all convinced he'd connected but the same umpire simply shook his head. Burge was in the seventies when I was absolutely certain I had him L.B.W, only for the umpire to again give not out. It was unbelievable, I was almost spitting blood I was so angry. Burge went on to make a ton, not long after I bowled him a pig of a yorker which ripped out two stumps sending the middle one cartwheeling across the pitch. I turned to the umpire and said, 'I nearly had him then!'
FRED TRUEMAN

Had his appeal. In the late 1940s Hylton Colliery Welfare CC (Durham) had a player by the name of L. B. W. Forten. A player always guaranteed to get into double figures.

Gloucestershire's Mike Procter is the only bowler to have achieved a hat-trick twice in English first-class cricket with all three wickets being lbw decisions, against Essex at Westcliff-on-Sea in 1972 and against Yorkshire at Cheltenham in 1979.

The League cricketers I played with and against took their cricket very seriously. I played against Crewe who had a bowler called Denis Cox. Having had several appeals for lbw turned down, at the end of our innings his cricket bag came through the dressing room window, followed by the tray containing the sandwiches, a sponge cake and a dressing room bench. It was a good job the Crewe chairman was a glazier.
SIR GARY SOBERS

The highest number of batsmen to be given out lbw in a one-day international is six. On 6 January 2007 at Auckland, New Zealand had six players lbw when making a total of 73 against Sri Lanka. Needless to say the Kiwis lost that one.

The highest number of players given out lbw in a single innings when playing for England is also six, in the ODI against Australia at Headingley on 18 June 1975.

The highest number of wickets taken lbw by a single bowler in Test matches is 155, by India's A. Kumble (1990–2008).

The highest number of wickets taken lbw by an England bowler in Test matches is 81, achieved by Ian Botham (1977–92).

Leicestershire's home is the County Ground, Grace Road in Leicester, commonly referred to simply as Grace Road.

The club has also played home matches at Aylestone Road in Leicester, Ashby-de-la-Zouch, Coalville, Hinckley, Loughborough and Melton Mowbray, as well as in neighbouring Rutland at Oakham and Uppingham.

The Leicestershire badge features a golden fox on a green background.

Leicestershire has won the County Championship on three occasions – 1975, 1996 and 1998. Other trophy successes include the Benson & Hedges Cup three times (1972, 1975 and 1985), the Sunday League twice (1974 and 1977) and the Twenty20 Cup twice (2004 and 2006).

The earliest known reference to cricket in the county appears in the *Leicester Journal* of 17 August 1776 (a match between two parishes). If this is the first instance of organized cricket in the county, the game appears to have reached Leicestershire rather late in comparison with other counties.

It is thought the Leicestershire and Rutland Cricket Club was formed around 1780. Certainly from 1781 the club was playing prestigious matches against the likes of the Marylebone Cricket Club, Sheffield and Nottingham.

Leicestershire County Cricket Club was formed on 25 March 1879.

Leicestershire's inaugural first-class match took place on 14–16 May 1894, against Essex. The following year the County Championship was officially reorganized and launched as a 14-team competition. Leicestershire were admitted along with Essex, Derbyshire, Hampshire and Warwickshire.

In 1899 Fred Geeson made the same score, 32, in three consecutive innings, first against Derbyshire and then in both innings in Leicestershire's following match against Warwickshire. Geeson may well have scored only 32, but it is the highest score to be made three innings in a row in English first-class cricket.

In 1906 Leicestershire scored 701 for 4 declared against Worcestershire at Worcester – the highest total in the history of the club.

In 1912 Leicestershire were dismissed for 25 by Kent at Grace Road – the lowest total made by the club in first-class cricket.

In 1929 George Geary took 10 for 18 against Glamorgan at Pontypridd. Geary ended with match figures of 16 for 96 – the best ever bowling figures in the history of the club.

Les Berry scored 2,446 runs (average 52.04) in 1937. Berry's Leicestershire career spanned the years 1924 to 1951, during which time he scored a total of 30,143 runs (average 30.32) including 45 centuries. All three feats are current club records.

In 1937 Berry scored seven centuries – a club record he shares with Willie Watson (1959) and Brian Davidson (1982).

Australian Jack Walsh took a club record 170 wickets (average 18.96) in 1948.

It is fair to say that for the first 70 or so years of their existence as a first-class county Leicestershire wandered up and down the middle and lower reaches of the County Championship table like a dog that had lost the scent. This was perhaps best summed up by Charles Palmer, the club's captain/secretary for most of the 1950s, who said, 'For the best part of the [twentieth] century, Leicestershire were a side those counties with championship aspirations had to beat . . . and often did.'

It was under Palmer's captaincy that Leicestershire enjoyed a fleeting renaissance, finishing third in the County Championship in 1953.

Leicestershire also enjoyed a comparatively golden period in the late 1950s. The cornerstones of the team then were Willie Watson, recruited from Yorkshire; local product Maurice Hallam, who proved himself to be a prodigious opening bat not only for the club but also for England; seamers Brian Boshier, John Cotton, Jack van Geloven and Terry Spencer; and spinner John Savage.

Willie Watson was the 'golden boy' of Leicestershire cricket in the late 1950s. A stylish left-hand batsman and fine outfielder, he moved from Yorkshire to captain Leicestershire and proved an inspirational skipper. From 1939 until his retirement in 1964 he scored 25,670 first-class runs (average 39.86), to which can be added 879 runs in 23 Tests for England (average 25.85). He was also a professional footballer of some note, happy at right-half, inside-right or outside-right, and a dual international, winning four caps for England.

 Following Yorkshire's home game against Leicestershire in 1957, I was having a pint with Leicester captain Charlie Palmer. Charlie told me he was retiring at the end of the season and asked if I knew anyone who might be interested in captaining Leicestershire the following season. I was 37 at the time and sensed Yorkshire were about to release me, so told him I might be interested. A couple of months later I agreed terms. Palmer told me Leicestershire were offering me a five-year contract. I nearly fell off my chair. In all my years with Yorkshire I'd never had a contract; I was paid if selected to play. Maurice Tompkin had died and Australian Jack Walsh, like Charlie, had retired, and I was asked what I was going to do about signing some batsmen. It suddenly occurred to me, I was in charge. As outgoing captain I asked Charlie if he had any advice for me. 'Yes,' he

said. 'Always be positive in your dealings with the players, the committee and the Leicestershire supporters. Be positive out there on the pitch, and when you haven't the faintest idea what to do next, just look positive.'
WILLIE WATSON

Two great captains of Leicestershire in the 1960s and 1970s were Tony Lock (Surrey, Western Australia and England) and, later, Ray Illingworth, who joined from Yorkshire. Lock skippered Leicestershire to a then unprecedented (for the county) runners-up spot in the County Championship, and Illingworth guided the club to its first title, in 1975.

You couldn't really have two more contrasting personalities than Tony Lock and Ray Illingworth. Lock was the consummate cricket professional, whereas Illingworth was the complete professional cricketer.
PETER WEST (BBC TV)

And you join us at Grace Road at a very appropriate time. Ray Illingworth has just relieved himself at the Pavilion End.
BRIAN JOHNSTON

Ivan D'Oliveira, brother of Basil (Worcestershire and England), played one season for Leicestershire (1967).

DON MOSEY: And then there were brothers Basil D'Oliveira and Ivan, erm . . . Ivan, um, erm—
FRED TRUEMAN: D'Oliveira?
MOSEY: Yes, correct, Fred.
TRUEMAN: Thought it might be.
TEST MATCH SPECIAL (BBC RADIO)

In 1971 Glamorgan were dismissed for 24 at Grace Road – the lowest score by a county side against Leicestershire. Also in 1971 Oxford University were dismissed for the same total at The Parks.

Roger Tolchard is Leicestershire's most successful wicket-keeper in terms of dismissals. Between 1965 and 1983 there were 903 of them (794 catches and 109 stumpings).

Arguably the most celebrated of all Leicestershire players is David Gower, a sublime left-hand batsman whose laid-back style was widely admired. He made his first-class debut for Leicestershire in 1975 and remained with the county until 1989. He was county captain from 1984 to 1986. In a playing career that lasted until 1993 he scored 26,339 first-class runs (average 40.09), and 8,231 (average 44.25) in 117 Tests for England, to which can be added 3,170 runs (average 30.77) in 114 ODIs. When Gower made his 100th Test appearance for England in 1988 he was four years younger than anyone else who had achieved that feat. He was awarded the OBE for services to cricket in 1992, and later became a regular panellist on the BBC's *They Think It's All Over*.

In 1996 Leicestershire scored 406 for 5 against Berkshire in the NatWest Trophy at Grace Road – the club's highest score in limited-overs cricket.

In 2003 Darren Maddy and Brad Hodge shared a club record stand of 436 (unbroken) for the third wicket, against Loughborough UCCE at Grace Road. The club record partnership against county opposition is 390 (for the first wicket), by John Steele and Barry Dudleston against Derbyshire at Grace Road in 1979.

In 2006 Hylton Ackerman hit 309 not out against Glamorgan at Cardiff – the highest individual innings by a Leicestershire player.

Leicestershire do not have the support or financial resources enjoyed by other counties, and the club now depends on developing its own young players. Part of current club policy is based on a report compiled by chairman Neil Davidson: 'An Evidence-Based Approach to the Identification and Development of England Test Cricketers in the County Championship'. Laudable in intent, the very title is too stuffy and elongated, akin to an academic paper – enough to put anyone off reading it. A far better title would have been a simple 'The Future of Leicestershire Cricket'. For all that the document may be a blueprint for the future, the fact the title of the report was accepted by the club may well offer a clue as to why Leicestershire endure rather than enlighten.

Most appropriately named player – George Ball (1933–36).

The club's limited-overs team is the Leicestershire Foxes.

Worth a visit for . . . a drink in the Foxes Bar, whose walls are adorned with fascinating photographs of past matches and players. The Charles Palmer suite also houses an excellent museum with an extensive collection of memorabilia; the content often changes in relation to which county is visiting. Locals should really give Grace Road a try. It's a good day out at one of the most convivial clubs on the county circuit.

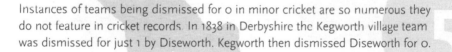

Instances of teams being dismissed for 0 in minor cricket are so numerous they do not feature in cricket records. In 1838 in Derbyshire the Kegworth village team was dismissed for just 1 by Diseworth. Kegworth then dismissed Diseworth for 0.

In 1872 the MCC were 7 for 0 against Surrey at Lord's, then collapsed to 8 for 9. Their last-wicket pair doubled their score to 16 all out.

The 'honour' of having the lowest total in English first-class cricket is shared by Oxford University and Northamptonshire. In 1877 Oxford were dismissed for 12 by the MCC, though they did bat one man short; Northamptonshire went for the same total against Gloucestershire at Gloucester in 1907 – the lowest total ever made in a County Championship match and the lowest by a team in which all 11 players batted (well, sort of).

In addition to Oxford University and Northamptonshire, seven other sides have been dismissed for 15 runs or fewer: Auckland (13), against Canterbury at Auckland in 1877–78; Nottinghamshire (13), against Yorkshire at Trent Bridge in 1901; Surrey (14), against Essex at Chelmsford in 1983; MCC (15), against Surrey at Lord's in 1839; Victoria (15), against MCC/England at Melbourne in 1903–04; Northamptonshire (15), against Yorkshire at Northampton in 1908; and Hampshire (15), against Warwickshire at Edgbaston in 1922.

In first-class cricket a team has been dismissed for less than 20 on 27 occasions.

The lowest match aggregate by two teams in a completed first-class match is 105 runs, in the match between the MCC and Australia at Lord's in 1878. The MCC made 33 and 19, and Australia 41 and 12 for 1. Proceedings began at 12.03 p.m. and it was all over at 6.20 p.m.

England's lowest total in a Test match is 45, in their first innings against Australia at Sydney on 28 January 1887.

In September 1888 Mullindillingong were dismissed for 10 in their first innings against Mummery, who in reply were dismissed for 0. Mullindillingong were then dismissed for 0 in their second innings, but sensationally again dismissed Mummery for 0. This is thought to be the only instance of a team being dismissed for 0 in both innings of a 'full' cricket match.

The lowest aggregate score by a team in the County Championship is 42, by Northamptonshire, who were dismissed for 27 and 15 by Yorkshire at Northampton in May 1908, though Northants batted with just 10 players as one withdrew through illness. In cricketing parlance, 'it was a good one to miss'.

The shortest completed innings in English first-class cricket in terms of balls bowled is 53, received by Hampshire when making 15 all out against Warwickshire at Edgbaston in 1922. Hampshire were asked to follow on and, incredibly, ended up winning the match.

The lowest match aggregate since 1900 is 157 (for a total of 22 wickets), in the match between Surrey and Worcestershire at the Oval in 1954.

The lowest aggregate in a completed Test match is 234 runs (29 wickets) – Australia v. New Zealand at Melbourne in 1931–32.

The lowest total in a Test match is 26, by New Zealand against England at Auckland on 28 March 1955.

In 1956–57, in a single day's play at Karachi, Australia scored a total of 80, followed by Pakistan making 15 for 2 before stumps were pulled for the day. Their combined total of 95 runs is the lowest number of runs scored in first-class cricket in an uninterrupted day's play.

The lowest match aggregate score by one team in first-class cricket is 34. In 1959–60 Border were dismissed for 16 and 18 by Natal at East London.

The lowest number of runs scored in a full day's play in a County Championship match is 134, by Glamorgan (134 for 3) against Hampshire at Portsmouth on 5 June 1964.

The lowest number of runs scored in a full day's play in a Test match in England is 151 – England v. New Zealand at Lord's in 1978. England began the third day on 175 for 2 and were all out for 289. In reply New Zealand were 37 for 7 when stumps were drawn.

The lowest post-war total in the County Championship is 14, by Surrey against Essex at Chelmsford in 1983.

On 25 March 1994 England scored their lowest post-war total in a Test match, 46, in their fourth innings against the West Indies at Port of Spain.

The shortest post-war completed innings in terms of balls bowled is 84, received by Lancashire when scoring 53 all out against Glamorgan at Liverpool in 1997.

England's lowest total in a one-day international is 86 (32.4 overs), against Australia at Old Trafford on 14 June 2001.

England has failed to make 100 runs on five occasions in ODIs: 86 v. Australia at Old Trafford (2001); 88 v. Sri Lanka at Dambulla (2003); 89 v. New Zealand at Wellington (2002); 93 v. Australia at Headingley (1975); and 94 v. Australia at Melbourne (1979).

On 15 March 2009 England achieved their lowest total in a Twenty20 international – 121, against West Indies at Port of Spain.

54

MCC stands for Marylebone Cricket Club, arguably the most famous cricket club in the world.

It is a private members club founded in 1787. The MCC headquarters is at Lord's.

The MCC was formerly the governing body of cricket in England (and across the world), until these powers were handed over to the ICC and ECB in 1993. The MCC, however, remains the framer and copyright holder of the Laws of Cricket. While just about every other sport has rules, cricket has laws.

The origins of the MCC are to be found in those of an even older club, The Nobleman's and Gentleman's Club, formed in the early eighteenth century. For many years the club was based at the Star and Garter on Pall Mall, which was essentially a social and gambling club but had sporting connections to the original London Cricket Club and the Jockey Club. The first known Laws of Cricket were issued in 1744 after a meeting at the Star and Garter.

What level of gambling went on at the Star and Garter? In 1751 it is written that £20,000 in bets was taken on the outcome of the cricket match between Old Etonians and an England team.

Members of The Nobleman's and Gentleman's Club formed the White Conduit Club for cricket in the early 1780s and played matches at White Conduit Fields in Islington. Members were dissatisfied with this site as, curiously, they considered it 'too public'.

Thomas Lord, a Yorkshireman, was a professional bowler for the White Conduit Club. Members gave him the task of finding a new, 'more private' ground and guaranteed him against any financial losses. In 1787 Lord found a suitable site in Dorset Fields (now Dorset Square), and the members renamed their club the Mary-le-bone Club. Today there is a blue plaque in Dorset Square to commemorate the site of Thomas Lord's original ground and the founding of the MCC.

The first 'great match' to be staged on Dorset Fields took place on 31 May and 1 June 1787 between Middlesex and Essex and resulted in a win for Middlesex.

In 1788 the members revised the Laws of Cricket and gradually took responsibility for the game throughout England. In essence, members were self-appointed governors and administrators of cricket in England but no other club possessed the will or wherewithal to object. Among the laws laid down were the various ways a batsman could be given out, and that the pitch should be one chain (22 yards) in length.

When the lease ran out on the Dorset Fields site in 1810, Lord was forced to move his ground to a field at North Bank Regent's Park on the St John's Wood estate. Three years later Parliament decided the Regent's Canal would pass through Lord's cricket field and Lord was given the task of finding yet another ground. (We know pros undertake all manner of tasks at a club, but, surely to goodness . . .)

In 1814 the club moved home for what proved to be the last time, to what we now know as Lord's in St John's Wood. Members were reported to be 'satisfied in the extreme' with the new site. Given this was the third ground he'd had to find, probably not as much as Thomas Lord.

The nobility were keen to see their cricketing sons play in the best possible surroundings, so a number of dukes and earls hired the ground for a match between Eton and Harrow Schools. This annual fixture between the schools is still played at Lord's.

On 22 June 1814, a year before the Battle of Waterloo, the inaugural match took place at the new ground. The MCC defeated Hertfordshire. (Given the aforementioned historical fact, somewhat appropriately one of the roads adjacent to Lord's is Wellington Road.)

In 1825 Thomas Lord (then 70) retired and sold the ground to William Ward, a director of the Bank of England. Lord died in 1832.

In 1827 the Lord's Pavilion, which housed all documents, scorecards, records and trophies, was destroyed by fire. Forty years of cricket history, moreover documentary evidence of the origins of organized cricket, literally up in smoke.

The club colours are world famous, often referred to as 'egg and bacon', sometimes as 'mustard and tomato' or 'rhubarb and custard'. The striped blazer in club colours makes Lawrence Llewellyn-Bowen appear a dowdy dresser.

Originally the club colours were sky blue but they changed between 1866 and 1867 to red and yellow. No one knows for sure why this decision was taken, but what about this? It was also during 1866–67 that William Nicholson loaned the club £18,333 6s 8d to purchase the freehold of the ground. Nicholson had made his fortune from distilling gin, and Nicholson's gin company colours were red and yellow. I leave the rest to you . . .

In 1868 a team of Aboriginal cricketers played at Lord's – the first Australian team ever to tour England. The team was promoted and captained by Charles Lawrence who had been a member of the first English team to visit Australia in 1861–62.

The Aboriginal team had an exhausting tour schedule of 47 matches and also gave exhibitions of athletics as well as native skills. Their team included Tiger Bonnibangeet, Mosquito Gronggarrong, Twopenny Murrumgunarriman and Dick-a-Dick Jungunjinnanuke.

Having assumed and been conceded lawmaking powers in its earliest days as a club, in the nineteenth century MCC members had no equal in terms of social status, patronage of the game and kudos in cricket. The club enjoyed unrivalled prestige as cricket's sole authority. In the 1870s the MCC even drew up the first rules of tennis.

The MCC wanted a greater involvement with county cricket, and in 1877 invited Middlesex to adopt Lord's as their home ground.

In 1887, the centenary year of the MCC, the club purchased the adjoining site of Henderson's Nursery Gardens. The site became the club's practice ground – hence 'The Nursery' and the 'Nursery End' at Lord's.

In 1889 the foundation stone was laid for a new pavilion, 'the grandest in all the world'. The cost of the new (present) pavilion was met by a £21,000 loan from William Nicholson. (Should such a thing happen today, the person making the loan would probably want the pavilion named after him.)

In 1890 the Lord's pavilion was opened for the new season. It had been completed to budget and on time. (Those were the days – prestigious buildings completed to budget and on time . . .)

In 1890 A. S. Worty painted a portrait of W. G. Grace. It was hung in the club boardroom where it remains to this day.

In 1903 the MCC assumed responsibility for the administration, organization and selection of all overseas tours. Until 1977–78 all England touring teams played under the banner of the MCC, with the exception of Test matches. Hence we read references to the '1970–71 MCC tour of Australia' – a term never used by the majority of cricket fans at the time for whom all tour matches were England matches.

 The refreshment department showed a profit of £463 15s 9d. In consequence of this satisfactory position it is proposed to make certain reductions in charges.
MARYLEBONE CRICKET CLUB REPORT, 1908

The MCC celebrated the centenary of the ground on its present site in 1914. One member is reported to have said, 'This will be the most important event of the year in England. What could possibly occur in 1914 to eclipse the Centenary of Lord's?'

In the 1920s the waiting list for membership to the MCC was 30 years, though it was rumoured certain individuals of import and standing in society at the time could be 'fast-tracked'.

The W. G. Grace Memorial Gates were erected in St John's Wood Road in 1923. The architect was Sir Herbert Baker.

In 1925–26 the second Grand Stand was built and the Father Time weather vane was presented to the MCC by Sir Herbert Baker.

In 1937 the MCC celebrated its 150th anniversary.

HRH The Duke of Edinburgh became president of the MCC in 1949, and 26 retired professional cricketers who had represented England were made honorary cricket members.

In 1953 HRH The Duke of Edinburgh opened the MCC Memorial Gallery to the memory of 'All cricketers of all nations, religion and creed' who lost their lives in the two world wars.

In 1967 the new Tavern was opened. The following year the 'New Stand' was erected on the site of the old Tavern.

In 1968 the Board of Control of Test Matches, Advisory County Cricket Committee and the Imperial Cricket Conference, which had been set up to cater for the growth of domestic and international cricket, were disbanded. In 1969 the first meeting took place of the Cricket Council, which comprised the MCC and the newly formed Test and County Cricket Board (TCCB) under the newly constituted Cricket Council.

The MCC Indoor Cricket School was opened in 1977 by Sir George 'Gubby' Allen.

FRED TRUEMAN: With all due respect, for what were you awarded your knighthood?
SIR GEORGE 'GUBBY' ALLEN: For services to the game of cricket, and for being among England's better fast bowlers.
TRUEMAN: Well, again with due respect, I too have given many years of service to the game of cricket. As for being just 'among' some of England's better fast bowlers, there you have me.

In 1985 the MCC opened the new MCC Library.

The bicentenary of the MCC was celebrated in 1987 with a match between the MCC and a Rest of the World XI. The Bicentenary Gates were presented by the Duke of Westminster in memory of Viscount Cobham, and the new Mound Stand was opened by HRH The Duke of Edinburgh.

In 1991 the MCC opened the Compton and Edrich Stands.

The ICC became independent of the MCC in July 1993. The ICC appointed its own administration but remained at Lord's into the new millennium, when it moved its headquarters to that hub of world cricket Dubai. The MCC's governance of English cricket was passed to the England and Wales Cricket Board.

In 1998 the MCC voted to admit women members for the first time. As there is such a long waiting list for membership there was no great influx, though the widely popular Rachael Heyhoe-Flint, former captain of the England Women's cricket team, was subsequently afforded the rare honour of an honorary life membership.

In 2003 the MCC's Young Cricketers programme included female players for the first time.

In 2004 Rachael Heyhoe-Flint became the first woman to be elected to the MCC Committee.

In 2006 Monty Panesar became the first male 'graduate' of an MCC University programme (Loughborough) to play for England. Also in 2006 Keith Bradshaw became the first non-Briton to become secretary of the MCC (also appointed chief executive).

The MCC currently has some 18,000 members and around 4,000 associate members. Members enjoy special privileges such as use of the pavilion and other stands for all matches played at Lord's.

Demand for membership exceeds the number of places available each year (there were some 400 places in 2007). There is an 18-year waiting list for full ordinary membership (managed to get it down from 30 years in the 1920s then). In order to join the membership waiting list one must obtain the vote of three members, and the sponsorship of a person on the List of MCC Sponsors, which consists of members of all MCC sub-committees, the MCC Committee, past, current and designate presidents, and MCC Out Match representatives ('Out Matches' being the many MCC teams which play in the UK and overseas to help foster and develop the game of cricket). You can circumnavigate the waiting list by becoming an umpire member, playing member or Out Match member, although these carry none of the privileges of full membership, apart from being eligible to play for the club. Alternatively, you may be awarded honorary life membership, but this is very rare. Honorary life members include Sir Garfield Sobers, Harold 'Dickie' Bird, Sunil Gavaskar, Alec Stewart, Henry Olonga and, as stated, Rachael Heyhoe-Flint.

The Honours Boards list the names of players who have scored a century or taken five wickets in a Test match at Lord's. The boards are mounted in the 'home' and 'away' dressing rooms. The 'home' dressing room contains the Batsmen's Honour Board, the 'away' dressing room the Bowlers'.

The MCC now has a women's team.

The MCC sponsors an annual lecture, the Cowdrey Lecture, in which a leading figure speaks on a cricketing topic, often related to the 'spirit' of the game. In 2008 the Cowdrey Lecture was delivered by Archbishop Desmond Tutu.

The MCC has to write to the ICC on an annual basis to seek permission for members and spectators to bring their own alcohol into Lord's. No other ground authority does this.

Middlesex's home is Lord's Cricket Ground, St John's Wood, London NW8, often referred to as the 'spiritual home of English cricket'. The ground is owned by Marylebone Cricket Club and has a capacity of 30,000.

The club also plays some matches at Southgate (Walker Ground), which hosts the Middlesex County Cricket Festival, Richmond (Old Deer Park) and Uxbridge.

The Middlesex badge is three seaxes (sabres).

Middlesex have always been at the forefront of English cricket. They have won the County Championship outright ten times – in 1903, 1920, 1921, 1947, 1976, 1980, 1982, 1985, 1990 and 1993 – and shared the title on two occasions (1949 and 1977). Other trophy successes include the Gillette Cup/NatWest Trophy in 1977, 1980, 1984 and 1988; the Sunday League in 1992; the Benson & Hedges Cup in 1983 and 1986; and the Twenty20 Cup in 2008.

Middlesex CCC was formed in 1864. In its early years the club was dominated by seven brothers by the name of Walker who in their time fulfilled just about every role within the club, on and off the pitch.

In the year of their formation (1864), Middlesex were dismissed for 20 by the MCC at Lord's.

Being London-based, in their formative years as a county club Middlesex were able to draw on some of the best amateur players in the country as many resided in the capital. This was not always to the advantage of the club, however. Availability of such players was sporadic and in the late nineteenth century players often declined to play outside London.

Rather than it being a case of 'the sun ain't gonna shine any more' for the Walker brothers, it was more a case of it dawning: they were active in the inception and organization of the County Championship and Middlesex were one of the founder members in 1890.

Too hot to Trott. In the 1890s Middlesex suffered from a lack of quality bowlers, but they addressed this problem with the acquisition of Albert Trott from Australia – the first overseas player of great repute to join an English county.

In 1898 the lively medium-pace bowler and batsman J. T. 'Jack' Hearne achieved match figures of 16 for 114 against Lancashire at Old Trafford – the best by any Middlesex bowler in the County Championship. (A G. Burton returned the same figures when playing against Yorkshire at Sheffield in 1888, in the days of the 'unofficial' County Championship.)

At the turn of the century, though the club boasted some fine players, notably Jack Hearne and stylish and prolific batsman Pelham 'Plum' Warner, Middlesex won the County Championship but once (1903). According to one contemporary report the inability of Middlesex to dominate the competition was due to 'the core of the side fading fast, whilst others have fallen victim to drink and weight gain'. (Was it ever thus in cricket?)

The involvement of the Walker family continued well into the twentieth century. When Middlesex won the County Championship for a second time in 1920, the club president was R. D. Walker, and three of his brothers held important positions within the club. Middlesex clinched the County Championship with victory over Surrey at Lord's in what was Plum Warner's last match for the club. Having at one time seemingly been out of contention, Middlesex triumphed courtesy of nine successive victories in their final nine matches.

In 1923 Middlesex scored 642 for 3 declared against Hampshire at Southampton – the club's highest total in a single innings.

It was in 1923 that Patsy Hendren scored a club record 2,669 runs (average 83.41). In a Middlesex career spanning the years 1907 to 1937, Hendren scored a club record 40,302 runs. Not content with being one of the most prolific batsmen in first-class cricket, he also took a club record total of 561 catches in the field. Following his retirement as a player he coached at Harrow School then Sussex before returning to Middlesex to act as scorer (1952–60).

In 1924 Middlesex dismissed Gloucestershire for 31 at Bristol – the lowest total the club has inflicted on first-class opposition.

The Oval, Canterbury, Brighton and Fenner's always produced good wickets; but Lord's was always terribly bad, and it was said that the only respect in which the pitch resembled a billiard table was the pockets.
HARRY ALTHAM

In 1929 George 'Gubby' Allen took 10 for 40 against Lancashire at Lord's – the best ever bowling figures in a single innings by a Middlesex player.

In the late 1930s it was a case of 'so near yet so far' for Middlesex: they finished runners-up in the County Championship in four successive seasons. The team included players who were to become club legends: Bill Edrich, Denis Compton, Patsy Hendren and Gubby Allen.

In the years immediately following the Second World War, people keen to see life return to 'normal' attended sporting events in great numbers. Nowhere more so than at Lord's, where Middlesex matches were often played in front of capacity crowds. In 1947, during one of the hottest summers on record, Middlesex won the County Championship for a fourth time. The star of their team was Denis Compton.

Denis Compton was a brilliant right-hand batsman and something of an unorthodox slow left-arm bowler. In Middlesex's Championship season of 1947 he scored, in all cricket, 3,816 runs (average 90.85) – still the record for the highest number of runs scored by an individual in the course of a first-class season. His tally included 18 centuries (13 for Middlesex), four in the Test series against South Africa, and one in a representative match for the MCC.

Compton charmed and thrilled huge crowds with his dashing strokeplay and brought glamour and glitter to a nation still very much suffering from the effects of war and rationing. He was the first British sportsman ever to acquire an agent, Bagenal Harvey. The most productive commercial deal Harvey negotiated on behalf of his client was to advertise Brylcreem (male hair gel), for which Compton was reputed to have received £1,000 per annum. His face adorned newspaper and magazine adverts and posters through the United Kingdom which, in an age before many people owned TV sets, made him the first truly nationally known star of British sport.

Compton's cricket career lasted from 1936 to 1964 in which time he amassed 38,942 first-class runs (average 51.85), including 123 centuries. He also took 622 wickets (average 32.27). He played 78 Tests for England (1937–57) and scored 5,807 runs (average 50.06), including 17 centuries.

Denis Compton was the only player to call his partner for a run and wish him good luck at the same time.
BARRY NORMAN (cricket writer and film critic)

In 1948 Bill Edrich and Denis Compton shared an unbroken third-wicket stand of 424 against Somerset at Lord's – the highest partnership in the history of the club.

In 1949 J. D. B. Robertson scored 331 not out against Worcestershire at Worcester – the highest individual innings by a Middlesex player.

It can be said that in the 1950s Middlesex suffered from some uninspired captaincy, though top-quality players emerged in wicket-keeper John Murray and spinner Fred Titmus.

Fred Titmus played his last match for Middlesex in 1982. His first game for the club was in 1949 so his career spanned five decades, albeit with a short spell as Surrey coach (1976–79) before returning to Middlesex.

In 1955 Fred Titmus took a club record 158 wickets (average 14.63). He also holds the record for the most wickets in a Middlesex career – 2,361 (average 21.27).

Fred Titmus begins his third over for Middlesex. He has two short legs, one of them square.
BRIAN JOHNSTON

In 1971 Mike Brearley was appointed captain and he inherited a side steeped in under-achievement. All was to change under Brearley, however: Middlesex won four County Championships including successive titles in 1976 and 1977. He also skippered Middlesex to Gillette Cup success in 1977 and 1980. With a formidable batting line-up which included Mike Gatting, Clive Radley, Graham Barlow and Brearley himself, and excellent bowlers in pacemen Wayne Daniel and Mike Selvey and spinners John Emburey and Phil Edmonds, the club enjoyed a golden period of success on the field.

Mike Brearley was an excellent tactical captain and an outstanding leader and motivator of players. He played for Middlesex from 1961 to 1983, was a very good opening bat and a specialist slip fielder. He scored 25,185 first-class runs, including 45 centuries. He played 39 Tests for England and was the second captain after Len Hutton to regain then successfully defend the Ashes, and the first to lead England to five wins in an Ashes series. He is widely regarded as the most intellectual cricketer since C. B. Fry, and this often showed in TV and radio interviews.

It was Jung, I think, who said we learned from our failures, success merely confirming us in our mistakes. What can I learn from my recent batting failures in Tests?
MIKE BREARLEY (1981)

Hello, is it possible to speak to Mike Brearley, please? He's just going out to bat? I'll hold.
EDDIE LARGE (comedian, telephoning Brearley during the 1981 Test at Lord's)

> ### And now, the familiar sight of a Middlesex captain lifting the Benson & Hedges Cup for the first time.
> JIM LAKER

In 1995 Middlesex set then equalled the club's record total in a limited-overs game: 304 for 7 against Surrey at the Oval, then 304 for 8 against Cornwall at St Austell.

Most appropriately named player – J. W. Box (four Studds also played for Middlesex).

The club's limited-overs team is the Middlesex Crusaders.

Worth a visit for . . . the experience of Lord's. Though subjected to much redevelopment in recent years, tradition and history seem to seep from every brick, no more so than from those that comprise the famous pavilion.

You do not have to wait for nearly two decades for MCC membership to enjoy the delights of Lord's and the famous Long Room in the pavilion. You can do this by becoming a Middlesex club member. Among other things, club membership entitles you to access to the pavilion, the Long Room and members' stands, access to the pavilion and members' enclosure at away games, and priority booking for Test matches, ODIs and Twenty20 fixtures. Oh, and you have the right to wear the Middlesex tie.

1709	First inter-county match, Kent v. Surrey
1769	**First known century scored, John Minshull for Duke of Dorset's XI v. Wrotham**
1771	Width of bat to be four and a quarter inches
1774	**First Laws of Cricket laid down, lbw law devised**
1776	First known scorecards produced at Vine Club in Sevenoaks, Kent
1787	**MCC formed**
1788	Laws of Cricket revised by MCC
1794	**First inter-schools match, Charterhouse v. Westminster**
1805	First Eton v. Harrow match
1806	**First Gentlemen v. Players match at Lord's**
1807	First known instance of round-arm bowling, by John Willes (Kent)
1811	**First Women's inter-county match, Surrey v. Hampshire**
1814	MCC move to current site at Lord's
1827	**First Oxford v. Cambridge match at Lord's**
1836	First county club formed – Sussex; batting pads invented
1837	**MCC Diamond Jubilee**
1838	First pavilion lit by gas, at Lord's
1845	**First match played at the Oval**
1848	Printing of match cards at Lord's
1850	**Wicket-keeping gloves introduced**
1850	John Wisden takes 10 wickets in an innings for North v. South

1858	Term 'hat-trick' devised for bowler taking three wickets in consecutive balls
1859	First overseas tour by an English team, to North America
1861	First tour by English team to Australia
1864	Over-arm bowling legalized
1864	John Wisden produces first *Wisden Cricketers' Almanack*
1868	Aboriginals the first Australian team to tour England
1873	W. G. Grace becomes first player to score 1,000 runs and take 100 wickets in a season
1877	First recognized Test match, Australia v. England, Melbourne
1880	First Test match in England, v. Australia at the Oval
1882	England lose to Australia for first time (Oval)
1887	MCC centenary
1889	Declarations authorized, but only on third day
1889	South Africa make Test debut
1890	County Championship formed
1895	Minor Counties formed
1899	England team to be chosen by selectors as opposed to invitation by host club
1900	Six-ball over replaces five-ball over
1905	Australian Board of Control formed
1921	Glamorgan admitted to County Championship, first from outside England
1926	Highest ever first-class total – 1,107, by Victoria v. New South Wales
1927	Lady Darnley presents 'Ashes' to MCC
1928	West Indies make Test debut
1930	New Zealand make Test debut
1931	Stumps regulated at height of 28 inches and optional wicket width of nine inches
1932	India make Test debut
1932	England 'Bodyline' tour commences in Australia
1934	First Women's Test, Australia v. England at Brisbane
1937	MCC's 150th anniversary
1947	Width of wicket regulated at nine inches
1948	First five-day Test in England, v. Australia
1948	Don Bradman plays last Test (finishes with average of 99.94)
1952	Pakistan make Test debut
1956	Jim Laker takes 19 wickets v. Australia in Old Trafford Test
1957	Declarations can be made at any time in match

56

1960	First tied Test, Australia v. West Indies at Brisbane
1962	Last Gentlemen v. Players match (Scarborough)
1963	Distinction between Gentlemen and Players (amateurs and professionals) abolished
1963	First Gillette Cup Final
1969	Sunday League introduced
1970	South Africa banned from international cricket due to government's apartheid policy
1971	First one-day international, Australia v. England at Melbourne
1972	Benson & Hedges Cup introduced
1975	First World Cup, won by West Indies
1976	First Women's Test match at Lord's, England v. Australia
1977	County Championship sponsored for first time
1977	Kerry Packer launches 'World Series'
1978	First helmet worn, by Graham Yallop (Australia)
1980	Eight-ball over in Australia abolished
1982	Sri Lanka make Test debut
1987	Bicentenary of MCC
1991	South Africa readmitted to Test cricket following abolition of apartheid
1992	Zimbabwe make Test debut
1992	Durham admitted to County Championship
1993	England Women's team win World Cup
1993	MCC cease to administer ICC which becomes an independent organization
1993	All county matches four-day duration
1997	ECB formed
1998	MCC votes to admit women members
2000	County Championship split into two divisions, promotion and relegation introduced
2003	Twenty20 Cup begins in England
2004	Rachael Heyhoe-Flint first woman elected to MCC Committee
2005	ECB in deal with Sky for broadcast of Test matches
2006	Shane Warne becomes first bowler to take 600 Test wickets
2007	Ashes urn returns to Lord's after exhibition in Australia
2008	Durham announce £40 million redevelopment of Riverside
2009	Sophia Gardens in Cardiff assumes Test status

Minor Counties

Minor Counties cricket is administered by the Minor Counties Cricket Association under the auspices of the ECB.

Five years after the formation of the County Championship in 1890, those counties not afforded first-class status formed a Minor Counties Championship competition. The league comprised seven teams in its inaugural season: Bedfordshire, Durham, Hertfordshire, Norfolk, Oxfordshire, Staffordshire and Worcestershire.

Three teams tied for the Minor Counties title in that inaugural season in 1895 – Durham, Norfolk and Worcestershire.

In 1896 Worcestershire became the first club to win the title outright, and retained the title in 1897 and 1898, thus becoming the first county to win three successive titles outright.

Some of the member counties left when elected to the County Championship: Worcestershire (member of the Minor Counties Championship 1895–98, afforded first-class status in 1899), Northamptonshire (1896–1904, first-class from 1905), Glamorgan (1897–1920, first-class from 1921) and, more recently, Durham (1895, 1897 and 1899–1991, elected to County Championship 1992).

Three teams from Wales other than Glamorgan were once members of the Minor Counties Championship: Carmarthenshire (1908–11), Denbighshire (1930–31 and 1933–35) and Monmouthshire (1901–14 and 1921–34).

Following a disagreement with Lancashire, Sydney Barnes played most of his cricket in the Minor Counties League, for Staffordshire. Barnes played in 27 Tests for England, and for 23 of those he was a Staffordshire player. In 1906 Sydney Barnes took 119 wickets for Staffordshire, which remains a Minor Counties record in the course of a single season.

Audley Miller also played for England when playing Minor Counties cricket, with Wiltshire.

Charles Coventry of Worcestershire played for England prior to Worcestershire being granted first-class status.

At various times in the history of the Minor Counties Championship, all County Championship clubs have fielded a Second XI in the competition. Lancashire Second XI were champions in 1907. From 1929 to 1959, the war excepted, County Championship Second XIs not only competed in the Minor Counties Championship but frequently won the title.

The majority of 'true' Minor Counties teams comprised amateur players, though a number did boast professionals from local professional leagues.

Traditionally Minor Counties teams played a minimum of eight two-day matches. Fixtures were usually organized on a regional basis to keep travel to a minimum and matches were often played in batches so amateur players could utilize holidays due to them from their respective workplaces.

In 1908 E. Garnett scored 282 for Berkshire against Wiltshire at Reading – the highest total by an individual batsman in the history of Minor Counties cricket.

In 1909 Cheshire were dismissed by Staffordshire for 14 at Stoke-on-Trent – the lowest total in the history of Minor Counties cricket.

The Minor Counties have traditionally fielded a representative team to play the tourists. The first Minor Counties representative team to play a touring side took on the South Africans at Stoke-on-Trent in 1912. The first and third days of the scheduled three-day match were lost to rain. The Minor Counties made 127 and in reply South Africa were 22 for 3 when the weather put an end to proceedings.

The Minor Counties' second first-class match was again against South Africa, in 1924.

In 1928 the Minor Counties met the West Indies at Exeter in a match that was to establish the fixture in the cricket calendar. The Minor Counties were asked to follow on but won the match by 42 runs, the pivotal performances coming from Staffordshire's Aaron Lockett, who scored 154, and Buckinghamshire's Edward Hazelton, who took six West Indies wickets in their second innings.

The highest ever total in the Minor Counties Championship is Surrey Second XI's 621 against Devon at the Oval in 1928.

David Townsend played for Oxford University and was chosen for England for the tour of the West Indies in 1934–35. On his return he played for Durham.

In 1959, when first-class counties formed their own Second XI competition, many teams withdrew from the Minor Counties Championship. Yorkshire Second XI were one of the few teams to continue membership and were the last County Championship club Second XI to win the Minor Counties title, in 1971.

In 1964 the top five Minor Counties teams of the 1963 season – Cambridgeshire, Cheshire, Durham, Hertfordshire and Wiltshire – were included in the first-round draw for the Gillette Cup alongside seven first-class counties. Durham were drawn against Hertfordshire in the first all-Minor Counties Gillette Cup tie. Durham won by seven wickets and thus became the first Minor County to reach round two of the competition, in which they lost to holders Sussex by 200 runs. Sussex went on to win the cup for a second successive season.

In 1972 two representative teams from the Minor Counties (South and North) were invited to participate in the Benson & Hedges Cup. From 1976 to 1979 the two Minor Counties teams were selected on a longitudinal basis, thus they became Minor Counties East and West. Of the 64 matches played by these four Minor Counties representative teams, 63 ended in defeat, the exception being a match involving Minor Counties South which due to bad weather was not completed and was categorized as 'no result'.

In 1973 Durham became the first Minor County to defeat a County Championship club in the Gillette Cup when they beat Yorkshire at Harrogate by five wickets.

In 1980 the Minor Counties were restricted to one representative team in the Benson & Hedges Cup.

The Minor Counties gained their first victory in the B&H Cup in 1980, against Gloucestershire. The following year they beat Hampshire. Curiously, both matches were won by the same margin of three runs.

Five Minor Counties teams competed every year in the Gillette Cup/NatWest Trophy until 1983 when the competition was revamped and all first-class counties participated in round one along with 13 Minor Counties, Scotland and Ireland.

The last Second XI of a first-class county club to compete in the Minor Counties Championship was Somerset Second XI, who withdrew after 1987. They were replaced by the Wales Minor Counties team.

In 1987 Cambridgeshire's S. Turner took 10 for 11 against Cumberland at Penrith – the best bowling figures in a single innings in Minor Counties cricket.

The Championship was decided not by points for matches won or drawn, but by the average points gained per team.

In 1983 the Minor Counties Championship was subject to a major overhaul when the present two regional divisions, East and West, were introduced along with a knock-out tournament. Each division consists of 10 teams. Initially each team played every other one in the division once; now six matches of three days' duration are played by each team. The divisional winners meet in a match to decide the Minor Counties champions.

When Durham were elected to the County Championship in 1992 their place was taken by Herefordshire.

With their title success of 1993, Staffordshire became the first county to win three successive Minor Counties titles since Worcestershire (1896–98).

M. C. C. A.

Minor Counties v. Australians

AT ASHBROOKE, SUNDERLAND

ON THURSDAY & FRIDAY, 4th & 5th AUGUST, 1977

Hours of Play: 1st Day 11-30 a.m. to 6-30 p.m.

MEMBERS' PAVILION ENCLOSURE

Ground Admission and Reserved Seat   (Under Balcony)

THURSDAY   Row ...A....

COMPLIMENTARY   Reserved Seat No. ..25...

Entrance   —   Rear of Pavilion

J. Iley, Secretary, Durham C.C.C.

Devon was the first (and to date only) county to win four successive Minor Counties Championships outright, from 1994 to 1997.

The MCCA Knockout Trophy is the name of the Minor Counties limited-overs competition. The final is staged at Lord's.

In 2005 the involvement of the Minor Counties in what was then the C&G Trophy ended when the competition changed to a league format comprising first-class counties, Ireland and Scotland.

Minor Counties clubs continue to play matches at venues throughout their respective counties. The county with the most grounds designated as venues for Minor Counties cricket is Staffordshire with 14 (Audley CC, Bignall End CC, Brewood CC, Cannock CC, Leek CC, Longton CC, Meir Heath CC, Old Hall CC, Michelin Sports Ground in Stoke-on-Trent, Porthill Park CC, Stone CC, Tamworth CC, Walsall CC and Wolverhampton CC).

The current members of the Minor Counties Western Division are Berkshire (2008 champions), Cheshire, Cornwall, Devon, Dorset, Herefordshire, Oxfordshire, Shropshire, Wales Minor Counties and Wiltshire. Eastern Division: Bedfordshire, Buckinghamshire, Cambridgeshire, Cumberland, Hertfordshire, Lincolnshire, Norfolk, Northumberland, Staffordshire and Suffolk.

The oldest club currently participating in the Minor Counties Championship is Norfolk, formed on 14 October 1876.

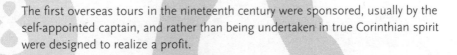

The first overseas tours in the nineteenth century were sponsored, usually by the self-appointed captain, and rather than being undertaken in true Corinthian spirit were designed to realize a profit.

In 1911 the first India team to tour England was sponsored by its captain, the Maharaja of Patiala, reportedly for £3,500.

In 1935 George Macaulay, who had been a mainstay of the Yorkshire bowling since 1920, was awarded a professional's benefit which raised £1,133. Born in Thirsk in 1897, Macaulay was educated at Barnard Castle School and every year as a pro took a team of notable cricketers to play the school First XI to raise money for school funds. The money raised by Macaulay over the years was considerably more than that raised in his benefit year, which was considered a disappointing sum. In an unprecedented gesture the Yorkshire CCC committee granted him an additional one-off payment of £250. When war was declared Macaulay joined the RAF as a pilot officer. Sadly he was killed in action in 1940.

 There is only one man who has made more appeals than you, George [Macaulay], and that's Dr Barnardo.
BILL REEVE (umpire)

In 1936 Thomas Goddard's benefit year realized £2,097 for the Gloucestershire spinner. In keeping with most benefit years, in addition to a benefit match various fund-raising activities took place through the calendar year, one of which was a sportsman's supper followed by a musical recital of extracts of Handel on a harmonium (you don't get sporting dinners like that any more). Goddard was awarded a second benefit in 1948 which raised £3,355, but this time Goddard's benefit committee obviously thought supporters should not have too much of a good thing: alas, no Handel on a harmonium.

No one had ever seen attendances or match receipts like those of the 1948 Australia squad's tour of England. The second Test at Lord's enjoyed a gross attendance of 132,000 and realized record receipts of £43,000.

Record attendances and receipts were recorded everywhere Bradman's Australians played. Their opening fixture against Worcestershire was watched by 32,080 spectators paying a total of £4,286. On 28 July a crowd of 17,211 attended the first day of the Australians match against Derbyshire at Derby, with receipts of £2,090.

When the Australians played squad players against non-county sides the attendances and receipts did not suffer as a consequence. A total of 25,800 spectators attended their match against Cambridge University at Fenners, producing total match receipts of £3,018. Due to rain only one day's play was possible against Durham at Ashbrooke, Sunderland, but the attendance was 17,548 (to this day a record for the ground) with then record receipts of £2,050.

The first major first-class competition in England to be sponsored was the inaugural Gillette Cup in 1963. It was reported the sponsorship was worth a total of £4,500 in the first season.

In 2006 Liverpool Victoria (financial services company) agreed a deal to sponsor the County Championship. The deal, from 2006 to 2009, was worth a total of £1.2 million.

In 2008 the winners of the Liverpool Victoria County Championship Division One received £100,000, the runners-up £40,000. The winners of Division Two received £30,000, the runners-up £15,000.

Twenty20 has proved immensely popular with spectators and provided county clubs with much-needed revenue. In 2003 the match receipts from a single Twenty20 match at Headingley exceeded the total gate receipts for all of Yorkshire's county matches – and Yorkshire were one of the better-supported teams in the County Championship.

In 2005 the Twenty20 match between Middlesex and Surrey at Lord's became the first ever match between two county teams (other than a cup final) to sell out in advance with total ticket sales of 29,000 and receipts in excess of half a million pounds.

In 2008 the winners of the Twenty20 Cup received £42,000, the runners-up £21,000, the two losing semi-finalists £10,000, and the four losing quarter-finalists £5,000 per club.

At the end of each group stage of Twenty20 there are awards for the leading player in each of seven categories: Most Runs, Most Sixes, Best Strike Rate (minimum 100 balls faced), Best All-Rounder, Best Wicket-keeper, Most Wickets and Best Economy Rate (minimum 100 balls). Each category winner receives £1,500; second-placed players receive £1,000.

In 2008 Friends Provident Trophy prize money was £43,000 for the winning team and £22,000 for the runners-up.

In 2005 the ECB did a deal with BSkyB which gave Sky Sports exclusive television rights to the live broadcast of England Test matches (2006–09 inclusive). The deal was worth £220 million over four years. Financially this was an astute piece of business on the part of the board but the deal incurred the wrath not only of cricket diehards but also the occasional fan, who took umbrage at England matches not being available on terrestrial TV.

In 2007 the annual income of the ECB was reported as £93 million, up from £77 million in 2006. In 2007 the ECB distributed £31.6 million in 'fee payments' to the 18 first-class counties, each county club receiving £1.75 million. Without this income a number of County Championship clubs would not be able to survive.

In 2007 the ECB conducted another profitable TV rights deal when it sold Asian rights for live English cricket to Asian broadcaster ESPN Star Sports. The five-year deal is worth £40 million.

In September 2008 ESPN Star Sports paid £527 million for the commercial and marketing rights to the inaugural Twenty20 Champions League in a deal set to run for 10 years.

In December 2008 Vodafone announced an end to its sponsorship of the England cricket team, a deal reportedly worth £16 million to the ECB.

The BCCI (India) enjoys the highest revenue of any international cricket board.

In 2006 the BCCI negotiated a media rights deal with Nimbus Productions that will last until 2010 and which is worth US$612 million. In addition to this deal the BCCI has a four-year (2006–10) kit sponsorship deal with Nike worth US$43 million; a four-year deal worth US$70 million with Air Sahara for the sponsorship of the India cricket team; a media rights deal for one-day matches with Zee Films worth US$219.5 million; and a deal worth US$450 million for rights to sponsorship of such areas as travel and ground advertising.

The Stanford Super Series, sponsored privately by Sir Allen Stanford, commenced in 2008 with a winner-takes-all (US$20 million) Twenty20 Championship match between Stanford Superstars (comprising an All-Star Caribbean XI) and England. The Stanford Superstars won by 10 wickets.

England was not the first choice to compete in the Stanford Super Series. Initially the plan was for Sri Lanka, India, Australia and South Africa to play an elimination tournament with the winners meeting an All Star Stanford XI in the final, but contractual issues with the ICC and other bodies rendered the deal unfeasible.

Another plan was for South Africa to play a Caribbean Superstars XI for a winner-takes-all prize of US$5 million, but the plan fell through as there were a number of caveats regarding the West Indies Cricket Board (WICB) which could not be resolved.

In 2008 the Stanford US$20 million was split as follows: each of the 11 members of the winning team (Stanford Superstars) received a million dollars; a million dollars was split among the squad members of the winning team who did not play in the Championship final; a million dollars went to the management team of the winning side; and the remaining $7 million was split between the ECB and the WICB. Following their ignominious defeat, the England players returned empty-handed.

In December 2008 the tournament looked unlikely to happen again when Sir Allen Stanford disbanded his team of 12 'Stanford Legends' who had been acting as ambassadors for the tournament, albeit the ECB had a five-year deal to compete in the Stanford Series which involved an annual Twenty20 with England (hosts), the West Indies and two invited teams worth US$9.5 million. Existing deals, however, appeared worthless in January 2009 when Sir Allen Stanford 'disappeared' and was later arrested by the FBI investigating allegations of fraud and misuse of monies. The ECB announced it 'highly unlikely the Stanford Legends competition would take place again', intimating England would not again be involved in such a venture.

ARLO WHITE (BBC Radio): You said from the start, Geoffrey, the Stanford Series would end quickly and in tears. The news just in is that Sir Allen Stanford has been arrested by the FBI amid allegations of fraud.
GEOFFREY BOYCOTT: There you go, then.

In 2008 it was reported in the *Asian Age* that India Test star Sachin Tendulkar was the greatest earner of any player in the history of the game. Tendulkar is estimated to make £14 every minute of every day – that is, £840 an hour, or £20,160 a day, or £7,358,400 per annum. In 2006 Tendulkar sold his image rights to Iconix (a subsidiary of Saatchi and Saatchi Advertising Agency) for £22 million in a three-year deal.

On 6 February 2009 England's Kevin Pietersen and Andrew Flintoff became the most expensive players in the Indian Premier League and cricket history. Pietersen signed for Bangalore and Flintoff for Chennai in deals reported to be worth £1.1 million each for the second IPL season. Essex's Ravi Bopara joined 'Kings' and Durham's Paul Collingwood Delhi, both reportedly for contracts paying £400,000.

Cricket was played in New Zealand prior to the country becoming a British colony in 1840. The earliest record of an organized match is dated March 1844, which is when Nelson played Surveyors of the Land Company at Nelson. Reports of the game appeared in a number of newspapers – as they would, Nelson always being good for a column

The first recorded 'important' match was contested by Wellington and Auckland and took place at Wellington in March 1860.

The inaugural first-class match was Otago against Canterbury at South Dunedin in January 1864.

The first New Zealand team to tour overseas was Canterbury, who visited Australia and Tasmania in 1878–79.

In 1887–88 Auckland were dismissed for 13 by Canterbury at Auckland – the lowest total in New Zealand first-class cricket.

New Zealand were granted Test status in 1928 and played their first Test against England at Lancaster Park, Christchurch in January 1930.

In 1935 P. E. Whitelaw and W. N. Carson shared a third-wicket partnership of 445 for Auckland against Otago at Dunedin – the highest partnership in New Zealand domestic first-class cricket.

In January 1940 Auckland scored 693 for 9 declared against Canterbury at Auckland – the highest total in a New Zealand inter-provincial match.

For all their relative geographical closeness, New Zealand did not play its first Test match against Australia until 1946.

In 1949 G. F. Cresswell took 6 for 168 against England on his Test debut.

New Zealand lost the 1949 series against England but, in a series comprising four Test matches, had the distinction of not having a single player out for a duck.

In December 1952 Bert Sutcliffe scored 385 for Otago against Canterbury at Christchurch – the highest individual score in New Zealand first-class cricket.

For many years New Zealand struggled in the Test arena and did not enjoy a Test match victory until 1956, when the West Indies were defeated at Auckland.

In 1969 New Zealand recorded their first ever Test series win, away from home against Pakistan. This ended a run of 30 consecutive series without a win.

New Zealand's prowess as a Test team developed apace throughout the 1970s and 1980s, as cricket in the country reaped the benefits of investment in the sport.

New Zealand's first Test victory against Australia came in 1974 at Christchurch in what was only the sixth Test match between the two countries.

Glenn Turner was the first New Zealand batsman to score two centuries in a Test match (101 and 110 not out), against Australia during the 1973–74 series.

New Zealand competed in the World Cup for the first time in 1975 and reached the semi-finals – a feat they repeated in 1979, 1992, 1999 and 2007.

Didn't whack a two. In October 1976 Wakatu CC were all out for just 21 against Nelson. At the end of the Wakatu innings, opening batsman John 'Jock' Sutherland was undefeated on 0 not out.

'Peejay' Petherick was the first New Zealand bowler to accomplish a hat-trick in a Test match, against Pakistan at Lahore in 1976–77.

In February 1978 the match between Central Districts and England ended in a tie. England tied the game when, with the scores level, Bob Willis delivered the last ball of the match and clean-bowled Central Districts' Terry Horne.

> **And for those of you watching who haven't television sets, live commentary of the England–New Zealand Test is on Test Match Special on Radio 3.**
> DAVID COLEMAN

New Zealand's first ever Test victory over England (at the 48th attempt) was at Wellington in 1978. New Zealand went on to win the series.

In February 1984 at Christchurch, New Zealand recorded their highest winning margin against England – an innings and 132 runs.

The record for the best bowling in a Test match is held by Sir Richard Hadlee who returned match figures of 15 for 123 against Australia at Brisbane in 1985–86.

No New Zealand bowler has taken 10 wickets in a Test match more times than Sir Richard Hadlee – nine times. He also holds the record for having taken five wickets in an innings the most times – 36.

That's not the end of Sir Richard Hadlee's records. He holds the record for the best bowling in an innings by a New Zealand bowler – 9 for 52, against Australia at Brisbane in 1985–86. The next best is, er, Hadlee's 7 for 23 against India at Wellington in 1975–76. In that 1985–86 Brisbane Test against Australia, Hadlee also became the first New Zealand bowler to take five wickets in both innings of a Test match – 9 for 52 and 6 for 71 (a feat he went on to accomplish on four further occasions). Hadlee's 9 for 52 might have been a 10-wicket haul – a feat no New Zealand bowler has achieved in a

Test match – but having taken nine wickets he took a rest for one over and brought on Vaughan Brown. Brown was not a recognized bowler but with the last ball of his only over he took his only Test wicket when he had Geoff Lawson caught at mid-on – by Richard Hadlee.

New Zealand is one of only two Test nations to have two players who have achieved the double of 3,000 Test runs and 200 Test wickets: Sir Richard Hadlee (3,124 runs and 431 wickets) and Chris Cairns (3,320 runs and 218 wickets). The other nation is South Africa, courtesy of Shaun Pollock and Jacques Kallis.

Chris Cairns shares another record with Shaun Pollock. Chris and his dad Lance and Shaun and his father Peter are the only father and son combinations to have each claimed 100 Test wickets.

Sir Richard Hadlee was the first bowler to reach 400 Test wickets, against India at Christchurch in 1990.

Priceless books. Sir Richard Hadlee possesses books containing the autographs of every international team to have toured New Zealand since Test status was granted. The books were first compiled by Sir Richard's grandfather, then his father, and Sir Richard has continued the family tradition.

In 1986, during a match between New Zealand and Brian Close's XI at Scarborough, New Zealand's Ken Rutherford scored 317 runs off 245 balls, of which 228 runs came in boundaries. In terms of balls faced it is one of the fastest triple centuries recorded. You can just imagine what Brian Close might have said to his team.

Having survived the 1986 tour of England without sustaining a single injury, Trevor Franklin finally succumbed when the New Zealand touring party were preparing to fly home from Gatwick airport. He was run over by a motorized luggage-train.

New Zealand's highest total in Test match cricket is 671 for 4, against Sri Lanka at Wellington in 1990–91. Martin Crowe scored 299 – the highest score in a single innings by a New Zealand batsman in a Test match. He shared a third-wicket partnership of 467 with Andrew Jones – the highest ever partnership by a New Zealand pair.

Martin Crowe also holds the record for the most Test centuries by a New Zealand batsman – 17.

Martin Crowe is the cousin of the actor Russell Crowe.

 So many batting reputations lie buried on the surface of this famous Christchurch wicket.
RADIO SPORT NEW ZEALAND

In 1997 at Harare, Stephen Fleming took five catches in a single innings against Zimbabwe – a joint world record for a Test match.

For decades the New Zealand team was affectionately known throughout the cricketing world as the Kiwis. In 1998 the team's sponsors, Clear Communications, for reasons known only to themselves, decided to hold a competition to find a new name for the national team. The winner was the Black Caps, the name by which the team is now known.

In 1999, playing against South Africa at Auckland, Geoff Allott faced 77 balls and was at the crease for 101 minutes. In itself nothing unusual, except when Allott's innings ended he was out for a duck.

In 2001–02 Nathan Astle reached 200 off 153 balls against England at Christchurch – Test cricket's fastest ever double century in terms of balls received. Astle's second hundred came off just 39 balls. He was eventually out for 222.

In 2002 at Lahore, New Zealand suffered their heaviest defeat in Test match cricket when they were beaten by Pakistan by an innings and 324 runs.

Stephen Fleming is New Zealand's most successful captain in terms of Test matches won. Fleming led New Zealand to 28 Test victories – more than twice as many as any other New Zealand captain.

In 2004, playing against England at Lord's, Chris Harris became the first New Zealand bowler to take 200 wickets in one-day internationals, and only the second bowler to achieve the double of 200 wickets and 4,000 runs in ODIs (the first was Sanath Jayasuriya of Sri Lanka).

New Zealand's record winning margin occurred in Harare in 2005 when they defeated Zimbabwe by an innings and 294 runs. New Zealand dismissed Zimbabwe twice in the same day, for 59 and 99, thus Zimbabwe became only the second team (after India at Old Trafford in 1952) to be dismissed twice in the same day of a Test match.

In the 2007 World Cup against Canada, Brendan McCullum scored the fastest World Cup fifty, reached off 20 balls.

Playing in New Zealand isn't like playing at the end of the earth, but you can just about see it from there.

WES HALL

59

Northamptonshire's HQ is the County Ground, Abington Avenue, Northampton. For 97 years, up to 1993, Northants shared their home with Northampton Town AFC and was the last county to share a home with a Football League club.

The current capacity of the County Ground is 6,500.

The club has also played matches at Kettering, Finedon and Wellingborough, and outside the county at Luton, Milton Keynes, Peterborough and Tring.

The traditional club badge is a Tudor rose in maroon and old gold, though in 2007 this was modified slightly to incorporate a white centre and edging to petals at the expense of much of the old gold.

Northamptonshire has never won the County Championship, Sunday/Pro40 League or Twenty20 Cup. They have, however, won the Gillette Cup/NatWest Trophy on two occasions – 1976 and 1992 – and the Benson & Hedges Cup in 1980.

The earliest known reference to cricket being played in the county dates back to 18 August 1741, a match at Cow Meadow near Northampton between two select elevens from Northamptonshire and Buckinghamshire, though the previous day a Bedfordshire XI played a combined Northamptonshire and Huntingdonshire XI at Woburn Park.

The official county club was formed on 31 July 1878 at a meeting at the George Hotel in Kettering. The constitution of the club was based on an existing one that dated back to 1820. The club operated as a Minor County until 1905 when, having been granted first-class status, it was successful in its application to join the County Championship.

Northamptonshire's inaugural match in the County Championship took place at Southampton on 18–20 May 1905, against Hampshire.

In 1907 Northamptonshire were dismissed for only 12 by Gloucestershire at Gloucester – the lowest total in the club's history, and in the history of the County Championship.

In the years immediately preceding the First World War, Northamptonshire enjoyed a period of relative success, finishing runners-up in the County Championship in 1912 and fourth in 1913. The strength of this team owed much to its bowling attack, which included 'Speedy' Sydney Smith and Billy 'Bumper' Wells, whose nomenclatures tell their own story.

In 1919 A. D. Denton returned to play for the county despite losing part of his right leg during the Great War.

In 1921 R. A. Haywood scored eight centuries for the county – never bettered.

Who is the only cricketer whose entire first-class career never involved him playing at home or in an away game for his county? The answer is, Northamptonshire's H. Wilson. Wilson made his debut for the club in June 1931 against New Zealand at Peterborough. Batting at number 11, he ran himself out for a duck in Northamptonshire's first innings. In the second innings Wilson came to the crease to partner Fred Bakewell. With Bakewell on 89 and looking good for a century, Wilson again ran himself out for a duck. Northants eventually lost by seven wickets and Wilson was never selected for the county again. Not only did he get a pair in his only first-class match and succeed in running himself out on both occasions, as the match was played at Peterborough, which is not in Northamptonshire, he also achieved the unique feat of playing his entire county career neither at home nor at an away venue.

During the inter-war years and in the seasons immediately following the Second World War the county endured a thin time in the County Championship, finishing above second last on only four occasions between 1923 and 1948, and finishing as wooden spoonists in every season from 1934 to 1938.

From May 1935 to May 1939 Northamptonshire endured a run of 99 matches without a single County Championship victory.

It was not all gloom and despair, however. In 1932 Vallance Jupp took all 10 Kent wickets for 127 at Tunbridge Wells – the existing club record for best bowling.

In 1947 E. W. 'Nobby' Clark retired with a career tally of 1,102 wickets (average 21.26) – a current club record. Clark had begun his career with the club in 1922.

In the early 1950s the club changed its recruiting policy, signing seasoned pros from other counties and overseas, such as Freddie Brown (Surrey), Raman Subba Row (Cambridge University), Jock Livingstone, Jack Manning, left-arm spinner George Tribe (Australia) and Peter Arnold (New Zealand), though the star of the Northamptonshire team was fast bowler Frank 'Typhoon' Tyson. The injection of new blood saw a great improvement in fortunes: by the late 1950s the club had become serious Championship contenders.

George Tribe made his Northamptonshire debut against Middlesex at Lord's in 1952 and took the wicket of Syd Brown with his very first ball, only to end the innings with figures of 1 for 90.

In 1952 Dennis Brookes scored a club record 2,198 runs at an average of 51.11 – the most runs accrued by a Northamptonshire batsman in the course of a season. Brookes was a Northants stalwart for a quarter of a century. His county career spanned the years 1934 to 1959 during which time he scored a club record 28,980 runs (average 36.13). His career tally of 67 hundreds is also a club record.

In 1954 Yorkshire played Northamptonshire at Northampton. Frank 'Typhoon' Tyson was bowling at a tremendous pace and very intimidating. Johnnie Wardle was batting, hopping about on the crease and very ill at ease with Tyson's pace. Eventually Johnnie played a daft stroke to get out. I was next man in. When I passed Johnnie I said to him, 'What kind of bloody stroke was that to play?' There was an unwritten rule amongst fast bowlers that we didn't bowl bouncers at each other. The first ball I received from Tyson was a bouncer. So I made a mental note that I owed him one. Tyson's next ball was a straight half-volley. I lost my footing and was bowled on the retreat. Back in the pavilion, I walked into the dressing room and Johnnie Wardle's grinning. He says to me, 'What kind of bloody stroke was that to play? Your feet were all over the place. What happened, Fred?' 'I'll tell you what happened,' I said. 'I slipped on that pile of shite you dropped on the crease.'

FRED TRUEMAN

In 1958 George Tribe returned match figures of 15 for 31 against Yorkshire at the County Ground – a club record. Tribe also holds the club record for the most wickets in a single season – 175 (average 18.70), in 1955.

One of my last games for Northamptonshire was in 1959, a repeat of my debut, against Middlesex at Lord's. Middlesex made 261 in their first innings and we were 230 for 9 when I was joined by Martin Dilley. Martin and I took our score on to 261, which was level. I was facing Fred Titmus and said to Martin, 'We're going to pass their total in some style. Look at the Long Room, I'm going to put the window out up there.' I hit Fred's next ball with a left-handed slog, a style later favoured by Rodney Marsh. The ball left the bat like a bullet, went over the top, but landed some three feet from the window and rolled back. Fred came down the wicket and said, 'George, if I pitch

another up will you have another go? I'd love to see
that window go.' Matches were keenly contested
but there was a camaraderie and repartee between
opposing players back then that doesn't seem to exist
nowadays.
GEORGE TRIBE

I see Northamptonshire have a new bowler called
Kettle [Michael Kettle]. May I suggest to Keith
Andrew that the best time to put him on would be ten
minutes before the tea interval.
LETTER TO *THE CRICKETER* (1959)

Opposition gave him the bird. In July 1963 Donald Ramsamooj, batting
against Surrey at the Oval, hit a shot that felled and killed a pigeon in full
flight. Undeterred, Ramsamooj went on to make 44 but declined the offer of
the deceased pigeon as a filling for a pie.

In 1968 former Northamptonshire (and Surrey) favourite Raman Subba Row was
one of the instigators in the creation of the Test and County Cricket Board, which
was to take over the running of first-class cricket in the UK from the MCC. He
later served as chairman of the TCCB, from 1974 to 1979.

Following a car accident in May 1969, Northamptonshire opening batsman
Colin Milburn lost his left eye, the leading eye for a right-hand batsman. It
was thought Milburn's career was over but he returned to play for the county
in 1973 and 1974. Courageous as he was, Milburn was not the only cricketer
to have played county cricket with the use of only one eye. Others include
William Clarke (Nottinghamshire), W. H. Fryer (Kent) and J. W. Sharpe
(Surrey).

Colin Milburn is as untidy as an unmade bed and as
devastating as a hand grenade.
CLIVE TAYLOR (cricket writer)

Dangerous off-drive. In June 1976 play was halted for almost 40 minutes during
Northamptonshire's match against the touring West Indies when a car went out

of control, careered through the crowd and on to the pitch. A raffle ticket kiosk was damaged, a teenage spectator sustained a broken leg, and the elderly driver of the car was treated for minor injuries and shock.

In 1977 Northamptonshire created a new club record for the lowest total inflicted upon first-class opposition when they dismissed Lancashire for 33 at the County Ground.

Northamptonshire's record score in one-day cricket is 360 for 2, against Staffordshire at the County Ground in 1990.

So, Northamptonshire are the 1992 [NatWest] Trophy winners, and I dare say the beer will be flowing like wine in the town tonight.
RICHIE BENAUD

In 1995 Northamptonshire scored a club record total of 781 for 7 declared against Nottinghamshire at the County Ground.

In 1998 Malachy Loye and David Ripley shared a partnership of 401 for the fifth wicket against Glamorgan at the County Ground – the highest partnership in the history of the club.

Northamptonshire supporters, unhappy with their team's run of indifferent form, have begun to let their voice be heard at the County Ground by staying away from matches.
TALKSPORT

In 2003 Australian Michael Hussey made the highest score in an innings by any Northamptonshire batsman – 331 not out, against Somerset at Taunton.

Over the years Northamptonshire has also enjoyed the services of such notable cricketers as Curtly Ambrose, Rob Bailey, David Capel, Brian Crump, Kapil Dev, Matthew Hayden, Anil Kumble, Allan Lamb, Wayne Larkins, David Larter, Dennis Lillee, Mushtaq Mohammad, Sarfraz Nawaz, Roger Prideaux, David Steele and Peter Willey. Their current stars are David Sales and England (ECB) contract player Monty Panesar.

Former England batsman Rob Bailey (1982–99) is now a first-class umpire, as are former Northants team-mates Neil Mallender, George Sharp and Peter Willey.

Most appropriately named player – A. Balls.

The club's limited-overs team is the Northamptonshire Steelbacks – a reference to the tradition of steel making in the county, particularly at nearby Corby.

Worth a visit for . . . though Northampton does not boast a Premiership or Championship football team, Northampton Town are in the Football League, and should fixtures fall kindly in September, enjoy the triple treat of watching County Championship cricket, top-flight rugby union at Franklin Gardens (Northampton RUFC) and Football League soccer at Sixfields Stadium over a single weekend.

61

The county home is Trent Bridge, West Bridgford, Nottingham.

Trent Bridge's current capacity is 15,350, though the club has plans to increase this to 17,500.

Nottinghamshire has also played matches at Newark and Worksop, and outside the county at Cleethorpes.

The club badge is the coat of arms of the city of Nottingham, comprising a heraldic shield flanked by two stags, though the county's one-day team sports a badge depicting a lone leaping stag.

Nottinghamshire have won the County Championship five times, in 1907, 1929, 1981, 1987 and 2005. Other major successes are the NatWest Trophy in 1987, the Benson & Hedges Cup in 1989 and the Sunday League in 1991.

The earliest known reference to cricket in the county dates back to 26–27 August 1771, a match between Nottingham and Sheffield Cricket Clubs at the Forest Racecourse. A contemporary report in the periodical *The White Mark Tablet* states, 'The outcome of the game was not determined on account of a dispute having arisen between players of both teams after a member of the Sheffield team was jostled.' Sadly the report does not state where exactly the jostling of the Sheffield player took place, or why. Any editor worth his salt would have asked the reporter in question to supply details, this being the real story of the match – black mark against *The White Mark*. It appears the periodical was short-lived. Given the omission of such crucial detail from a major story, it's little wonder readers stopped taking their *Tablets*.

Nottinghamshire owes its foundation as an informal county team to William Clarke, also its first captain. The club played its first inter-county match against Sussex at Brighton in August 1835. In 1838 William Clarke saw the potential of a little meadow at the back of the Trent Bridge Inn. It seems he was a man who would go to any lengths to stage cricket and find a permanent home for the Nottinghamshire club: he married the landlady of the Trent Bridge Inn (Mary Chapman) in 1838 and within a year was staging Nottinghamshire cricket matches in the meadow.

Clarke was something of a cricket innovator and obsessive. Not content with getting Nottinghamshire off the ground and a ground, he formed the All England XI (which, unsurprisingly, he also captained) – the team which, in turn, laid the foundations for the England international team.

In 1841 the formal creation of Nottinghamshire County Cricket Club was enacted by a committee chaired by guess who?

The All England team broke up in 1852 as some of the players believed William Clarke kept too much of the profits from matches for himself. The dissidents called a meeting with Clarke. It was alleged he was unable to attend on the day as he had a meeting with the architect of his new Nottingham home. (Sounds like they may have had a case.) The dissidents formed a rival team, the United All-England XI. The teams met at Lord's in 1856, the year after Clarke played his final game.

George Parr was Nottinghamshire captain from 1856 to 1870, and in 1859 he also skippered the first united England team to tour, to that emerging hotbed of cricket North America. Parr also captained England's second tour, to Australia and New Zealand in 1864, from which his side returned unbeaten. Curiously for a cricketer who played for a Midlands county, Parr was dubbed by the press 'The Lion of the North', which may say something for the way a London-based national press viewed Nottingham.

Nottinghamshire's inaugural first-class match took place in 1864.

In 1879 Nottinghamshire dismissed Derbyshire for 16 at Trent Bridge, and the following year Surrey for the same score at the Oval – the lowest total inflicted upon first-class opposition by the club.

Between 1896 and 1920 bowling stalwart Tom Wass took 1,653 wickets – the highest number of wickets taken by a bowler in a Nottinghamshire career.

In 1923 F. C. L. Matthews enjoyed match figures of 17 for 89 against Northamptonshire at Trent Bridge – a club record.

In 1929 Nottinghamshire won the County Championship for a second time. The spearhead of their bowling attack was hostile paceman Harold Larwood. Despite being only five feet eight inches (1.72m) tall, Larwood generated amazing pace, not least due to a superb action and the fact he had exceedingly long arms for a man of his size: standing upright with his arms before him he could touch his knees. He took over 100 wickets in a season eight times between 1926 and 1936. His most memorable season was 1932, when he took 162 wickets at an average of 12.86. Between 1924 and 1938 he took 1,427 wickets (average 17.51), and for a tail-ender proved himself more than useful with the bat, scoring 7,290 runs (average 19.91). He played in 21 Tests for England and took 178 wickets (average 28.41). Shamefully, he was made the scapegoat for the controversy that surrounded the 'Bodyline' tour of Australia in 1932–33 and was never selected for England again. Following retirement as a player he ran a sweet shop in Blackpool before emigrating to Australia in 1950. In 1993 he was belatedly awarded the MBE by cricket-loving Prime Minister John Major, who recognized his contribution to English cricket.

In Nottinghamshire's Championship season of 1929, 'Dodger' Whysall scored a club record 2,620 runs (average 53.46). The previous season Whysall had scored nine centuries, a club record he now shares with M. J. 'Mike' Harris (1971) and Chris Broad (1990).

All Gunns blazing. In 1931 George Gunn and his son George V. both scored centuries for Nottinghamshire in their match against Warwickshire – a unique feat in the history of English first-class cricket. George (the father) Gunn was the nephew of William Gunn, co-founder of the famed Nottingham-based cricket equipment manufacturer Gunn and Moore. George

Gunn played for Nottinghamshire from 1902 to 1932, and in 1929, on the occasion of his 50th birthday, scored 164 against Worcestershire. During his career with Nottinghamshire he amassed 31,592 runs – a club record.

Cereal run makers. Between 1931 and 1933 Nottinghamshire boasted players by the name of Oates (A. W.) and Wheat (A. B.).

1066 and all that. In 1956 Ken Smales took 10 for 66 against Gloucestershire at Stroud – the best single-innings bowling figures in the history of the club.

In the late 1960s Nottinghamshire enjoyed a major coup when they signed Sir Garfield Sobers (West Indies), arguably the greatest ever all-rounder.

In the late 1970s and early 1980s Nottinghamshire enjoyed the services of another great all-rounder and (later) knight in Sir Richard Hadlee (New Zealand). In 1981 Hadlee was a key member of Nottinghamshire's Championship-winning team, skippered by Clive Rice (South Africa) and featuring one of English cricket's greatest characters, Derek Randall.

Richard Hadlee has the appearance of a rickety church steeple and a severe manner which suggests women are not likely to be ordained yet.
PETER ROEBUCK

Derek Randall was indeed a great character. A columnist from a North Midlands newspaper once arrived at his home in mid-winter to interview Randall and was greeted at the door by the man himself wearing pads. On seeing the look of surprise on the face of the columnist, Randall felt the need to explain – 'I'm just breaking them in, come inside and meet my wife' – whereupon the columnist was treated to the sight of the Italian-born Mrs Randall sitting in an armchair in the lounge also wearing a set of pads.

In 1990 Nottinghamshire achieved their highest total in one-day cricket – 344 for 6, against Northumberland at Jesmond.

In 1998 Sir Garfield Sobers opened the Trent Bridge Cricket Centre, a state-of-the-art stand which incorporates a superb multi-purpose complex that includes the smartly named 'Bodyline' gym, though no amount of marketing and publicity has stopped fans (and commentators) referring to the stand by its original name, the Radcliffe Road End.

In 2000 Darren Bicknell and Gary Welton shared a club record (unbroken) partnership of 406 for the first wicket against Warwickshire at Edgbaston.

Having won the County Championship in 2005, the next year Nottinghamshire were relegated to Division Two – the first time a team has won the county title and been relegated the following season. In 2007 Nottinghamshire finished as runners-up in Division Two and were promoted back to Division One.

In 2007 Nottinghamshire achieved a club record total of 791 against Essex at Chelmsford.

Most appropriately named player – P. J. Hacker.

The club's limited-overs team is the Nottinghamshire Outlaws, after the original 'hoodie'.

Worth a visit for . . . the sight of the serene Trent Bridge pavilion. For all the tasteful redevelopment that has taken place at the ground over the years, happily it has been kept within the parameters of its 1889 foundation.

The first one-day international owed much to serendipity and rain. In January 1971 the first three days of the third Test between Australia and England at Melbourne were lost to rain which resulted in the Test being abandoned. Not wanting to totally disappoint Melbourne cricket fans, a one-off one-day match was hastily arranged.

That first ODI at Melbourne in 1971 consisted of 40 eight-ball overs per side. Australia defeated England by five wickets. The appeal of the one-day format was immediately apparent: the match was attended by a crowd of over 46,000.

The first ball bowled in an ODI was delivered by Australia's Graham McKenzie; England's Geoff Boycott received it. Boycott also became the first batsman out in an ODI when he was caught by Bill Lawry off the bowling of Jeff Thomson.

John Edrich was the first player to receive an ODI man of the match award, for scoring 82 for England against Australia in that inaugural ODI at Melbourne. In so doing he became the first batsman to score a fifty in an ODI.

The Melbourne ground thus holds a unique place in international cricket history: the first ground to stage a Test match and the first to stage a one-day international.

In 1972 Australia toured England and the scheduled sixth Test was replaced by three ODIs.

The first player to score a century in an ODI was Dennis Amiss (Warwickshire), for England against Australia at Old Trafford on 24 August 1972.

On 11 February 1973 New Zealand and Pakistan played their first ODI.

The first bowler to take five wickets in an ODI was Australia's Dennis Lillee, against Pakistan at Headingley in the 1975 World Cup.

In 1977 Kerry Packer launched the World Series on Channel 9 in Australia. Packer packaged the one-day game, introducing coloured clothing, coloured cricket balls and floodlights, innovations that would soon be adopted in official ODIs.

The first match in which players wore coloured clothing was the World Series match between WSC Australians and WSC West Indians at VFL Park in Melbourne in January 1979. The Australians wore gold and the West Indians coral pink.

Several players have represented more than one country in ODIs, including Warwickshire's Dougie Brown (England and Scotland), Anderson Cummins (West Indies and Canada), Clayton Lambert (West Indies and USA) and Kepler Wessels (Australia and South Africa).

The first bowler to accomplish a hat-trick in an ODI was Jalal-ud-Din, for Pakistan against Australia in 1982–83.

In 1993 Robin Smith scored 167 (not out) for England against Australia at Edgbaston.

In 1996–97 Pakistan's Saeed Anwar created a new record for the highest individual score in an ODI when he amassed 194 runs against India at Chennai.

In 1996–97 Shahid Afridi scored a century for Pakistan against Sri Lanka at Nairobi off only 37 balls.

In 1999–2000 Sachin Tendulkar and Rahul Dravid shared a second-wicket partnership of 331 for India against New Zealand at Hyderabad.

Sachin Tendulkar was the first batsman to score in excess of 30 centuries in ODIs.

Marcus Trescothick (Somerset) was the first England batsman to score 10 centuries in ODIs.

Pakistan's Wasim Akram was the first bowler to take in excess of 500 wickets in ODIs – 502 in 356 matches at an average of 23.52 – a record since broken by Sri Lanka's Muttiah Muralitharan.

In 2001 England were dismissed for 86 by Australia at Old Trafford – England's lowest total in an ODI.

In 2001–02 Chaminda Vaas (Worcestershire) took 8 for 19 for Sri Lanka against Zimbabwe at Colombo – the best bowling performance in an ODI.

In 2002–03 Australia set a new record victory margin for ODIs when they defeated Namibia by 256 runs (Australia 301 for 6, Namibia 45 all out).

The first England bowler to accomplish a hat-trick in an ODI was James Anderson (Lancashire), against Pakistan at the Oval in 2003. The following year Steve Harmison (Durham) equalled this feat against India at Trent Bridge.

The highest total in an ODI is Sri Lanka's 443 for 9 against the Netherlands in 2006.

The lowest total in an ODI is 35, by Zimbabwe against Sri Lanka at Harare in 2003–04.

In 2004–05 England were involved in their first tied ODI, against South Africa at Bloemfontein, both teams scoring 270 off 50 overs. In 2005 the match between England and Australia at Lord's also ended in a tie (Australia 196 off 48.5 overs, England 196 for 9 off 50 overs).

In 2005 Paul Collingwood (Durham) achieved the best bowling figures by an England bowler in an ODI – 6 for 31, against Bangladesh at Trent Bridge.

England's record total in an ODI is 391 for 4, against Bangladesh at Trent Bridge in 2005.

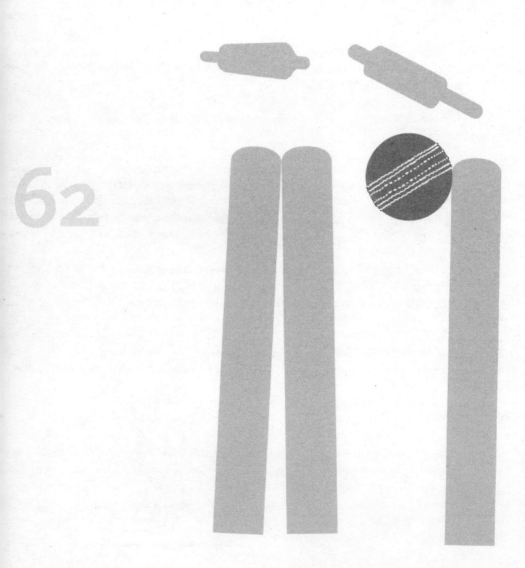

It was following the partition of India in 1947 and the establishment of Pakistan as an independent nation of two separate units, East and West Pakistan, that cricket in that part of the world developed at a rapid pace.

The first match to take place in the country following independence was between the Governors XI and Punjab University, at Lahore in February 1948.

The first player to score a century in Pakistan first-class cricket was Maqsood Ahmed, for Punjab University in the above-mentioned match

Initially Pakistan players continued to play for India. Amir Elahi and Gul Mahomed were part of the India team that toured Australia in 1947–48 though both would go on to represent Pakistan.

Though it did not enjoy Test status, the first representative team of Pakistan played its first match against the West Indies at Lahore in November 1948.

Pakistan first went on an official tour in 1949, to Ceylon (now Sri Lanka), though none of the matches enjoyed Test status.

On 28 July 1952, following a recommendation by India, Pakistan was granted Test match status at a meeting of the Imperial Cricket Conference at Lord's.

Pakistan played its first Test match in October 1952, against India at Delhi. The inaugural Test was part of a five-match series which India won 2–1.

In the second Test of that 1952 series against India, at Lucknow, Nazar Mohammad carried his bat through the Pakistan innings, scoring 124 not out as Pakistan won by an innings and 43 runs to record their first Test victory. Nazar Mohammad also gained the distinction of becoming the first player to be on the field for an entire Test match.

The Qiad-i-Azam Trophy, Pakistan's main domestic first-class competition, was first contested in 1953.

In 1954 Pakistan toured England for the first time and enjoyed a memorable victory at the Oval which owed much to the bowling of Fazal Mahmood, who took 12 wickets in the match. The series was drawn 1–1.

Due to the time it took to develop or construct grounds that met international standards, it was not until 1955 that Pakistan played their first Test on home soil, against India in Dhaka (now in Bangladesh) in January 1955.

The 1955 series against India consisted of five Tests, and every match was drawn – the first instance of this in Test history.

In 1958 Hanif Mohammad scored 337 against the West Indies – the first Pakistan player to score a triple century in a Test match.

In January 1959 Hanif Mohammad scored 499 for Karachi against Bahawalpur in Karachi – the highest individual innings in Pakistani first-class cricket and the highest individual innings for 35 years, until Brian Lara's 501.

ERIC MORECAMBE: I've been reading a book on self-defence.
ERNIE WISE: What's it called?
MORECAMBE: *A Guide to Karachi.*
WISE: Here, let me look at that. This isn't a self-defence book. It's about Karachi. Karachi is a city in Pakistan.
MORECAMBE: Is it? In that case, if you know of anyone going there for the Tests, I can show them around.

Worked up a head of steam. In 1964–65 Railways recorded the largest ever margin of victory in first-class cricket when they defeated Dera Ismail Khan by an innings and 851 runs at Lahore.

In 1969–70 Shahid Mahmood became the first bowler to take 10 wickets in a single innings in Pakistani first-class cricket when playing for Karachi Whites against Khaipur in Karachi.

Top Pakistan bowler of the 1970s Sarfraz Nawaz is credited with discovering and developing reverse-swing bowling. He then taught the technique to Imran Khan.

What a ball that was from Sarfraz. As soon as the ball left his hand it moved through the air. Extraordinary.
ALAN GIBSON (BBC Radio)

Had the crowd on the edge of their seats. In December 1977, against England at Lahore, Mudassar Nazar scored the slowest century in Test match history, reaching his hundred in nine hours 17 minutes. He was eventually dismissed for 114.

Asif Masood to bowl. And he approaches the wicket like Groucho Marx chasing after a pretty waitress.
JOHN ARLOTT (BBC Radio)

In October 1989 Imran Adil, some days short of his 19th birthday, took 10 for 92 for Bahawalpur against Faisalabad at Faisalabad.

In 1992 Pakistan won the World Cup for the first time.

Saqlain Mushtaq is credited with inventing a new type of off-spin delivery known as the 'doosra'.

In 2006 Mohammad Yousuf achieved the Pakistan record for the most Test runs in a calendar year – 1,788; the most centuries in a calendar year – nine; and also the record for the most centuries in successive Tests – six in five successive Test matches.

In July 2007 Pakistan appointed its third foreign coach for the national team, former Australian fast bowler Geoff Lawson.

On 3 March 2009 the coach containing the touring Sri Lanka cricket team was attacked by terrorists in Lahore as it journeyed to the Gaddaffi Stadium for the third day of the second Test. Five policemen were killed and eight Sri Lanka players and a member of the coaching team were injured. Unsurprisingly, the Test match and the series was called off by the Sri Lankan Cricket Board. The very serious nature of this incident led to Pakistan being unable to stage international cricket matches on home soil until the internal security situation improves considerably.

LI-LO have something for keen cricketers of all ages (and their less keen long-stop fielder companions). The hard-wearing Sorbo solid rubber composition cricket ball is ideal for practice, especially on hard wickets. In two sizes—Standard and Youth.

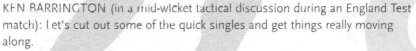

KEN BARRINGTON (in a mid-wicket tactical discussion during an England Test match): Let's cut out some of the quick singles and get things really moving along.
FRED TITMUS: OK. We'll cut out yours.

The highest partnership for any wicket is 624, by Kumar Sangakkara and Mahela Jayawardene for the third wicket in Sri Lanka's match against India at Colombo in 1997–98.

The highest partnership for any wicket in the County Championship is 555, by Percy Holmes and Herbert Sutcliffe for the first wicket in Yorkshire's match against Essex at Leyton in 1932.

At Leyton the scorers used to sit directly under the scoreboard and consequently could not see when it went wrong. With the Yorkshire total 555, Herbert Sutcliffe, with the new record achieved, took a swipe at a ball from Laurie Eastman and was bowled. Percy Holmes and Herbert Sutcliffe posed under the scoreboard for press photographers then the balloon

went up. The scorers said the Yorkshire total was
554 not 555. The Essex scorer Charles McGahey
asked if I would agree to the total being changed. The
umpires, very accommodating people, said a no-ball
had not been recorded. There was no doubt the extra
run was being 'found'. I told Charles I thought the two
batsmen had put up a magnificent performance and it
would be cruel luck if they were deprived of the
record, so the record it became. The Essex bowling
figures in that innings are also worth recalling:
Nichols none for 105, Daer none for 106, Peter Smith
none for 128.

CHARLES BRAY (Essex)

The record first-wicket partnership in first-class cricket is 561, by Waheed
Mirza and Mansoor Akhtar for Karachi Whites against Quetta at Karachi in
1976–77.

The record second-wicket partnership is 576, by Sanath Jayasuriya and Roshan
Mahanama for Sri Lanka against India at Colombo in 1997–98.

The record fourth-wicket partnership is 577, by Vijay Hazare and Gul
Mahomed for Baroda against Holkar at Baroda in 1946–47.

The record fifth-wicket partnership is 464 (unbroken), by Steve and Mark Waugh
for New South Wales against Western Australia at Perth in 1990–91.

The record sixth-wicket partnership is 487 (unbroken), by George Headley
and Clarence Passailaigue for Jamaica against Lord Tennyson's XI at
Kingston in 1931–32.

The record seventh-wicket partnership is 460, by Bhupinder Singh Jr and
P. Dharmani for Punjab against Delhi at Delhi in 1994–95.

The record eighth-wicket partnership is 433, by Victor Trumper and A. Sims
for Australian XI against Canterbury at Christchurch in 1913–14.

The record ninth-wicket partnership is also a County Championship record – 283, by Arnold Warren and J. Chapman for Derbyshire against Warwickshire at Blackwell in 1910.

The record tenth-wicket partnership is 307, by Alan Kippax and J. E. H. Hooker for New South Wales against Victoria at Melbourne in 1928–29.

Highest partnerships in the County Championship not yet mentioned:

Second wicket – 465 (unbroken), by John Jameson and Rohan Kanhai for Warwickshire against Gloucestershire at Edgbaston in 1974.

Third wicket – 438 (unbroken), by Graeme Hick and Tom Moody for Worcestershire against Hampshire at Southampton in 1997.

Fourth wicket – 470, by Alvin Kallicharran and Geoff Humpage for Warwickshire against Lancashire at Southport in 1982.

Fifth wicket – 401, by Malachy Loye and David Ripley for Northamptonshire against Glamorgan at Northampton in 1998.

Sixth wicket – 411, by Robert Poore and Edward Wynyard for Hampshire against Somerset at Taunton in 1899.

Seventh wicket – 344, by K. S. Ranjitsinhji and William Newham for Sussex against Essex at Leyton in 1902.

Eighth wicket – 292, by Robert Peel and Lord Hawke for Yorkshire against Warwickshire at Edgbaston in 1896.

Tenth wicket – 235, by Frank Woolley and in this instance the inappropriately named A. Fielder for Kent against Worcestershire at Stourbridge in 1909.

There have only been 11 last-wicket partnerships of 200 or more. The last in

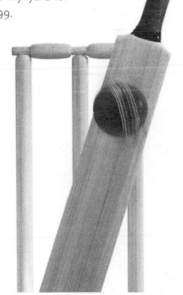

the County Championship was by Nick Knight and Alan Richardson (214) for Warwickshire against Hampshire at Edgbaston in 2002.

 I'd call, but often Tom Greenhough would be in two minds. I reckon Tom must have returned to the non-striker's end more times than the postman did to our house.
BRIAN STATHAM

64

 Morning, everyone.
RICHIE BENAUD

 Have I ever played cricket? Of course. I once delivered a simple ball which, I was told, had it gone far enough, would have been considered a wide.
LEWIS CARROLL

 Tha' sees two kinds of cricketers, them that uses a bat as if they were shovelling muck and them that plays proper, and like as not God showed them both how to play.
WILFRED RHODES

 Cricket does not pare a man down like a creed, political or religious, but reveals him.
HUGH DE SELINCOURT

TREVOR BAILEY: 13.5 runs per over required and I think they'll find that very difficult to get.
FRED TRUEMAN: Especially the point five.
BRIAN JOHNSTON: Oh, Fred, do give over.

 Cricket shouldn't be used as a political football.
DAVID GRAVENEY

 The ball came back, literally cutting Graham Thorpe in half.
COLIN CROFT

 Stand still in cricket these days and you go backwards.
SURREY OFFICIAL

 The wickets were pitched, and so were a couple of marquees for the rest and refreshment of the contending parties.
CHARLES DICKENS (Dingley Dell v. All Muggleton from *Pickwick Papers*, 1837, written in the Turk's Head, High Street, Exeter – still there, but sadly now a pasta restaurant)

 Tunnicliffe told me that Lord Hawke kept Emmott Robinson out of the Yorkshire county side till he was 35 years old because of a fear that Emmott's bowed legs would spoil the tidiness of the team.
WALLY HAMMOND

 Bowlers like Angus Fraser are the foot soldiers of cricket, the beetle crushers, the poor bloody infantry.
MICHAEL PARKINSON

 Once again we got a kick up the backside. Maybe it's the shot in the arm we needed.
ALLAN BORDER

What we are witnessing is a fascinating contest between bat and ball, with players involved of course.
ESPN COMMENTATOR

GARRY RICHARDSON: Can England win in Australia? Just say 'yes' or 'no'.
PHIL TUFNELL: Yes or no.

Even when we went 2–1 down in the series I never thought we would be whitewashed.
DEVON MALCOLM

Brian Toss won the close.
HENRY BLOFELD (BBC Radio)

He's got perfect control over the ball right up to the minute he lets it go.
PETER WALKER

Injuries of any sort are met with serious, concerned faces on football pitches. Injuries sustained in cricket tend to be a source for humour.
BENNY GREEN

I always liked to see melon on the menu during the lunch interval. You could eat, drink and wash your face all at the same time.
PETER PARFITT

You often see Pringles now instead of traditional crisps in dressing rooms at close of play. I think Pringle set out to make tennis balls, signed off a deal with the packing company, but on the day the rubber was supposed to turn up a big lorryload of potatoes arrived instead.
RODNEY MARSH

Do you have any superstitious routines before an innings? Like putting one pad on first then the other one?
TONY LEWIS

DON WILSON (in Yorkshire dressing room): A black cat has just walked across my path. Remind me again, what does that mean?
JIMMY BINKS: It means it's going somewhere.

Michael Vaughan has a long history in the game ahead of him.
MARK NICHOLAS

It's a Catch-21 situation.
KEVIN PIETERSEN

Mike Gatting often went with me to the gym, but his favourite machine was the vending machine.
IAN BOTHAM

Those buggers in high places made sure I'd only play once for my country. Mr Bloody Warner will go to bed when I've finished with him.
CHARLIE PARKER

Charlie Parker only played once for England because he was what was euphemistically described as 'outspoken'. He eventually consoled himself for the victimization he suffered at the hands of foolish selectors: he met Pelham Warner in a lift and thumped his patrician nose.
BENNY GREEN

It's an old maxim of cricket, older than when Jonah was in the Ark.
SIMON BATES

You could cut the atmosphere with a cricket stump.
MURRAY WALKER

Magnificent shot! No, out!
TONY GREIG (Channel 9)

Whenever anyone asks me if I ever batted against [Maurice] Tate I always think of the mother who asked the headmaster if her son had done trigonometry. 'Well, no, madam,' replied the headmaster, 'it would be an exaggeration to claim he has "done" trigonometry. The most we can say is that he has been exposed to it.' It was the same with me in my batting against Tate.
DON DAVIES (Sussex)

This pitch will produce plenty of up and down bounce.
TONY GREIG (Channel 9)

The police have infiltrated the crowd with plainclothes protectives.
KEN BARRINGTON

Play has ended here at Southampton, but they play until seven at Edgbaston, so over there now for some more balls from Rex Alston.
BRIAN JOHNSTON

I absolutely insist that all my boys be in bed before breakfast.
COLIN INGLEBY-MACKENZIE

The good news for England is that a brain scan has revealed Andrew Caddick is not, as feared, suffering from a stress fracture of the shin.
JO SHELDON

Peter Booth, who stands to break a personal milestone in this match.
PETER WALKER

 We apologize to the deaf and hard of hearing for the loss of subtitles during that cricket report.
ANGELA RIPPON

 In the 1950s A&BC gave away picture cards of cricketers with their bubble gum. One of the cards featured me, in the category of 'Batsmen'. There I am, playing forward. What the photograph doesn't show is that Alan Moss knocked my middle stump some 20 yards back. I can't think why I was featured as a batsman. I couldn't bat to save my life. They used to fight one another to grab the ball when they saw me coming out to bat.
BRIAN BOSHIER (Leicestershire)

 I thought they were only allowed two bouncers in one over.
BILL FRINDALL (*TMS*, commenting on a female streaker)

 Watching cricket is easy. All anyone needs is a deckchair, a pipe or knitting and a week off from the office.
TIME MAGAZINE

 What England need is a blessing that's not in disguise.
DAVID LLOYD

 I wish I was as cocksure of something the way Tony Greig appears cocksure of everything.
EDDIE BARLOW

It would be a surprise if the mirrors in Kevin Pietersen's house totalled anything less than the entire stock at one of the larger branches of B&Q.
MARTIN JOHNSON

I'm completely different from Pietersen. He would turn up for the opening of an envelope.
ANDREW FLINTOFF

Richie Benaud eyes the camera lens with the manner of a disdainful lizard.
BRIAN VINER

To be bowled by Tony Lock was like being mugged. To be dismissed by [Bishan] Bedi was akin to being handed a letter by a man in a frock coat saying your services were no longer required.
MICHAEL PARKINSON

Reginald Herbert Spooner led us through the wicket of fancy into Heaven's meadow and set us gathering stars.
DON DAVIES

Glamorgan played a key role in the outcome of this season's ProForty League. In fact they won it.
SIMON HUMPHRIES (Signal Radio)

MARK SAGGERS: Do you think England has a real chance of beating Australia today?
ALLAN LAMB: Not a real chance, but a chance.

Sir Len Hutton was on the England Selection Committee and had been quoted in the press saying some very complimentary things about me. When I

arrived at Lord's I saw him on the car park so went up to thank him for the opportunity he had given me and told him I hoped to repay his faith. He studied me for a moment then asked, 'Who the hell are you?'
GRAHAM GOOCH

 The West Indies total, 687 for 8 declared. Richards, a masterful innings of 291. He set the tone. His attitude, contagious, like the gladness of a happy child.
JOHN ARLOTT

 James Anderson says, 'I always use a daily moisturizer.' It's one of the great tragedies that Fred Trueman is no longer with Test Match Special, because Jonathan Agnew asking Fred what type of moisturizer he used in his day could have produced one of sport's truly great radio moments.
MARTIN JOHNSON

 Merv Hughes . . . an ordinary bloke trying to make good without ever losing the air of a fellow with a hangover.
PETER ROEBUCK

 And Sachin Tendulkar gets up on his toes to play that away, like a dwarf at a urinal.
NAVJOT SIDHU

 The crowd filled the ground, but so silent was it as Grace took his guard that one could hear the tink-tink of a hansom cab coming closer and closer along the Vauxhall Road.
NEVILLE CARDUS

Brian Congdon remains at the crease to frustrate England, like some lingering, unloved guest at a party.
JOHN ARLOTT

And there's the George Headley Stand, named after . . . George Headley.
TREVOR QUIRK

The clock on the flint tower of the church struck the half hour, and the vibrations spread slowly across the shimmering hedgerows, spangled with white blossom of the convolvulus, and lost themselves tremulously among the orchards.
A. G. MACDONNELL (*The Cricket Match*)

England's pace bowlers are making the helmet go out of fashion.
SCYLD BERRY

Well, we've now won one on the trot.
ALEC STEWART

I was stung by a bee at the Oval . . . paid 20 quid for a jar of honey.
PAUL BOARDMAN

They said to me at the Oval, come and see our new bowling machine. 'Bowling machine?' I said. 'I used to be the club's bowling machine.'
ALEC BEDSER

I once hit Australia's Rodney Hogg for three successive fours. He came down the wicket and snarled, 'I'm

going to knock that stupid head off your shoulders.'
I said, 'You're not quick enough, mate.' He said, 'I
wasn't thinking of using the ball!'
DEREK RANDALL

 Trying to find any little scandal about a player and
blowing it up happens all the time in football and it's
creeping into cricket. A reporter from a tabloid once
said to me, 'There's a rumour Graham Gooch, Mike
Atherton and another bloke got pie-eyed attempting
to empty a champagne cellar in Rheims by drinking it
dry.' I said, 'No rumour, dear boy, it's true . . . and I
was the other bloke.'
HENRY BLOFELD

 Twenty20 is the golden goose they're looking to
fleece.
ARLO WHITE

 On the India tour of 1981, Keith Fletcher held a team
meeting in which he told us his plan for dealing with
each Indian batsman, only for Ian Botham to have his
own ideas. 'Gavaskar?' said Both. 'He's the Ronnie
Corbett of Calcutta. You lot can pitch it up to him, but
not me. I'm banging it in just short of a length and
poking him in the throat with it.' So it went on:
whatever Keith said, Both had another plan. A heated
discussion took place. After some two hours we went
with Both. 'You'll not regret it, we'll be batting just
after tea,' Both told us. We were – on the second day,
India 625 for 4 declared.
GRAHAM GOOCH

At cricket matches, why do spectators sit in stands?
KEN DODD

You generally find the team who scores most in the first innings takes the lead in the game.
MARK SAGGERS

England's batting was like the weather, a shower that didn't last long.
BBC *SIX O'CLOCK NEWS* (31 July 2008)

Mark Ealham, 39 years of age now. He'll be 40 next year.
CHARLES COLVILLE (Sky Sports)

You're not God, you're a cricketer, and I'm a better one.
KEVIN PIETERSEN (to Yuvraj Singh, picked up by the stump mike, India v. England in December 2008)

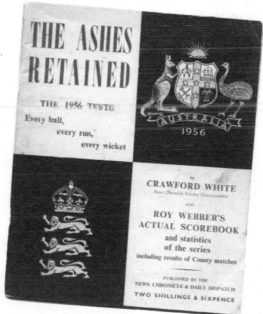

The only player to have given his name to a form of run-out is Vinoo Mankad. On 13 December 1947 during the second Test between Australia and India at Sydney, Mankad ran out Australia's Bill Brown when, as he was about to bowl the ball, he noticed Brown out of his crease, held on to the ball and whipped the bails off. This was the second time Mankad had run out Brown this way during the tour. In an earlier match between an Australian XI and India Mankad had warned Brown he would run him out should the Australian continue backing up before he had delivered the ball. Brown continued to walk down the wicket so Mankad ran him out. Following Brown's dismissal in the second Test, the Australian press dubbed this type of run-out a 'Mankad'.

Bill Brown's association with run-outs continued to dog him in that series against India. During the Melbourne Test in February 1948 he was run out when one run short of a century – the first player to be run out on the dreaded 99 in a Test match.

The Laws of Cricket relating to a bowler running out the non-strike batsman have since changed. They do not now allow a bowler to 'Mankad' a batsman once he has entered his delivery stride, though they do allow for a 'Mankad' should the bowler have started his run-up but not yet entered his delivery stride. The rules of indoor cricket still allow for a 'Mankad'. When this occurs the batsman is given out 'Mankad' rather than 'run out'.

Since the Brown incident in 1947 there have been three notable instances of 'Mankads' in Test cricket: Ian Redpath (Australia) by Charlie Griffith (West Indies) at Adelaide in 1968–69; Derek Randall (England) by Ewen Chatfield (New Zealand) at Christchurch in 1977–78; and Sikander Bakht (Pakistan) by Alan Hurst (Australia) at Perth in 1978–79.

The first batsman to be given out 'Mankad' in an ODI was Brian Luckhurst (England) by Greg Chappell (Australia) at Melbourne in 1974–75.

In 1987 Courtney Walsh (West Indies) declined to 'Mankad' last man Saleem Jaffa of Pakistan for backing up too early during a 1987 World Cup group match, opting instead to warn Jaffa of his intention to do so. Pakistan went on to win the match and the defeat cost the West Indies a place in the semi-finals.

The last batsman to be given out 'Mankad' in an ODI was Peter Kirsten (South Africa), run out by Kapil Dev (India) at Port Elizabeth in 1992–93.

Instances of batsmen being run out on 99 are numerous, but not necessarily in the same match. No fewer than three batsmen were run out for 99 in the Pakistan v. England Test at Karachi in 1973: Mushtaq Mohammad, Majid Khan and Dennis Amiss.

While playing for his country, Warwickshire and England skipper Mike (M. J. K.) Smith was run out four times in the nineties, and on two of those occasions he was on 99.

Two players who would go on to captain England missed out on what would have been their maiden Test century when run out on 99: Graham Gooch, against Australia at Melbourne in February 1980; and Mike Atherton, also against Australia, at Lord's in 1993.

Unlucky 13 – for him. In 2002 Neil McKenzie (South Africa) became the 13th player to be run out for 99 in a Test match when he was dismissed against Australia at Cape Town.

Nottinghamshire's Jason Gallian ran himself out on 199 twice in the same year. While playing against Sussex at Trent Bridge in April 2005 he chanced a quick single for his double century but was run out. The second occasion took place during the match against Kent at Canterbury in September. Gallian, on 196, hit the ball towards the lime-tree boundary, ran three, but in risking a fourth ran himself out. He is the only player in the history of cricket to be run out twice one run short of a double century (and in the same season) and the only player with two 199s in a career.

The highest number of run-outs from the field in a single innings of an international cricket match is five. The first side to reach this figure was the West Indies, in an ODI against Australia at Lord's on 21 June 1975. The Australian victims were Alan Turner (by Viv Richards), Ian Chappell (by Viv Richards), Greg Chappell (by Viv Richards, his hat-trick), Max Walker (by Vanburn Holder) and Jeff Thomson (by Deryck Murray). Australia (274) lost to the West Indies (291 for 8) by 17 runs.

There have been eight further instances of five run-outs in a single innings in international cricket, all in ODIs (team subjected to run-outs listed first): New Zealand v. Sri Lanka (Sharjah, 1988), Pakistan v. West Indies (Adelaide, 1992), Australia v. India (Mumbai, 1996), New Zealand v. India (Napier, 1999), Sri Lanka v. Pakistan (Dhaka, 2000), West Indies v. Zimbabwe (Perth, 2001), Australia v. Sri Lanka (Adelaide, 2006), and Zimbabwe v. South Africa (Bulawayo, 2007).

The most run-outs accomplished by England in a single innings is four, in the ODI against Australia at Lord's on 9 June 1979.

 There's only one word to describe that run-out by Randall. It was a fantastic pick-up, superb throw and deadly accurate.
TONY GREIG

The most run-outs sustained in a single innings of a Test match is four: India v. Pakistan at Peshawar (13 February 1955) and Australia v. West Indies at Adelaide (24 January 1969).

The most run-outs sustained in an ODI is eight: New Zealand (suffered five run-outs) against India (three run-outs) at Napier, 12 January 1999).

The most run-outs accomplished in a Twenty20 international is four – New Zealand v. India at Johannesburg on 16 September 2007, and Scotland v. the Netherlands at Belfast on 4 August 2008.

The 1911 Mowatt Cup Final between Great Northern Railway's General Managers Office CC (it rolls off the tongue) and Doncaster Locomotive Works CC ended in farce and a sensational run-out. In the final over the last pair were batting for Doncaster Locomotive Works with the scores level. The batsmen set off for what would be the winning run. The bowler, H. G. Rushton, ran to field the ball himself and, noticing the Works batsmen had stopped mid-wicket to shake hands and congratulate each other, threw down the wicket at the bowler's end to tie the match.

The equanimity of the Lord's Pavilion was disturbed when Gladwin, after being run out by his partner, accidentally put his bat through the dressing room window.
Wisden (1950 – Middlesex v. Derbyshire, 24–26 August 1949)

On 1 July 1958 Balliol College (Oxford) needed four runs to beat Marlborough College with three wickets in hand. The final over was bowled by Dennis Silk (later of Somerset). Three runs were scored off the first two balls then three Balliol batsmen were run out with consecutive balls and the match, sensationally, ended in a tie.

When it came to fielding, Colin Bland (South Africa, 1961–66) was anything but. In the 1960s Bland was rated as the best fielder of the ball in the world, particularly noted for his ability to hit a wicket side on from distance. He gave a demonstration of his accuracy on the BBC's Sportsview programme. In three attempts at picking up a running ball and throwing it 25 yards from the wicket he hit it side on every time.

On 10 July 1962, during the match between the MCC and Oxford University at Lord's, Oxford's David Pithey 'walked' thinking he had been bowled. The ball had in fact missed the wicket, but as Pithey left his crease he was run out.

A similar fate befell Dean Jones during the second Test between the West Indies and Australia at Guyana on 27 March 1991. Jones failed to hear the umpire call 'no-ball' and was bowled by Courtney Walsh. He began his walk towards the pavilion whereupon Carl Hooper, fielding in the slips, ran Jones out. Though in contravention of the Laws, Jones was 'run out' for 3.

Should a fielder want to run out a batsman it helps if he can throw from distance and with accuracy, though no player has yet beaten Robert Percival's record for the longest recorded distance for throwing a cricket ball. In 1882 Percival, renowned for his throwing, was challenged to throw a ball as far as he could at Durham Sands Racecourse in Durham. His throw was measured at 140 yards and two feet, beating the previous record of 140 yards and nine inches set by Ross Mackenzie in 1872.

In 1991 Middlesex and England bowler Angus Fraser made a valiant attempt to beat Percival's record at Chelmsford. Fraser's throw was measured at exactly 130 yards, which was the longest distance recorded for throwing a cricket ball since D. G. Foster's 131 yards and one foot in 1931.

All these years on I still have the scorecard, though, while I am able to recall the match in vivid detail, the scorecard cannot. Not even that we won.
H. E. BATES

The first *Test Match Special* scorer was Arthur Wrigley. In 1966 he was succeeded by Bill Frindall, affectionately known as 'The Bearded Wonder', who continued in the role until his untimely death in January 2009.

Bill was monarch of the moderns. If cricket scoring is an art, then Frindall was a Caravaggio of the game.
FRANK KEATING

Bill Frindall has done some mental arithmetic with a calculator.
JOHN ARLOTT

The oldest scorecard known to exist records a match between London and Kent at Finsbury Park in 1744.

The earliest known scorecards to appear on a regular basis were produced at the Vine Cricket Club in Sevenoaks, Kent in 1776.

Scorecards have always been treasured by supporters, primarily because they serve as a personal record of a match. County clubs and many minor clubs have long issued matchcards which supporters have taken great delight in completing as play unfolded.

 Arnold Long took an age coming out to the wicket, which gave me ample time to write next to the name of S. J. Storey 'c Boycott, b Wilson, 11', which I did in neat letters with a Winfield fountain pen purchased from Woolworths. I was in the process of adding Storey's score to my card when, suddenly, I heard a cry of voices followed by a smattering of applause. I looked up to see Long trooping back to the pavilion. I set about trying to keep abreast of events. What had started out as careful, neat script was deteriorating into scrawl. A weathered supporter tapped me on the shoulder and when I turned said to me, 'Next to "A. Long", be sure to write, "time coming but soon went".'
RICHARD BECKINSALE (actor, recalling a day at the Oval as a boy)

No one knows for sure when scorecards were first printed for county matches. The first scorecard printing machine was erected in a tent at Lord's in 1848, and matchcards were sold to supporters that season.

The matchcards were updated and printed for each day's play. Some clubs, such as Yorkshire, prided themselves on how quickly they could produce the matchcard for the following day's play, often issuing cards containing full details of the day's play only minutes after stumps had been pulled.

A club's matchcard was normally a single sheet of card, one side of which detailed the name of the home team and opposition, the dates of the match, and the batting line-ups for both teams, with spaces for supporters to write down how the batsman was out, his score for both innings, fall of wickets and bowling analyses.

Information on the reverse of the card varied from club to club. A Warwickshire matchcard of May 1953 simply contained adverts – 12 in total. Typically these adverts were parochial, small local businesses such as a confectionery shop and estate agent's that provided Edgbaston with a small but most welcome source of income long before major banks and multinational companies realized how they could benefit from an association with the game. Some counties used the reverse of the matchcard to detail First and Second XI fixtures, and in the case of the MCC and Middlesex in the 1950s and 1960s – the days before club shops – to print a price list for cricket-related products and books 'available from the Pavilion ticket office'. Some matchcards also carried on the reverse information regarding the times and availability on the day of lunch and teas, or information regarding the provision of a new ball.

Matchcards of yesteryear not only provide a detailed personal record of a game, fixture lists offer a snapshot of the variety of teams that enjoyed the facilities of a ground, and its social standing. A Middlesex matchcard of 1953 is particularly revealing in this respect. In addition to Middlesex, MCC and England games the following fixtures took place at Lord's that year: Oxford University v. Cambridge University, Eton v. Harrow, Royal Artillery v. Royal Engineers, Gentlemen v. Players, Beaumont v. Oratory, Clifton v. Tunbridge Wells, Rugby v. Marlborough, Cheltenham v. Haileybury, Southern Public Schools v. The Rest, Public Schools XI v. MCC Young Pros, Combined Services v. Public Schools, Royal Navy v. RAF, Army v. Air Force, RM Sandhurst v. RMA Sandhurst Old Boys, Barristers v. Barristers Clerks, MCC XI v. de Flamingos, Gentlemen of England v. Australians and House of Lords v. Eton Old Boys. All of which suggests that as late as the 1950s in cricket certain privileges were afforded to a certain class of people. No doubt the teams in question paid for the hire of Lord's, though one wonders what response a league club from, say, Nottinghamshire would have received from 'headquarters' should they have had the financial wherewithal to hire the venue.

67

Today many old matchcards and scorecards have become collectors' items. When it comes to collecting football programmes, the fact someone has written on one has a negative effect on price. The reverse is true of cricket matchcards: the most valued are those containing complete written details of a match.

In the 1950s and 1960s, prior to graphics technology, the BBC displayed handwritten calligraphic scorecards during their Test match broadcasts. The beautifully crafted cards were the work of Maurice Ryman, who had been introduced to the BBC by Brian Johnston. Johnners had once presented awards and certificates at a swimming gala in Brighton and had been so taken with the calligraphy on the certificates he recommended their creator to the head of BBC Sport Outside Broadcasts with a view to him writing the Test match scorecards.

The longest-serving scorer in international cricket is Bill Ferguson (1880–1957), who in addition to acting as official scorer was also baggage master on 43 Australian overseas tours in the days when one such tour was undertaken per year.

Any number of players assumed the role of their club's official scorer once they'd hung up their pads. Among the most notable are Clem Driver, Charlie Grove, Patsy Hendren, Andy Sandham, Harry Sharp, Jim Sims and Herbert Strudwick.

The battered tin number plates were rattled on to
their nails on the scoreboard by a zealous young
hobbledehoy who had undertaken the job for the day.

'Wodger say last man made?' he bawled, though the
scorer was only feet away.

'Last man, Blob.'

SIEGFRIED SASSOON

Spot of bother on verge of a century. The printed scorecard entry for G. E. V.
Crutchley, batting for Oxford University in the Varsity match against
Cambridge University on 8 July 1912, reads 'G. E. V. Crutchley . . . retired
suffering from measles . . . 99 not out'.

In 2008 Durham's official scorer, Brian Hunt, became the first county scorer to
be granted a benefit since Mac Taylor (Lancashire) in 1964.

The earliest known cricket match in Scotland took place at Alloa in 1785.

On 7 May 1849 a Scotland representative team played All England XI at Edinburgh. This is generally accepted as the first match contested by a Scotland international team.

Scotland played Surrey in 1865 – and won by 172 runs.

The Scottish Cricket Union was formed in 1879.

In 1882 Scotland caused a major upset when they beat the touring Australians by seven wickets.

The Scottish Cricket Union was beset by financial problems and internal disagreements, and became defunct in 1883. Grange CC took over the administration and organization of cricket in Scotland and ran things until 1909, when a new national body was formed.

Throughout the first half of the twentieth century cricket in Scotland had a relatively low profile. The game was given a major boost in 1948 when Australia played two matches, notable for being the last international fixtures played by Don Bradman, who signed off in some style with 123 not out.

A message to you Rudi. In 1961 Barbados-born Rudi Webster was studying medicine at Edinburgh University and playing for the university team when he was selected to play for Scotland against the MCC at Greenock. The game marked Webster's debut in a first-class match and he took a wicket with his very first delivery, bowling Carter Dodds (Essex). Webster repeated the feat with his very first ball of the MCC's second innings, clean-bowling Arthur Phebey (Kent). Webster returned match figures of 11 for 100, which persuaded him to seek a career in county cricket. Upon his graduation he signed for Warwickshire.

In 1980 Scotland competed in the Benson & Hedges Cup – their first appearance in English domestic cricket. In 1983 Scotland took part in the NatWest Trophy for the first time.

In 1986 Scotland celebrated their first victory over an English first-class county, defeating Lancashire in the Benson & Hedges Cup.

In 1992 Scotland severed ties with the TCCB and England. Two years later they gained associate membership in their own right of the ICC.

Scotland appeared in the ICC Trophy for the first time in 1997, finishing third, which led to qualification for the 1999 World Cup.

Scotland's debut in the 1999 World Cup was nothing to write home about: they lost every match. But competing in the tournament was considered to be an important step in the development and profile of Scottish cricket.

In 2004 Scotland won the inaugural Intercontinental Cup, and in 2005 the ICC Trophy for the very first time, defeating Ireland in the final.

Scotland continued to progress. In 2006 they competed in the C&G Trophy, winning three of their nine matches, and finished eighth in the Northern Conference.

The first Scotland match to be broadcast live and in its entirety on BBC Scotland was the ODI against India at Titwood in Glasgow in August 2007. India won by seven wickets.

Later in 2007 Scotland competed in the Twenty20 World Championship in South Africa. They lost to Pakistan by 51 runs, and the match against their other group opponents, India, was abandoned due to rain without a ball being bowled.

The Scotland team that competes in the Friends Provident Trophy is called the Scottish Saltires, a saltire being a diagonal cross such as the St Andrew's cross, which appears on the national flag. The Saltires play the majority of home matches at The Grange in Edinburgh, though some matches are scheduled for Titwood in Glasgow.

Notable Scottish players who went on to make a name in English cricket include Douglas Jardine (of 'Bodyline' infamy), Mike Denness (Kent and former captain of England), Brian Hardie (Essex) and Dougie Brown (Warwickshire). Former England captain Tony Greig can also lay claim to some Scottish blood: his father was Scottish.

Ian Peebles has the distinction of having played for both Scotland and England. His story is a curious one and serves to highlight the quixotic policies of past MCC/England selectors. Born in Aberdeen, Peebles moved to London in the late 1920s to take up a post as secretary of a cricket school run by South African Test player Aubrey Faulkener. While at the school he impressed Sir Pelham Warner with his off-break bowling and was invited to play in the Gentlemen v. Players match. He played some end-of-season matches at the Scarborough and Folkestone Cricket Festivals after which he was appointed 'Secretary to the Captain' for the MCC tour of South Africa in 1927–28, but was selected for four Tests. In 1928 he joined Middlesex, and in 1930 he went up to Oxford for a year. His 13 wickets in the Varsity match earned him an England call-up for the fourth Test against Australia at Old Trafford. In the fifth Test at the Oval he took 6 for 204, but that was in an Australia total of 695. He continued to play for Middlesex but during the Second World War lost an eye in an air-raid, which curtailed his effectiveness. On retiring as a player he wrote on cricket for the *Sunday Times* and penned a succession of popular books on the game. He remains Scotland's best-known cricket writer.

In 2009 Gavin Hamilton was appointed captain following Scotland's failure to qualify for the 2011 World Cup. Hamilton, formerly with Yorkshire and Durham, played in the 1999 and 2007 World Cups.

The knee's fine but my neck now hurts from watching
all those sixes hit by Australia.
MICHAEL VAUGHAN

The highest number of sixes scored in a single innings in the County
Championship is 16, by Andrew Symonds (254 not out) for Gloucestershire
against Glamorgan at Abergavenny in 1995. In the same game Symonds went on
to achieve the record for the most sixes by an individual batsman in a match – 20.

In June 2008 Graham Napier also hit 16 sixes, in a Twenty20 game for Essex
against Sussex. Napier scored 152 off 58 balls.

Seven other batsmen have hit 12 or more sixes in a single innings in English
first-class cricket: Majid Khan (13), for Pakistan v. Glamorgan at Swansea in 1967;
Gordon Greenidge (13), for D. H. Robins XI v. Pakistan at Eastbourne in 1974,
and for Hampshire v. Sussex at Southampton in 1975; Geoff Humpage (13), for
Warwickshire v. Lancashire at Southport in 1982; Ian Botham (12), for Somerset
against Warwickshire at Edgbaston in 1985; Roger Harper (12), for
Northamptonshire against Gloucestershire at Northampton in 1986; Dean Jones
(12), for Australia against Warwickshire at Edgbaston in 1989; and Graham Lloyd
(12), for Lancashire against Essex at Chelmsford in 1996.

In 1942 South African Test batsman Dudley Nourse hit nine sixes off consecutive balls, spread across two overs, while playing for South African XI against Military Police in that hotbed of cricket Cairo.

On 24 August 1951 Worcestershire needed six runs off the final ball of the match to beat Somerset at Taunton. Bob Wyatt, aged 50, hit Bertie Buse over the rope to win the match for Worcestershire.

In July 1955 South Africa's Paul Winslow reached his maiden century by hitting a six against England at Old Trafford.

In 1959 William Stewart scored 17 sixes for Warwickshire in a match against Lancashire at Blackpool.

Only two players have hit in excess of 50 sixes in a first-class season: Ian Botham (85), for Somerset and England in 1985, and Arthur Wellard (known affectionately to schoolboys as 'Walloper' Wellard), who accomplished this feat on no fewer than four occasions: 51 in 1933, 66 in 1935, 57 in 1936 and 57 in 1938.

DON MOSEY (BBC): Tell me, what happened out there?
IAN BOTHAM: Why, weren't you watching?

Six batsmen have scored in excess of 80 sixes in Test matches: Adam Gilchrist (Australia), 100; Brian Lara (West Indies), 88; Chris Cairns (New Zealand), 87; Viv Richards (West Indies), 84; Matthew Hayden (Australia), 82; and Andrew Flintoff (England) 81.

Sir Garfield Sobers was the first batsman in first-class cricket to hit six sixes off a single over, off the bowling of Malcolm Nash (Glamorgan) at Swansea in 1968, but he is not the only batsman to accomplish this feat. Ravi Shastri equalled Sobers' historic feat while playing for Bombay against Baroda in 1985, the unfortunate bowler being Tilka Raj. More recently Herschelle Gibbs hit six sixes for South Africa, against the Netherlands in the 2007 World Cup, and Yuvraj Singh did the same for India against England in the 2007 Twenty20 World Cup.

The bat used by Gary Sobers when he hit those sixes for Nottinghamshire against Glamorgan in 1968 was sold in 2000 at an auction in Australia for £54,257.

The ball Gary Sobers hit out of the Swansea ground to complete his sixth six was sold at auction at Christie's in 2006 for £26,400.

 ## Gary Sobers never had a nickname, he was always known as Gary . . . or 'The King'.
PAT POCOCK

On 27 August 1979 Mike Procter scored five successive sixes in the last five balls of the over and a six off the first ball of the next over he faced, so, as far as the scorebook is concerned, he hit six successive sixes albeit they were spread across two overs.

In the County Championship match between Kent and Glamorgan at Canterbury in August 2005, Kent's Darren Stevens hit a six which passed through the open flaps of the CAMRA real-ale tent and smashed four pint glasses containing beer. Not long after that Kent's Justin Kemp hit a six that zoomed into the president's marquee and felled waitress Danielle Weston-Webb. Concerned guests immediately went to Miss Weston-Webb's aid. Fortunately, other than shock, she appeared none the worse for her ordeal. The following day Justin Kemp tendered his apologies and presented Miss Weston-Webb with the ball that had hit her, which he had autographed – just what she always wanted.

Also in August 2005, during the match between Gloucestershire and Sussex at Cheltenham, Sussex's Matthew Prior hit a mighty six. The ball sailed into the crowd to where a spectator sat busily eating an ice-cream cornet – too busily to notice what Prior had done. The ball knocked the cornet out of the surprised spectator's hand and splattered his face with ice-cream.

The club is based at the County Ground in Taunton but also plays a number of matches at Bath. Somerset have also played at Frome, Glastonbury, Stratton-on-the-Fosse, Street, Wells, Weston-super-Mare, Yeovil and, curiously, two venues in Bristol: the Imperial Tobacco Athletics ground and Knowle CC.

The current capacity of the County Ground is 6,500, though redevelopment is ongoing and extensive. The club has acquired part of the neighbouring St James' churchyard that in time, in addition to affording spectators an iconic view, will allow the club to extend the boundary to meet international standards.

The club badge features the Somerset dragon.

Somerset is one of three county clubs never to have won the County Championship. Given the long history of the club, trophy successes have come only recently: the Gillette Cup/NatWest/C&G Trophy in 1979, 1983 and 2001; the Sunday League in 1979; the Benson & Hedges Cup in 1981 and 1982; and the Twenty20 Cup in 2005.

Stow-ball, a sport related to cricket, was played in the county during the sixteenth century, though the earliest known reference to cricket as many would recognize it dates from July 1751 – a match between two local teams in memory of the late Frederick, Prince of Wales.

The club was formed on 18 August 1875 by the Gentlemen of Somerset XI who met at an inn in Sidmouth, Devon following a match against a local team. (It's comforting, if not exactly in keeping, to think how many sports clubs have been formed in pubs and hotel bars.) This makes Somerset CCC unique in county cricket in that the club was formed outside the traditional boundaries of the county.

Somerset's inaugural first-class match took place on 8–10 June 1882 against Lancashire at Old Trafford. The club joined the then 'unofficial' County Championship.

In 1886 the club experienced financial difficulties, had problems recruiting players of the required standard, did not play any of the first-class counties and dropped out of the unofficial Championship. Somerset began playing against first-class counties once more in 1891, and in that year were admitted to what was by now the official County Championship.

In their second season (1892) Somerset finished third in the County Championship. *The Times* reported, 'Third place in the County Championship is a valiant effort and quite unlooked for at the advent of the season. The foundations have been laid for this fine, upstanding young club to perhaps soon secure the Championship itself.' It was to be 66 years before Somerset finished as high again.

It was also in 1892 that Lionel Palairet and H. T. Hewett shared an opening stand of 346 against Yorkshire at Taunton – still the highest partnership in the history of the club.

Another existing club record was set three years later, in 1895, when E. J. Tyler returned bowling figures of 10 for 49 against Surrey at Taunton.

In 1910 Somerset failed to win a single county match. Of the 18 matches they played they lost 15 and drew three.

Rippon yarn. Somerset opener Arthur Rippon (whose twin brother Albert often opened the batting with him) is the only known player to have played first-class cricket under an assumed name. Against Gloucestershire on 9–10 June 1919, Rippon was listed on the team sheet and scorecard as S. Trimnell, though no one knows why. As Albert also played in this match the family resemblance would surely have been evident. Arthur Rippon, aka S. Trimnell, made 92 and 58 not out – his best match batting figures of the season. Which leads one to think his jape could have backfired on him if the regulars in his local pub had read of the success of his 'replacement' and sung the praises of the new opener S. Trimnell, only for Rippon to remonstrate, 'No, no, you've got it wrong, that was me!' You can just imagine the incredulity of the regulars. 'Yeah, right, Arthur, course it was.'

In 1919 Somerset farmer Jack White returned match bowling figures of 16 for 83 against Worcestershire at Bath – the club's best bowling in a single match. White also holds the record for the most wickets taken in the course of a career with the club – 2,165 (average 18.03).

In 1920 Somerset dismissed Gloucestershire for only 22 at Bristol – the lowest ever total by first-class opposition against the club. Gloucestershire exacted their revenge, though, 27 years later: at Bristol in 1947, Somerset were dismissed for 25 – their lowest score in first-class cricket.

Between the wars it was rare for a Somerset player to be selected for England, which is why in 1924 there was much joy within the club following the selection of Jack White to play against South Africa. Unfortunately the match was a victim of rain and though White did appear in the field, he neither batted nor bowled and was never selected for England again – which must be some sort of record.

In May 1935 Harold Gimblett was called into the first XI at short notice for his county debut against Essex at Frome. Gimblett's debut was the stuff of dreams and legend. Coming to the wicket with Somerset on 107 for 6, Gimblett raced to his maiden century in only 63 minutes, going on to score 123 in 80 minutes in Somerset's first-innings total of 175. His efforts helped Somerset to win by an innings.

In 1936, playing against Northamptonshire at Bath, Harold Gimblett scored all of the final 84 runs of Somerset's total of 143. What's more, he did so entirely in boundaries.

Gimblett was the star of a Somerset team that in the late 1930s and for eight seasons after the Second World War often comprised just a handful of professionals. In a Somerset career that spanned the years 1935 to 1954 he scored a club record 21,142 first-class runs (average 36.96), including 49 centuries, and was a big favourite with Somerset supporters due to his cavalier batting style. Perhaps the fact he 'played to the gallery' and was from one of the 'unfashionable' counties is the reason why he played only three Tests for England. For a player whose batting style was described as 'swashbuckling and highly entertaining' he was considered by many to be a morose character and a depressive. He died at his Dorset home in 1978 having taken an overdose of prescription drugs.

In 1938 Arthur Wellard took 169 wickets (average 19.24) – the most by any Somerset bowler in the course of a season.

Fingers of fate are air-raising stuff. In June 1948, against Essex at Taunton, Arthur Wellard bowled to Essex opener T. C. Dodds, at the time on 75, who hit the ball straight back to the bowler. Wellard managed to get a hand to the ball, pushing it up in the air, and made to catch it at the second attempt only to lose his footing, but managing again to flick the ball into the air with his fingertips. Still struggling to execute the catch, Wellard got his fingertips to the ball for a third time to keep the ball in the air before finally, at the fourth attempt, diving forward to achieve a caught and bowled.

In 1949 slow left-arm spinner Horace Hazell bowled 105 consecutive deliveries against Gloucestershire at Taunton without conceding a single run. And they wondered why attendances were falling.

Somerset finished bottom of the County Championship in four successive seasons, 1952–55. The Somerset committee decided the culture within the club and dressing room, of 'happy-go-lucky cricket', had to change – a decision not in any small way prompted by the fact attendances were low and the club was in dire financial straits. A new policy was adopted with the aim of fielding a fully professional team aided by overseas players. Two of the first overseas players to arrive and help provide an upturn in fortunes were Bill Alley and Colin McCool from Australia. In 1958 Somerset finished third in the county table.

In 1961 Bill Alley, aged 42, scored 2,761 runs (average 58.74) – the most runs accumulated by a Somerset player in the course of a single season.

Affectionately referred to by Fred Trueman as Bill 'Bowling' Alley, he scored 19,612 first-class runs (average 31.88) and took 768 wickets (average 22.68) during his career. In his native country Alley had also been a renowned middleweight boxer, undefeated in all of his 28 bouts before deciding on a career in cricket. He was an unusual player, though far from unique, in that he batted left-handed but was a right-arm medium-fast bowler. He played his last and 350th match for Somerset at the age of 48, then became a first-class umpire for 16 years, officiating in 10 Tests and nine ODIs.

The Devon-based dramatist and novelist R. F. Delderfield was a keen follower of the fortunes of Somerset. In some ways mirroring David Powlett-Jones, the protagonist of Delderfield's last and most famous work *To Serve Them All My Days* (1972), the Somerset captain of the mid-sixties, Colin Atkinson, on leaving the club became a teacher at nearby Millfield School and eventually the headmaster. Coincidentally, five of the current Somerset team – Wesley Durston, James Hildreth, Craig Kieswetter, Robin Lett and Max Waller – all attended Millfield School.

Between 1972 and 1977 Somerset were captained by the inspirational and combative Brian Close, whose influence on Ian Botham was considerable. The team also included two other world-class players in Viv Richards and Joel Garner (both West Indies). Though the county title continued to elude Somerset and Close retired, to be succeeded as captain by the equally inspirational Brian Rose, for the first time in its long history the club became serious trophy contenders. Their first success was the 'double' of Gillette Cup and Sunday League in 1979.

 Brian Close is the hardest and toughest man I ever met. If he had gone into the ring with Muhammad Ali, Ali wouldn't have knocked him out. I remember a match between Somerset and Leicestershire. During the game Brian took over as wicket-keeper and flatly refused to wear the gloves.
IAN BOTHAM

When Peter Roebuck assumed the captaincy in 1987 he did so amid huge controversy among the supporters. Martin Crowe (New Zealand) was signed as overseas pro and Viv Richards and Joel Garner were released, some maintain sacked. Ian Botham resigned in protest and joined Worcestershire.

Sir Ian Botham is a true legend of cricket, a world-class all-rounder who, despite playing for Worcestershire (1987–91) and Durham (1992–93), will forever be associated with Somerset (1974–86, captain 1984–85). Born in Heswall on the Wirral, he was a batsman who would empty the bars and a hostile and highly effective swing bowler. Botham made his England debut in 1977 and within two years had 100 Test wickets to his name, achieving the double of 1,000 runs and 100 wickets in only 21 Tests – an England record. He went on to set numerous other records, among them 2,000 runs and 200 wickets in 42 Tests and 3,000 runs and 300 wickets in only 71 Tests. In 1985 he hit a record 85 sixes in a first-class season, on five occasions hitting the ball out of the ground. He also played football for Scunthorpe United, and over the years has raised millions of pounds for charity and worthy causes. In a career spanning the years 1974 to 1993 he scored 19,399 first-class runs (average 33.97), including 38 centuries, and took 1,172 wickets (average 27.22). His England record is also the stuff of legend: 102 Tests, 5,200 runs (average 33.54), including 14 centuries, and 383 wickets (average 28.40). He also played in 116 ODIs scoring 2,113 runs (average 23.21) and taking 145 wickets (average 28.54).

Ian Botham plays a net as if he is on Weston-super-Mare beach and the tide is coming in fast.

FRANK KEATING

They say Chris Lewis will take Botham's place in the England team. On the bus going to the ground, maybe, but that's about all.
FRED TRUEMAN

ERIC MORECAMBE: I once saw Ian Botham play for Somerset.
ERNIE WISE: And? Go on, or is that it?
MORECAMBE: That's it. You don't have to say any more really.

Other notable players to have played for Somerset include Bill Andrews (fast-medium pace bowler and later coach and member of the committee), Jamie Cox (Australia), Sunil Gavaskar (India), Sanath 'Batman' Jayasuriya, Ricky Ponting (Australia), Fred Rumsey (later of travel company fame), Harry Stephenson (legendary wicket-keeper, 1,007 dismissals), Roy Virgin (career total of 15,458 runs for Somerset) and Peter Wight (British Guyana), who arrived at Somerset from league cricket with Burnley and on his debut made 103 not out against Australia in 1953, and who is second only to Harold Gimblett in runs scored for the county with a total of 16,965. In recent years former England stars Andy Caddick and

Marcus Trescothick, and captain Justin Langer (Australia), have formed the backbone of the team.

In 1990 Somerset recorded their highest ever score in one-day cricket – 413 for 4 against Devon at Torquay in the NatWest Trophy.

In the opening match of 2007 Somerset recorded their highest ever score – 850 for 7 declared, against Middlesex at Taunton. Justin Langer created a new club record score by an individual player of 342, and three other Somerset players also scored centuries: James Hildreth (116), Cameron White (114) and Peter Trego (also 114). Four Middlesex players – Owais Shah, Billy Godleman, David Nash and Ed Smith – scored centuries in the game too. Eight centuries in a single match is an all-time County Championship record. In total 1,659 runs were scored in four days of cricket for the loss of just 13 wickets. The game ended in a draw.

Most appropriately named player(s) – J. W. Seamer and Brian Lobb. (Arguably the most unfortunately named player – E. W. Bastard.)

The club's limited-overs team is the Somerset Sabres.

Worth a visit for . . . OK, it's a cliché, but the cider is very good and very welcoming on a hot day. And many visit the County Ground without being aware of the Old Priory Barn, a multiplex centre that contains a host of cricket memorabilia and artefacts in the museum section. The club should flag it up more prominently – it's good.

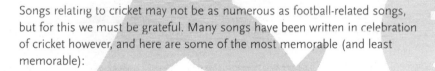

Songs relating to cricket may not be as numerous as football-related songs, but for this we must be grateful. Many songs have been written in celebration of cricket however, and here are some of the most memorable (and least memorable):

'Eton and Winchester' by Frederick Septimus Kelly, written prior to the First World War in celebration of the annual cricket match between the two schools. Perhaps not a dance hall favourite.

'How To Improve Your Cricket' by Jack Hobbs, one of three records made by the great Surrey and England man in the 1920s. Could well qualify as the most unromantic song title ever.

'How It's Done' by Don Bradman. Yes, the great man himself, released in 1930 – the record that is, not Bradman.

'Leg Theory' by Harold Larwood, recorded in 1933. The great Nottinghamshire bowler vies with Jack Hobbs for the most unromantic song title.

'Our Don Bradman' by Art Leonard. Very popular song of 1934 – at least very popular in Australia.

'Bradman' by Paul Kelly. 1989 tribute to the great man by Aussie singer-songwriter.

'Cricket Lovely Cricket' by Egbert Moore aka Lord Beginner. Iconic calypso cricket song of the 1950s.

'The Cricket Song' by Lord Kitchener. Another 'well-played' calypso song of the 1950s.

'Gavaskar' by Lord Relator (1970). West Indies tribute to the great India batsman.

'The Ashes Song'. One of the few cricket songs recorded by an actual cricket team, in this instance by the victorious MCC/England team following their 1970–71 series victory in Australia.

'When An Old Cricketer Leaves the Crease' by Roy Harper with the Grimethorpe Colliery Band, recorded in 1974. It often featured on the John Peel programme on Radio 1.

'The Ashes Song' by Bob Willis, released prior to the winter tour of 1978–79 in which Willis took 20 wickets – allegedly two more than the number of records sold.

'Soul Limbo' by Booker T and the MGs. Not specifically written with cricket in mind but as the theme tune for BBC Radio's *TMS* and formerly the theme of the BBC's Test match coverage (resurrected in the summer of 2009 for their Twenty20 World Cup highlights programmes), the tune that more than any other has become synonymous with cricket. Originally the 'B' side of the Booker T hit 'Time is Tight'.

'Theme from Bluey'. Again, not specifically written about cricket but became synonymous with the game as the theme tune for Australia's Channel 9 coverage of the World Series (originally the theme tune of the Australian cop series *Bluey*).

'Rally Around the West Indies' by David Rudder, the Trinidadian-born Canada-based singer-songwriter.

Cricket – An Operetta by Tim Rice and Andrew Lloyd Webber, written to celebrate the 60th birthday of Her Majesty the Queen and performed before the royal family at Windsor Castle. Curiously, not the only operetta devoted to the game: it was preceded by some years by *Batter Suite* composed by Vivian Ellis.

'It's Not Cricket' by The Twelfth Man. Cricket song containing imitation of Richie Benaud which reached number one in the Australian charts in 1984.

'N-N-N-N-Nineteen Not Out' by The Commentators (1985). Cricket song featuring talents of Rory Bremner, a parody of the Paul Hardcastle hit 'Nineteen'.

'The Shane Warne Song' by Kevin 'Bloody' Wilson. For DJs with decks, worth a spin.

'Marvellous' by Billy Birmingham and MCH Hammer (not to be confused with MC Hammer).

'Jazba' by Junoon. Official Pakistan song for the 1996 World Cup.

'I Made a 100 in the Backyard at Mum's' by Coodabeen Champions. Received lots of radio airplay in Australia, and probably at his mum's.

'Cricket Song' by Mark Radcliffe and Lard, former Radio 1 pairing, the latter of whom played with The Fall.

Top Twenty20. It has become the vogue among most county clubs to play music at various stages during Twenty20 matches, for example: when the Essex team takes to the field 'I Predict a Riot' by the Kaiser Chiefs booms out; when Middlesex take a wicket at Lord's 'Celebration' by Kool and the Gang is played. Should you also hear a motorized sound when such songs are played, it is probably W. G. spinning in his grave.

Jam Jah. Reggae band Big Bad Dread and the Baldhead include in their line-up former West Indies Test cricketers Courtney Walsh and Richie Richardson.

Fly fishing off the off-stump? McFly's concert at the Sheffield Arena in September 2006 was delayed due to a fire alarm. The band were playing cricket backstage when one band member hit the ball which struck and set off a fire alarm resulting in a two-hour delay.

Songs that are not about cricket but should have been: 'Howzat?' by Sherbert; 'Ashes to Ashes' by David Bowie; 'Bat Out of Hell' by Meat Loaf; 'In Da Clubhouse' by 50 Cent; 'Spinning Around' by Kylie Minogue; and anything by The Strokes.

Sussex is the only county club to have an official song, an adaptation of 'Sussex by the Sea' by Gerard Martineau.

The only county cricketer to sing on a song that reached number one in the UK charts is Sir Geoff Hurst, who played for Essex and sang on the England World Cup squad chart success 'Back Home' in 1970.

In 1978 10cc had a number one hit in the UK with 'Dreadlock Holiday' which featured the line 'I don't like cricket, I love it'.

While travelling by ship to the 1962–63 winter series in Australia, Ken Barrington, Colin Cowdrey, Ted Dexter, Tom Graveney, Ray Illingworth and Fred Trueman formed a band called 'Marylebone Calypso Club' and won first prize in the ship's talent contest. The group sang, in the main, self-penned calypso cricket songs, the lyrics for one of which were written by Fred Trueman, and which included the following lines:

> There's this man,
> Peter May is his name,
> Surrey his club and
> cricket his game.
> May may in May
> Play his opening shot,
> May may do well,
> May may do not.
> It all depends
> On this you see,
> How May may cope
> With FST!

It is generally accepted that cricket was introduced to South Africa by British troops in the late eighteenth century.

The first club to be formed was Port Elizabeth in January 1843.

The first tour of South Africa was undertaken in 1888 by an English XI captained by Sussex's C. Aubrey Smith.

In March 1889 C. Aubrey Smith captained the English XI against South Africa at Port Elizabeth. Though the English team was not truly representative of England and did not enjoy international standing, this match and the subsequent game against South Africa were granted Test status – thus these games were the first first-class matches in South Africa, which became the third Test nation. The year 1889 also marked the beginning of domestic cricket in the form of the Currie Cup.

In January 1890, during the match between Kimberley and Natal at Kimberley, all 11 Natal players had a spell bowling during Kimberley's total of 445.

Nourse King. A. W. Nourse was the first South African batsman to score a triple century (304 not out), for Natal against Transvaal at Johannesburg in April 1920.

Raise a steyn to that. In December 1929 Stephen Steyn scored his maiden century for Western Province against Border at Cape Town and went on to score 261. Steyn was selected for South Africa and was a member of the team that toured Australia in 1930–31 but never managed to be selected for a Test match.

Hail noble centurions. In November 1938 the MCC/England scored 676 against Griqualand West at Kimberley which included four individual centuries, from Eddie Paynter (158), Len Hutton (149), Norman Yardley (142) and Bill Edrich (109). Yorkshire's Hedley Verity took 7 for 22 in the first innings and 4 for 44 in the second. The MCC/England won by an innings and 289 runs.

Herculean effort in marathon. In March 1939 (part of the same tour as above) England scored a world record fourth-innings total. Set to score 696 to beat South Africa, England made 654 for 5 in a match spread over 12 days before a draw was declared. The match produced the record aggregate number of runs scored in a match in South Africa – 1,981.

The first player to be given out 'handled the ball' in a Test match was South Africa's 'Bill' Endean, against England at Cape Town during the 1956–57 series.

In 1968–69 South Africa's Prime Minister B. J. Vorster made it clear that the inclusion of Basil D'Oliveira in the England touring party was unacceptable. Protracted negotiations between the England officials, players and the South African Cricket Board and authorities proved fruitless. England players refused to play unless D'Oliveira, if selected for any game, was allowed to play. The South Africa government was unrelenting, which led to England returning home in protest. This major incident is seen as a watershed in the sporting boycott of South Africa.

In 1970 the ICC voted to suspend South Africa indefinitely from international cricket because of its government's apartheid policy, which only allowed South Africa to field white players and play against white nations whose teams comprised only whites.

A quirk of his. In 1978–79 Northern Transvaal's 'Tom' Quirk was given out 'obstructing the field' against Border at East London.

Hogged the limelight. In January 1980 Vince Hogg, playing for Zimbabwe–Rhodesia B against Natal B, batted for one hour and 27 minutes without scoring – and was then out for a duck.

In 1991 South Africa was reinstated as a Test nation following the deconstruction of apartheid in the country.

Following their reinstatement as an international team, South Africa played their first match, a one-day international, against India at Calcutta on 10 November 1991.

South Africa competed in the World Cup for the first time in 1992 and reached the semi-finals – a feat they replicated in 1999 and 2007.

In 1993 Darryl Cullinan scored 337 not out for Transvaal against Northern Transvaal – the highest individual score in first-class cricket in South Africa. Cullinan is also the youngest player to score a century in South African first-class cricket: he was 16 years and 304 days old in January 1984 when he reached 106 not out for Border against Natal B at East London.

Not taking anything away from Cullinan, because it was a superb innings, but, as a batsman, I don't think he could live with the late Dudley Nourse.
BILL FLESCH (Transvaal radio)

In 1998 South Africa won a gold medal in cricket at the Commonwealth Games.

In 2006, following an injury to Graeme Smith and Jacques Kallis, Ashwell Prince took over as captain of South Africa on a temporary basis – the first non-white to captain South Africa.

In March 2006 South Africa defeated Australia in an ODI after being set the highest ever run chase. South Africa reached their target of 438 for the loss of nine wickets in 49.5 overs. This game is widely considered to be the greatest ODI ever played. The aggregate of runs scored that day, 872, is a world record.

In 2007 South Africa was ranked the number one team in ODI cricket but failed to deliver in the World Cup that year. Having set out their stall with victories over England, the West Indies, Ireland, Scotland and Holland, they then lost to Australia, New Zealand and Bangladesh. In the semi-finals South Africa were dismissed for 149 by Australia – their lowest ever total in a World Cup.

The South Africa international team is known as the Proteas. A protea is a flowering shrub native to South Africa which may take on various shapes and forms, hence the term 'protean'.

For a time South Africa, like Zimbabwe, operated a 'racial quota policy', but this was removed in 2002 and the only criterion on which South African teams are now selected is 'ability'.

On 13 July 2008 South Africa's Graeme Smith (107) and Neil McKenzie (102 not out) shared an opening partnership of 204 against England in the first Test at Lord's – the highest opening stand by a team asked to follow on in a Test match. South Africa had made 247 in their first innings in reply to England's 593 for 8 declared.

On 29 December 2008 South Africa became the first team to win a Test series in Australia for 16 years (since 1992) following victory in the second Test in Melbourne. Graeme Smith became the first man to captain South Africa to a series victory in Australia.

Cricket was first introduced to what was then Ceylon in 1832 by the Reverend Brooke Bailey, who had arrived from England to take up a teaching position at Colombo Academy.

The first cricket club was Colombo CC, formed in 1832. In November of that year the first match took place, between Colombo CC and the 97th Regiment of the British Garrison, which resulted in a victory for the soldiers.

Between 1880 and 1912 the millionaire entrepreneur George Vanderspar promoted and funded cricket in Ceylon to international level. A former Somerset player, Vanderspar persuaded touring teams such as the MCC to play a match in Colombo on their way to tours in Australia.

The first overseas team to play in Ceylon was the All England team captained by Ivo Bligh (of Ashes fame), in October 1882.

The first overseas tour was undertaken by Colombo CC to India in 1884–85. This too was funded by George Vanderspar.

The Ceylon Cricket Association was formed in 1922.

The inaugural first-class matches by a touring team took place in January–February 1927. The MCC, captained by Arthur Gilligan, played a total of four matches.

In 1938 the first official domestic league was contested. From 1953 until 1975–76 a Ceylon national team competed for the Gopalan Trophy, a bi-annual fixture against Madras.

Ceylon became Sri Lanka in 1972.

The first tour by Sri Lanka was in 1975 to England, though this did not qualify as an official Test series.

Sri Lanka was granted Test status in 1981. Their inaugural Test match was against England at Colombo on 17–21 February 1982, a one-off Test which England won.

Sri Lanka's first success in a Test series (three matches) came with their 1–0 defeat of India in 1985. The series took place on home soil.

In 1993 at Colombo, Sri Lanka enjoyed their first ever Test success against England.

In 1996 Sri Lanka won the World Cup, defeating favourites Australia in the final. By virtue of this victory Sri Lanka also became the only nation to win the ICC Trophy and then go on to win the World Cup.

In August 1997 Sri Lanka recorded the highest ever total in Test cricket – 952–6, against India. Sri Lanka also holds the record scores in both ODI and Twenty20 international cricket: 443 for 9 v. Netherlands in Amstelveen (ODI, July 2006), and 260 for 6 v. Kenya at Johannesburg (Twenty20, September 2007).

In January 2002 Muttiah Muralitharan returned bowling figures of 9 for 51 against Zimbabwe – the best bowling figures in a single innings by a Sri Lanka bowler in a Test match.

Muralitharan holds the world record for the most wickets in Tests – 765 (1997–2009), at an average of 22.12. He has also set a record for ODIs with 494 wickets (average 22.72).

Mahela Jayawardene holds the record for the most runs in Tests for Sri Lanka – 8,251, average 53.23 (1997–2009). He also holds the record for the most Test hundreds (25) and the most catches in the field in Tests (142).

Sanath Jayasuriya holds the record for the most runs in ODIs for Sri Lanka – 13,085, at an average of 32.87 (1989–2009). He has also scored 341 runs in Twenty20 internationals (average 34.80).

In 2003, playing against Bangladesh, Chaminda Vaas became the first Sri Lankan bowler to take a hat-trick in a World Cup and went on to reach figures of 6 for 25 – the best by a Sri Lankan bowler.

In December 2004 cricket was suspended in Sri Lanka when the Indian Ocean tsunami killed over 30,000 Sri Lankans. First-class cricket resumed in February 2005 with the Inter-Provincial tournament, but such was the devastation cricket in Sri Lanka is still in the process of recovery

In 2006 Sri Lanka enjoyed their first 'whitewash' victory over England in an ODI series.

In July 2006 Mahela Jayawardene scored 374 against South Africa – the highest individual innings by a Sri Lanka player in a Test match. It was in this Test that Jayawardene shared a record Test partnership for Sri Lanka with Kumar Sangakkara (who scored 287) of 624 for the third wicket.

In March 2007 Lasith Malinga took four wickets in four consecutive balls in an ODI against South Africa.

On 5 February 2009 Muttiah Muralitharan became the highest wicket-taker in the history of ODIs when he claimed his 503rd against India at Colombo, overtaking the previous record held by Wasim Akram (Pakistan).

W. G. Grace was a man of formidable physique and presence, but blessed with a high-pitched voice, almost falsetto.

The only member of the royal family ever to have played in a first-class cricket match is Edward VII's nephew Prince Christian Victor, who, prior to Edward assuming the throne, played for I Zingari against the Gentlemen of England at Scarborough in August 1887. Not to the Victor the spoils, however: in the first innings the Prince made a respectable 35, but he was out for a duck in the second innings.

Couldn't hold a candle to Cave. Walter Cave, who played for Eton and Gloucestershire in the 1880s, was also an architect and interior designer, and he has a curious claim to fame: he is credited with the idea of placing candle holders on grand pianos, an idea which became the height of fashion in the late nineteenth century.

Batsmen crossing the Rubicon? In the nineteenth century Surrey boasted a player by the name of Julius Caesar.

On 8 June 1894 in the match between Yorkshire and Sussex at Dewsbury, Sussex appeared to be set fair for victory with five wickets remaining in their second innings when Yorkshire called upon Edward Wainwright to bowl. Wainwright took the last five Sussex wickets in seven balls, including a hat-trick.

George Beet and Fred Root often played together for Derbyshire prior to the First World War and on several occasions, no doubt much to the amusement of scorers, produced the scorebook entry 'caught Beet bowled Root'. Derbyshire later made claim to E. Coupe and R. T. de Ville.

Wood you believe it. In June 1911 in the match between Yorkshire and Leicestershire at Bradford, Leicestershire's C. J. B. Wood was on the field of play for every ball bowled in the match. Opening the batting for Leicestershire, Wood succeeded in carrying his bat through both Leicestershire innings, scoring a century in both (107 not out and 117 not out). He equalled the feat of H. Jupp, who in August 1874 at the Oval batted throughout two completed innings for Surrey scoring 43 not out and 109 not out – again the opponents were Yorkshire. The valiant efforts of both Wood and Jupp were in vain, however: Yorkshire won both matches.

Oliver Field, who played for Oxford University prior to the First World War and for whom a glittering career in cricket was predicted only for him to be killed in action in France in 1915, was a direct descendant of Oliver Cromwell.

In June 1921 A. Dolphin of Yorkshire broke his wrist when he fell off a chair while reaching for his clothes in the dressing room following Yorkshire's match against Middlesex at Lord's.

In July 1922 Miles Howell of Surrey was dismissed in successive balls while playing against Lancashire at Old Trafford, but in so doing won the match for Surrey. Surrey required two runs to win the match when Howell was caught off the bowling of V. Norbury, who was no-balled, which tied the match. Howell was caught once more off Norbury's next delivery, but once again the Lancashire bowler was no-balled. Hence Surrey won the match and Howell kept his wicket intact, for all that he was 'caught' off successive deliveries.

Jack MacBryan was selected for one Test, against South Africa at Old Trafford in 1924. He fielded, but is the only player whose Test career did not involve him batting, bowling or catching an opponent in the field.

In 1928–29 at Melbourne, Maurice Tate bowled 100 overs for England against Australia without taking a wicket (62–26–108–0 and 38–13–76–0).

Suits you, sir. On 23 May 1930, when the skip containing their whites went missing in transit, Nottinghamshire players took to the field against Hampshire at Southampton wearing their dress suits. This was not the first instance of a team playing a County Championship match in suits: on 10 June 1899, due to a flood in their dressing room which soaked their whites, Derbyshire players took to the field against Yorkshire at Dewsbury wearing their daywear shirts and suit trousers.

A total of 851 runs were scored in the match between Yorkshire and Norfolk at the Hyde Park Ground, Sheffield in July 1934, 128 of which were extras – 75 byes and 53 wides.

Somerset's Sydney Rippon was wounded at the Somme but carried on playing cricket until 1937. He was known for his 'swinging moods', from total introvert to outrageous extrovert, was often seen batting wearing his cap back to front, and occasionally, having seen the ball hurrying to the boundary, he would break from running between the wicket and express his joy by yodelling.

Sussex's Jack Oakes is the only player in the history of first-class cricket in England to have been named after a battle in either of the two world wars. His middle name was Ypres.

R. Cook, who captained Braintree CC (Essex) Second XI in the late 1940s, also led the bowling averages – a remarkable achievement as he played with two artificial feet, having lost his own in the Second World War.

In the 1950s film star Trevor Howard had a clause in his movie contract stating he could not be called for filming on the occasion of a Test match at Lord's.

Only two players have captained their county club's First and Second XIs to title success in their respective championships. Tom Dollery accomplished this feat when he led Warwickshire to the County Championship title in 1951 and then Warwickshire Second XI to the Minor Counties title in 1959. Yorkshire's Ronnie Burnet did the feat in reverse, first winning the Minor Counties title with Yorkshire Second XI in 1957, then captaining the First XI to County Championship success in 1959.

A man of letters. The man with the longest name to have played first-class cricket is Ilikena Lasurusa Talebulamaineiilikenamnainavaleniveivakabulaimainakulalakebalau, who played his cricket for Fiji in the 1950s and 1960s and who was probably responsible for Fiji completing more scorebooks than most during this period, until they finally decided to record his efforts under the name I. L. Bula.

In 1965 David Green scored 2,037 runs for Lancashire (and MCC and T. N. Pearce's XI) but never scored a century. His top score was 85.

Serves him right. On 28 January 1975 Aussie fast bowler Jeff Thomson suffered a back injury when serving while playing tennis on the supposed rest day of the fifth Test between Australia and England. He took no further part in that particular Test and also missed the sixth and final Test.

Not the best of Mates. In 1978 Conservative MP Michael Mates had his jaw broken by a policeman when playing for the House of Lords and Commons XI against West Indian Wanderers. The officer in question was Brian Mustill who, when bowling for the Wanderers, delivered a ball that reared up and hit Mates on the side of the face as he attempted to take evasive action. For once, an MP was lost for words.

Raining blows stopped play. Play was halted during the third Test between the West Indies and Pakistan at Bridgetown, Barbados on 27 April 1988 when Pakistan's Abdul Qadir was involved in a fight with a spectator while fielding near the boundary.

Nearly had his chips. A similar incident occurred during the Pakistan v. India Sahara Cup match in Toronto in 1997 when Pakistan's Inzamam-ul-Haq left his place in the field, grabbed a bat, and attacked supporter Shiv Kumar Thind, a Canadian of Indian descent who had been barracking Inzamam through a megaphone, loudly comparing him to various types of potato. Inzamam was arrested by the Toronto police who charged him with common assault and assault with a dangerous weapon (the cricket bat). The police subsequently dropped the charges but cautioned Inzamam, who received a three-match ban from international cricket by the match referee.

On 8 June 1983, following the first day's play of the County Championship match between Sussex and Kent, Sussex's Ian Greig broke an ankle when he fell from the window of his first-floor flat trying to gain entry after his key had snapped in the door lock. Four years later, on 3 May 1987, Greig broke a finger while batting for Surrey against Pakistan at the Oval. He was taken to hospital for an X-ray and treatment. After the X-ray he stood up, banged his head on the machine and sustained an injury that required stitches.

Top delivery. Don Topley missed the start of the 1989 season for Essex due to an injury sustained when a spring-loaded letter box trapped his hand as he delivered a birthday card to a friend.

On 8 July 1990 Surrey awarded county caps to Darren Bicknell, Chris Bullen and David Ward, prior to the club's Sunday League match against Warwickshire. All three contrived to be out for a duck on the day. To be fair, all three went on to offer sterling service to Surrey.

On 17 August 1992 at Bournemouth, Hampshire were sitting fair at 79 for 3 against Northamptonshire only to then lose six wickets for the addition of just one run. With Hampshire 80 for 9, Northamptonshire's Curtly Ambrose just couldn't finish off the last pair. He bowled a 13-ball over which included seven no-balls and conceded 12 runs in the process.

Without checking your wallet or purse, which is the only Bank of England note to feature a cricket match, and which match is it?
Answer: the £10 note, which features Charles Dickens, and alongside Dickens is a scene from Dingley Dell v. All Muggleton from *Pickwick Papers*.

No balls. Following Mahendra Singh Dhoni's 148 for India against Pakistan at Visakhapatnam in April 2005, Dhoni's parents were besieged at their home by eunuchs who proceeded to bestow upon them traditional blessings and refused to leave until the police arrived and dispersed them. This never happens in Barnsley – if only.

The bounder. In the County Championship match between Warwickshire and Middlesex at Edgbaston in April 2005, Scott Styris of Middlesex reached 50 by hitting 13 fours and one single in his total of 53 – the first player to score a first-class fifty with 13 fours.

On 24 July 2005 play was stopped in the Totesport match between Yorkshire and Warwickshire when a man wearing an Osama Bin Laden mask wandered on to the field of play.

Hair today gone tomorrow. In March 2006 15-year-old Carl Ferris was
excluded from his school, Westfield Community School in Yeovil, for refusing
to change his spiked haircut which he had adopted after his hero Kevin
Pietersen. Carl's father, Roy, claimed it was 'an invasion of human rights'.
When a local journalist pointed out to Mr Ferris that Pietersen no longer
sported a spiked haircut and had shaved his head, Mr Ferris was reported as
saying, 'Oh, forget it then.'

Also in 2006, Great Britain Transplant Cricket Club beat Australia Transplants in
a series to win the David Hookes Memorial Shield. Every player had been the
recipient of a heart, kidney, liver or bone-marrow transplant.

In September 2006 Muslim Imams XI beat a Christian Clergy XI by 27 runs
in a Twenty20 match at Grace Road to mark the fifth anniversary of the 9/11
attacks and to demonstrate inter-faith unity. The umpires were Jewish and
Hindu. The Imams' success in this cricket match followed their victory over
the Christian Clergy at football earlier in the year.

Three's a crowd. The Group A India Plate match between Himachal Pradesh and
Tripura at the HPCA Stadium in Dharmasala on 1 December 2006 was thrown
into chaos from the start when, to the amazement of the Tripura openers, two
different Himachal teams attempted to take to the field. The two home teams
had been selected by rival factions which had created a schism within the
Himachal Pradesh Cricket Association. The match referee gave permission for
the team chosen by the Pawar faction of the HPCA to take to the field, but the
match was abandoned when it was discovered the pitch had been sabotaged –
according to the Pawar faction, by their rival selectors of the Dalmiya faction.

The afternoon session of the final day of Lancashire's County Championship
match against Kent at Old Trafford in June 2007 was delayed due to burning
gravy. A pan containing gravy caught fire in the Old Trafford kitchen and,
with smoke billowing, the pavilion had to be evacuated and the fire brigade
called.

In 2008 Worcestershire's Ben Smith reached 1,000 runs for the season without
ever having scored a century.

You might think every number up to 300 has been achieved as an individual
total in Test cricket, but not so: no batsman has ever scored 229.

No team's innings in a Test has ever resulted in all 10 batsmen being bowled.

The only post-war players to play first-class cricket whose name begins with the letter 'X' are Xavier Doherty of Tasmania (2001–07) and Xavier Marshall of the West Indies (2008).

The team that never existed. In 1947 amateur cricketer Les Williamson and his brother-in-law invented a team by the name of St Pancras Spartans for which they filed 'reports' of matches to their local weekly newspaper for the duration of the season. Rather than invent names for the fictitious team, Williamson used those of the local amateur club he did actually play for, along with names of pals from his local pub. Williamson filed his weekly reports for another full season. His final submission in 1948 announced that St Pancras Spartans had to fold as their ground had been sold – an occasion marked by 'the presentation of a miniature silver lawn mower to groundsman Harry Susser in recognition of his 30 years' service.' A fitting coup de grass!

Matches between actual teams that bear curious names are not uncommon. Smokers v. Non-Smokers has already been mentioned; others include:

Players with One Arm v. Players with One Leg, 1863
Blackpool Gas Lighters v. Blackpool Sewerage XI, 1899
Ladies with Bats v. Men with Hunting Whips, 1894
Frothblowers v. Non-Frothblowers, 1927
W. W. Grantham KC XI v. Japanese Embassy, 1927
Ladies v. Gentlemen, Houghton Regis, 1949
Willie Watson XI v. Thompson's Shipbuilding Apprentices, 1955
Calm Men XI v. Easily Excited XI, Cumberland, 1961
Captain Pugwash XI v. Black Jake's XI, Cornwall, 1965
Hippies v. Straights, Cheshire, 1972
Maids of Hambledon v. Maids of Bramley, 1977
Men with Mincing Walks v. Men with He-Man Strides, Brighton, 1980
Woodseats Ladies v. Woodseats Not So Ladylike XI, Sheffield, 1981
George Andrew's Signal Radio XI v. London's Burning XI, Stoke, 1989
Flatulents v. Constipators, Manchester, 1994
Vegetarians v. Boiled Ham Lovers, Keswick, 1995
PhDs and MAs v. Thick As Pig-Shit XI, Leeds, 1996
Solicitors Clerks v. Court Clerks, Greenwich, 2000
Entomologists XI v. Etymologists XI, Sheffield, 2004

Handsworth Rap Artistes v. Handsworth R&B Artistes, Birmingham, 2006
Indian Take-Away Owners v. Pub Landlords, Bradford, 2007

A team by the name of the Goodwin Sands Pot Holing Club CC play a game on Goodwin Sands (a few miles off the Kent coast) every year when an exceptionally low tide allows. Kent also played a match on Goodwin Sands as part of Chris Cowdrey's benefit year. The teams used a hovercraft as the pavilion.

A right team of comedians. In the 1970s the *Sunderland Echo* printed the teams for the following day's fixtures in the Sunderland and District Cricket League. In 1976 the team for Victoria Gardens CC included C. Chaplin, O. Hardy. S. Laurel, E. Morecambe and J. Tarbuck.

75

Gloves were first worn by wicket-keepers in 1850.

Surrey's Ted Pooley was considered the greatest stumper of his era (1860s), but after an illustrious career with Surrey he fell on hard times. Described in the 1908 *Wisden* as having 'faults of private character' and being 'his own worst enemy', he spent his latter years in poor circumstances and was often compelled to seek the shelter of the workhouse. He died a pauper in Lambeth Infirmary on 18 July 1907.

The first wicket-keeper to achieve a hat-trick of stumpings was William Brain, for Gloucestershire against Somerset at Cheltenham in August 1893, off the bowling of Charlie Townsend, a 16-year-old schoolboy from Clifton. Brain was a 'keeper' in every sense of the word: as a student he also played in goal for Oxford University.

In August 1911 Fred Huish, playing for Kent against Surrey at the Oval, accomplished nine stumpings – a record for a wicket-keeper in a single match – four in Surrey's first innings and five in the second. He also took a catch in the second innings, but his efforts proved in vain: Surrey won by nine runs.

In a career that spanned the years 1895 to 1914, Fred Huish effected 377 stumpings – to this day second only to the record, held by Les Ames (Kent), who between

1926 and 1951 executed 418 stumpings in a career tally of 1,121 dismissals (703 caught).

In 1929 Ames achieved the record for the most dismissals by a wicket-keeper in an English first-class season – 128, of which 49 were stumpings. He also offered ample evidence of being just as effective in front of the wicket, scoring 1,795 runs for Kent that season.

Three years later Ames set the record for the highest number of stumpings in an English first-class season – 64, in a total of 104 dismissals for Kent in 1932. Ames is the only wicket-keeper to have achieved in excess of 50 stumpings in an English season. In addition to achieving this feat in 1932 he had also completed 52 stumpings in 1928.

In 1913–14 Herbert Strudwick (Surrey) executed six stumpings and took 15 catches for England against South Africa – the only wicket-keeper to have to his name as many as 20 dismissals in a series prior to the Second World War. It was also the then record for the number of stumpings in a Test series.

Strudwick, who played for Surrey for over 25 years, was one of the greatest and assuredly one of the most popular players of his time, a brilliant wicket-keeper noted for, among other things, his bravery – perhaps not a trait of his predecessor, Surrey wicket-keeper Frederick Stedman, who habitually protected his chest with a South Western Railway timetable stuffed into his shirt. On one occasion, after having received a particularly hefty blow, Stedman remarked to a team-mate, 'I'll have to catch a later train home tonight. That one knocked off the 7 30!'

On 2 July 1951 Hugo Arnold set a world record for the number of stumpings in a single innings of a first-class match. Playing for Worcestershire against Scotland at Broughty Ferry (near Dundee), Arnold accomplished six stumpings off the bowling of 'Roly' Jenkins and Michael Bradbury. He also took a catch to equal the then world record of seven dismissals in an innings, as set by Warwickshire's 'Tiger' Smith in 1926.

The career of Sussex and England wicket-keeper Jim Parks spanned 27 years (1949 to 1976) in which time Parks laid claim to 1,181 first-class dismissals of which only 93 were stumpings – by far the lowest of any wicket-keeper to have accomplished in excess of 1,000 first-class dismissals in English cricket.

Only eight English wicket-keepers have in excess of 300 first-class career stumpings to their name: Les Ames (418), Fred Huish (377), John Board (Gloucestershire, 355), David Hunter (Yorkshire, 347), George Duckworth (Lancashire, 343), Walter Cornford (Sussex, 342), Harold Stephenson (Somerset, 334) and Harry Elliott (Derbyshire, 302). Of these, the most recent is Harold Stephenson, who played his final match for Somerset in 1964!

Playing for Surrey against Lancashire at Old Trafford in 2004, Jonathan Batty achieved 11 dismissals which included four stumpings and seven catches – one dismissal short of Ted Pooley's English first-class record of 12 dismissals in a match, for Surrey against Sussex at the Oval in 1868.

The record number of stumpings in a single innings of a Test match is five, by Kiran More for India against the West Indies at Madras in 1987–88.

Stumped for a reason why. In 2001–02 Sri Nath, making his first-class debut, for Assam against Tripura at Guwahati, stumped a Tripur opener to claim his first dismissal. Nath went on to take seven catches to take his innings total of dismissals to eight, but never played another first-class cricket match.

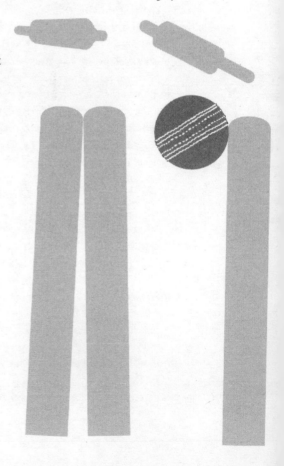

The Sunday League was the second limited-overs competition for county clubs. The inaugural year of the competition was 1969.

The Sunday League differed from the Gillette Cup as matches could not extend into a reserve day in the event of bad weather. It was also the only competition in which a restriction was placed on the bowler's run-up and in which a tie was an accepted final result.

The inspiration for the Sunday League was the Rothman's Cavaliers, a team comprising players and present players who from 1962 had played against first-class county clubs on a Sunday afternoon either in aid of the club's beneficiary or local charities. Matches involving the Cavaliers were first broadcast on BBC2 in 1965, though the majority of the UK did not receive the channel at the time. When BBC2 became available to most of the UK in the late 1960s, Cavaliers matches drew healthy audience figures and sizeable crowds. In 1967 the aggregate attendance for Sunday matches featuring the Cavaliers was 114,000. This was 31,000 greater than the best-supported County Championship side, champions Yorkshire, whose aggregate attendance was 83,000. It was the crowd figures that acted as the catalyst for the newly formed TCCB and county clubs to meet and formulate the Sunday League.

Deals were struck with the BBC for broadcasting rights, and with John Player and Sons, who agreed to sponsor the new league.

Each county was to play 16 matches – that is, all the other counties once. Matches consisted of 40 overs per team. Should matches be subjected to inclement weather, the overs for each team would be reduced, down to a minimum 10 overs per team.

The Pro40 was launched in 1999. In essence it was the Sunday League retitled to reflect the fact many matches were now being played on days other than a Sunday. From 1999 onwards the competition comprised two divisions with three teams relegated and promoted each way.

As part of the relaunch, in 2002 the competition was renamed the National League. Matches initially consisted of 45 overs and the competing first-class counties took on a suffix in the style of baseball or American football teams, such as Nottinghamshire Outlaws and Sussex Sharks.

In 2006 the competition was revised, each team playing its divisional opponents once as opposed to twice, with Scotland only competing between 2003 and 2005. Two teams from the First Division were relegated and two from the Second Division promoted. A third promotion/relegation spot was decided by a play-off match between the team third from bottom in Division One and the team third from top in Division Two.

The winners of the first Sunday League, in 1969, were Lancashire. They retained the title the following season, thus becoming the first county to win the Sunday League in successive seasons.

Led by example. It was hoped the Sunday League, like the Gillette Cup, would produce high-scoring matches, but the inaugural season produced some very economical bowling figures, none more so than those of Somerset captain Brian Langford against Essex at Yeovil: 8–8–0–0.

 For six days thou shalt push up and down the line, but on the seventh thou shalt swipe.
DOUG PADGETT (on the first season of the JP Sunday League)

Ducks and Drakes. In 1970 Derbyshire's Alan Ward took four Sussex wickets in four successive balls at Derby – a competition record equalled in 1999 by V. C. Drakes, for Nottinghamshire against Derbyshire at Trent Bridge.

Not one over the eight. In 1971 Keith Boyce took 8 for 26 for Essex against Lancashire at Old Trafford – the best bowling figures in the history of the competition.

At Headingley in 1974 Yorkshire dismissed Middlesex for 23 – the lowest ever total in the JP Sunday/Pro40 League.

Derbyshire's Bob Taylor dismissed seven Lancashire batsmen (six catches and one stumping) at Old Trafford in 1975 – the record number of dismissals by a wicket-keeper in a Sunday League match.

At Trent Bridge in 1983 Essex's Graham Gooch and Ken McEwan shared a second-wicket partnership of 273 against Nottinghamshire – a record partnership for the Sunday League.

In one-day cricket batsmen are as homogenous as baked beans.
PETER ROEBUCK

The mighty Both. Playing for Somerset against Northamptonshire at Wellingborough in 1986, Ian Botham hit 13 sixes in his total of 175 not out.

In 1990 Somerset recorded the largest margin of victory in the history of the competition when they beat Glamorgan by 220 runs at Neath.

In 1993 some bookies offered odds of 500–1 against Glamorgan winning the then AXA Equity and Law Sunday League, at the time a 50-overs-per-team competition – incredible considering Glamorgan had in their ranks Viv Richards (albeit 41 years old by then) and Hugh Morris. From 6 June to 12 September Glamorgan won every match they played in the competition, the sequence ended only by a rain-affected match against Essex. With one match of the season remaining the title was between Kent and Glamorgan, who coincidentally had to play each other at Canterbury on 19 September. A capacity crowd of 12,000 saw Glamorgan win the match, the title and their first one-day trophy, defeating Kent by two wickets.

Made his mark on the game. In 1995 Kent's Mark Ealham hit a century off only 44 balls against Derbyshire at Maidstone – the competition's fastest hundred.

Surrey's Alistair Brown holds the record for the highest individual score in the competition – 203, for Surrey against Hampshire at Guildford in 1997. Brown is also the only batsman to have scored a double century in the competition.

Almost a ton. The record for the most expensive spell of bowling in the competition belongs to Northamptonshire's Michael Strong. Against Gloucestershire at Cheltenham in 2001 he finished with match figures of 9–0–99–1.

Heave Hove. In 2003 Somerset scored 377 for 9 against Sussex at Hove – the highest total in the history of the competition.

In 2006 Essex became only the second county to win the Sunday/Pro40 League in successive seasons twice: Essex in 1984 and 1985, and 2005 and 2006; Lancashire in 1969 and 1970, and 1998 and 1999.

Durham and Northamptonshire are the only two county clubs never to have won the Sunday/Pro40 League.

M. C. C. A.

Minor Counties v. Australians

AT ASHBROOKE, SUNDERLAND

ON THURSDAY & FRIDAY, 4th & 5th AUGUST, 1977

Hours of Play: 1st Day 11-30 a.m. to 6-30 p.m.

MEMBERS' PAVILION ENCLOSURE

Ground Admission and Reserved Seat   (Under Balcony)

THURSDAY   Row ....A....

COMPLIMENTARY   Reserved Seat No. ...25...

Entrance ⌐ Rear of Pavilion

J. Iley, Secretary, Durham C.C.C.

The Sunday League has benefited from several major sponsorship deals – good for the game but often a source of confusion for some supporters: John Player 1969–86 (in 1969 the league was called John Player's County League, from 1970 to 1983 it was known as the John Player League, and from 1984 to 1986 as the John Player Special League); Refuge Assurance 1987–92; AXA Equity and Law 1993–98 (again this involved changes of name: AXA Equity and Law League 1993–96, AXA Life League 1997 only, AXA League 1998 only); CGU 1999 only; Norwich Union 2000–02 (which involved two changes of name: Norwich Union National League 2000 only, and Norwich Union League 2001–02); in 2003 the league was simply known as the National League; in 2004 and 2005 as the Totesport League; and in 2005 as the NatWest Pro40 League.

In July 2008 it was announced the Pro40 League would end in 2010 to make way for the English Premier League Twenty20 tournament. Following this announcement an official of the ECB was reported to have said, 'Another reason for the change is in recent years the Pro40 League does not appear to have enjoyed a defined identity, even among some sections of cricket supporters. Research has told us a proportion of the public who follow sport are not sure what the Pro40 League is.' Given the frequency of name changes, is it any wonder?

Surrey

Surrey's HQ is the Kennington Oval, Lambeth, London SE11, commonly referred to as the Oval, though due to a major sponsorship deal the ground is now officially the Brit Oval. One can't help thinking Ovaltine missed an opportunity there. 'And now it's over to the Ovaltine Oval' has a nice rhythm to it, don't you think?

The Oval has a current capacity of 23,000 with plans to increase this to 25,000. By tradition, the Oval (OK, Brit Oval) hosts the final Test of each British summer.

Surrey also play matches at Guildford (Woodbridge Road) and Croydon (Whitgift School).

The club badge features the three Prince of Wales feathers under which is inscribed 'Surrey Cricket'. In 1915 Lord Rosebery obtained permission to use this iconic symbol from the then Prince of Wales, owner of the land on which the Oval is situated. The land is still owned by the Duchy of Cornwall.

Surrey are one of the most successful county clubs, having won the County Championship on no fewer than 18 occasions: 1890, 1891, 1892, 1894, 1895, 1899, 1914, 1952, 1953, 1954, 1955, 1956, 1957, 1958, 1971, 1999, 2000 and 2002.

They also shared the title in 1950. Other major trophy successes: NatWest Trophy in 1982; Benson & Hedges Cup in 1974, 1997 and 2001; Sunday/Pro40 League winners in 1996 and 2003; Twenty20 Cup winners in 2003.

Although not considered the birthplace of cricket, Surrey can lay claim to the earliest known reference to the game. Legal documents dated 1597 note the game of 'kreckett' being played on land in Guildford dating back to 1550.

Cricket became a popular game in the county during the seventeenth century. It is believed that teams formed from Surrey villages played matches against one another as early as 1660. There is a record of a match between the Gentlemen of Surrey and Kent that took place in 1709, which is the earliest known reference to an inter-county match in England.

Surrey continued to play inter-county matches throughout the eighteenth century. This was an era of underarm bowling, the finest exponent of which was said to be one Edward 'Lumpy' Stevens. Given the lack of personal hygiene at the time, which often resulted in the population suffering from boils, warts, sebaceous cysts and similar ailments, it's a disconcerting thought that Stevens' nomenclature may not have been afforded as a result of his bowling technique.

Surrey CCC was founded on 22 August 1845 when representatives of some 100 Surrey cricket clubs met in the Horns Tavern (a pub, again) in South London. The motion that a Surrey County Cricket Club be formed was put forward by William Denison and voted upon unanimously by all representatives. (Cynics within the club are given to saying this was the first and last time all members agreed on anything.) A further meeting took place at the Horns Tavern on 18 October 1845 which formally constituted the club and appointed officers. William Denison was the club's first secretary. The meeting also agreed that club membership by way of 'yearly payment' and the issuing of cards be instigated – thus Surrey became the first county to enrol members by way of annual subscription.

Surrey's inaugural first-class match took place in May 1846 against the MCC at their new home, the Oval, which had been obtained on lease from the Duchy of Cornwall by a Mr Houghton of the Montpelier Cricket Club, and, of course, now of the newly formed Surrey CCC. The first inter-county match took place in June 1846, also at the Oval, against Kent.

Within a year the club was 'heavily in debt' to the tune of £70 and in danger of being wound up. The club's vice-president, the Honourable Fred Ponsonby (you couldn't make it up), proposed that six life members be created for a fee of £12 each. His motion was passed, six club members duly became life members, and the club survived.

Surrey were recognized as 'Champion County' seven times during the 1850s and continued to be a formidable force throughout the latter half of the nineteenth century. In 1872 what was believed to be a strong MCC XI was dismissed for 16 at Lord's.

Surrey won the first ever official County Championship in 1890 and were champions in five of the subsequent nine seasons, though this was hardly surprising as the club had dominated the unofficial Championship in previous years.

Tom Richardson was a prolific taker of wickets for Surrey in the late nineteenth and early twentieth centuries. In 1895 he took 252 wickets (average 13.94) – the first bowler to take in excess of 250 wickets in a first-class season. He played for Surrey from 1892 to 1904 and in that time took 1,775 wickets (average 17.87) – club records that remain unsurpassed.

More than Abel. In 1899 Surrey achieved their highest total in the history of the club – 811, against Somerset at the Oval. Bobby Abel lived up to his name, scoring 357 not out – the highest ever innings by a Surrey batsman. It was a fine year for Abel with the bat. With Tom Hayward he shared a fourth-wicket stand of 448 against Yorkshire at the Oval – the highest partnership in the history of the club.

In 1906 Tom Hayward scored 3,246 runs (average 72.13) – the most runs by a Surrey player in the course of a season. His tally included 13 centuries – a club record he shares with Jack Hobbs (1925).

The turn of the century saw a decline in fortunes on the field. Surrey's lone title success, in 1914, was not repeated until the 1950s.

In 1921 T. Rushby took 10 for 43 against Somerset at Taunton – the club record best bowling in a single innings.

The club's most famous player prior to the First World War and during the inter-war years was Jack Hobbs, who, having made his county debut in 1905, played for Surrey until 1934. Hobbs was widely acknowledged as 'The Master English Batsman', creating records that may never be surpassed. He scored an amazing 61,237 first-class runs (average 50.65), including 197 centuries, 98 of which were scored when he had passed the age of 40. In 1925 he scored 3,024 first-class runs (average 70.32) – a record later surpassed by Denis Compton (Middlesex). He formed formidable opening partnerships for Surrey with Tom Hayward and then Andy Sandham, making 40 and 66 century partnerships respectively with them. In 61 Tests for England Hobbs scored 5,410 runs (average 56.94), including 15 centuries. Hobbs was also a great cover fielder, and widely acknowledged as a 'wonderful man'. In 1953 he became the first professional cricketer to be knighted for services to the game.

People often refer to the number of centuries I scored, but such a score is often not nearly as valuable to a side as a 40 or 50 made in difficult circumstances. I made 49 in England's second innings of the third Test in Melbourne during the 1928–29 tour of Australia. If I may, with modesty, say so, I consider that to be one of my best performances as conditions were very difficult, the pitch was a crank and the pressure was on. But I stuck at it, chipped away at the runs and England, against all the odds, won the match.
JACK HOBBS

Jack Hobbs took the description 'unplayable' out of the category of pitches.
JACK FINGLETON

Opener Andy Sandham gave sterling service to Surrey both as a player and later as the club's official scorer.

Surrey enjoyed a period of cricket imperialism during the 1950s, winning seven consecutive County Championship titles from 1952 to 1958 inclusive. They also shared the title with Lancashire in 1950.

In 1955 Surrey won 23 of their 28 county matches – an existing record and, given the current structure of county cricket, one that will never be broken.

The side that dominated English cricket for much of the 1950s featured Ken Barrington, twins Alec and Eric Bedser, Jim Laker, Peter Loader, Peter May, Tony Lock and Micky Stewart (Alec's dad).

Peter May was an elegant batsman, considered the finest of his generation. He captained Surrey from 1957 to 1962 and also captained Cambridge University at football, though curiously not at cricket. He combined playing cricket for Surrey with work as an insurance broker. His daughter, Nicola, also excelled at sport: she won the European Junior Equestrian three-day event title in 1979. In a career that began in 1948 and ended in 1963 he scored 27,592 first-class runs (average 51.00), including 85 centuries. He played in 61 Tests (1951–61) and scored 4,537 runs (average 46.76), including 13 centuries.

Arguably the two most colourful characters of the Surrey team of the 1950s and early 1960s were Ken Barrington and Tony Lock.

In 1956 Tony Lock achieved the best ever match figures by a Surrey bowler – 16 for 83, against Kent at Blackheath.

Tony Lock was what these days one might term 'folically challenged'. During a cocktail reception that took place on an England tour of the West Indies, a British Embassy official engaged Lock in conversation, at one point belying diplomacy by remarking that Lock had lost a lot of hair since he had last seen him. 'I lost my hair when I was 27,' replied Lock. 'What a game of cards that was.'

Ken Barrington was also a ready wit and often delighted in taking the mickey out of members of the media. During England's tour of Australia in 1962–63 Barrington gave an interview to a young rookie reporter from an Australian radio station:

CUB REPORTER: Ken, the series is finally balanced. Both teams have one win to their names. Do you feel that, given those circumstances, the fact that the series is delicately balanced and could go either way, it's anybody's game and we know that. So, with all to play for, and the destiny of the Ashes up for grabs, do you feel, given your personal performances to date, which have been sterling without, and I say this with due respect, ever being startling –

by that I mean, for all you have batted well, you still, by your own standards, perhaps have not produced the form you may have hoped to produce – do you, all things considered, hope or believe you are capable of producing a big innings – and by that I mean a telling total, a century maybe, perhaps more? Or at least a score that is getting near to a ton? Do you feel you are capable of producing an innings that will tilt the series in England's favour? And by that I mean England going on, with the benefit of your run making, be it a century or thereabouts, to clinch the series? That is, beat Australia and seize the initiative which may allow your team, given your side's performances in the remaining Tests hold up, allow England to take back the Ashes, which Australia currently retain? In name only of course, as tradition dictates that the urn containing the Ashes of the burned bails of the very first Test match series should always remain at Lord's.

BARRINGTON: Sorry, could you repeat the question?

Paul Getty, once considered to be the richest man in the world, was at one time president of Surrey. Getty, a great lover of cricket and of Surrey in particular, built a replica of the Oval on his Wormsley Park Estate. To the best of anyone's knowledge it is still there.

In 1983 Surrey were dismissed for only 14 by Essex at Chelmsford – the club's lowest total in first-class cricket.

In 2007 Surrey achieved their highest total in one-day cricket, scoring a mammoth 496 for 4 against Gloucestershire at the Oval in the Friends Provident Trophy – the highest total achieved in the history of the competition in whatever guise.

Other notable Surrey players include George Lohmann and Bill Lockwood (who with Tom Richardson formed a formidable trio of bowlers in the 1890s), Douglas Jardine (of Bodyline fame – or should that be infamy?), Percy Fender, John Edrich, Geoff Arnold, Graham Thorpe, Alec Stewart and Alex Tudor. The current squad includes Alistair Brown, Mark Butcher, Asif Mohammad, Mark Ramprakash and Saqlain Mushtaq.

Surrey is the most financially successful first-class county, with a turnover in 2007 in excess of £24 million.

Most appropriately named player – S. A. Block.

The club's limited-overs team was once the Surrey Lions but is now known as the Surrey Brown Caps, in keeping with the club colours of chocolate brown and silver.

Worth a visit for . . . Lord's may be the 'spiritual home of English cricket' but one gains a sense that the Oval is at the heart of the game. Just sitting in the Oval, one is filled with a sense of great history and tradition, and one's eye keeps wandering to the mammoth and magnificent pavilion, completed in 1898. Unlike the tower block that overlooks Trent Bridge, the gasometers appear part of the Oval. In recent years there has been talk of them being demolished, but hopefully common sense will prevail and they will be saved, not just to preserve the traditional Oval vista but as a part of our national heritage.

BATS, BALLS & BAILS

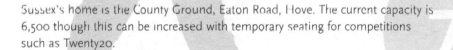

Sussex's home is the County Ground, Eaton Road, Hove. The current capacity is 6,500 though this can be increased with temporary seating for competitions such as Twenty20.

One of Sussex's earliest homes was on land donated by the Prince of Wales (Surrey may want to know why the then Prince of Wales consented to donate land to Sussex for a ground yet would only lease them the Oval). Unsurprisingly the club named this the 'Prince of Wales Ground'. It was situated in Hove, where Park Crescent now is.

Sussex also play matches at Arundel, Eastbourne and Horsham. The club's Second XI play matches at numerous venues throughout the county.

The club badge is the county arms of six martlets. The martlet is a mythological bird noted for having legs but no feet.

You know how some people have a complicated hierarchy of cleaning cloths in their kitchen, fathomable only to themselves? The situation at Sussex regarding capped and uncapped players is not dissimilar. Capped players sport six martlets on their sweaters, uncapped players wear just the club badge on the breast of their sweater. Capped players also wear caps that have the club crest trimmed with gold, whereas the caps of uncapped players have white trimming around the club crest. Yes, yes, the caps of uncapped players . . . the mind boggles as to how the club's cleaning cloths are organized.

Sussex had to wait more than 100 years for their first County Championship success. The club has won the title on three occasions, in 2003, 2006 and 2007. Other major trophy successes: Gillette/NatWest/C&G Trophy winners in 1963, 1964, 1978, 1986 and 2006; and Sunday/Pro40 League winners in 1982 and 2008.

Sussex, along with Kent, is widely recognized as the birthplace of cricket. Sussex county teams have been traced back to the seventeenth century, though a form of cricket was played in the county as early as the sixteenth century.

The earliest reference to cricket in the county can be found in ecclesiastical records dated 1611: two parishioners of Sidlesham (West Sussex) failed to attend church on Easter Sunday as they were playing in a grand cricket match. The record further notes the miscreants were fined 12d each and made to do penance. One Sussex wag suggested this may have involved having to watch Kent play.

Matches between Sussex parishes were common in the seventeenth century. In 1697 a 'great match' took place between two elevens chosen from various parishes for which each team received 50 guineas – so no financial incentive to win there, then. You may think this a considerable sum of money for the time, and it was, but sizeable sums were often at stake in these formative years of the game. In July 1797 the All England team played a representative team from the county of Norfolk, and the winners, All England, received 500 guineas.

In 1729 a Sussex XI beat a Kent XI in a game widely recognized as the first match involving a Sussex county representative side. However, Kent at the time laid claim to being the 'Champion County of 1728' so one assumes they must have previously played against another county in order to lay claim to such a title, or else they had a contemporary Max Clifford on board. Whatever the case, Sussex's victory in 1729 must surely have put the kibosh on Kent's claim.

More claims as to cricketing superiority were made throughout the eighteenth century. The famous Sussex club Slindon, whose team was often representative of the county during this period, was proclaimed to be the best team in England.

Occasionally records listed the profession or occupation of Slinden players. Presumably one Edward Aburrow would not have been best pleased with his: 'Known Smuggler'.

Records for 1792 note Sussex beating the MCC on three occasions, and also Middlesex.

In 1836 it was decided to form an official Sussex County Cricket Club – the first in cricket history. Sussex CCC was formally constituted on 1 March 1839. The club's inaugural first-class match took place later that year, against the MCC at Lord's.

In what was the unofficial County Championship, Sussex were 'Champion County' in 1845, 1848 and 1855, and shared the title in 1852.

In 1867 Sussex dismissed Kent for 18 at Gravesend – to this day the lowest total inflicted upon another county.

What's in a name? In the case of legendary Sussex player E. W. Dwyer, quite a lot. His full name was John Elicius Benedict Bernard Placid Quirk Carrington Dwyer. His great grandfather, Michael, led the Irish Rebellion of 1798 and was subsequently arrested and deported to Australia, hence E. W. Dwyer (Placid Quirk) was Australian.

In 1899 C. H. G. Bland took 10 for 48 against Kent at Tunbridge Wells – the best single-innings bowling figures in the history of the club.

In 1902 Sussex achieved their highest total in first-class cricket – 705 for 8 declared, against Surrey at Hastings.

In 1926 George Cox returned match figures of 17 for 106 against Warwickshire at Horsham – a club record yet to be surpassed.

In 1933 John Langridge and Ted Bowley shared an opening partnership of 490 against Middlesex at Hove – a club record partnership.

John Langridge holds a number of other club records: the most runs in a single season – 2,850 (average 64.77) in 1949; most centuries in a single season – 12, also in 1949; most runs in a Sussex career – 34,150 (average 37.69); most centuries in a career at the club – 76; and most catches in the field – 779. All of which must qualify him as one of the best cricketers of the twentieth century never to have been selected for a Test match. Born into a cricketing family, he followed his older brother, James, into the Sussex side of 1928 and remained a regular until his retirement in 1955. Only Alan Jones (Glamorgan) has scored more first-class runs and never played in a Test match, and no player who scored as many centuries as Langridge failed to be selected for England. Only five players in the history of English first-class cricket have taken more catches in a career. John Langridge did, however, finally realize his dream of Test cricket: on retirement he became a first-class umpire and stood in seven Test matches.

Another outstanding Sussex player of the 1920s and 1930s was Jim Parks, often referred to as Jim Parks senior as his son Jim Parks junior was a renowned Sussex wicket-keeper in the 1950s and 1960s. Jim Parks senior's brother also played for Sussex, and his grandson Bobby played for Hampshire. Jim Parks senior was a Sussex regular from 1927 to 1939 during which time he scored 1,000 runs in every season except one. In 1935 he did the double of 1,000 runs and 100 wickets, but his most memorable season was 1937, when he scored 3,003 runs and took 101 wickets.

In 1937 bowler Maurice Tate (1912–37) retired with two club records to his name that have yet to be broken: most wickets in a single season – 198 (average 13.47) in 1925; and most wickets in a career – 2,211 (average 17.41).

The Reverend David Sheppard, later to become Bishop of Liverpool, was batting against Roley Jenkins when the Worcestershire bowler, frustrated at the Reverend having played and missed on several occasions, let fly a stream of expletives. The following Sunday Sheppard chose as the theme for his sermon 'Faith is like facing Roley Jenkins. No hesitation – if you decide to go forward, go forward all the way.'

Sussex were the winners of the Gillette Cup in the inaugural year of the competition, 1963, and retained the trophy the following season.

The Sussex captain in both Gillette Cup successes was Ted Dexter, who was born in Milan. Dexter was a swashbuckling batsman and effective bowler who could have become a professional at golf but opted for cricket as a career. At Cambridge University he played rugby and golf for Jesus College as well as winning his cricket Blue. He was Sussex captain from 1960 to 1965, played in 62 Tests and also captained England on the tour to India and Pakistan in

1961–62. He lost the captaincy after losing the Ashes 1–0 at home in 1964 but remained in the Test side as a batsman. Between 1956 and 1968 he scored 21,150 runs (average 40.75), including 51 centuries, and took 419 wickets (average 29.92). In 1964 he stood (unsuccessfully) for Parliament against Jim Callaghan in Cardiff. He retired as a player in 1965 as the result of a bizarre accident: his car ran out of petrol in London and as he was pushing it to safety the car pinned him to a warehouse door, breaking his leg. He was persuaded to make a comeback in 1968 and made 203 not out in his first innings for Sussex, which earned him a Test recall for two matches against Australia. Following his definitive retirement at the end of 1968 he ran a successful PR company, and was chairman of the MCC and also chairman of the England cricket committee.

Dexter, such powerful straight driving. When you see him in this sort of form you know he is set for a big innings . . . bowled him!
BRIAN JOHNSTON (BBC TV)

In the late 1950s and 1960s the Sussex team included the brothers Mike and Tony Buss, which on one occasion, against Yorkshire, prompted the following memorable exchange in the slips following the dismissal of Mike Buss:
DOUG PADGETT: That's one Buss out.
FRED TRUEMAN: Don't worry. There'll be another one along in a minute.

Mike Buss survived two extraordinary near dismissals when batting against Yorkshire at Bradford in 1965. Facing a ball from Tony Nicholson in the first innings, he played and missed, the ball hit the off stump, but the falling bail lodged between the off and middle stumps so he was not given out. To Nicholson's chagrin the ball went for four byes. During the second innings Buss hit a ball from Chris Balderstone on to his boot, the ball ricocheted on to the stumps, and again a bail was dislodged but it never fell to the ground, prompting Balderstone to say, 'You know, Mike, nothing pisses me off so much as other people's good luck.'

South Africa-born Tony Greig was another notable Sussex captain. Educated at Queens College, Queenstown, he was coached, at various times, by ex-Sussex players Jack Oakes, Alan Oakman, Ian Thomson, Ron Bell, Richard Langridge and Mike Buss. At the age of 19 he was given a trial by Sussex and in his first match scored 156, against Lancashire. In 1974 he was chosen by England for the tour of the West Indies and ran into the sort of controversy that was to become a trademark of his career. On the second day of the first Test in Trinidad the last ball was bowled to Bernard Julian, who blocked it past Greig fielding close-in on the off-side. Julian headed off to the pavilion along with Alvin Kallicharran, only for Greig to whirl round and throw down the stumps. Umpire Douglas Sung Hue gave Kallicharran out, which resulted in a riot among the crowd with many spectators storming the pavilion. Technically the umpire was correct as he had not called time on the day's play, besides which the ball was in motion when Greig collected it and thus not 'dead'. However, England bottled it and decided to withdraw the appeal, the powers-that-be of the mind that Greig's action had been unsporting. Greig proved an excellent captain of both Sussex and England but was never far away from controversy, at no time more so than in 1977 when he signed up to Kerry Packer's 'Cricket Circus'. He now lives in Australia and continues to work as a TV commentator on cricket.

RUSSELL HARTY: How does a South African come to be captain of England?
TONY GREIG: I qualified to play for England by virtue of my father.
HARTY: And what nationality is he?
GREIG: Scottish.

In 1996 against Ireland in the NatWest Trophy in Belfast, Sussex achieved their highest total in a one-day game – 384 for 9.

Current player Robin Martin-Jenkins is the son of the cricket commentator and writer Christopher Martin-Jenkins. In 2002 Robin and Mark Davis shared an eighth-wicket partnership of 291 against Somerset at Taunton – an all-time club record for the eighth wicket.

In 2003 Murray Goodwin scored a club record highest innings of 335 not out, against Leicestershire at Hove.

In 2003 Sussex won their first ever official County Championship title and repeated the feat in 2006, a year in which the club also achieved their first double, winning the C&G Trophy as well.

Sussex won the County Championship for a third time in 2007 in what were unprecedented circumstances on the final day of the season. Sussex beat

Worcestershire, and their only rivals for the title, Lancashire, failed to beat Surrey, the match going beyond five p.m. Though Sussex's game against Worcestershire was over, a sizeable crowd remained inside the Hove ground to await the outcome of Lancashire's match, the events of the game being relayed over loudspeakers. When the Lancashire match finally ended there were jubilant celebrations around the Hove ground.

In 2008 Sussex staged a doughty comeback in the Pro40 Final to defeat Nottinghamshire, Murray Goodwin hitting a mighty six to seal what at one stage had looked a highly improbable victory.

Other notable Sussex players include Tony Cook, who also played football for Brighton and Hove Albion and Bristol Rovers and was manager of Brighton in 1947, Allan Donald (South Africa), Charles Fry, Ashley Giles, Nick Knight, Robin Marlar, Nawab of Pataudi, Alan Oakham, Shaun Pollock, Dermot Reeve, Jon Snow, Keri Suttle and Joseph Vine. The current squad includes Murray Goodwin, James Kirtley, Matt Prior and Michael Yardy.

In May 2009 Mushtaq Ahmed was released from his role as spin coach with the club in order to fulfil a similar role with England.

Sussex is the only county club to have a club song that is sung regularly by spectators at matches and by the players following victory. The song is a version of a military marching song composed by W. Ward for the Sussex Regiment during the First World War, entitled 'Sussex by the Sea'. The lyrics have been changed, and the opening verse is now as follows:

Good old Sussex by the sea,
Good old Sussex by the sea.
And we're going up to win the cup
For Sussex by the sea.

The team sing it in the dressing room after every victory, and the honour of leading the song is given to the player, named by the coach or captain, who is thought to have contributed most to victory.

Most appropriately named player – Ted Bowley.

The club's limited-overs team is the Sussex Sharks.

Worth a visit for . . . the great value for money and friendliness. At Hove there is free car parking next to the outdoor nets area. Head for the public seating section nearest to this car park – that is, at the far end of the ground to the Arthur Gilligan stand and main entrance. There is a nearby bar which, mercifully, is always well staffed, and the view of play from this section of the ground is every bit as good as from the neighbouring members' enclosure. In 2008 admission for a County Championship match was £13 but under 16s are admitted free if accompanied by an adult – very welcome for this author who has two young daughters who are starting to take an interest in cricket. Both stewards and supporters are exceedingly friendly, very welcoming of young children, and will readily engage in conversation about players past and present.

There are two designated intervals in first-class and Test cricket matches, lunch and tea, though in certain circumstances players may also enjoy a 'drinks break', which does not require the umpires, fielding team and two batsmen to leave the field.

Regulations have been laid down for when lunch and tea intervals may be taken. In first-class matches the umpires and respective captains agree prior to the match on when the tea interval will be; usually this will be a 20-minute break taken between 4 and 4.30 p.m. If a team that is batting has lost nine wickets by the agreed time for tea the interval may be delayed until the last wicket has fallen, or 30 minutes has elapsed. In one-day matches, teams usually agree to take tea between innings. As the thousands of non-first-class cricket clubs in Britain and Ireland play a limited-overs game there is no requirement for a lunch interval. Tea, however, is 'universal', with the obvious exception of those clubs that participate in evening mid-week leagues.

The tradition of cricket's tea interval as we now know it has its roots in the Victorian age. In nineteenth-century upper- and middle-class society it became fashionable to take a light meal each day between three and five p.m. This was known as 'afternoon tea', as opposed to 'high tea', which was eaten between five and six p.m., 'dinner' being the term given to a meal eaten after six p.m. The meal eaten between five and six p.m. was called 'high tea' because it was served on a dining-room table, whereas 'afternoon tea' was served on a lower table in a lounge and was a less formal affair in that people selected items of food for their plate which they consumed while sitting in the lounge. The profusion of cricket clubs that formed in the nineteenth century were administered by men who were accustomed to taking lunch and afternoon tea. Such meals were an intrinsic aspect of the society in which they lived and were adopted in the developing game of cricket.

 It was a very English thing to do, to have tea during a cricket match. But that was the Victorians for you. They introduced organized sport to the world but, in so doing, appeared loath to forgo simple pleasures enjoyed at home, so they simply transported their home comforts to the swards of England.

JOHN AMIS (writer/broadcaster)

Every club has its own idea as to what constitutes a cricket tea, and, it has to be said, the quality of teas may vary considerably from club to club. Some clubs are noted in their league not for their cricket but for the quality of their teas.

Traditionally, teas were organized and prepared by a club's 'Ladies Tea Committee', usually comprising wives and partners of officials and playing members of the club. Though women and many club members nowadays may feel this smacks of sexism, the tradition of women preparing teas still continues at many clubs.

In years gone by it was quite common for tips and suggestions to appear in women's magazines and books regarding what constituted the ideal cricket tea, such as the following from the now defunct *Woman's Own* in 1966: 'A selection of sandwiches, the crusts left on, with perhaps the exception of cucumber sandwiches. A selection of the following fillings will prove popular: corned beef, cucumber, cheese and tomato, grated cheese, fish paste, ham, Spam, tuna and mayonnaise. Shop-bought cakes are not popular, a simple home-baked Victoria sponge will go down a treat (though you may need at least three). Fruit cakes such as Dundee, Farmhouse and Madeira will also be appreciated, as will Battenberg. A tray of small home-baked cakes, fairy,

Yorkshire curd tarts and scones neatly displayed will disappear in no time. Then tea itself must be piping and not prepared too far in advance to prevent stewing. Stewed tea may give your club an unwanted reputation amongst other clubs. And, don't forget lemonade (home-made if you can) for the children.'

Today many clubs feel uncomfortable at the thought of asking the ladies to make tea for officials, players, opponents and spectators on match days, and they operate a rota system among club members. The cost of the tea either comes out of funds raised by the club or else members pay (and may be reimbursed from club funds).

Occasionally, such a system results in humorous advice being offered. In 2007 James Culverwell of Crawley CC penned a guide for players on the club's 'tea making rota', part of which reads as follows: 'To make egg sandwiches you need hard-boiled eggs. These can be purchased from shops ready-cooked. Simply buy Scotch eggs and remove the sausage meat from the outside. Bread does not come pre-buttered. Bread can, however, be purchased pre-sliced. Sandwiches are best made by placing a piece of bread butter side up on a flat board. Place filling on bread. Then place another slice of bread, butter side down, on top of the filling. Do not get these in the wrong order. If in doubt, ask. Do not cut into soldiers. Peanut butter and Marmite are popular sandwich fillers, but not together. To make tea you need milk. Milk comes from cows but for convenience sake can be purchased ready-made from shops. Please ensure that an adult person is present when you boil water.'

In 2008 Barhill CC also issued club members with 'Guidelines for Cricket Teas', though this guide was of the practical variety and included the following items: Purchase of teas should cost no more than £22.50 (excluding stock items). A receipt is needed to claim back the money you have spent.
Teas should not be purchased before the day of the game in case the game has to be cancelled.
Teas – composition: 4 loaves of medium-sliced bread (not Tesco variety); margarine, sandwich fillings, anything you desire but please ensure you include vegetarian varieties; milk; crisps (2 or 3 packets); sausage rolls and/or savoury nibbles; selection of cakes; fruit (optional).
REMEMBER NOT TO SPEND MORE THAN £22.50.
(Perhaps not noted in their local league for the quality of their teas, then.)

It appears Chipping Sodbury CC has an unusual attitude towards their supporters, particularly regarding the taking of tea. In 2008 the Chipping Sodbury 'Club Guide to Cricket Teas' contained the following advice: 'You are to cater for 22 players, 2 umpires and 2 scorers. Occasionally some supporters may like a cup of tea and a sandwich (there is usually plenty of them). Any food left by the players is put out for them to eat after the match.' (You can just see them now, can't you, gathered around the pavilion steps, tongues hanging out, waiting for the scraps.)

In 1977 Hendon Gardens CC (Sunderland) appeared to take a hard line where tea was concerned. The Hendon Gardens pub, in which the club was based, displayed the following advice on the cricket club's noticeboard: 'The club does not provide teas. If you want tea, bring your own.'

In recent years it has become the vogue among some clubs to provide a more cosmopolitan range of food, such as spring rolls, tortilla wraps, pitta bread with curried chicken filler, vegetable samosas and so on. No doubt all is consumed with relish, but somehow one can't help feeling such fare is simply not a cricket tea.

For a number of years the BBC's *Test Match Special* ran a 'Tea Lady of the Year' competition (presumably until someone pointed out this could be sexist). The competition, which ran into the new millennium, involved ladies being nominated by club members for the quality of the teas they prepared. In 2002 the winner was Mrs Kay Smart, provider of teas at Earls Barton CC in Northamptonshire. Perhaps BBC executives were prompted to question the ethics of this competition on hearing what Mrs Smart had to say when she was presented with her award: 'I can't stand cricket. I only have to turn up because my husband's here.'

Phil Tufnell (Middlesex and England) is a prolific tea drinker. It is said he would have three to four cups of tea during the tea interval.

In 2004 TV chef Delia Smith confessed to having cheated in the preparation of her lavishly praised teas for her husband's cricket club. Ms Smith came clean when she formally opened a new pavilion at Battisford and District CC (Suffolk), of which her husband, Michael Wynn-Jones, was a founder member. To reported 'gasps of surprise' from former and current players, Ms Smith said, 'I would make the teas every now and then, but when I was really busy I would get sandwiches from Marks and Spencer.' One former player was quoted as saying, 'The club was renowned as having fantastic teas because Delia often did them. But now it looks like she took a short cut.'

Tea toe-teller. On 2 May 2005, during the tea interval of Somerset's match against Surrey at Taunton, Surrey's Mark Ramprakash dislocated a toe on the pavilion steps when walking back to the dressing room with a cup of tea.

In March 2006 Margaret Parker announced her retirement as tea lady at Oulton Park CC in Cheshire, thus ending an 80-year family association with cricket teas at the club, one which involved only two people. Mrs Parker succeeded her brother-in-law as provider of teas, and he had prepared his first cricket tea for the club in 1926. Said Ms Parker, 'After enjoying myself so much over the years, deciding to retire was a difficult decision, but the idea had been brewing for some time.'

The first cricket match to be the subject of a radio commentary was Essex v. New Zealand at Leyton on 14 May 1927. The match was broadcast by the BBC Home Service and the commentator was Plum Warner, with 'inserts' from the Reverend Frank Gillingham (Essex).

Cricket is the slowest game in the world.

RADIO TIMES (1927 – that's the way to sell it)

Talk about own goals. In August 1927 Teddy Wakeham commentated on Surrey v. Middlesex from the Oval and reported to the BBC that 'cricket was impossible to commentate upon'. Cricket commentary all but disappeared from the airwaves until the mid-1930s. The BBC believed Test match cricket in particular was too slow for ball-by-ball commentary to be attractive to listeners.

In 1934 Seymour 'Lobby' de Lotbiniere, who was Head of Outside Broadcasts for the BBC, persuaded the Corporation to broadcast ball-by-ball commentary of Tests. The commentator was Howard Marshall. The broadcasts did not cover every ball but became increasingly popular with listeners.

The oldest surviving commentary in the BBC archives is of Howard Marshall commentating on the 1934 Test at Lord's, when Hedley Verity spun England to victory over Australia.

In 1938 BBC Television broadcast live coverage of England's Tests against Australia at Lord's and the Oval. The matches were not covered in their entirety, however, and as very few people in the UK had television sets, the audiences for these programmes would have been negligible.

The commentary for the Oval Test in 1938 is arguably the first iconic radio cricket commentary. Here's Howard Marshall describing Len Hutton's record innings: 'The total – Hutton's total 332. It sounds like the total of a whole side. The England total 707 for five and the gasometer sinking lower and lower. Here's Fleetwood-Smith again to Hutton. Hutton hits him. Oh, beautiful stroke, and there is the record.'

In 1946 BBC Radio broadcast commentary of the Victory Tests. The commentators were Howard Marshall and Rex Alston.

In 1948 BBC Radio broadcast full coverage of the Test series, but only for Australia; the UK received intermittent commentary. The commentators were Rex Alston, John Arlott, E. W. Swanton and Alan McGilvray of the Australian Broadcasting Corporation.

Like an old lady poking with her umbrella at a wasps' nest.

JOHN ARLOTT (on the batting of Ernie Toshack)

In 1950 BBC Television broadcast the Test match from Trent Bridge live; one of the commentators was Brian Johnston. The broadcast began at 11.25 on the first day in order to allow the commentators to set the scene. Producer Peter Dimmock asked umpires Frank Chester and Harry Elliot to come out at 11.30 and not 11.25. Chester and Elliot, however, took to the field as scheduled, at 11.25.

As I look around the ground I can see about 30 young girls all wearing Dutch caps.

JONATHAN AGNEW (commentating on a Holland game)

BBC Radio was the first broadcaster to cover every ball of a Test match. Throughout the 1940s and early 1950s the amount of ball-by-ball commentary on radio gradually increased, which led to the launch in 1957 of *Test Match Special*.

Test Match Special, or *TMS* as it is known to millions, was the idea of BBC producer Robert Hudson, who in 1956 persuaded the Head of Outside Broadcasts, Charles Max-Muller, that full ball-by-ball commentary on radio would be a 'winner'.

He played a cut so late as to be positively posthumous.
JOHN ARLOTT

The first *TMS* commentary team was Rex Alston, John Arlott and Ken Ablack, with comments from Bill Bowes and Gerry Gomez and close-of-play summary from E. W. Swanton. The producer was Michael Tuke-Hastings, who remained in that role until 1973.

Strangely, in slow motion replay, the ball seemed to hang in the air for even longer.
DAVID ACFIELD

Listeners had to 'channel hop' for the first *TMS* commentaries, which switched (during the same day's play) between the Light Programme (now Radio 2) and the Third Programme (now Radio 3), and, occasionally, the Home Service (now Radio 4).

In 1963 the BBC appointed its first 'cricket correspondent' – Brian Johnston. It was also in 1963 that the BBC switched *TMS* from the Light Programme to the Third Programme, where it was to stay for the next three decades.

The BBC's coverage of Gary Sobers hitting six sixes for Nottinghamshire against Glamorgan at Swansea in 1968 owes all to producer John Norman ignoring a request from the producer of *Grandstand* to shut down cameras and end coverage of the match. Norman, and cameraman John Lewis, continued filming, even though television coverage of the match had ended, as they wanted to capture Gary Sobers in action at Swansea for 'posterity'. What they captured was a truly historic moment in cricket. In 2007 it was reported the BBC was charging £17,000 for the rights to use the footage.

I don't think he expected it and that's what caught him unawares.
TREVOR BAILEY

In 1970 BBC Television dispensed with the commentary services of Brian Johnston, who joined the *TMS* team. Johnston's humour and obvious love of cricket introduced a new audience to *TMS* to add to the followers of the erudite talent of John Arlott.

Gatting at fine leg – that's a contradiction in terms.
RICHIE BENAUD

In 1978 *TMS* was broadcast on Radio 3's medium wave until 1992, when it switched to Radio 3 FM. In 1993 it moved to Radio 5 for the morning play and Radio 3 FM for the afternoon session, before eventually finding a home on Radio 4 long wave. With the advent of digital radio, *TMS* can also be heard on FiveLive Sports Extra and on the internet.

And Laird has been brought in to stand in the corner of the circle.
RICHIE BENAUD

From 1973 to 2007 *TMS* was produced by Peter Baxter, from 2007 by Adam Mountford.

The theme tune played at the beginning and end of *TMS*, which was also for 30 years the theme tune for BBC TV's Test match coverage, is 'Soul Limbo' by Booker T and the MGs. The music was chosen as the introduction is similar to the sound once made by West Indian cricket fans knocking tin cans together, which often happened during Test matches in the 1970s. (The MG in Booker T and the MGs stands for Memphis Group.)

In reply to Twyford's 220 for 3, Royal Doulton are 24 for 8. So, Royal Doulton still very much in that match.
JOHN KEARNEY (Signal Radio)

Notable *TMS* commentators include E. W. Swanton (BBC Radio 1938–75), Rex Alston (1945–64), John Arlott (1946–80), Robert Hudson (1958–68), Peter West (1958), Alan Gibson (1962–75), Brian Johnston (1966–1994), Don Mosey (1974–94), Tony Lewis (1977–85), Christopher Martin-Jenkins (1973 to present), Henry Blofeld (1971–91 and 1994 to present), Jonathan Agnew (1991 to present) and Simon Mann (1996 to present). Other notable contemporary commentators include Jonny Saunders, Jon Champion, Arlo White and Mark Pougatch. Notable *TMS* summarizers: Trevor Bailey, Fred Trueman, Mike Selvey, David Lloyd, Vic Marks, Graham Gooch, Geoff Boycott, Phil Tufnell and Ashley Giles.

Jonathan Agnew played for Leicestershire and England and began his broadcasting career with BBC Radio Leicester.

 In the rear, the small, diminutive figure of Shoaib Mohammed, who can't be much taller than he is.
HENRY BLOFELD

 Flintoff starts in, his shadow alongside him.
HENRY BLOFELD

 Trevor Bailey and myself knew we were on our way out of TMS when the producer called a meeting and we weren't invited. I was in Spain when I received the call from BBC Radio's Head of Sport. 'I don't know how to speak to a sporting icon,' he said. 'Oh quit the bullshit and get on with it,' I told him. That was it, the end of an era. What also irked was his call was routed through my phone in England, which meant I had to pay for it.
FRED TRUEMAN

 And we don't need a calculator to tell us that the run-rate required is 4.5454 per over.
CHRISTOPHER MARTIN-JENKINS

There is a tradition on *TMS* that every Saturday of a home Test match commentators wear a 'Primary Club' tie. Membership of the Primary Club is open to anyone who has been out first ball in any form of cricket. (Unbelievably, but true, the author does not qualify, but he is led to believe the editor of this book may qualify several times over.) Proceeds from the Primary Club are donated to a charity for the blind and partially sighted cricketers.

He could have caught that between the cheeks of his backside.
GEOFF BOYCOTT

Another feature of Saturday *TMS* is 'View from the Boundary' in which guests from all walks of life are interviewed. Originally the interview was conducted by Brian Johnston; nowadays most are hosted by Jonathan Agnew.

In 2008 BBC listeners voted Jonathan Agnew's comment during the Oval Test of 1991 that Ian Botham 'just didn't quite get his leg over' and the subsequent uncontrollable laughter and 'corpsing' of Brian Johnston as the 'Most Memorable Moment in the History of Sporting Commentary'.

This has been completely and utterly limp by England. They're playing with all the intensity of my drunk aunt playing Cluedo at Christmas.
JONATHAN AGNEW

In 1994 Sky bought the rights to ODIs and county cricket; BBC Television retained the rights to the broadcasting of Test matches. The deal was worth £60 million over four years.

In 1998 the BBC lost uninterrupted broadcasting rights for Test matches to Sky and Channel Four. The Sky/Channel Four deal was for four years and was worth £103 million to the ECB. The BBC was left with no coverage of major cricket.

Well, Andrew Strauss is certainly an optimist, he's coming out to bat wearing sunblock.
AUSTRALIAN COMMENTATOR (Channel Five highlights coverage)

In 2007 the BBC negotiated a deal to broadcast highlights from the 2007 World Cup, which was presented by Manish Bhasin, and the 2009 Twenty20 World Cup. (The BBC certainly knows how to win back viewers.)

Television shows with cricket as the theme:

P'Tang Yang Kipper Bang – Jack Rosenthal's script about a boy, Quack-Quack Duckworth, in post-war England who dreams of kissing Abigail and scoring the winning run in a Test match against Australia. The boy's daydreams of cricket are accompanied by commentary from John Arlott.

Arthur's Hallowed Ground – Jimmy Jewel plays a cantankerous old groundsman (is there any other type?) who so treasures his handiwork on the pitch he doesn't want anyone to play on it, let alone walk across it.

Bodyline – 1980s Australian TV movie offering excellent account of the infamous 'Bodyline' series – Jardine, Larwood, Bradman et al.

Outside Edge (1994) – TV series telling of the shenanigans at a minor cricket club, popular with viewers though one suspects not for the cricket scenes.

TV series that featured cricket in an episode:

Dad's Army, 'The Test' – Hodges challenges Captain Mainwaring's platoon to a game of cricket. Fred Trueman plays Ernie Egan, the 'ringer' in Hodges' team, the vicar and verger are the umpires
MAINWARING: That was my googly.
VERGER: From where I was standing it looked like a chuck, and don't argue with the umpire or you'll be sent off.
MAINWARING: You don't send people off in cricket.
VERGER: I do!
MAINWARING: I suppose I'm lucky not to have been given offside.
VERGER: Right, that's it, your name is going in the book.

Also: *Dr Who*, 'The Black Orchid' (1981); *Inspector Morse*, 'Deceived By Flight' (1989); *Midsomer Murders*, 'Dead Man's Eleven' (1999); *Kingdom*, season two, episode 4 (2008).

'The step up from county to Test cricket is a big one and a lot can't handle it. There have been many players who have excelled in domestic cricket who, for various reasons, just couldn't cut the mustard in Test cricket. Players from whichever era will tell you, playing Test cricket is very hard, the ultimate test of you as a player.
BRIAN STATHAM

The first ever international match, though not a Test match, was between Canada and the United States of America on 24–25 September 1844.

The term 'Test' is thought to originate from the notion that matches between representative teams from Australia and England were a 'test of cricketing strength and competence'.

The first known reference to 'Test' occurs in *Australian Cricket and Cricketers* by Clarence Moody, a book of the late nineteenth century detailing the earliest matches between Australian representative teams and touring teams from England, though few, if any, of the teams that participated in these matches were truly representative of either country.

The first ever official Test commenced on 15 March 1877, between Australia and England at the MCG (Melbourne Cricket Ground). Play began at just after one p.m. with England's Alfred Shaw bowling the first ball to Charles Bannerman. Bannerman became the first player to score a Test run, off Shaw's second ball. Having started at a little after one the first session was short: lunch was taken at two.

Allen Hill (England) was the first bowler to take a wicket in a Test match, and the first batsman to be out in a Test match was Australia's Nat Thomson. Charles Bannerman became the first player to score a century in a Test match, amassing 165 of Australia's first-innings total of 245. He added another first by becoming the first batsman to retire hurt in a Test.

Australia won this first Test by 45 runs. The attendance at the MCG on the final day of play was 3,000.

The teams for the very first Test match at Melbourne, 15–19 March 1877: AUSTRALIA: Charles Bannerman (New South Wales), John Blackham (Victoria), Bransby Cooper (Victoria), Thomas Garrett (NSW), David Gregory (NSW), Edward Gregory (NSW), John Hodges (Victoria), Thomas Horan (Victoria), Thomas Kendall (Victoria), William Midwinter (Victoria), Nat Thomson (NSW). ENGLAND: Thomas Armitage (Yorkshire), Henry Charlwood (Sussex), Thomas Emmett (Yorkshire), Andrew Greenwood (Yorkshire), Allen Hill (Yorkshire), Henry Jupp (Surrey), James Lillywhite Jr (Sussex), John Selby (Nottinghamshire), Alfred Shaw (Nottinghamshire), James Southerton (Surrey) and George Ulyett (Yorkshire).

The second Test also took place at the MCG. England won by four wickets to draw the series 1–1.

The first team to remain unchanged for the entirety of a five-match series was England, in the series against Australia in 1884–85, which England won 3–2.

The shortest ever completed Test match in England occurred on 30–31 August 1888, between England and Australia at Old Trafford. The match ended before lunch on the second day. Total playing time was six hours 34 minutes. Australia were dismissed for 70 in their second innings in 69 minutes – Australia's shortest innings in a Test in terms of time.

In 1891–92 Bobby Abel became the first England batsman to carry his bat through an innings in a Test. Abel made 132 not out in England's total of 307 against Australia at Sydney.

The 1912 Test between Australia and South Africa was the first Test to be held at Lord's which did not involve England. The match was also honoured by the presence of His Majesty King George V – the first occasion on which a reigning monarch attended a Test match.

The most wickets taken by an individual bowler in a Test series is 49, by Sydney Barnes, in four Tests for England against South Africa in 1913–14. It was all the more remarkable as Barnes played Minor Counties cricket.

In 1928–29 England defeated Australia at Brisbane by 675 runs – the largest victory by any team in a Test in terms of runs.

The highest number of runs scored by a batsman in a five-match Test series is 974, by Don Bradman for Australia against England in 1930.

Bradman also holds the record for the highest batting average in a five-match Test series – 201.50, against South Africa in 1931–32.

An aggregate of 234 runs was scored by Australia and South Africa in the Melbourne Test of 1931–32 – the lowest in a completed Test match. This was also the shortest ever Test match in terms of time, at five hours 53 minutes.

The first person to take five catches in a single innings of a Test is Victor Richardson, for Australia against South Africa at Durban in 1935–36.

In 1949 New Zealand achieved a record when they managed to play an entire series against England (four Tests) with not one player being out for a duck.

The only batsman ever to have been given out for 'obstructing the field' in a Test match is Len Hutton, against South Africa at the Oval in 1951.

The only Test player to have been hanged is Leslie Hylton, who played for the West Indies in the 1930s. In 1955 Hylton was tried and found guilty for the murder of his wife and subsequently executed.

The longest a team has gone without a victory is 44 Tests – New Zealand, from 1930 to 1956.

On 11 October 1956 only 95 runs were scored in an entire day's play in the Test between Pakistan and Australia at Karachi.

In 1959 England achieved their first ever 'whitewash' in a five-match Test series, winning all five Tests against India.

In January 1960 Gary Sobers (226) and Frank Worrell (197 not out) became the first batsmen to bat throughout two consecutive days in a Test match – the fourth and fifth days at Bridgetown against England.

There have only been two tied Test matches. The first was Australia (505 and 232) against the West Indies (453 and 284) at Brisbane in 1960–61; the second was Australia (574 for 7 declared and 170 for 5 declared) against India (397 and 347) at Madras in 1986–87.

The first bowler to achieve 300 Test wickets was Fred Trueman (Yorkshire). Trueman reached this milestone when he had Neil Hawke (Australia) caught by Colin Cowdrey (Kent) during the Oval Test on 15 August 1964. When Hawke began his walk back to the Oval pavilion, Trueman congratulated him on his efforts with the bat. 'A historic moment for you, Fred, and me,' replied Hawke. 'I always dreamed of one day my name appearing in the record books, and now, as your 300th Test victim, I've done it!'

In January 1965 all 20 outfield players were called upon to bowl in the Test between South Africa and England at Cape Town.

In 1966 Ken Higgs (63) and Jon Snow (59 not out) shared a partnership of 128 for the tenth wicket for England against the West Indies at the Oval.

From June 1968 to August 1971 England went 26 Test matches without defeat.

In 1976 Viv Richards scored 1,710 runs in 11 Tests for the West Indies – a record for the highest number of runs scored by an individual batsman in Test matches in a calendar year.

In 1977–78 Mudassar Nazar scored a century for Pakistan against England at Lahore, but it took him 557 minutes.

Terry Alderman (Australia) holds the record for having taken the most wickets on his debut in a six-match Test series. Alderman bowled 1,950 balls and took 47 wickets at an average of 21.26 against England in 1981.

Between 1977 and 1984 Ian Botham scored a century and took five wickets in an innings on five occasions for England. In 1979–80 against India he scored 114 and not only took five wickets in India's first innings (6 for 58) but also in their second (7 for 48).

Ian Botham is one of only two players to have scored a century and taken 10 wickets in a Test match; he accomplished this feat against India in 1979–80 (114, and 6 for 58 and 7 for 48). The only other player to have achieved this is Imran Khan (117, and 6 for 98 and 5 for 82), for Pakistan against India at Faisalabad in 1982–83.

The most consecutive Test appearances by an England player is 65, by Ian Botham, February 1978 to March 1984.

16 March 1984 was a historic day, for three Test matches took place for the very first time: Pakistan v. England at Faisalabad, West Indies v. Australia in Trinidad, and Sri Lanka v. New Zealand at Colombo.

Between 1984 and 1986 the West Indies enjoyed 10 successive Test match victories against England.

What would Health and Safety say nowadays? Malcolm Marshall broke his left thumb in two places and suffered severe bruising to his left forefinger on the first day of the third Test between England and the West Indies in 1984. He nevertheless came on to bowl during England's second innings and returned figures of 7 for 53. Earlier he had batted for the West Indies and, despite having his left hand in plaster, made four runs.

Mohammad Azharuddin (India) is the only batsman to have scored a century in each of his first three Tests, his first (110) coming against England at Calcutta in 1984–85.

In 1994 Allan Border created a record for the most consecutive appearances in Test matches when he played in his 153rd consecutive Test for Australia. The sequence began in March 1979 and ran to March 1994.

From 1999 to 2001 Australia enjoyed a record 17 consecutive Test match victories.

The most Test wickets taken by a bowler in a calendar year is 96 (15 Tests), by Shane Warne of Australia in 2005. Warne took 40 of those wickets in the series against England.

The first bowler to take 600 wickets in Test matches was Shane Warne (Australia).

 ### Shane Warne's idea of a balanced diet is a cheeseburger in each hand.
IAN HEALY

Only one batsman has scored in excess of 10 double centuries in Tests – Don Bradman (Australia), with 12.

What do England's Mike Atherton, Ken Barrington, Keith Fletcher, Graham Gooch, Len Hutton, Alan Knott and Maurice Leyland all have in common? All seven made a duck on their Test debut yet all went on to score over 2,500 runs in Tests for England.

The most ducks by a player in Test matches is 43, by Courtney Walsh (West Indies).

Ten players have scored in excess of 1,000 runs and taken in excess of 100 wickets in Tests for England – Trevor Bailey, Ian Botham, John Emburey, Andrew Flintoff, Ashley Giles, Tony Greig, Ray Illingworth, Wilfred Rhodes, Maurice Tate and Fred Titmus.

The Top Five Wicket Takers in Tests for England

383   Ian Botham, in 102 Tests
325   Bob Willis, in 90 Tests
307   Fred Trueman, in 67 Tests
297   Derek Underwood, in 86 Tests
252   Brian Statham, in 70 Tests

England have nothing to lose here, apart from this Test match.

DAVID LLOYD

In the Test between England and South Africa at the Oval in 2008, all five England bowlers – James Anderson, Stuart Broad, Andrew Flintoff, Steve Harmison and Monty Panesar – took at least one wicket in each innings.

The first Test in 2009 between England and the West Indies began at Lord's on Wednesday 6 May and concluded on the Friday with victory for England. This meant over 20,000 who had purchased tickets for play on Saturday were disappointed, albeit they did qualify for a refund. The ECB and MCC came in for severe criticism from supporters and media alike for having scheduled a Test to start on a Wednesday as opposed to the traditional Thursday. MCC chief executive Keri Bradshaw was unrepentant and seemed little concerned about supporters' grievances. He was quoted as saying, 'It's not the first Test to have started on a Wednesday and it won't be the last.' The Test began on the Wednesday to help accommodate a busy England fixture list which, in addition to the Test, ODI and Twenty20 series against the West Indies also involved the Ashes, ODI and Twenty20 series against Australia and the Twenty20 World Cup. Talk about over-egging the pudding.

Sixty-two batsmen have achieved the distinction of having scored in excess of 30,000 first-class runs in their career (a number of career totals have over the years been disputed, so alternative totals appear in brackets). They are, in descending order:

Jack Hobbs	61,237 (61,760)
Frank Woolley	58,969 (58,959)
Patsy Hendren	57,611
Philip Mead	55,061
W. G. Grace	54,896 (54,211)
Wally Hammond	50,551
Herbert Sutcliffe	50,138 (50,760)
Geoff Boycott	48,426
Tom Graveney	47,793
Graham Gooch	44,846
Tom Hayward	43,551
Dennis Amiss	43,423
Colin Cowdrey	42,719
Andrew Sandham	41,284
Graeme Hick	41,112
Len Hutton	40,140
Mike Smith	39,832

Wilfred Rhodes	39,802 (39,969)
John Edrich	39,790
Bob Wyatt	39,405
Denis Compton	38,942
Ernest Tyldesley	38,874
Johnny Tyldesley	37,897
Keith Fletcher	37,665
Gordon Greenidge	37,354
Jack Hearne	37,252
Leslie Ames	37,248
Don Kenyon	37,002
Bill Edrich	36,965
Jim Parks Jr	36,673
Mike Gatting	36,549
David Denton	36,479 (36,440)
George Hirst	36,323 (36,356)
Viv Richards	36,212
Allan Jones	36,049
William Quaife	36,012
Roy Marshall	35,725
George Gunn	35,208
Brian Close	34,994
Zaheer Abbas	34,843
J. G. Langridge	34,378
Glenn Turner	34,346
Cyril Washbrook	34,101
Maurice Leyland	33,660
'Wally' Hardinge	33,519
Bobby Abel	33,128
Alvin Kallicharran	32,650
Allan Lamb	32,502
Arthur Milton	32,150
Jack Robertson	31,914
Mark Ramprakash	31,894 (a work still in progress)
Joe Hardstaff Jr	31,847

James Langridge	31,716
Ken Barrington	31,714
Clive Lloyd	31,232
Mushtaq Mohammad	31,091
C. B. Fry	30,886
Dennis Brookes	30,874
Percy Holmes	30,573
Reg Simpson	30,546
L. G. Berry	30,225
Ken Suttle	30,225

The feat of taking 100 wickets in a County Championship season was achieved in every season from 1864 to 1971, war years excepted, when first-class cricket was suspended. In 1972 the County Championship season was reduced to 20 matches and no bowler achieved 100 wickets that season, or in 1976. In 1977 the county season was restored to 22 matches until 1982, and to 24 from 1983 to 1988, when four-day matches were introduced. In 2000 the County Championship took on the form of two divisions with each team playing 16 matches which made the feat of taking 100 wickets in a single season harder to achieve but not impossible.

Wilfred Rhodes (Yorkshire) holds the record for having scored 1,000 runs and taken 100 wickets in a season the most times – 16.

Others to have accomplished this feat eight or more times are George Hirst (Yorkshire, 14 times), V. W. C. Jupp (Northamptonshire, 10), William Astill (Leicestershire, 9), Trevor Bailey (Essex, 8), W. G. Grace (Gloucestershire, 8), Morris Nichols (Essex, 8), Albert Relf (Sussex, 8), Frank Tarrant (Middlesex, 8), Maurice Tate (Sussex, 8), Fred Titmus (Middlesex, 8) and Frank Woolley (Kent, 8).

The only player to have scored 3,000 runs and taken 100 wickets in a season is Jim Parks senior (Sussex), in 1937 – 3,003 runs and 101 wickets.

The only player to have scored 2,000 runs and taken 200 wickets in a season is George Hirst (Yorkshire), in 1906 – 2,385 runs and 208 wickets.

The last player to have scored 2,000 runs and taken 100 wickets in a season was Trevor Bailey, for Essex in 1959.

W. G. Grace (Gloucestershire) and Frank Woolley (Kent) hold the record for having scored 1,000 runs in a season the most times – 28.

Five other players have scored 1,000 runs in a season 25 times or more: Colin Cowdrey (Kent) and Philip Mead (Hampshire) – 27 times; Geoff Boycott (Yorkshire) and Jack Hobbs (Surrey) – 26; Patsy Hendren (Middlesex) – 25.

Frank Woolley scored 1,000 runs in a season on 28 occasions between 1902 and 1930, Hampshire's Philip Mead achieved the feat on 27 occasions between 1906 and 1936. Woolley also enjoyed 13 seasons in which he scored in excess of 2,000 runs with a peak of 3,352 at 60.94 in 1928.

Three players have achieved the feat of scoring 1,000 runs in May, then the first full month of the English county season: W. G. Grace (Gloucestershire), 9–30 May 1895 (22 days), 1,016 runs; Wally Hammond (Gloucestershire), 7–31 May 1927 (25 days), 1,042 runs; and Charlie Hallows (Lancashire), 5–31 May 1928 (27 days), 1,000 runs.

Fred Titmus was the last player to take 100 wickets and score in excess of 1,000 runs in a County Championship season, when playing for Middlesex in 1967.

Only two players have scored 1,000 runs and taken 100 wickets in a season since the reduction of County Championship matches: Richard Hadlee (Nottinghamshire) in 1984 and Franklyn Stephenson (also Nottinghamshire) in 1988.

The last player to take 100 wickets in a county season was Mushtaq Ahmed (103), for Sussex in 2003 and again in 2006 (102 wickets), thus helping Sussex to the County Championship and C&G Trophy.

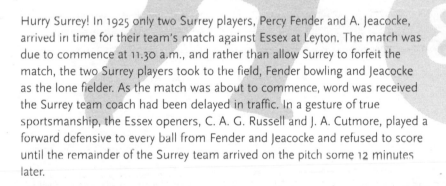

Hurry Surrey! In 1925 only two Surrey players, Percy Fender and A. Jeacocke, arrived in time for their team's match against Essex at Leyton. The match was due to commence at 11.30 a.m., and rather than allow Surrey to forfeit the match, the two Surrey players took to the field, Fender bowling and Jeacocke as the lone fielder. As the match was about to commence, word was received the Surrey team coach had been delayed in traffic. In a gesture of true sportsmanship, the Essex openers, C. A. G. Russell and J. A. Cutmore, played a forward defensive to every ball from Fender and Jeacocke and refused to score until the remainder of the Surrey team arrived on the pitch some 12 minutes later.

The first County Championship team to travel to a match by air was Lancashire, who on 26 July 1935 flew from their match against Glamorgan at Cardiff to Southampton for a game the following day against Hampshire.

The final Test in Durban between South Africa and England in March 1939 lasted 10 days (this was when Test matches had no time limit). The Test did, however, come to an end, with England needing only 42 runs for victory and with five wickets in hand, because England had to catch a train to Cape Town in order to arrive in time for the sailing of their ship home.

In 1949, I was 18 when I was called up at short notice to play for Yorkshire against the Minor Counties at Lord's. The Yorkshire team were already in London so I had to make my own way to the capital to join them. On the journey down it suddenly occurred to me I had not been given the name of the hotel where the team was staying. On arriving in London I asked a policeman where the Yorkshire team stayed when in London. He told me that for all he was well versed in the ways of London life and had received intense training at Hendon Police School, his training did not run to knowing the whereabouts of the Yorkshire cricket team. Eventually a taxi driver told me Yorkshire stayed at the Bonnington Hotel in Southampton Row and took me there. I presented myself at the hotel reception and informed the clerk I was a member of the Yorkshire cricket team and had arrived a little late. 'You're telling me,' said the clerk. 'Yorkshire hasn't stayed at this hotel since 1937!'
FRED TRUEMAN

In his early days with Yorkshire, Fred Trueman was playing for Second XI when he received a telegram informing him of his inclusion in the Yorkshire First XI for the match against Hampshire at Bournemouth. Having to make his own way to the south coast, Fred caught a train from Leeds to King's Cross and, needing then to catch a connecting train at Waterloo, hailed a taxi. 'Waterloo, please,' said Fred, unaware of the London taxi driver's aversion to driving south of the river. 'The station?' enquired the incredulous driver. 'Well I'm too bloody late for the battle,' confirmed Fred.

Travel to away matches in the 1950s was always hectic and fraught with anxieties. We played back-to-back three-day County Championship matches in those days and no sooner would a home match be

over than we would load everything into the wicker
skip and, depending on where we were playing the
following day, race like mad to either Piccadilly or
Central station. It was always a rush. Away matches
against Sussex, Hampshire and Kent were always
problematic. We'd catch a train to London, arrive at
Euston then hump the skip and all our gear across to
Waterloo, Charing Cross or wherever to catch a
connecting train. Often we didn't arrive at our hotel
until the early hours of the morning, but would
always be there at the ground by ten the next day,
ready to play. In those days Lancashire tried to see
off the opposition in two days so we could have a day
off. I knew some teams who, if they were batting and
the game was truly beyond them, would throw away
their last two or three wickets in order to catch a
train home at a decent time.

BRIAN STATHAM (Lancashire)

In June 1963 Lancashire's Ken Howard returned home in the evening after
having batted in his team's match against Derbyshire at Liverpool. The following
morning Howard missed his intended train to Liverpool and did not arrive at
the ground until after midday. He was noted in the scorebook as being 'retired
out . . . 1'.

Also in June 1963, only three Middlesex players were present at Tunbridge
Wells for the second day (Monday) of the match against Kent, two of whom
were ineligible to bat as Peter Parfitt had already been dismissed and Eddie
Clarke was down as 12th man. The only player able to play was Robert White,
who was 43 not out when stumps were drawn on the Saturday. Kent appealed
to the umpires under the then Laws that the Middlesex innings should be
closed at 121 for 3 as they were unable to commence play. Robert White
remained 'not out 43'; his absent partner at the wicket, Ron Hooker, was
noted in the scorebook as 'out, absent . . . 13'. Ten minutes after the
Middlesex innings was closed, Don Bennett and John Price arrived at the

ground, 12th man Eddie Clarke was given permission to play, and the match recommenced with Kent batting against the five Middlesex players and six fielders recruited from the Kent ranks. Eventually the remainder of the Middlesex team arrived and the status quo of the match was restored, at least until the close of play. The third day was abandoned due to rain and the match ended in a draw.

Nine players wide of the mark. In June 1990, due to a misinterpretation of travel arrangements, only two players of Synthonia CC (Billingham) turned up for their match against Darlington CC at Feethams. The two Synthonia players went in to bat but Steve Eland was bowled in the first over for a duck. Synthonia then took to the field with their two players plus nine Darlington players as substitute fielders. Eland opened the bowling for Synthonia and his fourth delivery was wide, thus Darlington won without any of their players having to score a run.

The Warwickshire team were abandoned on their way to a C&G Trophy match against Holland on 3 May 2005. The venue for the game was the VOC Club ground in Rotterdam, but the ground was so new it did not feature on their coach driver's satnav. Having asked for directions from a well-meaning passer-by, the Dutch coach driver was directed to the old VOC ground, which is derelict and three miles from the new ground. Having been left at the old ground with their equipment, the Warwickshire party, realizing they were at the wrong venue, called for directions and were advised to walk through woods which would take them to the new VOC ground. Unfortunately the woods were large and un-signposted. The party became lost in pouring rain and had to be rescued by their hosts.

Warwickshire's nightmare trip to Holland was far from over. Having arrived at the new VOC ground, a storm blew up. The Warwickshire party took shelter in a large tent allocated for their use but the wind was so strong it blew the tent from its moorings and pegs. It was not all bad news, though: Warwickshire won by 23 runs.

Twenty20s are fine, but my solution would be to let the players drink before a game, not after it. That always works at our picnic matches.
PAUL HOGAN

In Twenty20 cricket a bowler may bowl a maximum of four overs.

Umpires have the power to award five penalty runs if they believe a team is guilty of time wasting.

If the fielding team does not start their 20th over within 75 minutes of the start of the innings, the batting side is credited six runs for every entire over bowled after the 75-minute mark.

If the match ends in a tie, five bowlers from each side will deliver one ball each at an unguarded wicket. The team that hits the wicket the most times wins the match. If the number of wickets is equal after the first five balls per team, bowling continues on a 'sudden death' basis.

Should a bowler bowl a no-ball, one run is credited to the batting side and his next delivery is designated a 'free hit', meaning the batsman can only be dismissed from this ball by a run-out, obstructing the field or handling the ball.

Twenty20 cricket was formally introduced by the ECB in the inaugural Twenty20 Cup competition. The first matches took place between county teams on 13 June 2003.

The first player to score a century in the Twenty20 Cup was Ian Harvey (100 not out), for Gloucestershire against Warwickshire at Edgbaston in 2003.

The first winners of the Twenty20 Cup were Surrey Lions, who defeated Warwickshire Bears by nine wickets in 2003.

The first Twenty20 match staged at Lord's was between Middlesex and Surrey on 15 July 2004. The attendance was 26,500 – the largest for any match involving county teams other than a limited-overs cup final since 1953.

The first Twenty20 match in Australia took place on 12 January 2005 at the WACA between Western Warriors and Victorian Bushrangers. It attracted a crowd of 20,750.

The first official Twenty20 international took place on 17 February 2005; Australia triumphed over New Zealand at Auckland. Both teams sported clothing as worn in the 1980s and some players adopted 1980s hairstyles. Glenn McGrath even evoked memories of the Trevor Chappell incident from the 1981 ODI between the two countries by bowling one ball underarm.

The first Twenty20 international in England was between England and Australia at the Rose Bowl, Southampton on 13 June 2005. England won by 100 runs – their largest margin of victory by runs in a Twenty20 international.

In July 2006, 19 West Indies regional teams participated in the Stanford Twenty20 tournament, funded to the tune of US$28 million by billionaire businessman Allen Stanford.

In 2006 Somerset scored 250 for 3 off their 20 overs against Gloucestershire at Taunton. Justin Langer and Cameron White shared a second-wicket partnership of 186.

In 2007 the inaugural ICC Twenty20 World Cup tournament was held in South Africa. India defeated Pakistan in the final.

On 5 January 2007 a crowd of around 10,000 was expected for the Twenty20 match between Queensland Bulls and New South Wales Blues at the Gabba, Brisbane. However, nigh on three times the expected number of spectators arrived to see the match. With thousands of fans still outside the ground at the appointed time for the match to start, chaos and confusion reigned. To appease the disgruntled fans and to start the match at a reasonable time, Gabba staff decided to allow free entry to many supporters. The final attendance figure was 27,653.

On 1 February 2008 the crowd at the match between Australia and India at Melbourne was 84,041 strong.

In 2008 it was reported Mahendra Dhoni (India) signed a contract worth US$5.8 million over three years to play for Chennai in the Indian Premier League.

On 26 July 2008 at the Rose Bowl, Middlesex won the Twenty20 Cup when Kent failed to score four runs off the final ball of the match. Middlesex amassed 187 for 6 – the highest total in a Twenty20 Cup Final – Owais Shah scoring 75 off 35 balls, including five sixes. Kent made 184 for 5, making this the highest aggregate Twenty20 Cup Final score.

On 11 April 2009 Afghanistan defeated Ireland by 22 runs in the Super 8 phase of the Twenty20 World Cup qualifiers in South Africa. Afghanistan had only been playing ICC cricket for three years.

The 2009 Twenty20 World Cup hosted by England was won by Pakistan who, in the final at Lord's, beat Sri Lanka by eight wickets. Pakistan had been runners-up in the previous and inaugural Twenty20 World Cup held in South Africa in 2007. In the 2009 match, England did not live up to their reputation as bookies' favourite, failing to reach the semi-finals following a five-wicket defeat (DL method) against the West Indies in the Super Eight stage.

Twenty20 Cup Winners
2003	Surrey
2004	Leicestershire
2005	Somerset
2006	Leicestershire
2007	Kent
2008	Middlesex

The Twenty20 Champions League was scheduled to begin on 3 December 2008 with £3.4 million prize money on offer for the eight teams which included England's Twenty20 Cup holders Middlesex. The tournament, however, never got off the ground, and had to be rescheduled.

The MCC has also inaugurated a Twenty20 competition called the British Asia Cup, with the winners of the IPL facing off against the Twenty20 Cup holders.

I see Twenty20 not Tests as being the future of cricket.
CHRIS GAYLE (WEST INDIES, 2009)

The umpire signals a bye with the air of a weary stork.
JOHN ARLOTT

The word 'umpire' comes from the old French 'nompere', meaning not equal, or impartial.

Professional matches have umpires and a match referee, who may be called upon to make a decision that has a bearing on the outcome of the match but who in the main is there to ensure the ICC Cricket Code of Conduct is adhered to.

Test matches have four umpires: two on the field, a third to assess video replays of incidents, and a fourth who looks after the match balls, organizes drinks for the on-field umpires and is responsible for arranging the travel, accommodation and meals of all the umpires.

The scorebook of the match between Benenden and Penshurst in 1892 contains the note 'Umpire ducked in pond for giving unsatisfactory decision'.

You says 'How's that?' and I says 'Hover', and hover it is said the umpire.
W. E. W. COLLINS

Umpire Harry Bagshaw, who died in 1927, was laid to rest in accordance with his own carefully defined wishes: in his white coat, with six pebbles in one pocket and a cricket ball in the other.

During a tour game in 1948, umpire Alec Skelding turned down a number of appeals from Australian players. Minutes later a dog ran on to the field. It was eventually caught by Australia's Ray Lindwall, who handed it over to umpire Skelding saying, 'Here you are, Alec. All you need now is a white stick.'

Leg bye misnomer. On 22 August 1949 at Clacton, umpire McCanlis awarded four leg byes when a delivery from Essex's Trevor Bailey hit Somerset's G. E. S. Woodhouse on the head and the ball carried on down to the boundary. It was then that the Essex players drew the attention of the umpires to the fact the bails were on the ground, and appealed. McCanlis and the square leg umpire, C. Woolley, both had their attention focused on the ball hitting Woodhouse on the head and were at a loss as to whether he'd hit his wicket or not. After conferring, the umpires ruled they had been 'unsighted' and Woodhouse was given not out – and not knocked out either.

The Bramall Lane crowd prided themselves on being very knowledgeable about cricket and had a reputation for giving terrible stick to umpires. And quite right too.
DOUG PADGETT

Umpires will vary in what they take out with them to record every ball of an over. There is a little contraption, used for many years, that contains six spikes that can be depressed after each delivery. Nowadays a digital 'calculator' is available, but most umpires prefer their own method of marking off balls. Some have resorted to pebbles. Jack Crapp used six Victorian pennies, as did Arthur Jepson. Barry Meyer preferred 10p pieces. Johnny Arnold used conkers, and Dickie Bird had six miniature beer barrels given to him by a major brewery.

I was once on an England tour with the Bedser twins. One night, after I had been out for a few drinks with some journalists, I returned to the hotel and presented myself at reception for my room key. There had been plenty written of the England party in the local press, so I thought the receptionist would know of me. 'Bed, sir?' she enquired. I believed she thought I was one of the Bedsers so I said, 'No, Crapp.' 'Gentlemen's toilets are to your right, sir,' she informed me.

JACK CRAPP

Stood the test of old Father Time. In 1962 one of the umpires in the match between Lord's Taverners and Old England XI at Lord's was Joe Filliston, who was 100 years old – the oldest man ever to have umpired a match at Lord's, and probably in the world.

Arthur Fagg stood in 18 Tests and seven one-day internationals. At one stage during the England–West Indies Test at Edgbaston in 1973, Fagg refused to take to the field after some of the West Indies players questioned one of his decisions.

 You need big pockets in those white coats, and plenty of them. These days an umpire takes out with him: whatever he uses to mark off balls, so six of whatever it is; a spare ball, light meter, rag for cleaning the ball if required, spare bails, rulebook of whichever competition it is, copy of the Laws of the game, little notebook, pens, penknife, safety pins, two or three elastoplasts, and two handkerchiefs, one for himself and one in case a player needs one, a packet of Polos or Murray Mints being optional.

DUSTY RHODES

DERBYSHIRE OFFICIAL: Do you have any specific requirements, Mr Rhodes?
DUSTY RHODES: At the end of each session, big pot of tea, preferably brown enamel and bottomless.

In 1980 it is alleged umpire David Constant was involved in a scuffle with MCC members when he delayed the start of the Centenary Test between England and Australia at Lord's when of the mind the outfield was still waterlogged following heavy rain. It is also alleged that the respective captains, Ian Botham and Greg Chappell, had to step in to protect Constant.

One of the most infamous exchanges between an umpire and player took place during the second Test between Pakistan and England on 9 December 1987 at Faisalabad. The third day of play was lost following umpire Shakoor Rana's decision to stop play as he believed England captain Mike Gatting had been moving David Capel at square leg without informing Pakistan batsman Salim Malik. Gatting was of the mind Rana was 'overstepping his bounds', and the pair became embroiled in a heated exchange, at one point their faces inches from each other. Rana refused to participate further in the match until Gatting issued an apology. Pakistan captain Miandad called his batsmen in prior to the last 20 overs and the umpires drew the stumps. A strict interpretation of the Laws should have resulted in England being awarded the match. Needless to say, they weren't.

I cannot for the life of me see why the umpires, the only two people on a cricket field who are not going to get grass stains on their knees, are the only two people allowed to wear dark trousers.
KATHERINE WHITEHORN

Harold 'Dickie' Bird, so beloved of all umpires, played in the same Barnsley CC team as writer/broadcaster Michael Parkinson and Geoff Boycott. He stood in his first first-class match in 1970 and his first Test, England against New Zealand at Headingley, in 1973. In all, Bird stood in 66 Tests, his last in 1996. Two years later he officiated at his last county match.

My only complaint with Dickie Bird is that he requires a degree of certainty that is almost neurotic; like the man who has to keep going to the front door to make certain that he's locked it.
MIKE BREARLEY

In June 1998 Mr Bryn Derbyshire received a three-month suspended sentence and was ordered to pay £400 compensation to his victim by Nottingham Crown Court after being found guilty of reversing his car at Mr Joseph Purser, one of the umpires who had officiated at the match between Old Park CC and Blyth CC (Nottingham). It appears Mr Derbyshire was incensed at being given out lbw by Mr Purser during the said match.

David Shepherd stood in 92 Tests, his last in 2005, and officiated at three World Cup finals. One of Shepherd's quirks was to raise one foot off the ground when a batsman reached 111. The score is known as 'Nelson' and considered to be unlucky as the number resembles three wickets without bails. A number of old pros believed the way to avoid bad luck when 'Nelson' appeared on the scoreboard was to lift one leg off the ground, though no one is sure how or why this superstition originated.

Following his retirement, David Shepherd became president of Devon CCC.

Rudi Koertzen (South Africa) is not immune to moments of controversy but, like his fellow umpires, upholds high ethical standards. In 1999 Koertzen was approached by an individual who asked for his co-operation in 'fixing' the outcome of some international matches in return for financial gain. Koertzen declined, and reported the incident to the ICC, who launched a major investigation.

Steve Bucknor (West Indies) is the only man to have officiated in the cricket and football World Cups. Bucknor stood in five cricket World Cup Finals and as a fully qualified FIFA referee was involved in the qualifying stages of the 1978 football World Cup.

Steve Bucknor also became the first umpire to stand in 100 Test matches, including 14 Ashes Tests. He stood in his first Test in 1988–89 and passed the 100 mark in 2005. He retired in March 2009, having stood in his 128th Test, between South Africa and Australia at Cape Town. Bucknor's last match as an umpire was the ODI between the West Indies and England on 29 March, at the end of which both teams formed a guard of honour to applaud him from the field.

During the first Test between New Zealand and Sri Lanka at Napier in April 2005, New Zealand's Hamish Marshall complained he could not see the ball when delivered by Sri Lanka bowler Lasith Malinga because of the umpire's trousers. The issue was taken up by New Zealand captain Stephen Fleming, who informed the umpires Malinga had such a low-slung action, late in the day when the weather was overcast his batsman lost the ball against the umpire's trousers. They requested a change of clothes but the umpires declined, though both agreed to remove their dark ties, and umpire Bucknor tied a sweater around his waist as a personalized sightscreen.

In 2002 the ICC introduced the Elite Panel of Umpires and Referees, two of which stand in a Test match while one officiates with the home umpire, who is chosen from the Supplementary International Panel in limited-overs internationals.

In 2009 the Elite Panel comprised Steve Davis, Daryl Harper and Simon Taufel (Australia); Mark Benson and Ian Gould (England); Billy Bowden and Tony Hill (New Zealand); Aleem Dar and Asad Rauf (Pakistan); Rudi Koertzen (South Africa); Billy Doctrove (West Indies); and Asoka de Silva (Sri Lanka).

Most first-class umpires in England are former players. In 2009 the list included Rob Bailey (formerly Northamptonshire), Mark Benson (Kent), Barry Dudleston (Leicestershire), Ian Gould (Middlesex), Peter Hartley (Warwickshire and Yorkshire), Vanburn Holder (Worcestershire), Richard Illingworth (Worcestershire and Derbyshire), Trevor Jesty (Hampshire), Neil Mallender (Northamptonshire), Tim Robinson (Nottinghamshire), John Steele (Northamptonshire and Derbyshire), Peter Willey (Northamptonshire and Leicestershire) and Martin Bodenham, the first man to qualify as a first-class cricket umpire and a top-flight football referee.

 What a great country this would be if every man, whatever his station, concentrated half as much on the smallest detail of his work as an umpire is compelled to do, from high noon to dewy evening.
NEVILLE CARDUS

Bird felled. Dickie Bird was felled when a straight drive by Graham Gooch off a ball delivered by Bob Holland struck him on the ankle during a Test match between England and Australia in 1985.

Umpire Dickie Bird is gestating wildly.

TONY LEWIS (BBC TV)

On 31 May 1986 Jerry Daykin sustained a broken neck when, while umpiring at the striker's end, he was hit by a rising straight drive during a match between Long Eaton and Nottinghamshire Amateurs.

On 5 February 2009 a system of 'referral' to the third umpire was trialled in the first Test between the West Indies and England. The first instance of referral occurred when Ramnaresh Sarwan was given out lbw off the bowling of Steve Harmison. The decision was overturned following referral to the third umpire but resulted in an eight-minute delay in proceedings. The delay made it unpopular with umpires, players and spectators alike, and for that reason alone the system may never officially be adopted in Test matches.

BATSMEN	ENGLAND v AUSTRALIA 2ND INNINGS OF AUSTRALIA	HOW OUT	BOWLER	TOTAL	MINS
1 C.C. McDONALD		c Oakman	Laker	89	341
2 J.W. BURKE		c Lock	Laker	33	106
3 R.N. HARVEY		c Cowdrey	Laker	0	2
4 I.D. CRAIG		lbw	Laker	38	263
5 K. MACKAY		c Oakman	Laker	0	8
6 K.R. MILLER		b	Laker	0	17
7 R.G. ARCHER		c Oakman	Laker	0	3
8 R. BENAUD		b	Laker	18	107
9 R.R. LINDWALL		c Lock	Laker	8	144
10 I.W. JOHNSON		not out		1	27
11 L. MADDOCKS		lbw	Laker	2	8
WIDES				TOTAL EXTRAS	16
BYES				TOTAL	205
LEG BYES					
NO BALLS					

FALL OF WICKETS 1 28 2 55 3 114 4 124 5 130 6 130 7 181 8 198 9 203 10 205

BATSMAN Harvey Burke Craig Mackay Miller Archer Redmond Benaud Lindwall Maddocks

Four university teams are considered first-class teams when playing against other first-class sides – Durham UCCE (University Centre of Cricketing Excellence), Cambridge University, Loughborough UCCE and Oxford University, all of whom play three county teams on an annual basis. In addition to these four teams, Cardiff (UWIC and Glamorgan) and Leeds (with Bradford and Leeds Metropolitan University) also play three matches against county teams, but these matches do not enjoy first-class status.

Cambridge University is a first-class team that plays all but one of its first-class matches as part of the Cambridge UCCE.

Cambridge play their home matches at Fenners.

The earliest reference to cricket at Cambridge University dates back to 1710. Cambridge's first match against Eton was in 1754.

In May 1817 Cambridge University first played Cambridge Town CC (later Cambridgeshire CCC) in what was to become an annual meeting between the two teams. The 1817 fixture against Cambridge Town marked the first-class debut of Cambridge University.

As with Cambridge, Oxford University is now subsumed into the university's Centre of Cricketing Excellence, retains its independence and enjoys first-class status.

Oxford play their home matches at The Parks.

The earliest reference to cricket being played at Oxford University dates back to 1729. According to Dr Samuel Johnson, he played cricket at the university in that year.

The annual Varsity match between Cambridge and Oxford is the oldest first-class cricket fixture in the world. The first ever Varsity match took place in 1827 and was Oxford University's first-class debut. The match ended in a draw.

Players who have played in the four-day Varsity match are eligible for a Blue.

In 1877 Oxford were dismissed for 12 by the MCC – the joint lowest total in English first-class cricket.

The lowest total recorded in the Varsity match is Oxford's 32 at Lord's in 1878.

Ivo Bligh (he of Ashes urn fame), later Lord Darnley, played in the Cambridge team that beat the touring Australians in 1878.

In 1890 Cambridge recorded their highest total when playing against Sussex at Hove – 703 for 9 declared.

In 1895 Oxford recorded their highest ever total – 651 all out, coincidentally this too against Sussex at Hove.

Both Tony Pawson (later Kent) and his father Guy captained Oxford University teams to an innings victory against Cambridge. Tony's uncle, Clive Pawson, also played in the winning Oxford side in the Varsity match of 1901.

The Oxford team (captained by Tony Pawson) that won the Varsity match in 1948 defeated a Cambridge side which contained four future Test players: Trevor Bailey, John Dewes, Hubert Doggart and Doug Insole.

Peter May, widely considered one of England's best post-war batsmen, played in three Varsity matches and never made a fifty.

Peter May played in a Cambridge side that included David Sheppard, Cuan McCarthy, Raman Subba Row and Gerry Alexander, all of whom went on to play Test cricket.

There appears to be something about Varsity teams and Sussex (and Hove): in 1950 John Dewes scored 212 for Cambridge against Sussex at Hove.

Too good for Oxford, too good for Cambridge. In 1985 G. J. Toogood scored 149 and took 10 for 93 in the match against Oxford. Only one Oxford player had previously achieved this notable double, P. R. le Couteur (160 and 11 for 66) in the match of 1910.

The 1988 fixture became the first Varsity match ever to be abandoned due to bad weather.

In 2001, as part of the ECB's reorganization of university cricket, the venue of the annual Varsity match was removed from Lord's. Cambridge hosted the match against Oxford for the very first time.

In 2005 Oxford made the highest total in a Varsity match against Cambridge – 610 for 5 declared, at Fenners.

Notable Cambridge University players include Gilbert Jessop, Stanley Jackson, K. S. Ranjitsinhji, Cuthbert Burnup, Frank Mann, Arthur Gilligan, Percy Chapman (who captained the England side that regained the Ashes in 1926), George 'Gubby' Allen, Walter Robins, Ken Farnes, Wilfred Wooller, Trevor Bailey, Doug Insole, Peter May, Robin Marlar, Raman Subba Row, Ted Dexter, Gammi Goonesena, Tony Lewis, Mike Brearley, Deryck Murray (62 Tests for West Indies), David Acfield, Roger Knight, Phil Edmonds, Paul Parker, Robin Boyd-Moss, Derek Pringle, Ian Greig, Mike Atherton and Ed Smith.

Notable Oxford University players include Lionel Palairet, C. B. Fry, Plum Warner, Bernard Bosanquet – gained half Blue at billiards(!), played professional ice hockey(!!), father of Reginald(!!!) – Douglas Jardine, R. Robertson-Glasgow, Ian Peebles, Tony Pawson, Abdul Harfeez Kardar (who captained Pakistan in their first 23 Tests), Donald Carr, Colin Cowdrey, Mike Smith, Alan Smith, the Nawab of Pataudi, Jahangir Khan, Tim Lamb, Imran Khan, Chris Tavaré, Vic Marks and John Carr.

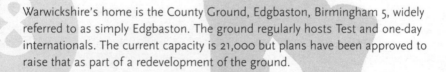

Warwickshire's home is the County Ground, Edgbaston, Birmingham 5, widely referred to as simply Edgbaston. The ground regularly hosts Test and one-day internationals. The current capacity is 21,000 but plans have been approved to raise that as part of a redevelopment of the ground.

In the past, Warwickshire has also played at Coventry, Dudley, Nuneaton and Warwick.

The club badge features a bear standing on hind legs and holding a wooden staff.

Warwickshire have been county champions six times (1911, 1951, 1972, 1994, 1995 and 2004), Gillette Cup/NatWest Trophy winners on five occasions (1966, 1968, 1989, 1993 and 1995), Sunday League winners three times (1980, 1994 and 1997) and Benson & Hedges Cup winners twice (1994 and 2002).

It is believed cricket was first played in the county towards the end of the seventeenth century. Historical documents of the mid-eighteenth century make reference to the landlord of the Bell Inn, Birmingham, advertising for matches for his tavern team. There was also a prominent club in Coventry towards the end of the eighteenth century. Reports exist of two matches played by Coventry against Leicester in 1787 and 1788.

The first known match contested by a so-called Warwickshire XI took place in August 1843. Leicestershire were defeated at Gosford Green, on the site where Coventry City's football stadium now stands. It is doubtful, however, that this team was wholly representative of the best players in the county.

On 8 April 1882 a meeting led by a Birmingham schoolmaster, William Ansell, was held at the Regent Hotel in Leamington attended by representatives of various clubs. It was at this meeting that Warwickshire County Cricket Club was formally established.

In 1884 Warwickshire played its inaugural first-class match, against Nottinghamshire at Trent Bridge.

Warwickshire began as a county club towards the end of the Victorian age, during the reign of Queen Victoria.
GEORGE ANDREWS (Signal Radio)

The club at this time did not have a permanent home, playing matches at various grounds throughout the county. In 1886 it was decided the club should have a permanent base in Birmingham and meadowland was acquired by the banks of the River Rea on the Calthorpe Estate.

The first match to take place at what was to become Edgbaston was against the MCC in 1886. There was a sizeable crowd, and no doubt they and the Warwickshire players were left dumbfounded when the MCC players walked off the field in the late afternoon as they wished to take an early train back to London. Warwickshire were further chagrined when, as a result of this action, the club received notification from Lord's that the match had been declared a 'draw'.

From 1900 to the advent of the First World War, Warwickshire yo-yo'd between the upper and lower reaches of the county table, the one exception being 1911 when the club won the County Championship for the very first time.

In 1903 S. Hargreave returned match figures of 15 for 76 against Surrey at the Oval – a club record.

In these formative years no fewer than eight members of the Foster family played for the club, the most successful being Frank Foster, a dashing batsman (in every sense of the word) and a highly effective fast bowler. Foster was the mainstay of the Championship-winning side of 1911, in which year he headed both the club's batting and bowling averages. A superb all-rounder, he scored 6,548 runs for the club and took 718 wickets, his career ending with the start of the war. After the war he was invited to return to the club but by this time was beset by domestic problems and ill health as the result of an accident, and never played for Warwickshire again.

In 1913 Warwickshire were dismissed for their lowest ever total – 16, against Kent at Tunbridge Wells.

The club could have done with some Fosters in 1919. The season proved small beer with Warwickshire ending it at the bottom of the county table for the first time.

In 1922 Warwickshire dismissed Hampshire for just 15 at Edgbaston – the lowest total the club has inflicted upon a first-class county.

The most wickets taken in a single season by a Warwickshire bowler is Eric Hollies' haul of 180 (average 15.13) in 1946. Hollies' career (1932–57) haul of 2,201 (average 20.45) is also the best by any Warwickshire bowler.

Well, I'll go to the top of our stairs. Right-arm fast-medium bowler John Bannister took 10 for 41 against the Combined Services at Edgbaston in 1959 – the club's best bowling figures for a single innings.

In the same season Mike Smith hit 2,417 runs (average 60.42) – the most runs by a Warwickshire player in a single season.

In the 1950s and 1960s Tom Cartwright was a swing and seam bowler of great repute and a gracious and self-effacing player. When he was selected for England at the expense of Fred Trueman in 1965, Cartwright telephoned Trueman and said, 'I think they've got themselves in a muddle, Fred, they've picked the wrong man.'

Cartwright inadvertently precipitated the sporting isolation of South Africa. He withdrew from the England squad to tour South Africa in 1968–69 due to a shoulder injury and his place was given to Basil D'Oliveira (Worcestershire), which sparked the controversy that led to South Africa not participating in a Test for 22 years.

On retirement as a player, Cartwright coached at Warwickshire and Somerset, at the latter having a great influence on the swing bowling of a certain young Ian Botham. He then became coach for the Welsh Cricket Association. He played his last game of cricket at Broadhalfpenny Down in 2005. Tom died of a heart attack in 2007.

Alvin Kallicharran (West Indies) and Geoff Humpage shared a club record partnership of 470 for the fourth wicket against Lancashire at Southport in 1982.

Geoff Humpage has the sort of look on his face of a man who is yet to make a big score in this match, which he hasn't done as yet.
KEN BARRINGTON (BBC TV)

In 1984 Warwickshire scored their highest total in one-day cricket – 392 for 5, against Oxfordshire in the NatWest Trophy.

Dennis Amiss is Warwickshire's best ever homegrown batsman. He scored 35,146 runs (average 41.64) for Warwickshire – the most runs in a career (1960–87) at the club. He also holds the record for the most centuries – 78. On twenty occasions he amassed in excess of 1,000 runs in a season, and he scored at least one century and more than 1,000 runs against every other first-class county – a unique feat in the history of the club. His Test haul was 3,612 runs (average 46.30).

Warwickshire's record total is 810 for 4 declared, against Durham at Edgbaston in 1994. Brian Lara (West Indies) created not only a club record for the highest individual innings but also a record for English first-class cricket by scoring 501 not out. The backbone of Warwickshire's innings was an unbroken fifth-wicket stand of 322 by Lara and wicket-keeper Keith Piper. It was also in 1994 that Lara equalled Alvin Kallicharran's club record of nine centuries in a single season (1984).

In 1994 Warwickshire created English cricket history by becoming the first county to win a 'treble' of major trophies – County Championship, Sunday League and Benson & Hedges Cup. The following season the club achieved the 'double' of County Championship and NatWest Trophy.

Duggie Brown is one of that rare breed of cricketers, a UK dual international. A member of Warwickshire's 'triple' side of 1994, he was selected for England's one-day team in 1997 and 1998 and played for Scotland in the 2007 World Cup. He is now the club's Academy director.

M. J. K. 'Mike' Smith was also a dual international. Captain of Warwickshire and England, he also played rugby union for England at fly-half against Wales at Twickenham in 1956.

Other notable Warwickshire players include Dick Lilly, the first Warwickshire player to be selected for England (1896), a wicket-keeper who also occasionally bowled in matches and took 40 wickets with what he described as his 'right-arm hopefuls'; Billy Quaif, affectionately known as 'Twinkle Feet'; Tom Dollery, known by team-mates as 'Centsy' (think about it); Khalid 'Billy' Ibadulla (Pakistan); Bob Barber, who at the age of 17, as a pupil at Ruthin School, achieved the 'double' of 1,012 runs and 108 wickets; Lance Gibbs (West Indies), the original 'Spin Doctor'; Bob Willis, Allan Donald (Australia), Ashley Giles, Nick Knight, Tim Munton, Dermot Reeve and Gladstone Small. The current squad includes Ian Bell, Sanath Jayasuriya (Sri Lanka), Darren Maddy, Shaun Pollock (South Africa) and Jamie 'Jim' Troughton.

Billy Ibadulla had more edges than a cracked pisspot.
FRED TRUEMAN

RICHIE BENAUD: You didn't wear a helmet?
DERMOT REEVE: No. No brain no pain.

I was facing Malcolm Marshall who came down the wicket, held up the ball for me to see and said menacingly, 'See this? It's small and red like a sports car, and like a sports car it's going to come at you at a hundred miles an hour.' I hit his next delivery for

four, walked down the wicket and said to him, 'I've just parked it on the other side of the boundary.'
GLADSTONE SMALL

Most appropriately named player – C. H. Cort.

The club's limited-overs team is the Warwickshire Bears.

Worth a visit for . . . the pasties: wholesome, bulging and no overly greasy pastry as you find at some grounds. As one Bears supporter remarked, 'I once had a pasty at Southport, the meat was something else. I don't know what it was, but it wasn't meat, that's for sure.'

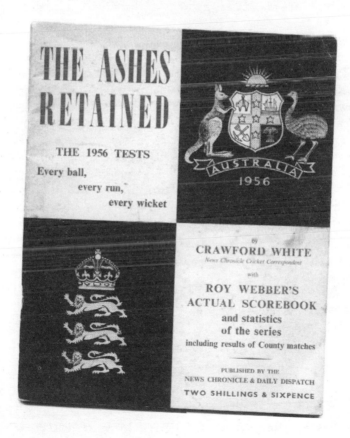

> Those of you who believe beach cricket is a jolly romp
> would have found no place in my father's team. He
> approached our matches in an entirely scientific
> manner, employing tidal charts and weather forecasts
> in his game plan.
> MICHAEL PARKINSON

The wind was so bitingly cold during the match between the MCC and Oxford University in May 1893, fielders not only wore two jumpers but also coats and gloves.

The only man to have swum across a county cricket ground is George Gillingham, who played for the Gentlemen of Worcestershire prior to the First World War and later became honorary secretary of Worcestershire CCC. In the winter of 1929 Gillingham was serving as honorary secretary when the River Severn flooded the County Ground. Gillingham swam across the field to gain access to the pavilion and returned with the club's account books, which were required by auditors. Gillingham was a man of the cloth for 52 years but can be regarded as something of a loose 'cannon'. He left his post at Worcestershire CC and that of vicar of St Martin's to fulfil a similar role in Coventry, which he combined with running the Barley Mow pub, where he formed the 'Hooligans Club' for teenage boys whom he coached in cricket and boxing as well as giving Bible classes.

Bad light then light white. On Christmas Day 1947 a match took place between Noel Bennett's XI and Yule Logs at Preston Park, Brighton. Much of the match was played under dark clouds, then it snowed, but they carried on.

Hail the champions! On 8 May 1948 a hailstorm beset Arms Park, Cardiff during the lunch interval of Glamorgan's match against Essex, who were batting. Undeterred, Essex went on to make their highest total of the season, 374, while Glamorgan ended the season as county champions.

Play was interrupted on the first day of Yorkshire's match against Gloucestershire at Bramall Lane in July 1953 due to 'ice on the pitch'. The ice had fallen in lumps from the sky, landing about the ground and on the actual pitch. It later transpired an aeroplane had jettisoned water as it flew over Sheffield and the water had frozen at high altitude. The second day's play was abandoned as the result of something else falling from the sky – rain.

The second day's play of Derbyshire's match against Lancashire at Buxton on 2 June 1975 was abandoned due to a snowstorm.

Long rain results in very short reign. In 1988 Worcestershire were due to play a Benson & Hedges Cup tie at Haden Hill Park in Old Hill (West Midlands) – the first ever first-class match at this venue. Unfortunately, due to incessant rain the match was abandoned without a ball being bowled and the venue has never been chosen since.

In May 2005 the match between Babington CC and Ditcheat (Somerset) was brought to a stop by a 'man-made wind' caused by an air-ambulance landing at the Babington House Hotel, which overlooks the Babington ground, to take an injured man to hospital.

In June 2005 play was stopped in the match between Olney Town Second XI and Willen Second XI when a strong gust of wind blew one of the sightscreens on to the banks of the nearby River Ouse. The players retrieved the sightscreen just before it was about to be blown into the river, and having returned it to the boundary ensured there would be no repetition by tying it to a tree.

After days of torrential rain in July 2007, Worcestershire's New Road ground was under four feet of water for several days when the nearby River Severn broke its banks.

Worried about rays. In June 2008 sun stopped play for 83 minutes during Derbyshire's Twenty20 match against Durham at Derby. The setting sun was considered problematic for batsman which resulted in the match being subjected to the Duckworth-Lewis method.

England's one-day international against South Africa at the Riverside scheduled for 19 August 2008 was postponed on the 18th because the Durham pitch was under water after eight consecutive days of rain, prompting South Africa coach Micky Arthur to say, 'They should rename this ground because it's not by the riverside any more, it's in it.'

On 20 March 2009 England won the first one-day/night international of the series against the West Indies due to a calamitous misreading of the regulations governing rain when coach John Dyson waved his batsmen in when they were offered the light. The West Indies needed 27 runs off 22 balls for victory but on the instructions of Dyson remained in the pavilion, only to lose the match on the Duckworth-Lewis method.

SPIN or SWING with Sorbo

LI-LO have something for keen cricketers of all ages (and their less keen long-stop fielder companions). The hard-wearing Sorbo solid rubber composition cricket ball is ideal for practice, especially on hard wickets. In two sizes—Standard and Youth.

The first 'important' cricket match to take place in the West Indies was between Barbados and Demerara (now one of the three counties of Guyana) in Bridgetown on 15–16 February 1865.

The first West Indies team to go on tour visited North America in 1886, where they played 13 matches. In a reciprocal gesture, a North America representative team toured the West Indies the following year.

The West Indies Cricket Board joined what was then the Imperial Cricket Council in 1926 and was granted Test status in 1928.

The West Indies is the only Test nation not to have adopted a national flag. As the West Indies represent a number of independent and dependent states, the WICB created an insignia on a two-tone maroon background comprising a small island on which is a set of wickets and a palm tree overseen by a full sun.

The current West Indies team represents the independent states of Antigua and Barbuda, Barbados, Dominica, Grenada, Jamaica, St Kitts and Nevis, St Lucia, St Vincent and Grenadines, and Trinidad and Tobago; also the British dependencies of Anguilla, Montserrat and British Virgin Islands; also the US Virgin Islands and St Maarten.

A number of these also have national teams which participate in the Carib Beer Cup/Regional Four Day Competition, formerly known as the Busta Cup and, initially, the Shell Shield. The Shell Shield was first competed for in 1965–66. The winners of the inaugural competition were Barbados, who retained the Shield the following season. Barbados is the most successful team in the history of the competition. Jamaica, however, won the tournament in successive seasons (2007–08 and 2008–09).

Extra, extra! Read all about it! In 1909 at Georgetown, William Shepherd's XI conceded 74 extras in a single innings against Demerara.

Karl Nunes was the first player to captain West Indies in a Test match, in 1928.

For all that the West Indies produced some great individual players, such as Sir Learie Constantine in the 1920s, who was knighted for services to his own people and later created a life peer, and George Headley from the 1930s onwards, it was not until the mid-1950s that they began to assert themselves as a Test team of note.

In 1928 at Lord's, Learie Constantine took seven Middlesex wickets in their second innings and scored 86 (in under an hour) and 103 (in an hour).

I never wanted to make a hundred. Who wants to make a hundred anyway? When I first went in my immediate objective was to hit the ball to each of the four corners of the field. After that I tried not to be repetitive.
LEARIE CONSTANTINE

In the 1930s the West Indies were captained by Jackie Grant, who was succeeded as skipper by his brother, Rolph.

In 1945–46 Clyde Walcott and Frank Worrell shared an unbroken fourth-innings partnership of 574 for Trinidad against British Guyana. Walcott scored 314 not out and Worrell 255 not out.

George Headley (father of Ron – Worcestershire) played in 22 Tests from the 1930s to the 1950s. His Test batting average was 60.83.

Towards the end of George Headley's career he had been living in the Midlands and in summer playing in the Birmingham League. In 1953 the Jamaican people raised over £1,000 to bring him back to Jamaica just so he could play in the series against England. It had been tough for those people to raise that sum of money but they did it and believed the sacrifices they had made would be worth it just to see George play against England. So you can imagine what they thought of me when, in his first game playing for Jamaican Parishes, I broke his arm.

FRED TRUEMAN

In October 1956 Jamaica's Alf Binns, on 151 against British Guyana, got himself in a tangle and connected with the ball twice with his bat. He was given out for having hit the ball twice.

In 1957–58 the West Indies scored their highest Test total – 790 for 3 declared, against Pakistan in Kingston. In this innings Gary Sobers scored a then world record Test score of 365 not out.

Oh my word, what a rout,
365 not out,
King Cricket, King Cricket,
Garfield Sobers is his name.

CALYPSO SONG (1958)

Frank Worrell made such a contribution to the 1960–61 series in Australia, a new trophy to be presented to the series' winners between the two teams was named after him. Frank Worrell was knighted for services to cricket and the Jamaican people, and following his death at the age of 42 from leukaemia he was the first cricketer to be honoured with a memorial service at Westminster Abbey.

During the second Test against Australia in Melbourne in 1968, Seymour Nurse was caught at deep fine leg from a ball that rebounded off the head of a fielder at backward short leg.

Sir Garfield Sobers is arguably the greatest all-rounder of all time. He scored 8,032 runs in 93 Tests (1954–74) and took 235 wickets and 117 catches. His first Test century was his 365 not out against Pakistan in 1957–58, and in 1968 he hit six sixes in an over while playing for Nottinghamshire against Glamorgan at Swansea. As a bowler he began as an orthodox left-arm spinner but soon added chinamen and googlies to his armoury, and then pace. He was quick enough to open the bowling for the West Indies.

 Gary Sobers was happy to stand or fall by his belief that cricket, even at Test level, should be entertaining.
RAY ILLINGWORTH

 I was batting with Wes Hall in Kingston and Chandrasekhar was bowling. Wes said, 'I can't read this guy, but you read him well, skipper.' Chandrasekhar was mainly bowling leg breaks but would throw in a googly which flummoxed Wes. I told Wes when I spotted his googly coming I would tug on my pants. The signal worked really well: Wes went on to make a good score at tea. During the interval, Wes was bragging to all the boys about how great he was at reading Chandrasekhar's googly when our recognized batsmen couldn't. After tea, I spotted a googly coming from Chandrasekhar but stood bolt still, and Wes was bowled. As he passed me he said, 'What's up? Didn't you see that one coming, skipper?' I said, 'I read it well enough, Wes, only with you being so great at picking them, I figured you didn't need my help no more.'
SIR GARY SOBERS

 It's fascinating to watch Gary Sobers in action. You learn things you never knew.
BILL LAWRY (Australia)

In 1976 at the Oval, Michael Holding achieved match figures of 14 for 149 against England – the most wickets taken by a West Indies bowler in a Test match.

Michael Holding had an almost silent run-up. The first umpires were aware of his presence was when they felt a swish of air at their shoulder. Dickie Bird nicknamed him 'Whispering Death'.

The West Indies have won the World Cup twice, in 1975 and 1979 – the first two competitions.

 After their 60 overs, West Indies have scored 244 for 7, all out.
FRANK BOUGH (BBC TV)

George the first. In January 1986 while playing for Barbados against Windward Islands, George Linton became the first batsman in West Indies first-class cricket to be given out for handling the ball. Following a dead bat stroke, Linton picked up the ball and handed it to bowler Desmond Colleymore, whose appeal was upheld by the umpire.

Viv Richards played 121 Tests for the West Indies, averaging 50.23 with the bat.

 My one and only match as captain of England was against the West Indies in 1988. Their captain was the great Viv Richards. Prior to the game we met in the middle to toss the coin to see who would bat first. I said to Viv, 'I bet you don't know who I am.' 'Sure I do,' said Viv. 'You're the rabbit we bowl out for a duck every time we come down to Kent.'
CHRIS COWDREY

In 1994–95 Courtney Walsh achieved match figures of 13 for 55 against New Zealand in Wellington.

In 2003–04 Brian Lara scored 400 not out in a West Indies total of 751 for 5 declared against England at St John's – a world record highest individual innings in a Test match. On the same ground against the same opposition in 1993–94 Lara had scored a then world record 375.

The West Indies won the ICC Champions One-day Trophy for the first time in 2004.

You could have told me. It was only on 29 June 2006, the day before the final Test match between the West Indies and India, that Brian Lara discovered he had been a West Indies Test selector for over a month. Due to an administrative mix-up Lara had never received any official communication to this effect and no one on the West Indies Cricket Board had thought fit to mention the fact to him.

The first West Indies bowler to achieve a hat-trick was Jerome Taylor, against Australia in the ICC Champions Trophy league match at Mumbai on 19 October 2006.

The West Indies defeated England in the 2008–09 winter Test and ODI series, only for England to exact revenge in both the Test and ODI series in England in the summer of 2009.

All-rounder – someone of similar girth to Mike Gatting.

Appeal – what happens to skin on hot days should you not apply sunblock.

Average – quality of most county players.

Averages – collective noun for county cricketers.

Away Swinger – in minor cricket, what a bowler calls a wide.

Beamer – a ball bowled at terrific speed straight at the batsman's head after which the bowler says, 'Sorry, it slipped out of my hand.'

Benefit – what all journeyman county players desire more than anything. Members spend a whole year, and fellow pros give of their time, raising money. After it is presented to the player he feels duty bound to justify it every time he crosses the white line.

Boundary – who actually makes rope that long and circular?

Bowl – according to the Laws, 'to propel the ball fairly to the striking batsman's wicket'. As far as bowlers in minor cricket are concerned, they missed out the word 'near' after 'fairly'.

Bumper – bowlers expect it to do what it says on the tin.

Bye – an extra run awarded to the batting team while the batsman swears blind he connected with the ball.

Central contract – piece of paper that ensures a player is a county cricketer in name only.

Cow shot – unorthodox stroke played across the line of the ball with near horizontal bat which, curiously, minor cricketers have perfected but professionals have not.

Day-nighter – limited-overs match, the starting time of which has been changed from when most people are at work in the morning to when most people are at work late in the afternoon.

Declaration – opportunity for a team that has made a good total to large it.

Dolly catch – anyone who has taken one will tell you there is no such thing.

England tour – in the past, while everyone busied themselves watching football, the England team went on an overseas tour and were never seen again until they returned the following April. Nowadays, while everyone busies themselves watching football, the England team embarks on lots of tours and, unless you have Sky, are not seen again until they return the following April – and only then if you have Sky.

Gardening – sweeping crumbs of soil off the pitch with a bat – one of the few things an international cricketer does that a minor club cricketer can also do.

Googly – an off-break bowled with a leg-break action; the ball that characters in films and books say their father or uncle taught them to bowl.

Gully – fielding position between point and slip formerly known as backward point, renamed in honour of Gubby Allen by a dyslexic fan.

'He looks set for a big innings' – he'll be out before the over's out.

High fives – opportunity for the third man to come in out of the cold and get himself on TV.

Hook – in first-class cricket, a stroke made off the back foot as a result of which a short, fast ball is hit to leg with a cross bat. In minor cricket, what a player hangs his clothes on in the dressing room.

King pair – how the former player who never fully pronounces his words describes the new opening batsmen.

Leg-break – to your smug satisfaction, what your pal who went on the skiing holiday you could not afford comes home with.

Leg theory – theory put forward during dressing-room discussion as to what is physically preferable in a woman.

Long-hop – what the fielder at short leg does when the ball hits him with force on the kneecap.

Long-off, long-on – fielding positions near the boundary at either side of the sightscreen at the bowler's end which the bowler never asks to be taken up but the captain does.

'Loyal county player' – never been approached by another county club.

Nightwatchman – opportunity for the captain to reveal who he believes is the worst batsman in the team.

Off break ball – a ball that suddenly turns from off to leg when pitching and which, if the batsman is not wearing a box, may live up to its name in reverse.

'One of the modern game's real characters' – wears an earring.

Opening batsman – most likely winner of 'Man of the Match' award in a limited-overs game by virtue of the fact he will have taken an age to make a decent score leaving his team-mates minutes in which to recklessly score runs in the hope of making a decent team total.

Over rate – what the media will now do to any young England batsman or bowler who has a half-decent international debut.

Reduced target – modernism of cricket whereby statistical superiority may be achieved by way of practical inferiority.

Required run-rate – a figure per over which upper-order batsmen have set their tail-enders to score in order to win the match.

Round the wicket – method of bowling which bowler resorts to when he has tried everything else.

Seam bowler – seemed to think he could bowl.

Sightscreen – large white wooden board placed on the boundary behind the bowler's arm by the captain of the fielding team to prevent the batting team in the pavilion from seeing what's going on.

Silly mid-on – the closer the fielder gets to the bat the sillier he is.

Single – what a married cricketer thinks he is when on tour.

Skier – opportunity for two fielders to indulge in some knock-about comedy.

Spinner – slow medium pacer off short run-up.

Square cut – a shot practised by club cricketers in between deliveries but never executed when actually facing a ball.

Stanford Tournament – pie-in-the sky multi-million-pound cricket competition that ended as many supporters predicted it would, in tears.

Sticky wicket – a wet pitch which has begun to dry out under the sun, forming a hard crust over a soft, damp soil. Also sometimes referred to as 'Beckham's brain'.

Stumped – state of mind of a Minor Counties bowler when up against a seasoned first-class county batsman.

Sweep – the funny one in *The Sooty Show*.

Test match – a match you used to be able to pay on the gate to see, but alas, no more. Also a match you used to be able to see for free on TV, but alas, no more. Also a type of match that used to be played the most by England against the tourists, but alas, no more.

Tourists – once the annual visit to England by one overseas team; now anything up to four teams come every summer.

Twelfth man – drinks waiter.

Twenty20 – when the ECB decided to end the Sunday League, the decision was taken to retain the type of cricket played in the final few overs and create a whole new game out of it.

World Cup Final – Australia against some other team.

Yorker – ball from a bowler which makes the batsman stub his bat into the ground with such a jolt it nigh on tears both biceps in two. Usually followed by the sound of falling ash wood.

M. C. C. A.

Minor Counties v. Australians
AT ASHBROOKE, SUNDERLAND
ON THURSDAY & FRIDAY, 4th & 5th AUGUST, 1977
Hours of Play: 1st Day 11-30 a.m. to 6-30 p.m.

MEMBERS' PAVILION ENCLOSURE
Ground Admission and Reserved Seat   (Under Balcony)

THURSDAY
Row .....A.....

COMPLIMENTARY
Reserved Seat No. ...25...
Entrance   Rear of Pavilion
J. Iley, Secretary, Durham C.C.C.

'Can I practise wicket-keeping by myself?' I am often asked. I always reply, 'Yes, even when you are at home. Use a chair as a wicket, stand behind it, don a pair of gloves and practise all your usual movements in the comfort of your own lounge for an hour or so.'
ARTHUR McINTYRE (Surrey coach, 1959 – well, not that many people had televisions in those days)

The only wicket-keeper to accomplish 12 dismissals in a County Championship match is Ted Pooley, for Surrey against Sussex at the Oval in 1868. Pooley's achievement comprised eight catches and four stumpings.

Hands not just together on Sundays. In July 1899 Hampshire scored 672 for 7 declared against Somerset at Taunton, yet not one of Hampshire's 672 runs came from a bye. The Somerset wicket-keeper was the splendidly named Reverend Prebendary Archdale Palmer-Wickham, the vicar of Martock, who was coming up to his 44th birthday.

The most dismissals in a County Championship season is 128, by Leslie Ames of Kent in 1929. Ames's tally comprised 79 caught and 49 stumped.

Godfrey Evans was the first wicket-keeper to achieve 200 dismissals in Test matches. His 200th Test victim was Collie Smith (West Indies), at Headingley in July 1957.

On 16 June 1958 Derbyshire wicket-keeper George Dawkes achieved a hat-trick of catches against Worcestershire at Kidderminster (the bowler who also achieved a hat-trick was Les Jackson). Dawkes's feat was equalled in 1986 by Gloucestershire's Jack Russell against Surrey at the Oval, albeit Russell's hat-trick was accomplished off the bowling of two bowlers, Courtney Walsh and David Lawrence (two).

In 1959–60 at Brisbane, wicket-keeper Wally Grout (Queensland) dismissed eight Western Australian batsmen in a single innings, all caught.

 The true mark of the esteem in which an Australian cricketer is held is not in having a stand named after him, but a bar in the ground. Better still, a urinal, as in 'The Wally Grout Gents' in Sydney.
FRED TRUEMAN

In 1960 Yorkshire's Jimmy Binks took 96 catches.

 Arguably the Yorkshire player subjected to the greatest injustice in the 50s and 60s was Jimmy Binks. Season after season Jimmy produced great performances behind the stumps and was a very good batsman, after Godfrey Evans the best in the country, but only selected for England twice. When Godfrey Evans finished, the England selectors seemed happy to pick anybody over Binksy in those days. If he'd had a Blue from Oxford or Cambridge, he'd have been one of the first names down on the England team sheet.
FRED TRUEMAN

In July 1964 Surrey's Arnold Long held 11 catches in the match against Sussex at Hove, seven in Sussex's first innings and four in their second – a feat since equalled by several wicket-keepers, including David Bairstow for Yorkshire in 1982, Warren Hegg for Lancashire against Derbyshire in 1989, Alec Stewart for Surrey against Leicestershire in 1989, and Keith Piper for Warwickshire against Derbyshire in 1994.

In 1965 Warwickshire captain Mike Smith, frustrated at some obdurate batting by the Essex openers in their second innings at Clacton, called upon wicket-keeper Alan Smith to try his hand at bowling. Smith dismissed both openers, Gordon Barker and Geoff Smith. Alan Smith then took the wickets of Keith Fletcher and one Trevor Bailey to end with four wickets.

East sent them west. On 27 July 1985 David East (Essex) dismissed eight Somerset batsmen at Taunton. East took eight catches while Somerset's ninth wicket fell to a run-out conducted by East before Somerset captain, Ian Botham. East thus created the record for the most dismissals by a wicket-keeper in a single innings of a County Championship match, later equalled by two other wicket-keepers, and in all instances their victims were caught: Steven Marsh for Kent against Middlesex at Lord's in 1991, and Jonathan Batty for Surrey against Kent at the Oval in 2004.

The Top Five Wicket-keepers by Dismissals in English First-class Cricket

	Career	Catches	Stumpings	Total
Bob Taylor (Derbyshire)	1960–88	1,473	176	1,649
John Murray (Middlesex)	1952–75	1,270	257	1,527
Herbert Strudwick (Surrey)	1902–27	1,242	255	1,497
Alan Knott (Kent)	1964–85	1,211	133	1,344
Jack Russell (Gloucestershire)	1981–2004	1,192	128	1,320

In 1979–80 England's Bob Taylor equalled the record for the number of dismissals by a wicket-keeper in an innings of a Test match – seven, all caught, against India at Bombay. Taylor went on to make 10 dismissals in the match, eight of which were off the bowling of Ian Botham. Taylor shares the record with Wasim Bari, the first wicket-keeper to dismiss seven batsmen in a single innings of a Test, for Pakistan against New Zealand at Auckland in 1978–79; Ian Smith (New Zealand); and Ridley Jacobs (West Indies).

He's played well, but he's no Bob Taylor. Then again, who is?
JEREMY CONEY (BBC Radio)

In 1982–83 Australia's Rodney Marsh achieved 28 dismissals, all caught, in the series against England.

In 1992 Tahir Rashid created a world record for dismissals by a wicket-keeper in a single innings when he claimed nine Pakistan Automobile Company wickets when playing for Habib Bank in a BCCP Patron's Trophy match (eight catches and one stumping).

In 1995–96, in the Test against South Africa at Johannesburg, Jack Russell dismissed 11 South African players (all caught) – the highest number of dismissals by an England wicket-keeper in a Test match.

Why is it funny to see a wicket-keeper running to field the ball?
H. E. BATES

Most Wickets in a Career – the Top Twenty

	Career	Wickets	Average	Matches
W. Rhodes	1898–1930	4,204	16.72	1,110
A. P. Freeman	1914–36	3,776	18.42	592
C. W. L. Parker	1903–35	3,278	19.46	635
J. T. Hearne	1888–1923	3,061	17.75	639
T. W. J. Goddard	1922–52	2,979	19.84	593
A. S. Kennedy	1907–36	2,874	21.23	677
D. Shackleton	1948–69	2,857	18.65	647
G. A. R. Lock	1946–71	2,844	19.23	654
F. J. Titmus	1949–82	2,830	22.37	792
W. G. Grace	1865–1908	2,809	18.14	870
M. W. Tate	1912–37	2,784	18.16	679
G. H. Hirst	1891–1929	2,742	18.73	826
C. Blythe	1899–1914	2,503	16.81	439
D. L. Underwood	1963–87	2,465	20.28	676
W. E. Astill	1906–39	2,432	23.76	733
J. C. White	1909–37	2,355	18.58	472
W. E. Hollies	1932–57	2,323	20.94	515
F. S. Trueman	1949–69	2,304	18.29	603
B. J. Statham	1950–68	2,260	16.37	559
R. T. D. Perks	1930–55	2,233	24.07	595

The bowler who has taken 100 wickets in a season on the most occasions is Jack Hobbs, who achieved this feat 23 times between 1898 and 1929.

The last bowler to take 200 wickets in a season was Tony Lock (Surrey). In 1957 he took 212 wickets at an average of 12.02.

Five bowlers have taken four wickets in a single over when playing for England (curiously, on three occasions this was achieved on the same ground – Headingley): Maurice Allom, v. New Zealand in Christchurch (1929–30); Ken Cranston, v. South Africa at Headingley (1947); Fred Titmus, v. New Zealand at Headingley (1965); Chris Old, v. Pakistan at Edgbaston (1978); and Andy Caddick, v. West Indies at Headingley (2000).

The earliest known report of a women's cricket match appeared in the *Reading Mercury* on 26 July 1745. It concerned a match on Gosden Common near Guildford, Surrey between Maids of Bramley and Maids of Hambledon. The latter won by 'eight notches'.

In an era of underarm bowling, in the early 1800s Christina Willes (sister of John Willes) adopted roundarm bowling, as pioneered by Tom Walker in the 1790s, to avoid her arm being ensnared in her skirts.

The first women's cricket club was the White Heather CC, formed in 1887 at Nun Appleton in Yorkshire.

In 1890 a team called the Original English Ladies Cricketers embarked on a tour of England, playing in exhibition matches. The team played before sizeable crowds but had to disband when their manager absconded with the profits – and, it has been said, with one of the team members. James Lillywhite's *Cricketers' Annual* of 1890 carried a photograph of the team, and for years people have been surmising as to which member of the team it was who did a flit with the manager.

In 1905 the Victorian Women's Cricket Association was formed in Victoria, Australia.

The Women's Cricket Association was formed in 1926.

In 1931 the Australian Women's Cricket Association was formed.

The first overseas tour by an England Women's team was made to Australia and New Zealand in 1934–35. It was on this tour that the first women's Test match took place, between Australia and England in December 1934. England won the three-match series 2–0.

England's highest ever total is 503 for 5 declared, against New Zealand at Christchurch on 16 February 1935. It was during this innings that Betty Snowball scored 189 – the highest individual innings by an England player in a Test match.

After the suspension of cricket due to the Second World War, England resumed Test cricket overseas in 1948–49 when a three-Test series was played against Australia. England, whose team included seven players making their international debuts, lost the first Test and drew the remaining two, and therefore lost the 'Women's Ashes'. England's star players were Molly Hide, who batted throughout the final day of the third Test to ensure a draw and was the only England player to score a century, and Myrtle Maclagan, who in the second Test scored 77 and was England's leading wicket taker on the tour with nine wickets. England concluded their tour by defeating New Zealand.

In 1951 Australia toured England for the first time since 1937. Australia defeated England before a large crowd at Scarborough, but England won the final Test by 137 runs, Mary Duggan taking nine wickets. The series was drawn 1–1, so Australia retained the Ashes.

In 1954 England toured New Zealand and enjoyed their first series win since their inaugural series victory in 1934–35 against Australia.

In 1957–58, against Australia on 21 February at Melbourne, Mary Duggan set a women's Test record with bowling figures of 7 for 6 off 14.5 overs – a record that was to stand for 38 years. It was during this series that Australia's Betty Wilson became the first player to score a century and take 10 wickets in a Test match.

The International Women's Cricket Council was founded in 1958. One of the remits of the IWCC was to co-ordinate and help in the administration and development of women's cricket in member countries Australia, Denmark, England, Holland, New Zealand, South Africa and the West Indies.

England became a world force in women's cricket in the 1960s, remaining undefeated in 14 Tests. In 1963 England regained the Ashes by defeating Australia.

In 1966 Rachael Heyhoe (later Heyhoe-Flint) assumed the England captaincy for the series against New Zealand. Heyhoe-Flint's career spanned the years 1960 to 1979 during which time she scored 1,814 runs (average 51.82), including three unofficial internationals against Jamaica in 1971. She was England captain from 1966 to 1977, during which time England never lost a Test match and won the World Cup (in 1973). She hit four Test centuries, with a top score of 179 against Australia in 1976, and scored 643 runs in ODIs (average 58.45). In 1963, against Australia, she became the first player to hit a six in women's Test cricket. She was a dual international, having played four times for England at hockey. In 1971 she married Derrick Flint and added his name to hers. She was awarded the MBE in 1973 for services to cricket and sport in general, was the first woman member of the MCC, and when her playing days were over became a highly respected journalist and cricket writer. She was sports editor of the *Wolverhampton Chronicle* in the 1970s. Her name is still synonymous with cricket though she is now PR director for Wolverhampton Wanderers.

In 1967 Jan Molyneaux, playing for Olympic against Northcote in the Melbourne A Grade Final, scored a world record 298.

In April 1970 the first women cricketers, Sian Davies and Sally Slowe of Cheltenham Ladies College, attended the MCC Easter Coaching Classes at Lord's. Their attendance was seen at the time as being indicative of the 'breaking of the gender barrier'.

The first Women's World Cup was held in 1973. It was won by host nation England.

In 1979 the first women's Test match to be staged at Lord's took place between England and Australia.

On 16 June 1979 Julia Greenwood achieved match figures of 11 for 63 against the West Indies at Canterbury – the best match bowling figures by an England player.

On 19 July 1991 Jo Chamberlain took 7 for 8 in the ODI against Denmark at Haarlem in Holland.

On 12 December 1997 England scored 376 for 2 against Pakistan in the ODI at Vijayawada in India – England's record total in an ODI.

Four days later, on 16 December, 17-year-old Charlotte Edwards scored 173 not out against Ireland at Puna – the highest individual ODI innings by an England player.

In 1998 the ECB took over from the Women's Cricket Association as the governing body of women's cricket in England with female representation.

In 2005 the International Women's Cricket Council was integrated under the umbrella of the ICC. The ICC Women's Cricket Committee was formed.

England have always sent a 'development' squad to every European Championship and have won the tournament on six occasions and been runners-up once (2001). England's European Championship successes came in 1989, 1990, 1991, 1995, 1999 and 2005.

In 2005 England defeated Australia to win the Ashes for the first time since 1963.

In 2005 Clare Connor not only led England to victory in the Ashes but also Sussex to their third consecutive County Championship.

In 2005 Holly Colvin made her Test debut for England aged 15 - the youngest player to be capped by England Women.

On 2 September 2008, against the West Indies at Taunton, at 19 years old Sarah Taylor became the youngest woman to pass 1,000 runs in ODIs.

The Women's County Championship comprises 12 teams split into three divisions of four. County teams who are not members of the County Championship compete in the County Challenge Cup, which comprises five groups each of four teams and is organized on a regional basis; also the ECB Knock-out Cup.

Between 1992 and 2002 inclusive, Yorkshire won the Women's County Championship in 10 of the 11 seasons. Kent triumphed in 2006 and 2007, Sussex in 2008.

England are currently ranked number one in the world and are the holders of both the World Cup and Twenty20 Cup. Captained by Charlotte Edwards, England regained the Ashes in 2008, the year in which Edwards was voted ICC Women's Player of the Year. On 21 March 2009 she led England to victory in the Women's World Cup Final in Sydney, in which England defeated New Zealand by four wickets in Sydney.

In 2009 Charlotte Edwards was named one of the top five cricketers in *Wisden* – the first woman ever to be afforded this distinction.

94

Worcestershire's home is the County Ground, New Road, Worcester, current capacity 7,000. The ground is low-lying near the River Severn and is often subject to flooding, even in summer. The floods in the summer of 2007 submerged the ground resulting in the club having to play the majority of their 'home' matches away from New Road – and an estimated loss in revenue in excess of a million pounds.

The club has also played matches at the Bournville Cricket Ground in Birmingham, Dudley, Evesham, Hereford, Halesowen, Kidderminster, Stourport-on-Seven (at the wonderfully named Chain Wire club) and Stourbridge.

The club badge is a shield, argent bearing fess between three pears sable.

Worcestershire has won the County Championship five times, in 1964, 1965, 1974, 1988 and 1989. Other major trophy successes: NatWest Trophy in 1994; Benson & Hedges Cup winners in 1991; Sunday/Pro40 League winners in 1971, 1987, 1988 and 2007.

Worcestershire no longer award traditional county caps. Players are awarded county colours when they make their Championship debut.

The earliest reference to cricket in the county is, compared to other counties, rather late – 1829.

The earliest known record of a match involving a Worcestershire representative side, against Shropshire at Hartlebury Common, is dated 28 August 1844. In 1846 a 22-man Worcestershire team played William Clarke's All-England XI at Powick Hams.

Worcestershire County Cricket Club was formed on 11 March 1865 at the Star Hotel in Worcester.

In the 1880s Paul Foley, who hailed from a family of iron masters in Stourbridge, was a key member of the club and helped establish the Minor Counties Championship in 1895.

Worcestershire shared the inaugural Minor Counties title with Durham and Norfolk in 1895 before winning it outright in the three subsequent seasons (1896, 1897 and 1898).

Worcestershire's quadruple success in the Minor Counties Championship led to the club successfully applying for first-class status. Worcestershire entered the County Championship in 1899.

The club's inaugural first-class match was against Yorkshire in May 1899.

Worcestershire's early years in the Championship can best be described as moderate. It is said that weak bowling on 'perfect New Road pitches' was responsible for this. The club's leading player at the turn of the century was Reginald 'Tip' Foster, one of seven members of the Foster family (other notables were Harry and Bill) to play for the county at this time. Tip, Harry and Bill Foster all played in Worcestershire's inaugural first-class match against Yorkshire.

In 1899 Tip Foster and his brother Bill scored 134 and 140 respectively in the first innings against Hampshire. In the second innings they shared a partnership of 219, with Tip 101 not out and Bill 172 not out. This was the first time in first-class cricket that two brothers had each scored two hundreds in the same match – a record that stood alone until Ian and Greg Chappell each scored centuries in both innings for Australia against New Zealand in 1974.

In 1903 at Huddersfield, Yorkshire skittled out Worcestershire for their lowest ever total – 24 all out. Coincidentally, in the same season Worcestershire dismissed Hampshire for 30 at New Road – the lowest total inflicted on first-class opposition.

Worcestershire's regular wicket-keeper between 1900 and 1910 was George Gaukrodger, who prior to joining the club had managed to gain an international cap at football for Ireland, against Wales at Belfast in 1895, scoring the first goal for the Irish in a 2–2 draw. Seemingly, Gaukrodger had no qualms about playing football for Ireland even though he was not Irish. A mix-up led to him being invited to play for Ireland as the Irish FA believed him to have been born in Belfast. He was actually born in Belfast Street, in Leeds, in 1877.

Following the First World War the club experienced so much difficulty recruiting players of the required standard they did not compete in the County Championship in 1919.

The club returned to the County Championship in 1920, but created an unwanted and lasting record for the Championship when they lost three successive matches each by an innings and over 200 runs.

Fox runs with the wolves. In 1923 the MCC, in particular Lord Harris, disputed the registration of Worcestershire's Len Crawley and Vic Fox. This resulted in Fox being unable to play county cricket for Worcestershire until 1926 following a three-year 'qualification period' with Dudley in the Birmingham League, during which time he signed for Wolverhampton Wanderers, making a total of 49 first-team appearances for them. He was also Wolverhampton AAA sprint champion two years in succession.

Worcestershire continued to struggle in the County Championship until the early 1930s. One of the club's few quality players at this time was Fred Root, one of the first exponents of leg theory bowling. At one stage in 1925 – a season in which he took 207 wickets to become the first Worcestershire bowler to take in excess of 200 wickets in a season – Root remarked, 'We have a strong team. We're holding up the rest of the league.' (Could this have been the first cracking of this old chestnut?) Root holds the club record for best bowling in an innings – 9 for 23, against Lancashire at New Road in 1931. He never managed 10 wickets in a single innings, but he took nine wickets on three occasions. He also holds the club record for most wickets in a season – 207 (average 17.52), in 1925. Following his retirement as a player Fred Root became an umpire then a journalist noted for witty and informed cricket pieces for the Sunday Pictorial.

Just what the doctor ordered. In 1934 Harry 'Doc' Gibbons scored 2,654 runs (average 52.03) – a club record, and more than Don Bradman totalled for the touring Australians that summer.

Leg-break bowler Roly Jenkins always bowled wearing a cap. He was a surprise call-up for the England/MCC tour of South Africa in 1948–49 and had to postpone his wedding in order to go. Jenkins enjoyed a very successful tour, finishing on top of the England Test averages with 16 wickets. Back with Worcestershire in 1949 he enjoyed a terrific season with bat and ball, making 1,183 runs and taking 183 wickets, but was not selected for England that summer.

Perks of the job. Between 1930 and 1955 Reg Perks took a club career record 2,143 wickets (average 23.73) for Worcestershire.

Reg Perks' father Reg senior (one-time assistant to New Road groundsman Fred Hunt) played at Crystal Palace for the MCC against a London County XI in 1902. Included in the MCC team was Sir Arthur Conan Doyle.

Reg Perks was the first professional to captain Worcestershire, appointed in 1955.

Worcestershire had a mediocre time of it in the 1950s. Their form throughout the decade can best be described as 'indifferent'.

Worcestershire's fortunes continue to go up and down like a pendulum.
BBC RADIO HEREFORD AND WORCESTER

All changed for the club in the 1960s under the presidency of Sir George Dowty and the captaincy of Don Kenyon. Indeed the county emerged as a true force in first-class cricket. In 1962 Worcestershire finished runners-up in the County Championship – their highest placing since 1907. The following year they were beaten finalists in the Gillette Cup, and then in 1964 won the first of what was to be successive Championship titles. The club's success was primarily down to a strong, well-balanced side that included Len Coldwell, Basil D'Oliveira, Jack Flavell, Norman Gifford, Tom Graveney, Martin Horton, Ron Headley, Ted Hemsley and Jim Standen.

Martin Horton played his first match for the club's Second XI at 15 years old but had actually played against Worcestershire's second string at the age of 14 in a friendly for Northamptonshire Second XI.

Don Kenyon ended his Worcestershire career (1946–67) with 34,490 runs (average 34.18) – a club record. He shares a Worcestershire record of 124 century partnerships, 22 of them with Peter Richardson, whom he succeeded as captain in 1959. He was a member of the Worcestershire committee (1968–82) and became the first former professional to be elected president of the club, a post he held until 1990.

In 1964–65 Don Kenyon led Worcestershire on a tour of Rhodesia and, wait for it, Hollywood. In keeping with the song 'It Never Rains (in Southern California)', it 'just pours' (Tony Toni Tone, 1969), both Worcestershire's scheduled matches in California were postponed without a ball being bowled due to incessant rain.

In 1970 New Zealander Glenn Turner scored a club record 10 centuries, later equalled by Graeme Hick (1988).

On the first morning of Worcestershire's match against Lancashire in 1977 the umpires reported the New Road pitch as 'unfit for first-class cricket'. After much discussion between umpires, officials and the respective team captains it was agreed the game would go ahead. Ted Hemsley scored a career best 176 not out and shared a fourth-wicket partnership of 213 with Glenn Turner.

In 1987 Worcestershire achieved their highest total in one-day cricket – 404 for 3, against Devon at New Road in the NatWest Trophy.

Graeme Hick created a new record for the highest score in an innings when he made 405 not out against Somerset at Taunton in 1988.

In 1997 Graeme Hick and Tom Moody created a club record partnership when the pair put on 438 (unbroken) for the third wicket against Hampshire at Southampton.

In 1998, playing against Derbyshire at Derby in the Sunday League, Graeme Hick struck a delivery from Kevin Dean that broke and dislodged a tile on the roof of the Derby pavilion before the ball rolled back and became lodged in the guttering. A ladder was required in order for officials to retrieve the ball and the game was held up for some minutes.

Graeme Hick has scored the most centuries in the course of a career (1984–2008) with the club – 106. He also holds the club record for the most catches in the field – 543. Hick arrived from his native Zimbabwe in 1984 and was selected for his country on the tour of England in 1985. He was a prolific run maker in county matches, in Tests (for England) and in one-day matches, scoring his 100th century against Sussex at New Road in 1998 days after his 32nd birthday – just two weeks older than the youngest batsman ever to score 100 hundreds, Wally Hammond (Gloucestershire).

Other than his mistakes, Hick hasn't put a foot wrong.
SIMON HUGHES

In 2007 Worcestershire scored their highest ever total against a rival county – 701 for 6 declared, against Surrey at New Road.

Other Worcestershire notables include Roy Booth (1956–70), the last wicket-keeper to take 100 dismissals in a season (1964); Ian Botham; Brian Brain (the typist's nightmare); Jim Cumbes; Tim Curtis; Duncan Fearnley, who began his bat-making business in the back room of ex-player Fred Poole's fishing tackle shop; Glenn McGrath (Australia); the wonderfully named Percy Tarbox, who was weeks short of his 30th birthday when he made his first-class debut for the club in 1921 but went on to play in 226 matches; and Younis Ahmed, who was asked to leave the club after he put a bet on Worcestershire to lose against Leicestershire in 1983 – a match that was abandoned due to rain. The current squad includes Kabir Ali, Gareth Batty, Simon Jones, Ben Smith and Vikram Solanki.

And how long have you had this lifelong ambition to play for Worcestershire?
BBC HEREFORD AND WORCESTER (interview with Richard Jones following his first-class debut in 2007)

Most appropriately named player – R. I. Scorer.

The club's limited-overs team is the Worcestershire Royals, though some supporters refer to whatever Worcestershire team as 'the Pears'.

Worth a visit for . . . if you can gain entry to the members' enclosure, as you sit, the teas served in the green building to your right are a must: sumptuous, sandwiches freshly made, cakes home-baked, evocative of times gone by.

The World Cup is organized by the International Cricket Council. The competition consists of a qualifying stage for non-Test nations leading to the finals, which are staged every four years. The official name of the competition is the ICC Cricket World Cup.

The World Cup is the world's third most viewed sporting event on television, after the Olympic Games and the football World Cup.

The current cup was created for the 1999 competition and is the tournament's first permanent trophy. It is made of silver and gold and features a golden globe standing on three columns of silver shaped like stumps and bails. The three columns signify the three fundamental aspects of cricket: batting, bowling and fielding. The trophy is 60cm high and weighs 11kg. The names of the winning teams are engraved on shields that ring its base. The trophy was designed and created by Garrard and Co. of London. A replica is permanently awarded to the winning team.

Nations keen to host the World Cup submit bids, which are examined and voted upon by the ICC Executive Committee.

England hosted the first three competitions. England was awarded the inaugural World Cup in 1975 because at the time it was the only cricket nation with the resources and wherewithal to organize such a tournament.

Eight teams participated in the inaugural World Cup in 1975: Australia, England, India, New Zealand, Pakistan and the West Indies, plus non-Test nation (at the time) Sri Lanka, and a representative team from East Africa.

The original World Cup was sponsored by Prudential and called the Prudential Cup. The trophy featured a silver cup with two handles (not dissimilar to the FA Cup), a silver top, and a plinth ringed by a silver band on which the names of winning teams could be engraved.

Matches consisted of 60 overs per team.

Dennis Amiss (Warwickshire) scored 137 for England against India at Lord's – still the record score by an England batsman in a World Cup. England's total was 334 for 4, and they defeated India by 202 runs.

India's Bishan Bedi achieved bowling figures of 12–8–6–1 against East Africa at Headingley.

England were dismissed for 93 by Australia at Headingley.

The first ever winners of the World Cup were the West Indies, who defeated Australia by 17 runs in the final at Lord's before a crowd of 27,000.

The 1979 World Cup spawned the ICC Trophy, a tournament for non-Test-playing nations that would also act as a qualifying stage for the World Cup finals. The first two teams to qualify for the World Cup (1979) via the ICC Trophy were Canada and Sri Lanka.

The West Indies became the first nation to retain the World Cup when they won the tournament for a second time in 1979, defeating England in the final by 92 runs.

India volunteered to host the third World Cup in 1983, but the ICC awarded it to England because the longer periods of daylight in June meant matches could be completed in a single day.

Sri Lanka, as a Test nation, qualified automatically for the 1983 tournament. Zimbabwe qualified via the ICC Trophy.

England's Vic Marks took 5 for 39 against Sri Lanka at Taunton. England's total against Sri Lanka was 333 for 9.

The most expensive bowling figures recorded in a World Cup are those of New Zealand's Martin Snedden, against England at the Oval in 1979 (12–1–105–2).

The West Indies reached the final for the third consecutive time but were beaten by India, by 43 runs.

India and Pakistan hosted the 1987 World Cup – the fourth tournament and the first to be held outside England.

Matches were reduced from 60 to 50 overs per team.

India's Chetan Sharma achieved the first hat-trick in a World Cup, against New Zealand at Nagpur.

England's Graham Gooch scored 471 runs in the tournament – the record for an England batsman in a World Cup.

England reached the World Cup Final for a second time, but lost to Australia by seven runs – the narrowest margin of victory in a World Cup Final.

The 1992 finals were held in Australia and New Zealand.

The 1992 finals not only saw the introduction of a new trophy, it was also the first World Cup to feature coloured clothing, day/night games, white cricket balls and changes to fielding restrictions.

South Africa participated in the World Cup for the first time following the end of apartheid in the country which resulted in the lifting of the worldwide sports ban.

Australia defeated India by one run at Brisbane – the second occasion on which Australia had gained victory over India by a single run in World Cup tournaments.

In 1992 England reached the World Cup Final for a third time, and lost for a third time, on this occasion to Pakistan, by 22 runs.

The 1996 World Cup was held in Asia for a second time. Sri Lanka staged some of the group matches.

Gary Kirsten scored 188 not out for South Africa against the United Arab Emirates at Rawalpindi to create a new World Cup record for the highest individual innings.

Sri Lanka scored 398 for 5 against Kenya at Kandy.

The 1996 World Cup was plunged into controversy when riots broke out during the semi-final between India and Sri Lanka at Eden Gardens in Calcutta when India, chasing 254, slumped to 120 for 8. As police struggled to restore order the match was awarded to Sri Lanka by default.

Sri Lanka, with their cavalier approach to batting, proved the 'surprise package' of the tournament, beating Australia by seven wickets in the final at Lahore.

Sri Lanka is the only host nation to have won the World Cup, albeit a co-host (the final was held in Lahore, Pakistan). England is the only other host nation to reach a World Cup Final (1979).

The 1999 World Cup was staged in England, with group matches also being held in Ireland, Scotland, Wales and Holland. The tournament featured a Super 6 stage.

India's Rahul Dravid and Sourav Ganguly shared a second-wicket partnership of 318 against Sri Lanka – the record partnership for the World Cup.

Having defeated South Africa in the final over of their Super 6 encounter, Australia again overcame South Africa in the semi-final in dramatic circumstances. With the match tied, there was a mix-up between South African batsmen Allan Donald and Lance Klusener. Donald dropped his bat, was stranded between wickets and was run out, giving Australia victory by virtue of having lost fewer wickets.

In the final, Australia defeated Pakistan by eight wickets.

The 2003 World Cup was held in South Africa; matches were also played in Zimbabwe and Kenya. A record number of teams participated in the finals – 14.

Thirty-seven years after World Cup Willie (a lion) was the mascot for the 1966 football World Cup in England, in 2003 a mascot was adopted by the Cricket World Cup for the first time – 'Dazzler', a zebra.

There was a sensational and unique start to the game between Sri Lanka and Bangladesh at Pietermaritzburg, when Sri Lanka's Chaminda Vaas achieved a hat-trick with the first three balls of the match.

Australia's wicket-keeper Adam Gilchrist dismissed six Namibia batsmen in the match at Potchefstroom – all caught.

The 'surprise package' of the 2003 World Cup was Kenya, who reached the semi-finals following victories over Sri Lanka and Zimbabwe and a forfeit on the part of New Zealand, who refused to play in Kenya due to concerns over security.

Kenya was the first associate member of the ICC to reach the semi-finals of a World Cup.

Canada were dismissed by Sri Lanka for 36 – the record for the lowest total by a team in the World Cup.

Australia's Glenn McGrath took 7 for 15 against Namibia – the best ever bowling figures in a World Cup.

India's Sachin Tendulkar scored 673 runs in the tournament.

Australia won the 2003 World Cup, becoming the first nation to win the World Cup three times. Australia amassed the highest ever total in a World Cup Final – 359 for 2 – and defeated India by 125 runs.

The 2003 World Cup was attended by 626,845 spectators.

The 2007 World Cup was staged in the West Indies.

The mascot for the tournament was 'Mello', a raccoon which, for reasons known only to the designers, was orange in colour.

The 'surprise package' of the 2007 World Cup was Ireland, who in their first appearance in the finals of a World Cup tied with Zimbabwe and defeated Pakistan to progress to the second stage, where they defeated Bangladesh, who had previously defeated India and in the second stage enjoyed victory over South Africa.

The format for the 2007 World Cup was cumbersome. Sixteen teams were divided into four groups of four. The top two teams from each group progressed to the Super 8 stage with the Super 8 teams playing six teams that had progressed from other groups. Teams earned points as they did when playing group matches, but carried their points forward from previous matches gained against other teams who qualified from the same group to the Super 8 stage. Many fans didn't understand what was going on, and the format was described in one newspaper as 'a muddled mess'.

The 2007 World Cup sold 672,000 tickets, though a number of matches did not attract good attendances. Not having learned from previous football World Cups, the tournament was too weighty by far with too many matches, the admission price for which was beyond the budget of most local cricket supporters. The sheer number of matches played diluted the drama and excitement generated by straight knockout matches.

Glenn McGrath took 26 wickets – a record for the World Cup – was named player of the tournament, and ended it as the leading wicket taker in the history of the competition with 71 wickets (1996–2007).

India's Sachin Tendulkar ended the 2007 tournament with a total of 1,796 runs (1992–2007) – the most runs scored by any batsman in the history of the World Cup.

India achieved the highest total in a World Cup match – 413 for 5, against Bermuda.

Australia became the first country to win three successive World Cups when they defeated Sri Lanka in the final by 53 runs courtesy of the Duckworth-Lewis method. Australia's victory saw them create a record of 29 consecutive World Cup matches without defeat.

The 2007 World Cup was televised in 200 countries to an estimated 2.2 billion viewers.

Following criticism of the format of the 2007 World Cup, the ICC announced that the format for the 2011 tournament would be simplified. Teams will now be allocated into groups and play in a round-robin format, the top four teams in each group progressing to a quarter-final knock-out stage.

The 2011 World Cup is scheduled to be held on the Indian subcontinent with matches to be played in India, Pakistan, Sri Lanka and Bangladesh. The final will take place in Mumbai. Due to concerns about terrorism there is, however, serious disquiet regarding certain venues, such as Pakistan. The ICC is monitoring the situation and is compiling contingency plans.

The 2015 World Cup is to be held in Australia and New Zealand, the 2019 World Cup in England.

The ICC has negotiated television rights for the 2011 and 2015 World Cups in a deal worth US$1.1 billion. A deal for sponsorship rights was agreed worth US$500 million.

World Cup Winners

1975	West Indies
1979	West Indies
1983	India
1987	Australia
1992	Pakistan
1996	Sri Lanka
1999	Australia
2003	Australia
2007	Australia

The Ten Worst First-Class Career Bowling Averages

	Career	Matches	Balls	Runs	Wkts	Ave
Mark Lawrence (Oxford U.)	1982–86	30	5,364	2,979	42	70.92
Sachin Tendulkar	1988–2008	250	7,221	4,101	67	61.20
Stuart Saunders (Tasmania)	1979–89	60	7,186	4,016	70	57.37
Xavier Doherty (Tasmania)	2001–07	27	5,614	3,374	60	56.23
Asif Din (Warwickshire)	1981–97	211	6,573	4,393	79	55.60
Richard Pearson (Essex etc.)	1991–97	51	10,356	5,516	100	55.16
Ian Swallow (Somerset etc.)	1983–91	88	11,215	5,798	106	54.69
Usman Afzaal (Northants etc.)	1995–2008	203	7,971	4,422	83	53.27
John Fitton (Lancashire)	1987–92	52	8,391	4,359	82	53.15
Suresh Mahadevan (Goa)	1985–96	44	5,774	3,162	60	52.70

In September 2008 the 11th worst first-class career bowling average belonged to England captain Kevin Pietersen – 127 matches, 5,377 balls bowled, 3,104 runs conceded, 60 wickets taken at an average of 51.73.

The most runs conceded by a bowler in a single innings in a Test match is 298, by Chuck Fleetwood-Smith, playing for Australia against England at the Oval in August 1938.

The worst thing that can happen to a batsman in a Test match is for him to be out for a pair on the same day. This happened to Pakistan's Ebbu Ghazali against England at Old Trafford on 24 July 1954. What's more, his two dismissals occurred within two hours of each other.

The worst day so far for watching runs in a Test match in England was 26 August 1978 at Lord's when just 151 runs were scored in the Test between England and New Zealand. England contributed 114 runs (in a total of 289), and at the close of play New Zealand were 37 for 7.

The worst sequence of results England have endured against another Test nation occurred between 1984 and 1986 when they lost 10 successive Tests against the West Indies.

The most overs bowled without taking a wicket is 72, accomplished by Denis Atkinson against England at Edgbaston in 1957. Atkinson's 72 overs yielded him figures of 0 for 137.

England's worst sequence without a series win in a five-match Test series is 11 years. From the 1986–87 series win in Australia, England did not win another series until the defeat of South Africa in 1998.

Yorkshire's home is Headingley in Leeds. As the result of a major sponsorship deal with Leeds Metropolitan University in 2006 the ground is now called Headingley Carnegie Stadium. As laudable and worthwhile as this partnership is, you just feel no amount of publicity and marketing will ever penetrate the consciousness of the nation's cricket lovers for whom the ground is, and will always be, simply 'Headingley'.

Headingley's capacity is 17,000, though the club has plans to rebuild the stand next to the rugby ground which will increase capacity to 20,000.

Yorkshire also plays at Scarborough (North Marine Road), which hosts the annual Scarborough Festival.

In the past the club was always keen to 'spread' matches throughout the county, notably Sheffield (Bramall Lane, also Abbeydale Park), Bradford (Park Avenue), Middlesbrough (Acklam Park), Harrogate, Huddersfield, Hull (The Circle), and Dewsbury and Barnsley. It would appear the majority of Yorkshire supporters would like to see a return to these 'out matches' rather than for every game to be staged at Headingley.

Bramall Lane, Sheffield and Park Avenue, Bradford were shared with Football League clubs Sheffield United and Bradford Park Avenue respectively, albeit the latter dropped out of the Football League in 1970.

The Yorkshire badge is a white rose.

In terms of County Championships won, Yorkshire is the most successful of all counties. Since 1890 the club has won the title 30 times – 1893, 1896, 1898, 1900, 1901, 1902, 1905, 1908, 1912, 1919, 1922, 1923, 1924, 1925, 1931, 1932, 1933, 1935, 1937, 1938, 1939, 1946, 1959, 1960, 1962, 1963, 1966, 1967, 1968 and 2001 – in addition to which they were joint champions in 1949. Other major trophy successes: Gillette Cup/C&G Trophy winners in 1965, 1969 and 2002; Sunday League winners in 1983; and Benson & Hedges Cup winners in 1987.

The earliest known reference to cricket in Yorkshire relates to local matches between Sheffield parishes in 1751. The first game of any note was played in August of that year between the Duke of Cleveland's XI and Earl of Northumberland's XI at Stanton, near Richmond (one wonders if there was a Yorkshireman in the crowd that day who sat there saying, 'The game's nowt like it were in ma day').

In September 1757 Wirksworth entertained Sheffeld at Brampton Moor, near Chesterfield. It is thought this is the earliest reference to the Sheffield club that eventually became Yorkshire CCC.

Sheffield regularly played first-class matches, as they then were, into the nineteenth century. The team was referred to as Yorkshire for the first time in 1849, for a game against Lancashire – the first 'Roses' encounter.

In March 1861 a Match Fund Committee was instigated in Sheffield with a view to running and funding Yorkshire county matches. In 1863 Yorkshire Cricket Club was formed at a meeting of the Match Fund Committee at the Adelphi Hotel in Sheffield. The club was originally based at Bramall Lane.

Yorkshire's inaugural first-class match took place in June 1863, against Surrey at the Oval.

In 1867 Yorkshire won their first unofficial County Championship.

Lord Hawke was appointed captain in 1883 and held this position at the club for 23 years. He later became president of the club, then president of the MCC.

In 1893 the club moved its headquarters to Headingley, Leeds.

Yorkshire dominated the early years of the official County Championship. In 1896 they achieved their highest ever total – 887, against Warwickshire at Edgbaston. This is also the highest total ever achieved in the County Championship. Four players hit centuries in one innings of this match: Bobby Peel (210 not out), Lord Hawke (166), Ted Wainwright (126) and Stanley Jackson (117).

From 1900 to 1902 Yorkshire played 80 Championship matches and lost only two.

In 1901 Yorkshire dismissed Nottinghamshire for only 13 at Trent Bridge.

In 1905 George Hirst scored 341 against Leicestershire at Grace Road – the highest innings by a Yorkshire batsman in the County Championship.

Yorkshire won the first post-war Championship in 1919, a season which saw the debut of two players who were to become legends: Herbert Sutcliffe and Emmott Robinson.

Having served as a commissioned 2nd Lieutenant in the First World War, Herbert Sutcliffe was 24 years old when he made his debut for Yorkshire, but quickly made up for lost time. He scored 1,839 runs in 1919 – a record for a debut season in first-class cricket. After that he kept the scoreboard clicking over, amassing over 1,000 runs each season up to 1939, including over 2,000 runs each season from 1922 to 1935 – a feat he repeated in 1937. In 1928, 1931 and 1932 he scored in excess of 3,000 runs in all matches. Sutcliffe still has the best record of an English batsman against Australia – 2,751 runs (average 66.85) – and still holds a number of club records: most runs in a County Championship season – 2,883 (average 80.08); most runs in a career at the club – 38,558 (average 50.20); most centuries in a season – 12, in 1932; and most centuries in a Yorkshire career (1919–45) – 112.

Some batsmen can play fast bowling, some can't. But if truth be known, no one likes to play fast bowling.
HERBERT SUTCLIFFE

In 1921 Yorkshire beat Northamptonshire by a record innings and 397 runs at Harrogate.

Another Yorkshire great, all-rounder Wilfred Rhodes, retired from cricket in 1930. In his final season he made 478 runs and took 73 wickets – he was 53 years old. Rhodes was one of a rare breed of cricketers: he bowled against both W. G. Grace and Don Bradman. He scored 39,802 first-class runs (average 30.58) and took 4,187 wickets (average 16.71). He holds the club record for the most wickets in a season – 240 (average 12.72), in 1900 – and most wickets in a Yorkshire career (1898–1930) – 3,597 (average 16.02).

In 1932 Percy Holmes and Herbert Sutcliffe shared an opening partnership of 555 against Essex at Leyton – the highest in the history of the club and of the County Championship. When the partnership was finally broken and the next man in, Wilf Barber, came down the steps, he remarked to Essex members, 'Here I go, just the man for a crisis.'

It was also in 1932 that Hedley Verity returned the amazing bowling figures of 10 for 10 against Nottinghamshire at Headingley – a first-class record. The following year Verity returned match figures of 17 for 91 against Essex at Leyton – a club record.

In 1946 over 47,000 spectators attended the three days of the Roses match against Lancashire at Bramall Lane.

Having dominated the County Championship in the 1930s, Yorkshire won the first post-war Championship. The side included the mercurial spinner Johnnie Wardle, a replacement for the great Hedley Verity, who had been killed in the Second World War.

In 1951 Bob Appleyard became the first bowler to take 200 wickets in his first full season in the County Championship.

Len Hutton's career spanned the years 1934 to 1960. From 1937 to 1953 Hutton averaged at least 48 in every season, with a peak in 1949, when he scored 3,429 runs (average 68.58). In scoring 1,294 runs that June he created an all-time record for the most runs scored in a single month in first-class cricket. Hutton was widely regarded as the complete batsman on all types of wicket. His Test debut was nothing to write home about – he made 0 and 1 against New Zealand in 1937 – but the following year, at the age of 22, he compiled the then highest ever Test score of 364 against Australia at the Oval. He scored 40,140 first-class runs (average 55.51), including 129 centuries. He played in 79 Tests scoring 6,971 runs at 56.67, including 19 centuries. He was the first professional to captain England and the second (in 1956) to be knighted for services to cricket.

If my mother hadn't thrown my football boots on to the fire, I might have become as famous as Denis Compton.
SIR LEN HUTTON

In 1954 Yorkshire were involved in a tied County Championship match against Leicestershire at Huddersfield, a result repeated against Middlesex at Bradford in 1973. Three years later Yorkshire beat Middlesex, again at Bradford, on this occasion by one run.

Yorkshire appointed Ronnie Burnet as captain in 1958. He was 39 years old and had never played a match for the Yorkshire first team.

In August 1958 Johnnie Wardle, who had been selected for the MCC/ England winter tour of Australia, was sacked by the club for his 'general behaviour' and for a ghosted article that appeared in the *Daily Mail* deemed to be critical of Ronnie Burnet and other Yorkshire players.

In 1959 Ronnie Burnet led Yorkshire to the County Championship title. In their final match, in order to win the title Yorkshire had to beat Sussex at Hove and were set a seemingly impossible target of 215 in less than two hours. Openers Doug Padgett and Bryan Stott took the score to 100 after only 43 minutes, and to 150 after 61 minutes. Yorkshire wickets started to fall as batsmen took chances but they reached their target of 215 in 95 minutes for the loss of 5 wickets.

To win the match and the county title we had to score at almost two runs a minute. At one point, Brian Close hit the ball out of the ground for six, but the five minutes it took to retrieve the ball and return it to the bowler's hand only served to up the ante. I must be the only captain to get a message out to a batsman in the middle saying, 'God's sake stop hitting the ball out of the ground.'
RONNIE BURNET

The sixties saw a new team emerge and dominate the County Championship. Brian Close was made captain in 1963 of a side that included Padgett, Fred Trueman, Ray Illingworth, Phil Sharpe, Geoff Boycott, wicket-keeper Jimmy Binks, Jack Hampshire, Ken Taylor, Don Wilson and Tony Nicholson. The squad also contained Chris Balderstone and Richard Hutton, son of Sir Len.

Brian Close, Fred Trueman and Ray Illingworth were often referred to as the 'Holy Trinity' of the Yorkshire team of the fifties and sixties.

It was said that Brian Close thought about cricket 24/7. When captain of Yorkshire, if an idea came to him about the technique of a certain player he would ring that player irrespective of the time of day. Having had an idea as to why Tony Nicholson was having problems with his bowling delivery, Close rang Nicholson – at two a.m. A bleary-eyed Nicholson answered the phone and hearing the voice of his captain said, 'Skipper, do you know what time it is?' Unabashed, Close turned to his wife Vivienne and said, 'Vivienne, love, Tony wants to know what time it is. Clock's on your side.'

RICHARD HUTTON (tongue-in-cheek): You must have bowled the lot today, Fred. Inners, outers, yorkers, slowers. Tell me, Fred, have you ever bowled a straight ball?
FRED TRUEMAN: Aye, I tried that once, against Peter Marner [Lancashire]. It went straight through him like a stream of piss and flattened all three stumps.

Brian Close was controversially sacked in 1970 as the great Yorkshire team of the 1960s began to break up. In 1973 an even greater connection was severed when Bramall Lane, the club's original home, was closed as a cricket ground after over 400 first-class matches.

Brian Close was also an excellent footballer, he signed for Arsenal and also played for Bradford City but chose cricket as a career. He was a highly effective batsman and bowler and also an outstandingly brave close-to-the-wicket fielder.

 When I'm in Leeds I don't have to read a newspaper to know when the cricket season has started. I just listen for the sound of Brian Close being hit with the ball.
ERIC MORECAMBE

Brian Close should have played many more Tests for England than he did, but that was a Yorkshire player's lot back then. The MCC selection committee preferred southern players, would pick a player from the north when pushed and one from Yorkshire only when they had to.

FRED TRUEMAN

Fred Trueman was one of the greatest fast bowlers of all time, aggressive, strong and with a perfect action, a bowler who always bowled side on. He was also a hard-hitting lower-order batsman and a brilliant fielder, particularly at short leg or in the deep. He matured into a fine captain of Yorkshire whom he served from 1948 to 1968. He also played Sunday League cricket for Derbyshire in 1972. Following his retirement as a player he became a TV presenter, a regular on BBC Radio's *Test Match Special* and arguably the greatest sporting after-dinner speaker of them all. He was the first bowler to take 300 Test wickets (1964), took 2,304 first-class wickets (average 18.29), and scored 9,231 first-class runs (average 15.56). As a tail-ender who normally batted at number 10, he scored three centuries, one for England. He played in 67 Tests taking 307 wickets (average 21.57).

I smile when I hear myself referred to as a 'tail-end batsman'. Apart from the wickets taken, I scored shy of 10,000 first-class runs, my career average was 15.56, and I hit three centuries and took over 500 catches. Nowadays a player with such a record would be referred to as a good all-rounder.

FRED TRUEMAN

Famous and much-loved umpire Harold 'Dickie' Bird began his playing career with Yorkshire before moving on to play for Leicestershire.

Geoff Boycott captained the team for most of the 1970s but success eluded a team whose club rules did not allow the signing of overseas players. In the late seventies the club was riddled with problems, not least disagreements within the committee and the dressing room.

In 1982 Ray Illingworth (who had been at Leicestershire) returned to captain the team, at the age of 50.

In 1983, for the first time ever, Yorkshire finished bottom of the County Championship but won the Sunday League for the first time. There was more controversy within the club when Geoff Boycott was not offered a new contract which resulted in a public outcry and the resignation of the club's General Committee. Boycott was eventually reinstated as a player and elected to the new committee, chaired by Brian Close.

Throughout its history Yorkshire was unique among county clubs in that it had a rule that it only recruited players who had been born within the historic boundaries of the county. At first the rule was modified to allow players not born but educated within the county to play for the club, then in 1992 it was scrapped altogether. One of the first players to benefit from this was Michael Vaughan, born in Salford and educated at Silverdale School in Sheffield, who made his Yorkshire debut in 1993. And one of the first overseas players to take advantage was Sachin Tendulkar (India).

In 1997 Yorkshire forswore their traditional policy of spreading matches throughout the county and decided to play only at Headingley and Scarborough.

It was at Scarborough in 2001, under the captaincy of David Byas, that Yorkshire defeated Glamorgan to win their first County Championship title since 1968.

In 2002 Yorkshire were relegated to Division Two of the County Championship but won the C&G Trophy.

In 2004 Yorkshire scored their highest total in limited-overs cricket – 411 for 6, against Devon at Exmouth in the C&G Trophy.

In 2005 Yorkshire remained unbeaten in Division Two until the final match of the season, and won promotion to Division One.

It was also in 2005 that Yorkshire purchased Headingley cricket ground for £12 million – with the help, it was reported, of a £9 million loan from Leeds City Council.

Prior to the start of 2006 Yorkshire-born Chris Adams, captain of Sussex, was unveiled as the new club captain but withdrew citing the role was too much for him.

What do Stanley Jackson, Len Hutton and Michael Vaughan have in common? They all captained England to victory in an Ashes series but none was ever club captain at Yorkshire.

Other notable Yorkshire players include David Denton (33,282 runs, 1894–1920), second only to Herbert Sutcliffe (38,501) as the most runs in a Yorkshire career; Clarrie Grimmett; Maurice Leyland, an outstanding middle-order batsman and later coach at the club; Bill Bowes, Norman Yardley, Brian Sellars, Chris Old, David Bairstow, Younus Khan, Richie Richardson, Martyn Moxon, Michael Bevan, Simon Katich and Chris Silverwood. The current squad includes Tim Bresnan, Matthew Hoggard, Anthony McGrath, Jacques Rudolph (South Africa) and Craig White.

Most appropriately named player – Brian Bolus. Also, G. N. Duck played for the Gentlemen of Yorkshire.

The club's limited-overs team is now called Yorkshire Carnegie.

Worth a visit for . . . an all-sporting weekend in August, should fixtures fall kindly: county cricket at Headingley, rugby league at Headingley (Leeds Rhinos), League One football at Elland Road, and top-notch rugby union with Leeds. All four would be unusual, but three is possible.

For sale. Complete set of Encyclopaedia Britannica. No longer needed – I have a teenage son who knows everything.
EVENING SENTINEL (classified advertisement)

 The match programme referred to me as a 'veteran cricketer'. I told them, 'I'll have you know, I'm but in the youth of my cricketing senility.'
BENNY GREEN

The youngest player to have played first-class cricket in England is the appropriately named Charles Young, who was 15 years and 131 days old when he played for Hampshire against Kent at Gravesend in 1867.

The oldest player to have made his Test debut for England is James Southerton, 49 years and 119 days old, against Australia at Melbourne in 1876–77.

The youngest man to have captained England is Monty Bowden (Surrey), in 1889 against South Africa, at the age of 23 years and 144 days. Strangely, Bowden went out to South Africa as a member of the team led by Major Wharton but did not return with the England party, remaining in South Africa until his untimely death three years later. He died of fever in a makeshift mud hut hospital in Umtali where a constant guard had to be kept over his body to protect it from marauding lions. Equally bizarre is the fact his coffin was made from old whisky cases.

George Canning was 60 years and 151 days old when he played for Kent against All India at Catford in July 1911. Canning had been captain of England in the very first Test match in England, against Australia at the Oval in 1880.

In 1920 a 12-year-old scored 115 not out in a total of 156 for Bowral High School against Mittagong High School in Australia. The boy's name was Donald Bradman.

The oldest player to have made his Test debut for England after 1900 was Rockley Wilson, who was 41 years and 337 days old when he played against Australia at Sydney in 1920–21.

The Reverend Reginald Moss is the oldest player to have appeared in the County Championship. He was 57 years and 89 days old when he played for Worcestershire against Gloucestershire at Worcester in May 1925. It was his only appearance for the county.

Jack Hobbs was 46 years and 82 days old when he scored his last century for England, against Australia at Melbourne in March 1929 – the oldest batsman to have scored a Test century.

The youngest player to have represented the West Indies in a Test is Derrick Sealy, who was 17 years and 122 days old when he made his Test debut against England at Bridgetown in 1929–30.

The oldest player to have played for England in a Test match is Wilfred Rhodes, who was 52 years and 165 days old when he played in his final Test against West Indies at Kingston in 1929–30.

The oldest player to have taken 100 wickets in his debut season in first-class cricket is George Brook, who was 41 years old in 1930 when he took 132 wickets for Worcestershire having joined the club from Kidderminster CC in the Birmingham League.

The oldest player to have kept wicket for England is Frank Woolley (Kent), who deputized for the injured Leslie Ames against Australia at the Oval on 22 August 1934. Woolley was 47 years and 87 days old, and the choice of him as wicket-keeper proved not to be inspired: he conceded 37 byes – a record number for a Test match.

The youngest batsman to score 1,000 runs in his debut season is Denis Compton, for Middlesex in 1936. Compton was 18 years and seven days old when he first appeared for Middlesex against Sussex at Lord's in May. He batted at number 11.

The youngest player to achieve the double of 1,000 runs and 100 wickets in his debut season is Brian Close, who was 18 years old when he achieved this feat for Yorkshire in 1949, a summer in which he also became the youngest player ever to make his Test debut for England, aged 18 years and 149 days, against New Zealand. Close was 45 years and 140 days old when he played his final Test for England, against the West Indies at Old Trafford in 1976 – 27 years between his first and last Test.

The oldest player to have played a Test match for England since the Second World War is Gubby Allen, who was 45 years and 245 days old when he played in his final Test against the West Indies at Kingston in 1947–48.

The oldest man to appear in first-class cricket is Raja Maharaj Singh, who was 72 years old when he captained the Bombay Governor's XI against the Commonwealth at Bombay in November 1950.

The youngest player to have played for Australia in a Test is Ian Craig, who was 17 years and 239 days old when he made his Test debut against South Africa at Melbourne in 1952–53.

In February 1961 Mushtaq Mohammed, at the age of 17 years and 82 days, scored a century (101) for Pakistan against India at New Delhi.

Former cricketer Edward Apsley died in September 1966. Two months earlier he had watched, on television, England win the football World Cup by defeating West Germany. Apsley had made his Hampshire debut in 1898 when the County Championship was only eight years old. He was born on 1 January 1864, when the American Civil War was still raging, Bismarck was only a minister in Prussia, and Germany had yet to be united as a nation.

Jack Cleaver took 9 for 45 for Glenfrith CC (Leicestershire) against Hallaton in 1986, when he was 73 years old.

When Hasan Raza took to the field for the Test match between Pakistan and Zimbabwe at Faisalabad in 1996–97, it was claimed he was just 14 years and 227 days old. The Pakistan Cricket Board rejected the claim as there was no official record to verify Raza's date of birth.

Sachin Tendulkar was 16 years and 205 days old when he made his Test debut for India against Pakistan at Karachi in 1989–90 – and that's official.

In May 1991 Jackie Watson achieved a hat-trick for Bearpark CC (County Durham). He was 70 years old.

Took half as many wickets as his age in a single innings. In 1994 Richard Johnson, at 19 years and 185 days, became the youngest bowler to take 10 wickets in a single innings in the history of the County Championship. Playing for Middlesex against Derbyshire at Derby on 2 July, Johnson returned figures of 10 for 45.

Daniel Vettori was 18 years and 10 days old when he made his Test debut for New Zealand, against England at Wellington in 1996–97 – the youngest player to have represented New Zealand in a Test.

Not the oldest, but the current game does boast some seasoned and senior players of note, such as Mark Ramprakash (40 in 2009), whose first county club was Middlesex in 1987; Shaun Udal (also celebrated his 40th birthday in 2009), who initially signed for Hampshire in 1988; Sanath Jayasuriya (Warwickshire – 40 in 2009); and Lancashire's Stuart Law (41 in 2009), who made his debut for Queensland in 1988 though now enjoys British citizenship. Graeme Hick (Worcestershire) announced his retirement in 2008 at the age of 42 having played his first first-class game in 1983 when Spandau Ballet's 'True' topped the UK charts, Bob Paisley was still manager of Liverpool and Ray Illingworth, at the age of 50, was in his second spell as captain of Yorkshire.

How old are you? Seventeen? You do realize there are people in this room who have underpants and socks that are older than you.

FRED TRUEMAN (during Q&A at a sporting dinner)

Zimbabwe is a full member of the International Cricket Council (ICC) with Test and one-day international status. However, due to internal problems in the country the number of matches played in the new millennium has been severely limited.

The history of Zimbabwean cricket has very close links to that of South Africa. Cricket was introduced in the late nineteenth century by employees of a company owned by Cecil Rhodes, the Prime Minister of the Cape Colony.

The oldest record of a game is of a match between Police and Civilians at Salisbury in 1891.

The Rhodesian Cricket Union was formed in 1898.

In March 1905 Rhodesia competed for the first time in the Currie Cup, South Africa's national tournament, in which Rhodesia played their inaugural first-class match against Transvaal in Johannesburg. Rhodesia were not to compete in the Currie Cup again until 1929–30.

Rhodesia's inaugural first-class match on home soil was against the touring H. D. G. Leveson-Gower's XI at Bulawayo in 1909–10.

As cricket was only played by a small percentage of the population between the wars, Rhodesia struggled to field a team of sufficient quality to make an impact on first-class cricket until the 1950s. Domestic matches would not be afforded first-class status until 1993–94, when the country was Zimbabwe.

In 1980 President Mugabe ordered Zimbabwe to end their association with the Currie Cup after the team competed as Zimbabwe-Rhodesia.

In March 1981 Zimbabwe were dismissed for 56 by a Leicestershire XI at Salisbury (now Harare).

In July 1981 Zimbabwe was elected as an associate member of the ICC.

In 1992 Zimbabwe was granted Test status and played their first Test against India at Harare in the same year. The match ended in a draw.

In 1994–95 Grant Flower created a new record for the highest first-class aggregate by a Zimbabwean batsman – 983 runs (average 57.82).

Also in 1994–95 Zimbabwe achieved their record total in a Test match – 544 for 4 declared, against Pakistan at Harare. It was in this match that Zimbabwe recorded their first Test victory, and Grant and Andy Flower shared a fourth-wicket partnership of 269 – a world record partnership by brothers in a Test match.

Zimbabwe's historic victory over Pakistan in 1994–95 was not televised as, rather than paying for the broadcasting rights to screen the match, the government-controlled national television network demanded a fee from the Zimbabwe Cricket Union to screen the game which the ZCU could not afford.

In addition to the Flower brothers, in the 1990s Zimbabwe also produced top-class cricketers in Alistair Campbell, Murray Goodwin, Paul Strang, Heath Streak and Eddo Brandes, whose occupation was chicken farmer.

In 2003 Zimbabwe, South Africa and Kenya were joint hosts of the World Cup. The competition went smoothly in South Africa, but Zimbabwe's contribution was marred by internal political interference, a 'quota system' selection policy effectively based on colour as opposed to ability, and England forfeiting their match against Zimbabwe citing 'security concerns'.

During the tournament Andy Flower and Henry Olonga wore black armbands to symbolize the mourning of 'the death of democracy in Zimbabwe'. Both were immediately banned from playing for Zimbabwe and eventually both applied for political asylum overseas.

Henry Olonga came to England and was afforded the rare honour of being awarded honorary life membership of the MCC.

In 2004 Zimbabwe captain Heath Streak was sacked by the ZCU amid allegations the union had been pressured into this by the Zimbabwe government. Fourteen players walked out on the national team in protest against political influence in the team's management and selection policies. Subsequent Zimbabwe teams consisted of 'fringe' players. In 2005 Heath Streak was reinstated.

Zimbabwe suffered a series of humiliating defeats. In 2005, against New Zealand, they became only the second team in the history of Test cricket (after India in 1952) to be bowled out twice in a single day's play.

Following another crushing Test defeat, to India in September 2005, Heath Streak announced his retirement from international cricket.

In November 2005 the new Zimbabwe captain, Tatendu Taibu, resigned citing political interference in the management of the game and selection policy.

On 6 January 2006 the Sports and Recreation Commission, a division of the Zimbabwean government, took over the offices of the Zimbabwe Cricket Union. The chairman of the SRC, Brigadier Gibson Mashingaidze, oversaw the sacking of all whites and Asians in the ZCU, 'because of their racial connotations and saving their own agendas and not government policy' he was quoted as saying.

Later in 2006 an interim board was appointed as the new body of cricket in Zimbabwe, and it announced the suspension of the playing of Test cricket for the remainder of the year.

Zimbabwe competed in the 2007 World Cup but was eliminated in the first round.

The ICC has not supported Zimbabwe's return to full Test status and has said it will not do so until 'the national team can perform consistently at that level'.

In 1993–94 the Logan Cup was competed for by seven first-class teams: Mashonaland, Mashonaland Country Districts, Mashonaland Under-24s, Midlands, Masuingo, Manicaland and Matabeleland. It seems the main criterion for qualification for this tournament was a team's name had to begin with the letter 'M'. It's surely the first time a first-class cricket competition has involved entrants all of whose names begin with the same letter.

 Regarding investment in the game, the government has promised Zimbabwe cricket they can expect change. As yet we don't know if that will be a couple of one- or two-cent coins.

PAUL BOARDMAN